India's New Economic Policy

India's New Economic Policy

A Critical Analysis

Edited by

Waquar Ahmed

Amitabh Kundu

Richard Peet

RAWAT PUBLICATIONS

Jaipur · New Delhi · Bangalore · Hyderabad · Guwahati

ISBN 978-81-316-0411-3

First Indian Reprint, 2011

This edition published by arrangement with Routledge. Routledge is an imprint of the Taylor & Francis Group, an informa business.

First published in 2010 by Routledge, 270 Madison Avenue, New York, NY 10016. Simultaneously published in the UK by Routledge, 2 Park Square, Milton Park, Abingdon, Oxon OX14 4RN

Published by
Prem Rawat for Rawat Publications
Satyam Apts, Sector 3, Jawahar Nagar, Jaipur 302 004 (India)
Phone: 0141 265 1748 / 7006 Fax: 0141 265 1748
E-mail: info@rawatbooks.com
Website: www.rawatbooks.com

New Delhi Office
4858/24, Ansari Road, Daryaganj, New Delhi 110 002
Phone: 011 2326 3290

Also at *Bangalore, Hyderabad* and *Guwahati*

Printed at Chaman Enterprises, New Delhi

Dedicated to
the masses of poor people in India
who struggle for social justice.

Contents

Tables

Figures

Introduction

Waquar Ahmed, Amitabh Kundu, and Richard Peet

In 1991 India launched a New Economic Policy. The new policy framework mirrored standard structural adjustment measures, advocated universally by the International Monetary Fund (IMF) and World Bank, following a basically neoliberal approach to economic policy. Conventional interpretations see these measures of economic liberalization transforming the structure of the Indian economy and resulting in substantial increase in the rate of economic growth. Aggregative growth figures, however, cannot be taken to be the sole, or even main, indicators of the developmental performance of a large and socioeconomically diverse country like India. For, the question also has to be: who benefits from the new growth regime? And can it significantly improve the conditions of livelihood for India's 800 million people whose incomes are below $2.00 a day? The present volume looks at the international neoliberal policy regime, and its adoption at the national level in India, under strategic conditions of economic crisis and coercion, and within longer-term structural changes in the power calculus of global capitalism. It looks at long-term growth tendencies, poverty and employment rates at the national, regional, and local levels in India; the main growth centers; the areas and people damaged; the advantages and deficiencies of the existing policy regime; and alternative economic perspectives for India.

A developmental approach to understanding the growth scenario would imply evaluating policy in terms of its effect on the living standards and the conditions of livelihood of the majority of the people. Economic growth is not enough. It must lead to development. Thus the immediate question is: what have been the socioeconomic effects of India's turn to encouragement of private entrepreneurship in the 1980s and adoption of neoliberalism in the early 1990s? On the one hand, the secondary and, especially, tertiary sectors of the economy have assumed positions of dominance within the Indian economy since 1991—such is a well-publicized aspect of the "Indian Miracle". On the other hand, growth has been highly uneven among regions, between urban and rural areas, and across different size classes of urban settlements. Far more seriously, neoliberal growth has come at the expense of high levels of smallholder indebtedness, mounting unemployment, and a declining natural resource base. These have contributed to large-scale agrarian distress, reflected in high and persistent levels of malnutrition, illiteracy, and preventable illnesses.

The 1990s also saw fundamental changes in the previous state policy, as input subsidies, credit, and extension services in agriculture were rolled back, several infrastructure and services were privatized, and domestic markets were opened to international trade. This raises the longer-term question: can neoliberal policy regimes deal effectively with social problems that have resulted in the persistence of distress to millions for several decades after Independence? India is important not so much because it is portrayed as a poster child for neoliberal success in the face of an entrenched state bureaucracy (the license Raj). India is uniquely important because it is a country with a population numbering over one billion: it will soon be the most populous country on earth. It has as many people living in hunger as in the whole of sub-Saharan Africa. Examining the Indian model of development is instructive in itself, as well as for its considerable implications for policy in other developing countries.

Undoubtedly, the case of India's recent development needs critical analysis. The idea is to look particularly at the neoliberal economic policy regime that began to be articulated in the 1980s but was reinforced and institutionalized as a result of the 1991 economic and political crisis in India. This necessitates a detailed examination of the international and domestic origins of India's New Economic Policy, its institutional and discursive structure, its application and results, and the contentions that have met and changed this regime. The present volume attempts to do this. It particularly looks at neoliberal economic growth as a process of uneven development. It focuses on regions, sectors, and spaces that have grown at a tardy pace, have not grown at all, or have declined. It probes into the issue of why only certain sections of people have benefited from this growth dynamic, while others have been adversely affected? This book, based on interdisciplinary, international, and comparative research, underlines the need for a comprehensive analysis of the key premises of the neoliberal policies in India particularly and the world generally.

The basic argument of the book unfolds in the following way. Chapter 1, "Neoliberalism, Inequality, and Development" by Richard Peet, sets India's New Economic Policy in the context of the neoliberal economic growth regime spread across the globe. Putting it bluntly, the claim made by governments, intellectuals, business, and the media that neoliberal growth produces development, in India as elsewhere, is one huge confidence trick. Economic growth under neoliberalism consistently, persistently, in a broad array of contexts, benefits a minority of the population. Neoliberal growth has spectacular effects, in the way of building tall office buildings, opulent houses, high levels of conspicuous consumption, "modern-looking" young people, new cultural styles, cosmopolitanization, and so on. This has convinced even some critical minds that a process of development that is widely beneficial is occurring now and will include everyone very soon. State power, therefore, must be exercised ruthlessly when necessary, because the powerful have seen the future, and it (apparently) works, whereas resistance merely blocks the way toward progress for all.

Things, however, look differently from the other side—from the perspective of people who, rather than being "left out" or "left behind" (as the conventional statements have it), have instead been massively ravaged by neoliberal growth. Neoliberal development is predicated on the underdevelopment of the vast majority of people, as dependency theory puts it strongly and accurately. Statistical evidence on this is overwhelming. It should be perfectly clear to those who care to examine the growth process from the perspective of the excluded majority that neoliberalism's main socioeconomic product is inequality (because it is intended to produce it). In turn, the main outcome of inequality is poverty, because inequality is exploitative, emanating from the strengthening of the power and capability of some to benefit *at the expense of others*. In a phrase, neoliberalism cannot solve social problems because it causes them.

Chapter 2, "From Mixed Economy to Neoliberalism: Class and Caste in India's Policy Transition" by Waquar Ahmed, more exactly links global neoliberalism to the specific case of India. Neoliberal transformation, Ahmed says, is not simply a top-down, outside to inside, process. The hegemonic neoliberal policy discourse at the global level has an ally in the Indian elite, producing sub-hegemonic power centers and more specific forms of class-biased economic growth. Employing a case study of the electric power industry, Ahmed substantiates how the coercive power of global institutions of governance has worked in tandem with the interest of the local elite to produce neoliberal changes in the country. It is in this context of intra-class and inter-class and caste contestation that India's transformations of economic and electric power policy have to be understood. Neoliberalism has been accompanied by a disproportionate increase in the political and economic power of the urban elite and marginalization of the poor, who live in villages and the vast slums of India's cities. Further, class position within Indian society intersects with caste position. The higher castes in India have greater access to education and wealth and have benefited most from India's New Economic Policy. This re-assertion of class and caste power has been fundamental to the New Economic Policy in India. So, while neoliberalism was thrust on India due to imperatives of global capital market, and by the World Bank, the IMF, and the U.S., its continuance has been ensured by large sections of the class and caste elite. In other words, the exogenous power of the global institutions of governance has worked in tandem with the interest of the local elite to produce, what Gramsci calls, hegemony—consent through non-physically coercive means.

Chapter 3, "Urban System in India: Trends, Economic Base, Governance and a Perspective of Growth under Globalization" by Amitabh Kundu, begins by overviewing trends and patterns of urbanization in post-colonial

India, in the context of the demographic and economic trends in Asia. Kundu's chapter critically examines the urban scenarios projected by international and national agencies in the context of their methodological predispositions. He analyzes trends in employment, unemployment, wages, and so on and stipulates the thesis of the 'formalization of informal sectors'. Recent increase in the rates of unemployment (along with high growth in employment) and stagnation or decline in real wages are explained in terms of this process of 'informal formalization'. Increasingly, the illiterate rural-to-urban migrants, dispossessed farmers, and rural artisans, who do not have the minimum level of conversation skills or market smartness, are being denied a foothold in the urban job market. Under the new system of urban governance in India, attempts are being made to open up the land and capital markets to enable local bodies, para-statal agencies, and private developers access to land at preferred sites and mobilize resources for their residential, business, and infrastructural activities in "select global centres of the future". This is accomplished by simplifying the legal and administrative procedures for changing land use and by flushing out "low valued" activities from these sites. Removal is often carried out indirectly, and discreetly, through slum improvement schemes, "rehabilitating" the poor out into the peripheries and strengthening, thereby, the process of exclusionary urbanization. The new system of urban governance has increased the dependence of urban local bodies on institutional resources and market borrowings. This has ensured that the new urban infrastructures and civic amenities meet the requirements of the class that can pay for them and make them self sustaining. Initiatives promoting participatory planning through preparation of 'vision documents', encouragement of civil society organizations and other stake holders, and so on, have resulted in elite capture of urban planning. These measures have been responsible for the segmentation of India's cities, the accentuation of intra-city inequalities, and a strengthening of the process of degenerated peripheralization.

Chapter 4, "New Urbanism, Neoliberalism, and Urban Restructuring in Mumbai" by Swapna Banerjee-Guha, also looks at how the consolidation of a worldwide regime of disciplinary neoliberalism is showing up in the recent re-modeling of Indian cities into 'world class cities', that function as nodes for the circulation of global capital. Projected as the epitome of the 'urban efficiency' these cities, along with their counterparts elsewhere, embody the imperatives of capitalism, achieved through practices of 'flexibilization' and 'disaggregation' that reflect a wider restructuring of the economy. These "world class cities" increasingly concentrate a disproportionate share of the poor and the marginalized and emerge as key sites of their devalorization. Banerjee-Guha's chapter examines a process of neoliberalism in Indian cities that is not only molding the entire concept of the current 'urban' but intensifying unevenness at the intra- and inter-urban levels as well. The chapter discusses diverse manifestations of neoliberal urban policy in contemporary India, but finally takes up the case of

Mumbai more elaborately. In general, the chapter examines the imperatives and associated contradictions of neoliberal urbanism in India.

Chapter 5, "Economic Liberalization and Urban Governance: Impact on Inclusive Growth" by Shipra Maitra, argues that the current urbanization risks harboring economic and spatial inequalities that are not automatically neutralized through flows of rural-to-urban migration. The labor force in urban areas remains rooted to the land through various sociocultural factors that are not guided by economic reason. Macroeconomic policies that stimulate overall national growth are not sufficiently re-distributive to neutralize the adverse impact of location-specific growth. The cities tend to attract high-value investments and create shortage of common urban resources, like land. As the competitive value of urban land is beyond the reach of the vulnerable sections of society, direct government intervention is needed—in terms of the demarcation of land for the deprived section. This ought to be backed up by speedy provision of basic services for the reduction of vertical and spatial inequalities. The current urban agenda, followed by the Government of India, unfortunately emphasizes efficiency and competitiveness for overall economic development. This chapter asks whether such an agenda is in tune with the concept of inclusive growth.

Chapter 6, "The Right to Waste: Informal Sector Recyclers and Struggles for Social Justice in Post-Reform Urban India" by Bharati Chaturvedi and Vinay Gidwani, examines waste picking and other informal sector livelihoods, such as vending and street hawking, that are often stigmatized in urban contexts. It examines the nature of the interdependence between informal and formal economies against the backdrop of India's New Economic Policy, and the trend toward privatization and formalization of municipal solid waste management. The authors argue that urban policymakers and municipal authorities are extremely reluctant to acknowledge these informal services as essential, and often display a visceral mistrust of the urban poor and unorganized workers in their programs and administrative decisions. They often ignore the fact that these services are the essential elements in ensuring the efficiency of urban economy, as well as the lifestyles demanded by its elites. The global trend toward privatization and formalization of informal sector activities, in which the city of Delhi (their main focus of interest) is an active participant, is misguided for a number of reasons: (a) it fails to confront the issue of employment generation and urban poverty; (b) it blithely ignores that the urban poor—despite their precarious access to employment and housing—have as much right to make claims on city resources as the urban elite; and (c) it fails to see that they are economic actors and entrepreneurs, whose work sustains the urban system in critical ways. Chaturvedi and Gidwani argue that among the waste collectors, numbering over 150,000 in Delhi, mostly in the informal sector, a large majority fall way below the poverty line, and their working conditions are often abject and inhuman. It is important that their work and contributions to the city's economy are officially recognized and legitimized. Unless policymakers safeguard their work, they will lose out to large private companies, who are often privileged players in urban politics. Alternately, they will continue to work in extreme poverty under hazardous conditions, with illness as a hallmark of their survival. The future livelihoods of Delhi's informal sector waste collectors, thus, foregrounds profound questions of social justice.

Chapter 7, "From Red Tape to Red Carpet? Violent Narratives of Neoliberalizing Ahmedabad" by Ipsita Chatterjee, finds both champions of neoliberal reform and critics of neoliberal policy, converging in their assessment that markets and states are undergoing re-organization. The process of neoliberal re-organization entails all kinds of state-market negotiations that in turn have diverse imprints on society. Since society, and the space it occupies, is not tabula rasa, neoliberalism-generated state-market re-organization works on the existing sociogeographical terrain to produce 'new' spaces that reflect how 'quasi-climatic' neoliberalism has been socio-spatially embedded. With an increase in national border porosity, cities are important sites for embedding 'new' configurations of state-market reorganization. As the national state reconfigures itself to accommodate market rule, it simultaneously urges local states (city governments) to fend for themselves. City governments must trim public spending, relinquish goals of social equality, and become astute entrepreneurs on behalf of their urban space. Such entrepreneurs, however, have color, race, gender, and class positions. Therefore, their economic 'rationality' is not ideologically neutral. In their pursuit of profit, they often embed neoliberalism through elitist and racial configurations. Through case studies of city planning documents, and urban renewal projects, like the Green Partnership Program, the Riverfront Development Program, and various public housing schemes in the globalizing city of Ahmedabad, India, Chatterjee demonstrates how neoliberalism is embedded in class- exclusion, ethno-racism, and Islamophobia. The state and the market, thus emerge in ideological cohabitation as the 'market-state', with a blurring of the hyphen.

Chapter 8, "Neoliberalism, Environmentalism, and Urban Politics in Delhi" by Rohit Negi, argues that, in addition to structurally adjusting the political economy, the New Economic Policy in India has led to the formation of a complex urban space. The underlying goal, in the metropolitan cities of India, has been gaining membership in the elite list of the so-called "global" or "world" cities. One way of conceptualizing and activating the shift is the creation of a 'post-industrial' city. This translates on the ground in terms of a shift toward a service-economy, away from 'traditional' manufacturing activities. Urban transformations in Delhi, for instance, confirm this general process. But this is only a part of the story since a large number of interest groups and actors are involved, in either facilitating or resisting such changes. In the case of Delhi, a certain kind of environmentalism has formed a key element of the neoliberal spatial changes. Activists have asked the judiciary to help enforce environmental and, increasingly, planning laws that the state is thought to be ineffective in implementing, left to its devices. This judiciary-mediated process unfortunately has led to thousands of workers and city-residents being progressively disenfranchised. They continue to seek access to the spaces of the post-colonial state to advance their claims and resist the exclusionary impacts of neoliberal urban change, often without much success.

Chapter 9, "Coping with Challenges to Food Security: Climate Change, Biofuels, and GMOs" by Suman Sahai, holds that India's current food crisis has emerged from a past of thoughtless domestic policies, coupled with an inequitable international environment. A discriminatory framework at the World Trade Organization (WTO) continues to block attempts by developing countries to make agriculture and food production more viable at home. The emergence of climate change and global warming have raised a new and more immediate set of challenges for agriculture and food production in India and other developing countries. According to assessments linked to climate change, agriculture in the productive areas of South Asia will be among the worst affected. A quick response and a proactive approach are therefore urgently required to ensure that agriculture and food production are maintained at satisfactory levels. Exacerbating a delicate food situation is the current trend of biofuels. Not to be left behind in the global craze, India has also begun biofuel programs. A vocal 'biofuel lobby' argues that bioenergy crops producing agrofuels would only be grown on degraded or waste land, which is empirically questionable. The author argues that it is not possible to grow plants like *Jatropha* or other oil-bearing crops in a commercially viable manner without adequate soil nutrients (fertilizers) and irrigation. Further, if the "wasteland" is capable of supporting *Jatropha* cultivation, it can be used for cultivating food crops or at least fodder grasses for livestock. Agrofuel crops will thus take land out of food production and increase the price of agricultural commodities, jeopardizing the livelihoods of small and marginal farmers. Furthermore, the genetic engineering (GE) industry is lobbying with the argument that food security cannot be met without GE foods. Empirical research in this area reveals that GE crops in India are linked with a high-risk technology. In addition, the food safety question resulting from production of toxic and allergenic proteins, that can neither be predicted nor controlled, is harder to settle than was anticipated. Given this scenario, the country diverting precious resources to the transgenic craze and neglecting proven methods of food production would be a matter of concern. The chapter shows how, with the right policies and intelligent planning, it is possible not just to overcome the food crisis at the micro level but also to create big food surpluses for the country. Has the New Economic Policy been good for the poor in countries like India? The number of poor has increased, not decreased, and the rates of malnutrition are appalling, with states like Jharkhand and Madhya Pradesh now ranking below sub-Saharan Africa on the number of children suffering from acute malnutrition. The agricultural economy is so adverse that more than half the farmers in India would abandon farming if they had an alternative. Biofuels in the name of clean energy are being promoted at the cost of food security; the poor will get hungrier as common grazing lands are diverted to produce biofuels. Agriculture credit has plummeted, squeezing institutional credit to farmers and making them dependent on private moneylenders at usurious interest rates. The resulting indebtedness crushes any prospect of food security for the vulnerable.

Chapter 10, "Imperialism, Resources, and Food Security, with Reference to the Indian Experience" by Utsa Patnaik, analyzes the reasons for declining incomes and nutritional intakes of agriculture-dependent populations in developing countries under recent neoliberal economic reforms, by taking up the case of India. Located mainly in tropical areas, developing countries can produce a qualitatively different primary output vector, with a much larger range of products, compared to cold temperate regions, comprising the advanced countries of today. This fact underlies the author's critique of David Ricardo's theory of comparative advantage leading to mutual benefit from trade. The latter is shown to be based on a material fallacy since it assumes that the two countries entering into trade can produce both goods, something that is factually untrue. Past demands by northern countries on limited tropical lands under colonial plantation systems for expanding exports, always led to declining food grains availability for local populations. The same outcome is seen at present in countries opening up to trade. The demands from advanced countries on tropical lands have increased manifoldly and encompass a range of perishable products whose rapid expansion for export entails a decline in foodgrains output and energy intake per head of the agriculture-dependent population. The past mechanism for releasing the land and resources required for an export thrust was heavy taxation by the colonial state reducing the purchasing power of local populations and the use of taxes to purchase export goods from them. The present mechanism too relies on expenditure-deflating policies by the national state following the advice of the IMF and World Bank. These policies raise unemployment levels and reduce the purchasing power of the agriculture-dependent population, which leads to a decline in their foodgrains absorption and energy intake. The official and World Bank claims of decline in poverty in India are shown to be untenable, since the original nutrition norms for estimating poverty lines have been abandoned. The present method of estimation of poverty follows a fixed, over-three-decades-old consumption basket, updating it by only the recent prices which results in gross underestimation of poverty. Correctly measured poverty, linked to fixed nutrition intake, would, on the contrary, show a markedly rising trend over the economic reforms period.

Chapter 11, "Special Economic Zones: Space, Law, and Dispossession" by Rupal Oza, attempts to understand the geography of neoliberalism in India by looking at the creation of Special Economic Zones (SEZs). SEZs are spaces acquired by the state for private capital to set up industrial enclaves at a low cost. Oza aims at mapping the altered geography generated through the creation of these enclaves. Efforts to govern and secure these enclaves have resulted in a series of rules and provisions that give them exemptions from a range of juridical statutes governing labor, industry, environmental assessments, and taxes. In effect, these zones exist separately from the surrounding areas and, for the purposes of trade and tariff, are designated as 'foreign territory'. As 'spaces of exception', territorially within the Indian state, yet legislatively outside it, Oza says that SEZs offer an ideal opportunity to critically examine the geography of India's recent neoliberal experiment.

Chapter 12, "Thinking Militant Particularisms Politically: Resistances to Neoliberalism in India" by David Featherstone, interrogates emerging forms of resistance to neoliberalism in India. It positions these resistances in relation to debates around the contestation of neoliberal globalization, with particular attention given to the possibilities for solidarities between different place-based struggles. Following the British Marxist theoretician Raymond Williams, Featherstone terms these diverse place-based struggles, emerging in relation to neoliberalization, as 'militant particularisms'. Drawing on Partha Chatterjee's work, the chapter emphasizes the importance of understanding militant particularisms politically. It explores ways in which militant particularisms have contested neoliberalization, and the practices through which militant particularist struggles have been articulated and networked. This draws on discussion of a range of struggles, including mobilization against the Coca Cola Corporation and the resistance to neoliberalization articulated by the Indian New Farmer's Movements. The chapter concludes with some reflections on the possibilities for left political strategies in the current conjuncture.

Chapter 13, "Radical Peasant Movements and Ruaral Distress in India: A Study of the Naxalite Movement" by Raju J. Das proposes that since its inception in the late 1960s, the Naxalite movement (Maoist) in India has been transformed from a local flare-up to regional, and some would argue, national-scale, movement. Das examines the causes behind the Naxalite movement's continued existence. In many ways, the Naxalite movement, including its geography, provides a window to an Indian countryside in perpetual developmental distress, which has only been worsened by the neoliberal New Exonomic Policy. Much of the discussion in the chapter, therefore, is organized around the theme of development. The chapter relates the emergence and continuation of the Naxalite movement to two developmental failures: the basid failure of capitalist develpment; and the failure of the post-colonial state—both in terms of hte state policy interventions and in terms of state form—to bring significant benefits to the rural poor. The continuation of the movement is also due to the fact that the Naxalites address the contradictions of society by providing some relief to the suffering masses and help them stand up for their rights which are being trampled on by neoliberal capital. But the movement suffers from serious theoretical and tactical problems which have adversely affected its social and spacial spread.

What is our overall conclusion? Neoliberalism in the form of the New Economic Policy in India has not meant a triumph of the new over the entrenched habits of the old, as the conventional (pro-business) media always phrase it. Instead it has meant lots more money and power for a relative few, located in the elite spaces of India's glittering cities, and utter deprivation and exploitation for the masses, sleeping on the streets, encamped in urban slums, and struggling to survive in over half a million villages. This policy regime must be changed. We, the editors, believe that the book can contribute in promoting a more comprehensive discussion on the paradigm of globalization which might change the ongoing growth process. Our propositions are simple and straightforward: Read the book. Think on the issues debated. Argue. And get engaged in building a better world.

1 Neoliberalism, Inequality, and Development

Richard Peet

Who directs the development of economies? Who benefits most from each new form that development takes?

The question "Who directs?" is not easy to answer with capitalism. For in capitalism, millions of decisions by selfish actors collide in markets to produce an economy. The answer therefore appears to be "the market directs"—as though the market "itself" is a collective actor. Yet as Karl Polanyi (1944) demonstrated, markets are social constructions, with states playing a big part in making, shaping, and directing them. So the longer answer for capitalist economies is: markets as directed by states—states of many kinds, at different scales, and with the state "writ large" as governance and governmental institutions.

The question "Who benefits?" is a little easier to answer, once the notion that economies are important not just as producers of goods and services, but also jobs and incomes. Different types of economy produce different income distributions, some more egalitarian than others, with most being extremely skewed in favor of rich people. The main problem here is getting behind the ideological disguise of an economy. Because, if states indeed regulate the markets that organize economies, and governments are "freely elected" by virtually everyone, then potentially states can be instructed to regulate economies in the interests of all. And indeed democratic states must make this claim, even when they mainly are regulating economies in favor mainly of already-wealthy people. Economic development policy must, as a result, take an ideological form, often claiming to do the reverse of its real practice—for example, claiming that rewarding entrepreneurship creates more jobs for broad sections of the population, when what is really happening is capital and wealth are being accumulated by a few people, who do what they want with their money.

So these are complex, vital issues—who controls the economy, through what institutional and ideological means, in whose interest, to benefit whom? This chapter pretends only to provide a few analytical terms that can be used in answering such questions, along with some of the recent historical evidence on who benefits most from different types of economy.

POLICY REGIMES

States intervene to direct capitalist economies along trajectories that yield entirely different typical distributions of incomes among classes. We can use the term "policy regime" to describe typical sets of policies. The term "policy regime" indicates: a systematic approach to policy formation by a set of government or governance institutions, and their financial allies; dealing with a definable, limited range of issues; that prevails, as the dominant interventionary framework; over an historical period lasting at least several decades; and stretching over global space to include, in somewhat different regional forms in multiple societies. Policy regimes are lent coherence by an underlying political-economic interpretation of the causes of a set of related socioeconomic problems. This interpretation is not scientifically neutral. Instead it represents the interests of certain elements of economic and political power, such as a fraction of capital, like finance capital, represented by a definable set of institutions, inhabited by a certain group of people, like investment bankers. Further, the ideologies that lend consistency, cohesion, and believability to policy regimes are constructed over long time periods by experts residing in geographic centers of ideological power, with ideas for new regimes thought up in prestigious, elite institutions. Change often comes from elite institutions that were previously peripheralized—as with the Chicago School of Economics in the U.S. Several policy regimes may co-exist in time, as past, present, and future versions of a given approach to solving a limited range of problems. Regimes may co-exist in space, as regionally variant approaches to somewhat differently experienced problems, with relations of dominance and subordination between the regional approaches—at any time one approach dominates—as with the Anglo-American neoliberal model. Indeed the co-existence in time, but separation in space, of more than one policy regime, makes the dominant regime dynamically effective—any effective policy regime contains elements of its alternatives and variants as co-opted, but potentially conflictive, elements—the "concern for poverty" in contemporary Anglo-American neoliberalism for instance. All this produces an overall, global policy regime that has been well described, in the case of neoliberalism, as a contradictory process, existing in historically and geographically contingent forms, produced during a period of institutional searching (Tickell and Peck 1995; Peck and Tickell 2002, 383; Peet 2007).

FROM KEYNESIANISM TO NEOLIBERALISM

Since World War II, the capitalist world has seen two main political-economic policy regimes: Keynesian Democracy, predominating between 1945 and 1973; and Neoliberal Democracy predominating between 1980 and the present; the years 1973–1980 represent a transitional period, when the two regimes contended for dominance, while the years since 2007 are another major crisis, that might alter Neoliberal Democracy—push it slightly toward Keynesianism or produce more of a state-banking sector synthesis.

The Keynesian policy regime was characterized by countercyclical macroeconomic management by an interventionist state committed to achieving full employment and high incomes for everyone. This regime responded to the Depression of the 1930s, a crisis that de-legitimized the theoretical rationality and the persuasive claims of the previous, long-lasting Liberal (free-trade) regime, by using state authority to stabilize accumulation and democratize economic benefits. Regional differences in theoretical-interpretative and political-economic tradition informed three main variants in the capitalist world: Social Democratic Keynesianism in Western European countries and their former settler colonies; Liberal Democratic Keynesianism in the U.S.; and Developmental State Keynesianism in Japan and many industrializing Third World countries (Chang and Rowthorn 1995; Kohli 2004), although we might add a fourth variant in the case of India, which combined socialism with Keynesianism into "one of the most heavily regulated economies in the world" (Nayer 1998).

The convention is that Keynesianism entered into crisis in the 1970s characterized by problems associated with stagflation—high rates of inflation coinciding with high rates of unemployment. But crises do not produce new policy regimes. Dominant actors do. So changes in policy regime might be seen as "interpretive moments", when interpretations of crisis, reflecting contending interests, represented by institutions and leading individuals, clash in the court of economic and social opinion. To the victor goes the right to spoil the newly emerging regime. I return to this shortly.

The successor to Keynesianism, the Neoliberal policy regime, revives late nineteenth century, free trade Liberalism by reconstructing the state so that it serves business interests. Neoliberalism employs monetarist economics under the conceptual belief that macroeconomic problems, like inflation and debt, derive from excessive government spending (fiscal deficits) on social programs. While regional variations in speed of adoption, and level of commitment, persist, the neoliberal regime responded positively to the globalization of economy, society, and culture of the late twentieth century. Indeed neoliberalism helped to organize the emergence of a particular kind of globalization that benefits a newly re-emergent, super-wealthy, financial-capitalist class, mainly living in the leading Western countries, especially the U.S., but operating transnationally in terms of investment activity.

GROWTH, INEQUALITY, AND POVERTY

If we divide the post-World War period into these two periods, the Keynesian-Social Democratic policy regime up to 1980 and the Neoliberal policy regime dominant since 1980, we can compare the social and economic results of the two policy regimes. The measure used by conventional economists to measure societal well-being is economic growth—let us, for a moment, accept this measure at face value (i.e., "growth is good"). Economic growth in the Organisation for Economic Co-operation and Development countries, the richest countries in the world, averaged 3.5% a year in the period 1961–1980, basically during Keynesianism, and 2.0% a year in 1981–1999, basically during neoliberalism. In developing countries excluding China (excluded because it was neither Keynesian nor neoliberal), the equivalent figures were 3.2% and 0.7% (Pollin 2003, 133). In other words, Keynesianism vastly out-performed neoliberalism in conventional (mainstream economics) terms. Now, looking at aspects of the economy more important to the well-being of the people than economic growth, let us compare the two periods in terms of inequality. Using data collected by the University of Texas Inequality Project on national structures of pay, Galbraith (2007, 587) finds "a worldwide pattern of declining inequality from 1971 until 1980, followed by a long and sharp period of increasing inequality from 1981 through the end of the century", a tendency that he associates with changing "global macroeconomics". In 1960 the 20% of the world's people living in the richest countries had 30 times the income of the 20% of the world's people living in the poorest countries; in 1973 the figure was 44 to 1; and in 1997 the ratio was 74 to 1 (UNDP 1999, 36–38). According to the World Bank (2008, 353), 1,056 million people living in the "high-income" countries and making up 16% of the world's people receive $39.6 trillion in income, or 75.3% of the global income of $52.6 trillion, while 1,296 million people in the "low-income" countries, making up 19.6% of the world's people, receive $0.75 trillion, or 1.4 % of global income. Putting this a little differently the "average person" living in the high-income countries gets 53 times as much as the "average person" living in the poor countries—or recalculating this in PPP terms (i.e., taking purchasing power into consideration), 20 times as much. National poverty rates in the low-income countries are in the range of 45% to 70% of the population, while the percentage of people living on less that $2 a day varies from 50% to 90%, depending on the country.

Yet geographic inequality only begins this sorry tale. Class, caste, ethnicity, region, and gender distribute incomes extremely unequally *within* countries. Of the 80% of income going to rich countries, 50% typically goes to the 20% of the people with the highest incomes, while the 20% of the people with the lowest incomes get 5% to 9%, again depending on the country. In the low-income countries, the richest 20% typically get 50% to 85% of national income, while the poorest 20% typically get 3% to 5% of the 1.4% of global income that these poor countries receive (World Bank 2008). The richest 2% of the world's adult population now owns more than half of global household wealth; the bottom half of adults own barely 1% (UNDP 2007). The great, unmentioned fact about global income distribution is this: poverty results from inequality. National poverty increases as the world becomes a more unequal place. The poor are poverty stricken because the rich make so much. So, what has been happening to inequality under neoliberalism?

Take the case of the leading capitalist society, the U.S., set up as a neoliberal model copied by the rest of the world". Between 1947 and 1973, under the Keynesian policy regime, every income category of people experienced real income growth, with the poorest families having the highest rate of growth of all. After 1973 average real income not only remained stagnant but reflected high income growth for the top 20% of families and a significant income decrease for the poorest 20%, so that almost half of all families received lower real incomes by the mid 1990s than they had in 1973 (Leone 1995). The key factor causing these secular changes in class incomes was an even greater divergence in the ownership of wealth, especially financial wealth—that is bank accounts, ownership of stocks and bonds, and life insurance and mutual fund savings. Particularly important is ownership of stocks and mutual fund shares. Despite "democratization" (retirement savings invested in mutual funds, etc.), only 27% of U.S. families own stocks. While 78% of the richest families own stocks and mutual funds, 3% of the poorest families do so. The equalizing trends in wealth ownership of the entire, state interventionist period between the 1930s and the 1970s (New Deal, War Economy, Keynesianism), reversed sharply in the neoliberal 1980s, so that by 1989 the richest 1% of households owned almost half the total financial wealth of the U.S. (Wolf 1995), a concentration of ownership that has only become more extreme since (Harvey 2005, 16–17). Within this rich 1%, the super-rich—that one-thousandth of the population (145,000 people) making an average of $3 million a year—doubled its share of total national income between 1980 and 2002, to 7.4%, while the share earned by the bottom 90% fell (Johnston 2005, 1). All this produces the defining U-shape to the distribution of incomes over the last hundred years under liberalism, Keynesianism, and neoliberalism. Figure 1.1 shows the percentage of income going to the highest income 0.1%, 0.5%, and 1.0% of the U.S. population—it is based on tax returns, that tend to understate income going to the rich, if only because they hide it better and employ tax accountants more skilled than the bureaucratic accounts used by state bureaucracies. A major reason for this extremely skewed distribution of income is that neoliberalism is a way of running an economy that produces dramatic upsurges in the stock exchange, where the rich put their money to earn even more (Figure 1.2). And note that stocks are a relatively safe bet compared with neoliberalism's other "irrational exuberances", like derivatives. Liberalism and neoliberalism produce economic growth that almost exclusively benefits the super-rich. State intervention, even by the relatively non-interventionist, "liberal-democratic" U.S. state, reduces the proportion of income going to the super-rich and re-distributes income and state-subsidized services to the poorer sections of the population. Neoliberalism is development for the already-rich. This can be taken as indubitable fact.

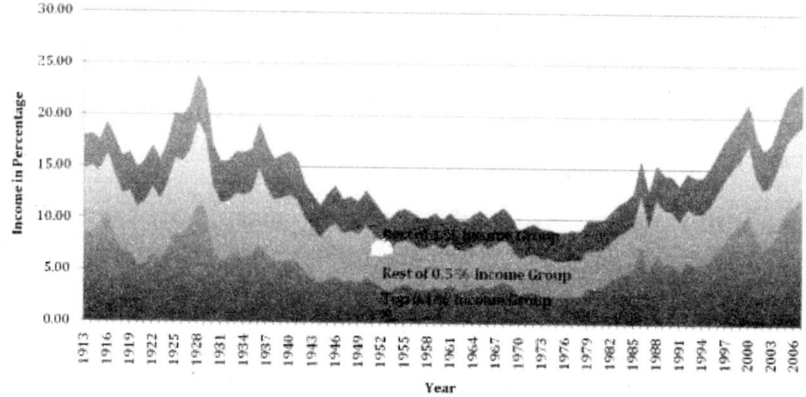

Figure 1.1 Top fractiles income sharing (including capital gains) in the U.S., 1913–2007. Statistical Source: Saez 2007

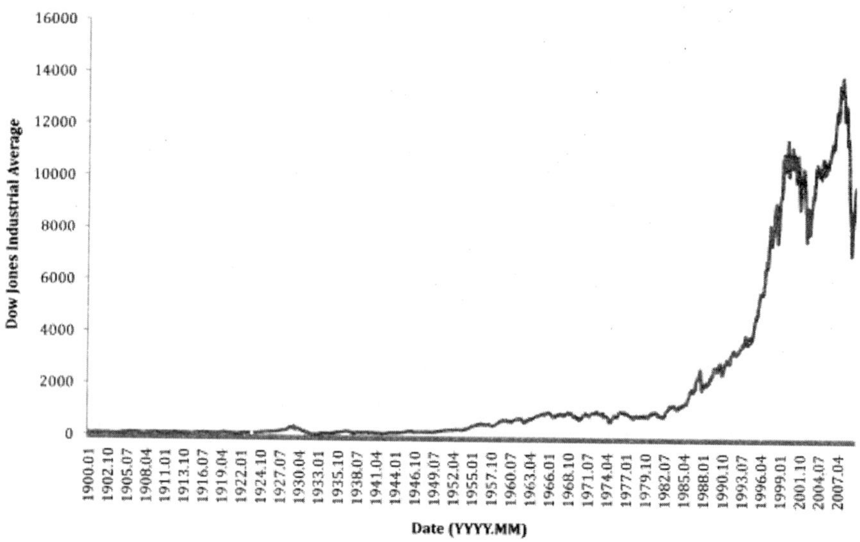

Figure 1.2 Dow Jones industrial average, 1900–2009. Source: Dow Jones, Wren Research (http://www.wrenresearch.com.au/downloads/files/mdowj.csv)

Examining the data for 15 countries with comparable time series, Atkinson et al. (2009) find this U shape to be typical for 9 countries (U.K., U.S., Canada, Australia, New Zealand, India, Argentina, Sweden, Norway), by comparison with a group of 6 countries where the share of the top 1% has remained relatively "flat" since World War II (France, Germany, Switzerland, Netherlands, Japan, Singapore). They find the share of total gross income received by the top 1% of income earners, strikingly similar for 18 countries for which comparable data are available—countries as diverse as India, Norway, France, New Zealand, and the U.S., the top 1% had on average between 8 and 12 times the average income. Or looking at the percentage of total income received by the top 0.1% of taxpayers, of 18 countries for which there is comparable data, 12 countries have around 3.25% of income going to this tiny group, and the top 0.1% had between 26 and 39 times the average income (Atkinson et al. 2009, 27). Putting this more starkly, the result of decades of unequal growth is that the assets of the 200 richest people in the world are greater in value than the assets of the 2.6 billion poorest people on earth. These are important facts. Economies can be structured to distribute income in a number of different ways. The Keynesian economies of the period 1945–1980 directed income to the working class because, following the depression of the 1930s, lack of demand was seen as the fundamental deficiency of capitalism. The neoliberal economies that followed deliberately channeled income to the capitalist class because lack of investment was seen as the fundamental deficiency of capitalism. An economy where 20% of the income produced goes to the richest 1% of the population moves along a fundamentally different trajectory than an economy where 5% of the income produced goes to this richest 1%.

Neoclassical economics predicts that such inequalities will be erased over time by the functioning of markets. In the meantime differences are due to "human capital deficiencies", like lack of education (Kuznets 1955; Tinbergen 1995). But the inequalities created by neoliberalism are too great to be accounted for by conventional criteria, like educational differences. The basic tenet of Marxist economic theory, by comparison, is that owners of money (capitalists) control the conditions under which labor makes commodities, by controlling factories, offices, land, and so on (the means of production), so that surplus value can be expropriated (or taken) from the real producers of value (human workers), to form the profit that is the real purpose of capitalist production—Marx (1973) calls this "exploitation". More wealth is extracted from labor by extending the number of workers employed in capitalist production, through globalization for instance, but more forcefully, neoliberal growth also extracts resources from poor people—what David Harvey (2005: 178) calls "accumulation by dispossession", through privatization, indebtedness, environmental degradation, the loss of traditional rights to common property, and so on. Accumulation by dispossession, as with taking land from peasants, requires intervention by the state, in what is inevitably an act of violence—because the state is taking away peoples' means of existing, killing their children, and condemning their aged to a retirement into misery. It also requires legitimation from powerful ideologies phrased in terms of the inevitability of progress, the necessity for development, or "this may look bad now but its good for everyone in the long run". (These ideologies appeal to some Marxists imbued with notions of technological growth and stages of history.) Then too, neoliberal growth produces glittering cities, with ostentatious new, tall buildings, streets full of cars, shopping centers, and well-dressed young people who are incessantly on the cell phone, all of which make it look like "everyone is doing well". This visual evidence overwhelms the statistical evidence, even when (rarely) data on inequality are presented, in the popular and expert opinion. On the one hand, we have to realize that statistical information is collected, understood, analyzed, and distributed by a technical elite acting in the interests of power, and not by dedicated, neutral scientists. But also that counter-evidence can be presented to limited audiences, in universities and other centers of the intelligentsia—positivism has its moments. On the other hand, the mass of the population sees more video than statistics. The video seen by the masses is subject to the most intensive editing, that excludes the few critical frames mistakenly captured by errant camera-persons, and is distributed by center-right to right media organizations that now include not only the obviously biased outlets, like Fox News, but even once venerable state corporations like the BBC World News.

IDEOLOGY

The main question that needs an answer is: why would a majority of the electorate vote for political parties that are committed to a neoliberal development model that disproportionately benefits a small minority? The convention is that, during the 1970s, Keynesianism entered into crisis. The term used to describe this is "stagflation"—high rates of inflation coinciding with high rates of unemployment. Further, the convention is that Keynesianism was replaced by a more effective neoliberal policy regime. However, as intimated earlier, analytic conventions are made from competing, interest-based interpretations, each given differential purchase on decision making by the political and cultural temper of the times. Recall that governments, economies, social systems, and cultures in the Western political democracies faced massive and continuous protests in the 1960s and early 1970s. Beginning with the Civil Rights movement, and opposition to the Viet Nam War, protest escalated into mass rejection of the consumptive values of a Fordist capitalism increasingly seen as contradictory with an overwhelmed natural environment. In face of escalating contentiousness that threatened social, cultural, and political order, the capitalist elite committed itself to counter-revolutionary activity. "During the 1970s, the political wing of the [U.S.] nation's corporate sector staged one of the most remarkable campaigns in the pursuit of power in recent history" so that by the early 1980s "corporations had a level of influence not seen since the boom days of the 1920s" (Edsall 1985, 107; Harvey 2006). An essential part of this was an interpretation of economic crisis that found the main structural contradiction to lie in lack of investment in sluggish economies. In the U.S., to take but one example, the state responded through neoliberal economic policies centered on redistribution of income toward rich investors. So, the Economic Recovery Tax Act of 1981 cut the marginal tax rate on the highest income bracket to 50%, followed soon after by the Tax Reform Act of 1986 further reducing the top rate to 28%, from which it rose during Democratic administrations in the 1990s to 39.6%, only to be cut again to 35% by the Economic Growth and Tax Relief Reconciliation Act of 2001. Compared with Keynesian marginal tax rates of 70% to 90%, the neoliberal policy regime brought marginal tax rates on high incomes down to a range of 28% to 50%.

The ideological guises of this redistribution were "recovery, reform, investment, growth", terms that suggest (to voters) a policy regime stimulating investment to serve broad, popular national and international interests. The reality was stagnation in the real incomes of working class and poor people—disguised by cheaper goods produced by a globalized economy. In Third World countries, the investment imperative is mixed with a fetish of the foreign to produce an ideology of the utter necessity for specifically foreign investment. It is dependency in new ideological guise. Under the control of this ideology, entire societies are re-structured to make them more appealing to the almighty white people—pimping for foreign investors—or, perhaps worse, setting up local investors as national, anti-imperialist heroes, while in fact they are just making money that could end up anywhere—New York, Dubai, the Cayman Islands; these people do not care. In brief, under neoliberalism, investment is the key to growth, and growth produces development, and we should let the rich do what they want with the money produced by social labor.

INEQUALITY AND CRISIS

Therefore, in the neoliberal policy regime since 1980 income was deliberately re-directed toward people who could not spend it, no matter how hard they tried ($20 million apartments in financial centers that became real-estate price multipliers); they could only save and invest it. So under neoliberalism $1 trillion a year flows into the investment accounts of a few hundred thousand already very wealthy people in the U.S. alone (Johnston 2005). Financial institutions compete to use the investment funds over-accumulated by "high net worth individuals" and by workers' savings in pension funds, insurance contributions, and so on. But there is a problem with private investment—the line between productive investment to improve efficiency and speculative investment to produce immediately high returns is so thin as to hardly exist. Even this thin line has broken under neoliberalism. Corporations compete to attract investment capital from this huge financial accumulation not so much by offering high dividends over the long run, which would be evidence of successful investment strategies, but by rapidly increasing the price of their shares in the short run, evidence of successful gambling. CEOs and corporate boards come and go, prosper or not, largely on the basis not so much of how effectively they run the corporation, but how much they can run up the price of the corporation's shares over a short period of time (re-visit Figure 1.2). Countries compete for investment from finance capital not on the basis of development in the long term, but how high a rate of return they can offer over the next year. Corporate and national capitals experience this competition for funds as an external compulsion originating in the dominant financial fraction of capital. CEOs who fail to deliver are subject to scrutiny by private equity firms that make their money by buying up "non-performing" corporations, ruthlessly restructuring them (i.e., firing workers), and then selling to make a quick profit that yields high returns to investors. So national economies, and indeed the global economy, are playgrounds for the speculative rich. Countries that fail to deliver are deemed to be out of touch with the new reality, full of red tape, without the right, competitive attitude. As this suggests, the reach of financial power (in all its aspects) has expanded outward, from its original, capitalist bases in the advanced industrial countries, onto a global playing field, where trillions of dollars range daily with ease and speed in search of high returns. Clearly, this global playground for capital is lined still with political and cultural boundaries. But increasingly, within the established, global investment space, countries are adjudicated merely as risk/benefit ratios, and by being included that way in the profit calculus, states are reduced in significance, except as they act as minders to the profit-seeking actions of global capital. This new version of finance capitalism is centered on the deployment of large accumulations of wealth by specialized institutions, like investment banks and risk assessment firms, concentrated in a few centers of financial power—the upper rank of "global cities".

So we live in societies where the dynamic of the economy is formed by the pursuit, by any means, of more money for those who already have too much. This reckless pursuit of money for the sake of more money is societal madness. It can only result in disaster. For the price of high returns is . . . eternal risk. Any investment fund, or any country, that does not generate high returns and, thereby, does not present extreme risk, suffers dis-investment in highly competitive markets, where money changes hands in computer-quickened moments. So, there is a competitive compulsion to take increasingly daring risks in search of higher returns that temporarily attract investment. Speculation, risk and fear, are structurally endemic to finance capitalism. Fear itself becomes the source of further speculation—buying gold or futures, for example. Speculation and gambling spread from Wall Street into all sectors of society—house prices, state lotteries, casinos, sweepstakes, Pokemon cards, "a chance to win with every purchase"—everyone gambles, even little kids. The interlocking of speculations is the source of their intractability and the widening space of their effects. The financial crisis of 2007–2010 has the following moments: vastly over-priced housing particularly near booming financial centers; competition among financial institutions to offer easy credit to everyone; the bundling of home mortgages into tradable paper; very high levels of leveraging; and the use of assets whose value can disappear in an instance to securitize other, even more risky, investments. It is not just that crisis spreads from one area to another. Its more that crisis in one (like the inevitable end to the housing price bubble) has exponential effects on the others (investment banks over-extended into high risk speculations) to the degree that losses accumulate that are beyond the rescuing powers of states and governance institutions. Hence the tendency in neoliberalism toward global catastrophe.

However, there is a bit more to it than this. What seems to have happened in the period since the middle 1990s is that small groups of financial experts contrived instruments that are so arcane, so riddled with difficulty, that only their creators, and a small inner group of insider-traders, can understand them or, more importantly, manipulate them, in markets with highly restricted access. For example, a small "tribe" of experts at the New York investment bank J. P. Morgan devised the instrument "credit derivative", essentially a contract by which Bank A pays a fee to Bank B in return for B assuming some of the risk on a loan granted by A. These credit derivative contracts are then bundled and sold to investment funds, while Bank A goes on to make more loans. Also necessary was intense, expensive lobbying that prevented the state and its regulatory apparatuses (the Securities and Exchange Commission in the U.S.) from overseeing this risky business (Tett 2009). When it went sour with the burst of the housing price bubble in 2006–2007, the state had to come to the rescue using taxpayer funds to bail the system out. This was an advance on mere "financial expertise"; in the Cities of Greed a new form of financial manipulation was created, that we might call "contrived expertise". To coin a phrase, "all expertise corrupts, and absolute expertise corrupts absolutely".

And finally, the discourse on neoliberalism has always been accompanied by a discourse on poverty that makes it look like something is being done for the poor even in societies that become more unequal by the day.

ANTI-POVERTY DISCOURSE

Under the neoliberal policy regime, income flows predominantly to the super-rich, causing poverty for the very poor. This central fact of neoliberal growth cannot be widely recognized because of its explosive social and political potential. Hence, we see the exclusive emphasis, among mainstream economists, on economic growth, rather than income distribution. The media focuses exclusively on the new glistening cities of the neoliberal earth and on the celebrities of wealth, the financiers and entrepreneurs, the corrupt politicians, the movie stars, the beautiful, tall, pale-faced, plastically enhanced "model" people. Hence the emphasis is on neoliberal growth as the wave of the future, and resistance to it . . . as the weight of the past. While the rich cannot recognize that their wealth causes poverty, at least in public, they are aware of it in private, and they have a conscience. In several traditions, philanthropy is the way rich people salve their consciences. This applies to rich individuals (Bill Gates, Warren Buffet, George Soros, Bono, Ratan Tata, and Narayana Murthy, to name a few), to the state apparatuses of the rich countries, and to the global governance institutions, as with the World Bank. Philanthropy toward poor people and low-income countries has its moments of sincerity. But it is encased within neoliberal beliefs that the rich earn, and deserve, their wealth. So the rich countries look down on the poor and, in pitying them, devote themselves to "ending global poverty" through safe means like education, funding anti-HIV-AIDs activities, and mosquito nets. Academic experts like Jeffrey Sachs (2005) are the "organic intellectuals" of the philanthropic elite and are well, and much, recognized, for their efforts in saving capitalism. Anti-poverty policy is an ideology aimed at reducing interregional tensions between rich and poor countries. And "ending global poverty now" is a disguise for the extension of the domain of global finance capital. It pacifies new regions of exploitation; it dominates societies behind a sympathetic face; or, in a word, it creates hegemonic space in a kindly way. In such ways, and more, are global finance capital, neoliberalism, and anti-poverty policy linked.

Anti-poverty policy is administered by the "international community" rather than any particular state. However, that "community" is the International Financial Institutions (IFIs) and, behind these, the Secretary of the U.S. Treasury Department, the British Chancellor of the Exchequer and the Finance Ministries of the other Western powers, and behind these the financial interests that control the leading capitalist states. The policies judged sound follow essentially a Washington consensus neoliberal agenda. Here we find the G7/8 countries, or rather their finance departments, in collusion with the IFIs, telling poor countries how they must run their economies if they want to receive debt relief. Just as the "deserving poor" are made to do the repentance shuffle to earn a charitable handout, or the homeless pretend instant arm-waving Christian conversion to get a bed for the night, now we find the rich countries telling the poor countries of the world how to "reform" to get their debt relief. This is the way global poverty is "solved".

But it is exactly this IFI insistence on neoliberal Washington consensus policies that brings demonstrators onto the streets in protest whenever the World Bank and the IMF meet. Why? First, it's the imperialism of economic policy, the undemocratic notion that a few thousand Western experts, steeped in neoclassical/neoliberal economics, know what policies work best for a world of diverse others in countries they have not visited. The recent versions of structural adjustment are particularly nasty because they disguise an imperialism of expertise in the wondrous garb of world humanity's most generous impulse, the elimination of global poverty.

Second, if the neoliberal policies prescribed by the IFIs actually worked for the poor, their elitism might possibly be forgiven. To get their money, poor countries have to agree to open their markets to foreign competition, privatize public enterprises, withdraw the state from service provision, reduce state budget deficits, reshape their economies toward export-orientation, "flexibilize" their labor markets, reduce marginal tax rates (on the rich), open their borders to capital movements, secure property rights for all property owners, domestic and foreign, and so on down a list written under the belief that markets, free competition, entrepreneurialism, and (especially foreign) investment can guide any economy into the magic realm of economic growth (Williamson 1997). But opening markets means losing protected jobs—that is, creating unemployment in the name of "efficiency" in countries where labor is already under-used. Privatization means introducing the profit motive into, for example, water or electricity supply, and cutting off anyone who cannot, or will not, pay higher rates—a lot of people have been shot for protesting that little number. Reducing swollen state deficits in the name of fiscal responsibility may sound fine until it is remembered that desperate people rely for their lives on state-supported food subsidies and free health care. As for exporting more, the problem is "export what?" China monopolizes cheap labor manufacturing and the prices of coffee, cocoa, and cotton are volatile, and have declined in the long run, so that small farmers break their backs working for less than nothing. (Note at the same time that local food production is undercut by focusing on export crops and removing tariff protections, producing a dangerous mass vulnerability to episodes of starvation.) Labor market flexibility means attacking the unions, paying lower wages, and eliminating what few laws might exist to protect workers—a great way to "eliminate poverty"! "Reducing marginal tax rates" on the rich is supposed to stimulate risk-taking, as though that was automatically admirable, but instead it is simply the state re-paying its owners. Opening borders and securing property rights reveal the real intent behind the Washington consensus—which is, to allow complete freedom of investment to create a form of economic growth that benefits capital most, especially foreign capital. And finally, even the supposed outcome, economic growth, when it happens, does not necessarily reduce poverty, especially when growth follows the neoliberal design. Instead it produces a replica of its U.S. homeland—wage stagnation for the majority, and more income for the already wealthy. In other words, to earn debt relief, supplicant countries have to restructure their economies neoliberally, so that they reward foreign capital. Debt relief in its present form, under the tutelage of the IFIs, produces the poverty it supposedly ends. Benevolence is beneviolence. Anti-poverty policies perpetuate poverty.

Has poverty actually decreased recently as the IFIs and United Nations Development Programme claim? An analysis by Sanjay Reddy and Camilia Minoiu (2007) concludes that, because of uncertainties in the methods used to measure levels of poverty ($1 and $2 a day incomes per person) and deficiencies in the data collected, "global poverty may or may not have increased. The extent of the estimated increase or decrease in world poverty is critically dependent on the assumptions made". In a major review of the World Bank poverty data Robert Wade (2004) concludes: "The magnitude of world population increase over the past 20 years is so large that the Bank's poverty numbers would have to be *huge* underestimates for the world poverty rate not to have fallen. Any more precise statement about the absolute number of the world's people living in extreme poverty and the change over time currently rests on quicksand."

What we know more certainly is that neoliberal economic growth increases social inequality. In a 2007 report, *Inequality in Asia*, the Asian Development Bank (ADB) finds that over the last decade most Asian countries have experienced increases in inequality, especially absolute inequality (i.e., absolute differences in the incomes of the richest 20% of the population versus the poorest 20%). As the ADB puts it, mildly: "Increases in inequality dampen the poverty-reducing impact of a given amount of growth". We might add the obvious, although they do not: because nearly all the income produced by neoliberal growth goes to rich people.

As the institutions regulating capitalism have globalized, with increased power going to the IMF, the World Bank, the World Trade Organization, the UN agencies, the European Union, so has policy. Hence we see global "concern" about poverty. Recently, a more emotive, idealistic, moralistic veneer has been added to this "science-based" policy discourse because, in the Fordist age of consumerism and advertising, people are attuned to image, suggestion, and subjective exaggeration in all spheres of life, especially the political. Particularly in the case of the global poverty discourse, the use of image, media, and spectacle plays on popular concern, apparently to build support for philanthropic action by states, charities of nongovernmental organizations, but less obviously to channel what could mount into mass anger into safe and responsible, institutionally contained intervention. Much of the poverty discourse takes the superficial form of an optimistic, hand-wringing, moralistic blather. Nevertheless the message pushed by organizations like (singer) Bob Geldof's "Make Poverty History"—"we are telling the rich countries that The World Can't Wait. They must deliver on their promises and take decisive action against poverty and climate catastrophe now"—has been constructed into the predominant popular form taken by public debate. Their notion of the causes of global poverty—"it isn't chance or bad luck that keeps people trapped in bitter, unrelenting poverty. It's man-made factors like a glaringly unjust global trade system, a debt burden so great that it suffocates any chance of recovery and insufficient and ineffective aid"—have sufficient purchase on the immediate causes as to be believable. Such well-intentioned efforts raising mass consciousness about poverty might have some positive effect. The media intermittently carry stories about "poverty in Africa" especially when there is some good footage of crying babies and shriveled refugees available, before quickly moving on to happy trivia before the next ad-break—all the news that's fit to entertain. But we have to go further in criticizing the misleading analysis of the causes of poverty and the superficiality of the proscribed remedies. Is the positivity of mass awareness worth the necessary deviation into superficiality? My own position on this has changed over time to the point where I think that superficiality of causal analysis produces a temporary, easily diverted mass awareness.

NEOLIBERALISM IN INDIA

The New Economic Policy adopted in India in 1991 includes standard structural adjustment measures, under the tutelage of the IMF and World Bank (after a relatively small 1991 emergency loan), including the devaluation of the rupee, increase in interest rates, reduction of public investment, reduction in public sector food and fertilizer subsidies, restructuring of the industrial sector, increase in imports and foreign investment in capital-intensive and high-tech activities, and abolition of the cash compensatory support for exports. Many interpretations see this program of economic liberalization as transforming the economy for the better, and leading to a substantial increase in the rate of India's economic growth. India is frequently used as the leading recent success story for neoliberal reform of a country's economic policy regime (Das 2006; Aiyar 2008). The change from what neoliberal economists call the "License Raj" to the "New Economic Policy" in 1991 is seen as resulting in some of the highest growth rates for any economy in the world. India's gross domestic product grew at a rate of 5.8% a year in the period 1980–1990 and 5.9% a year in the period 1990–2005, with annual rates of growth of 8.5, 7.5, and 8.1% in the budgetary years 2003–2004, 2004–2005, and 2005–2006 (Government of India 2007). Even so, when posed in terms of social justice, the question is not growth, but who benefits from the new growth regime and whether it can significantly improve the conditions of livelihood for India's 350 million people with incomes below $1.00 a day, or the 800 million people with incomes below $2.00 a day. Using the conventional understanding this should be an economy that has grown rapidly enough, over a period long enough, to enable social problems, like poverty, to show significant signs of being reduced. At first sight this appears to be the case. Quoting the World Bank:

> [. . .] estimates for India indicate a continuing decline in poverty. The revised estimates suggest that the percentage of people living below $1.25 a day in 2005 (which, based on India's PPP rate, works out to Rs 21.6 a day in urban areas and Rs 14.3 in rural areas in 2005) decreased

> from 60% in 1981 to 42% in 2005. Even at a dollar a day (Rs 17.2 in urban areas and Rs 11.4 in rural areas in 2005) poverty declined from 42% to 24% over the same period. Both the dollar a day and $1.25 measures indicate that India has made steady progress against poverty since the 1980s, with the poverty rate declining at a little under one percentage point per year. (World Bank 2009)

However there is considerable skepticism about the accuracy of the poverty estimates—to the extent that poverty rates may be twice as high using one method of measurement as they are using another. It is impossible to tell, from the data available, whether poverty in India has increased or decreased since 1991 (Palmer-Jones and Sen 2001). Or, in another example, a report by the government-appointed N. C. Saxena committee in 2009 concluded that at least half India's rural population lives in poverty, nearly doubling the Planning Commission's previous estimate that 28% of Indian villagers are poor. The Saxena committee also found that though the official poverty count fell from 56% in 1973–1974 to 28% in 2004, there had been no real decline in the number of the poor (Paul 2009, 1).

So, as the World Bank (2009) is forced to conclude:

> the number of very poor people who lived below a dollar a day in 2005 has come down from 296 million in 1981 to 267 million in 2005. However, the number of poor people living under $1.25 a day has increased from 421 million in 1981 to 456 million in 2005. This indicates that there are a large number of people living just above this line of deprivation (a dollar a day) and their numbers are not falling. To achieve a higher rate of poverty reduction, India will need to address the inequalities in opportunities that impede poor people from participating in the growth process.

In other words the poverty rate is going down according to the revised definition, but the numbers of poor people are increasing, because whether its $1.00 or $1.25 a day, the definition of poverty is arbitrary, and there is a huge mass of poor people who live around this artificial level, and will be "deprived" anyway. Yet the World Bank uses this morass of statistical confusions to authoritatively claim that poverty results from "inequalities in opportunities to participate in the growth process", as though that growth process is aimed at benefitting everyone if only they can "participate"—a new version of blaming the victim. The power of policy expertise lies exactly in its near monopoly control over the production of statistics, over publication, and, most of all, over media dissemination. The release of the "latest figures", covered extensively by the media, who love tables and leagues, is used as opportunity to slip in a lecture on the causes of poverty. And the lecture is always conventional—neoliberalism produces growth, growth grants opportunities for those who can grasp them, and we should approach the poor, benighted people, mired in the past, by reaching down with extended helping hands to pull them into the future. In the meantime, poverty is what conventional expertise makes of it. When they want it to be reduced to show that neoliberal policy is "succeeding", miraculously, hey presto, down goes poverty, and out comes the stock footage of fat, smiling babies and happy shoppers. Poverty measurement is expertise for sale.

What we do know with more certainty is whether inequality has changed since the neoliberal reforms of the early 1990s. As one author puts it: India's "outstanding aggregate growth" comes with growing inequality (Basu 2008), and as others show regional inequality in India remained largely unchanged during the 1980s but rose dramatically after the adoption of the 1991 reforms (Kar and Sakthivel 2007). Using tabulations of tax returns published each year by the Indian tax administration Banerjee and Piketty (2005, 1–2) conclude:

> The data show that the shares of the top 0.01 percent, 0.1 percent, and 1 percent in total income shrank substantially from the 1950s to the early to mid-1980s but then rose again, so that today these shares are only slightly below what they were in the 1920s and 1930s. This U-shaped pattern is broadly consistent with the evolution of economic policy in India: From the 1950s to the early to mid-1980s was a period of "socialist" policies in India, whereas the subsequent period, starting with the rise of Rajiv Gandhi, saw a gradual shift toward more probusiness policies . . . the results are consistent with an important role for policy in shaping the distribution of income. In particular, there is evidence of a substantial decline in the share of the elite during the years of socialist planning and a comparable recovery in the post-liberalization era.

So neoliberal growth in India is consistent with the world-wide pattern of channeling income to the super-rich (Figure 1.3). India has the U-shape curve of decreasing proportions of income going to the super-rich during socialism, followed by increasing proportions under the neoliberal NEP. And the Bombay stock exchange shows why—a bubble in stock prices in the 2000s, then a crash, then instability (Figure 1.4). That is neoliberalism's purpose—the rich are rewarded in the hope that they will be entrepreneurial. And that is its function—to provide them capital with which to be entrepreneurial . . . or speculative. At least grant the IFIs and the Government of India a certain audaciousness for their claim, in effect, that "inequality cures poverty". For us it's the reverse: utter, total corruption of the society's economic morality.

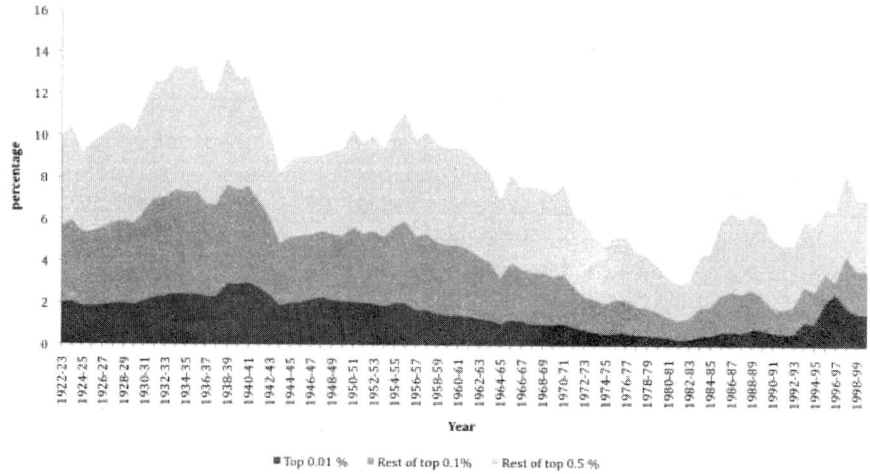

Figure 1.3 Percentage of income earned by top 0.05% of taxpayers in India, 1922–2000. Source: All India Income Tax Statistics, 1922–2000.

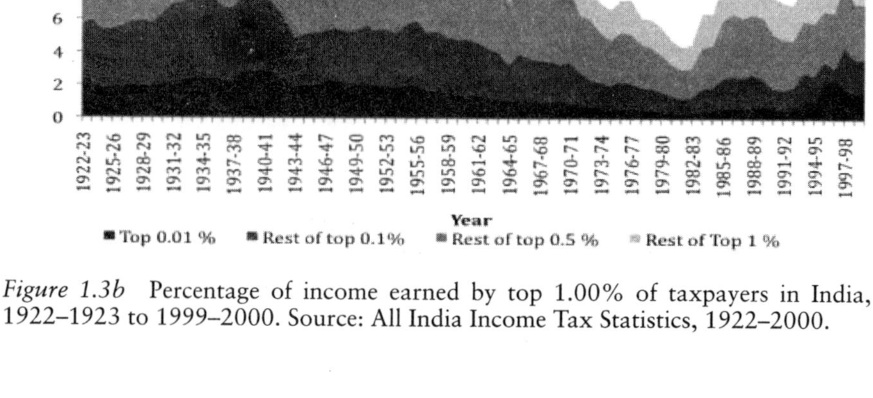

Figure 1.3b Percentage of income earned by top 1.00% of taxpayers in India, 1922–1923 to 1999–2000. Source: All India Income Tax Statistics, 1922–2000.

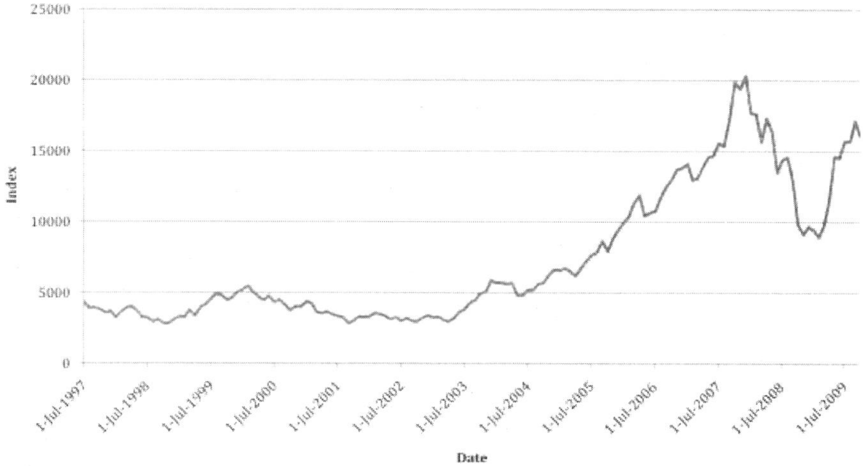

Figure 1.4 Bombay stock sensitive exchange index, 1997–2009. Source: All India Income Tax Statistics, 1922-2000. Source: Yahoo! Finance (http://finance.yahoo.com/q/hp?s=%5EBSESN&a=06&b=1&c=1997&d=09&e=30&f=2009&g=m)

CONCLUSION

The claim that neoliberal growth produces development in India and elsewhere is one huge confidence trick. Economic growth under neoliberalism consistently benefits a minority of the population: in India, the business elite and people with an education who can speak English. Such growth has spectacular effects in the way of "world cities" with tall, new office buildings, opulent houses, high levels of conspicuous consumption, "modern-looking" young people, new cultural styles, cosmopolitanization, and so on. It produces a "razzle-dazzle" effect that convinces even critical minds that a process of development that is widely beneficial is indeed under way now, and will include everyone . . . soon. So visitors go to Mumbai and somehow see only the colonial waterfront, framed by hills dotted with elegant residences, and amazingly not the streets clogged with plastic-sheeted hovels where millions sleep and defecate every night. The visitor, the beneficiary, the policymaker, the bureaucrat, the media personality, even the reader of "serious newspapers", all are members of a cultural/social/economic elite that lives, experiences, and reflects in cloistered spaces, even when passing through India's streets of misery. The people who usually comment on a policy regime lie within a circle of responsible spokespersons that benefits from those policies—by high salary and stock ownership, for example. And everyone is affected by the rays of affluent modernity emitted from the centers of power, influence, and persuasion. Can it be that this kind of socially constructed affluent reality is more persuasive than poverty-ridden material reality? Does affluence put optimistic, rose-colored spectacles on the eyes of the world's elite?

It is essential that dominant power presents neoliberalization as modernization rather than exploitation. Modernization allows the possibility that everyone eventually will benefit from an economic growth conceived as societal evolution. This kind of drive to modernity convinces that power must be exercised ruthlessly when necessary, because the powerful have seen the future, and it (apparently) works, whereas resistance ignorantly blocks the way toward progress for all. However things look differently from the other side, from the perspective of people who have not passed through the looking glass, even while they might be dazed by its reflected light. Here material reality, in the form of the enormous inequalities and massive deprivation produced by neoliberal growth, bursts through the most sophisticated ideological disguise as the upsurge of peasant and worker movements, the outbursts of direct action, the constant flow of moments of disgust. It looks differently too from the perspective of that tiny intellectual minority who have, to a degree, evaded or transcended neoliberal mesmerization. For "the truth" is that neoliberal development is predicated on the underdevelopment of the vast majority of people, as dependency theory would have it. The trouble is, this alternative version of the "truth" is difficult to reach. Critical theory, deconstruction, and alternative data are the tools of this tiny intellectual minority. Speaking from within the small elite that reads, understands, and can criticize statistical data, the evidence is overwhelming: it is perfectly clear, to those who care to examine, to those who think in a caring way, that neoliberalism's main socioeconomic product is inequality (because it's intended to produce it), and that inequality's main product is poverty (because inequality is exploitative—the rich benefit *at the expense of* the poor). So while neoliberalism may bring growth, even spectacular over-abundance in some places, it cannot bring development, in the sense of growth that particularly benefits the poor. Neoliberalism cannot solve social problems ("challenges" in their optimistic lexicon) because it causes them at a faster rate than it appears to solve them. In the Marxist sense, neoliberalism is fundamentally contradictory, with the opposition between growth and poverty being foundational, irresolvable within neoliberal relations of production. That is why neoliberalism must be abandoned. To all people of conscience: unite, you have nothing to loose except your illusions.

REFERENCES

Aiyar, S .S. A. 2008. India lets success happen. *The American Spectator* July 1.

Asian Development Bank. 2007. *Inequality in Asia*. Manila: ADB.

Atkinson, A. B., Thomas Piketty, and Emmanuel Saez. 2009. Top incomes in the long-run of history. Chap. 13 in *Top incomes: A global perspective*.

Banerjee, A., and T. Piketty, 2004. Are the rich growing richer? Evidence from Indian tax data. In *Data and dogma: The great Indian poverty debate*, edited by A. Deaton and V. Kozel, 598–611. London: McMillan Press.

———. 2005. Top Indian incomes, 1922–2000. *World Bank Economic Review* 19: 1–20.

Basu, K. 2008. India's dilemmas: The political economy of policymaking in a globalised world. *Economic and Political Weekly* 43 (February).

Chang, H-J., and R. Rowthorn, eds. 1995. *The role of the state in economic change*. Oxford: Clarendon Press

Das, G. 2006. The India model. *Foreign Affairs* (July/August).

Dow Jones, 2009. Dow Jones Industrial Average (DJIA) History.

Edsall, T. 1985. *The new politics of inequality*. New York: Norton.

Galbraith, J. K. 2007. Global inequality and global macroeconomics. *Journal of Policy Modeling* 29: 587–607.

G8 Finance Ministers' Conclusions on Development London June 10–11 2005.

Government of India. 2007. *Economic survey*. New Delhi: Ministry of Finance.

Harvey, D. 2005. *A brief history of neoliberalism*. Oxford: University Press.

Johnston, D. C. Richest are leaving even the rich far behind. *New York Times*, pp. 1, 17, June 5, 2005.

Kar, S., and S. Sakthivel. 2007. Reforms and regional inequality in India. *Economic and Political Weekly* 42 (November 30).

Kohli, A. 2004. *State-directed development: Political power and industrialization in the global periphery* .Cambridge: University Press

Kuznets, S. 1955. Economic growth and income inequality. *American Economic Review* 45(1): 1–28.

Leone, R. C. 1996. Foreword. In *Top Heavy: A Study of Increasing Inequality of Wealth in America* by E. N. Wolf. New York: The New Press.

Marx, K. 1967. *Capital* Vol. 1. New York: International Publishers.

Nayer, B. R. 1998. Political structure and India's economic reforms of the 1990s. Pacific Affairs 71: 335–358.

Palmer-Jones, R. W., and K. K. Sen 2001. On India's poverty puzzles and the statistics of poverty. *Economic and Political Weekly* 36: 211–217.

Paul, C. Count puts poverty at 50%, riles govt. *The Telegraph* (Calcutta), p. 1, September 21, 2009.

Peck J., and A. Tickell. 2002. Neoliberalizing space. *Antipode* 34: 380–404.

Peet, R. 2007. *Geography of power*. London: Zed Books.

Piketty, T., and E. Saez. 2006. The evolution of top incomes: A historical and international perspective. *American Economic Review* 96: 200–205.

Pollin, R. 2003. *Contours of descent: U.S. economic fractures and the landscape of global austerity*. London: Verso

Polanyi, K. 1944. *The great transformation*. Boston: Beacon Press.

Reddy, Sanjay, and Camilia Minoiu. 2007. Has world poverty really fallen? Social Science Research Network. www.socialanalysis.org.

Sachs, J. 2005. *The End of Poverty: Economic Possibilities for Our Time*. Foreword by Bono. New York: The Penguin Press.

Saez, E. with Thomas Piketty. 2007. Income inequality in the United States, 1913–1998. *Quarterly Journal of Economics* 118(1), 2003: 1–39. |FCO|HyperlinkLonger updated version published in A. B. Atkinson and T. Piketty, eds., Oxford University Press, 2007 (updated August 2009). |FCC| http://elsa.berkeley.edu/~saez/.

Tickell, A., and J. Peck. 1995. Social regulation after Fordism: Regulation theory, neoliberalism and the global-local nexus. *Economy and Society* 24: 357–386.

Tett, G. 2009. *Fool's gold: How the bold dream of a small tribe at J. P. Morgan was corrupted by Wall Street greed and unleashed a catastrophe*. New York: Free Press.

Tinbergen J. 1995. *Income distribution: Analysis and policies*. Amsterdam: North-Holland. UNDP (United Nations Development Programme). 1999. *Human Development Report*. New York: UNDP.

———. 2007. *Human Development Report*. New York: UNDP.

Wade, Robert Hunter. 2004. Is globalization reducing poverty and inequality? *World Development* 32: 567–589.
Williamson, J. 1997. The Washington consensus revisited. In *Economic and social development into the XXI century*, edited by Louis Emmerji. Washington, DC: Inter-American Development Bank.
Wolf, E. N. 1996. *Top heavy: A study of increasing inequality of wealth in America*. New York: The New Press.
World Bank. 2004. *World development report*. New York: Oxford University Press
———. 2008. *World development report*. New York: Oxford University Press.
———. 2009. New global poverty estimates: What it means for India. 2http://go.worldbank.org/51QB3OCFU0.
Yahoo! Finance. http://finance.yahoo.com/q/hp?s=%5EBSESN&a=06&b=1&c=1997&d=09&e=30&f=2009&g=m.

2 From Mixed Economy to Neoliberalism

Class and Caste in India's Policy Transition

Waquar Ahmed

INTRODUCTION

This chapter examines the evolution of India's neoliberal economic policy regime by embedding it in the broader social, political, and economic transformation of the country. It also provides a brief case study of the electric power industry.

After gaining independence from British rule, India adopted an indigenously altered variant of Keynesianism, a 'mixed-economy' approach to development, with major investments in the public sector, yet with some sectors remaining open to private capital. In 1990–1991, India underwent a balance of payment crisis. To overcome this crisis, India borrowed money from the World Bank and the International Monetary Fund (IMF). These loans came with conditionality. India had to implement structural adjustment—that is, adopt neoliberal economic policies. Even though India's policy change was sudden, and a result of U.S.-backed IMF's coercion, this policy change was not bereft of endogenous support. Neoliberalism had the support of the Indian elite, represented in class, but also caste, power. Here I look at the transition from Keynesianism to neoliberalism, as the dominant developmental discourse at the global level, and examine how this influenced India's economic policy change. I look more specifically at the agents involved in the transformation of India's economic and electricity policy in the direction of neoliberalism. The chapter is divided into six sections. The first section, "Agriculture and the Societal Basis of Economic Transformation", deals with the overall exercise of class, caste, and spatial power in rural India in the transformation of India's economic/development policy. Similarly, the second section, "Industry and the Societal Basis of Economic Transformation", focuses on urban-industrial society and economic change. The next section, "Global Policy Regimes", examines dominant and alternative development discourses and policy regimes at the global level and sets the background to understand how India was drawn into the neoliberal regime. The fourth section, "Shock Therapy", examines India's balance of payment crisis that allowed the International Monetary Fund and the World Bank to intervene in India's economic policy. The fifth section "Power Policy in India", examines India's electricity sector, which is representative of, and formative in, India's neoliberal transformation. The final section presents a set of conclusions.

AGRICULTURE AND THE SOCIETAL BASIS OF ECONOMIC TRANSFORMATION

India gained independence from Britain in 1947. The new Government of India faced numerous, immediate problems. Consolidation of the significantly different regions and the greatly varying identities into a single nation-state was among the more important problems. India had a semi-feudal[1] social structure (Bhaduri 1973), and the caste system prevented socioeconomic mobility for a large section of the population (Dumont 1970; Namboodiripad 1977; 1981). The transformation of a caste-based, exploitative social structure into a more egalitarian social order was another major problem. Improving living conditions for the general population, and uniting diverse regions and identities, was interpreted in terms of a state-led agenda of development and progress. In 1951 about 83% of India's people lived in rural areas. Policymakers believed that India needed a strategy of balanced growth: that is, simultaneous development of the industrial and the agricultural sectors. While industrial growth was given priority, rural and agricultural development was deemed vital for India's food security and the overall development of the nation. The fact that independent India emerged as a democracy compelled the state to draw support from poor and rural people. Even the elites drew substantial power from ownership of land in rural India. The problem of poverty and landlessness of the poor in rural India and the transformation of the sub-human conditions to which lower caste population had been relegated (Ambedkar and Moon 1979; Ilaiah 1996) were issues that the state needed to address immediately. The survival of democracy in India depended on the electoral support of the poor and deprived castes.

According to Rudolph and Rudolph (1987), state intervention in post-colonial (and pre-neoliberal) India has been partly successful in improving the lives of socially and economically deprived sections of the society, and class polarization has diminished as a result. India no longer has an agrarian upper class anything like England's landed aristocracy, Prussia's Junkers, or the Latin American latifundistas. The first wave of land reforms in the 1950s nominally, and to a considerable extent actually, abolished "intermediaries," the quasi-feudal landlord class, standing between the state and the cultivator, by acting as revenue agents while performing some local government functions. Since then, no prominent political party, at least until the late 1980s, dared to exclusively represent the interest of urban and rural capitalists at the expense of alienating the poor.

In the 1960s, two producer groups occupied the dominant position in the countryside left vacant by the forced demise of the quasi-feudal landlords. Some landlords, with variously sized holdings, had successfully blocked or evaded land ceiling legislation, and rented to sharecroppers or tenants, or employed attached or casual labor. Members of the other group, termed 'bullock capitalists' (Rudolph and Rudolph 1987), made up of small to medium-sized, self-employed, independent agricultural producers, were the main beneficiaries of reform. The balance of power between these groups lay with the landlords in the 1960s. But in the 1970s, power shifted toward the bullock capitalists. Electrification of villages became an important means for the state, and the ruling political alliances, for garnering support from these powerful groups. India entered a period, now referred to as the Green Revolution, involving the widespread use of high-yielding crop varieties, with significant increases in inputs of water and fertilizer in fields that had hitherto been almost solely dependent on rainfall. Much of the early irrigation projects were large and publicly funded, involving surface water resources. Later groundwater pumping on individual farms, using electrical or diesel pump-sets, became increasingly prevalent (Dubash and Rajan 2001). Subsidized electricity began to be used as a political tool for garnering the support of powerful sections of the rural population in the mid-1970s. To a degree, this subsidy benefited the poor farmers and led to broader rural development. But the richer farmers benefited most and paid little, or nothing, for the resource they consumed. Over time, the substantial subsidies became a liability for the state exchequer. But farmers had become so used to the subsidy that any discussion among policymakers about removing it drew protests, jeopardizing chances of the ruling political party in subsequent elections.

In the 1980s, more than 70% of the population continued to live in rural areas. The contribution of agriculture and allied activities, however, to the sectoral share of the national income, declined from 59% in 1950–1951 to 41% in 1980–1981 (see Figure 2.1). The industrial and the service sectors, primarily located in urban areas, made up 65% of the total gross domestic product of the national economy by 1990–1991 (see Figure 2.1c). These figures portray tremendous shifts in economic power between regions (urban/rural) and sectors of the economy. It was among people with economic interests in non-agricultural sectors, who did not benefit much from agricultural subsidies, that a mindset against state control developed—this section of the population became supporters of neoliberal policies. Rural India, including the rural bourgeoisie, however, continued to favor a developmental state—they had benefited from state policy of subsidized electricity, seeds, fertilizer, and so on. Neoliberalism, evidently, has harmed the agricultural sector—post-1991, agricultural growth rate in India declined sharply (see Table 2.1). In the wake of policy changes in 1991, Indian farmers organized several anti-globalization rallies: the second *Lucknow Panchayat* (meeting of the village community in the city of Lucknow) in

January 1992 to protest against the hike in fertilizers and electricity rates; the *Dunkel Dunk* or *Beej* (seed) *Satyagraha* of 1992–1993 to pressurize the government and stop the entry of multi-national corporations in the agricultural sector; and several others. The Dunkel Dunk was a movement in opposition to the Dunkel Draft text of the Uruguay round of the General Agreement on Tariffs and Trade (GATT). Arthur Dunkel, then director general of GATT, had drafted a treaty which supported the patenting of seeds and liberalization of agricultural imports and exports—more than 500,000 farmers and activists took part in the anti-globalization march in the city of Bangalore in October 1992 and more than 200,000 farmers and activists marched to the historic Red Fort in Delhi on March 1993 (Shiva 2005). In other words, support for neoliberalism is an urban (elite and middle-class) phenomenon. Despite being the numerical minority, the urban elite has been able to exercise greater power over India's economic policy formulation because of the shift in India's economic base from the rural to urban. Additionally, the urban elite control India's media and intellectual space, vital in producing consent in favor of neoliberal policies, and have a stranglehold over India's economic policy. On account of rural opposition, the neoliberal transformation of rural India has been relatively slow.

INDUSTRY AND THE SOCIETAL BASIS OF ECONOMIC TRANSFORMATION

Social contestations in rural India, within and around the agricultural sector, formed the early background to India's overall policy transformation. But the centers of struggle for economic liberalization were located in India's cities, within the manufacturing and service sectors. As evident from Figure 2.1, the manufacturing and service sectors of the India economy had gained positions of prominence by the 1980s and 1990s. Individuals and associations representing the interests of the manufacturing and service industries were now in a position, more than ever before, to influence India's economic policies to their advantage. Thus, it is also important to examine the historic rise of India's industrial-entrepreneurial class.

Indian big business had not played a crucial role in India's independence struggle between 1917 and 1947 (Kochanek 1987). India's development strategy was, at least theoretically, designed to ensure that the economy would grow rapidly in a planned and self-reliant direction; the private sector would invest only in high-priority industries approved by the government; monopoly and the concentration of economic power would be forestalled; the state would come to control the commanding heights of the economy; and steep tax rates for individuals and corporations would provide resources for the plan, check the conspicuous consumption of the rich, and create a society based on social justice. Industry's share in India's gross national product (GNP) was only 18.8% in 1978, though it was growing

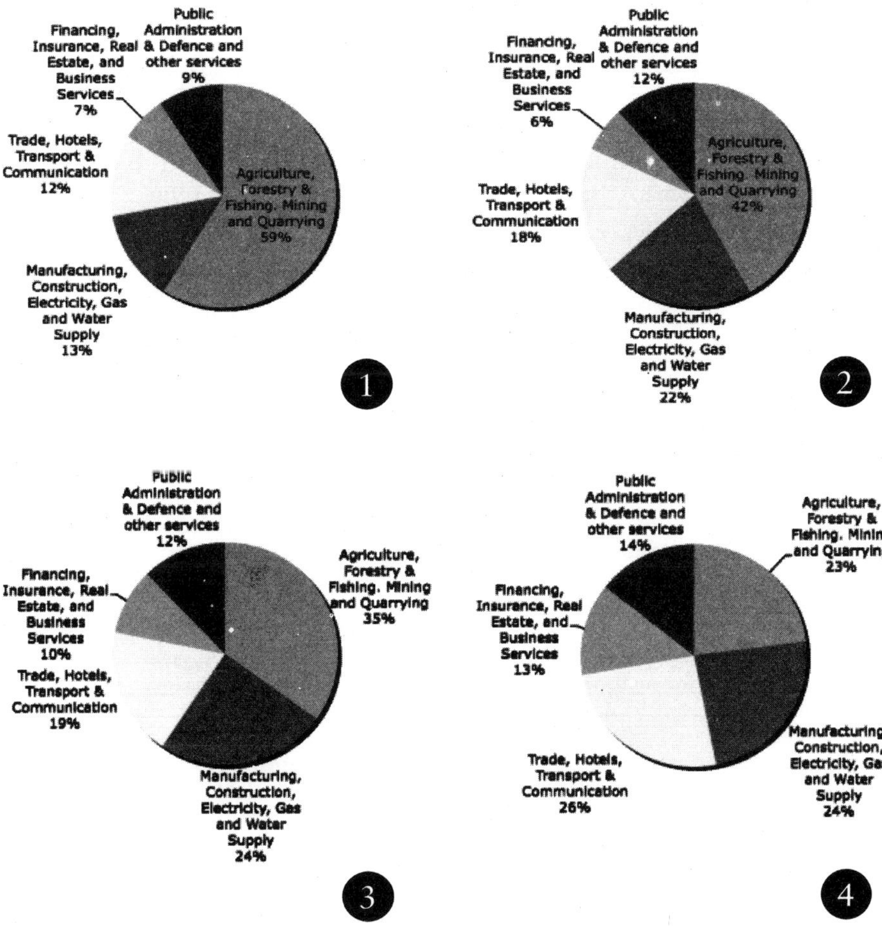

Figure 2.1 Proportion of gross domestic product at factor cost by industry of origin.

rapidly, increasing to 28% in 1983 (*Seminar* 1985). In 1985, of the total paid-up capital held in large-scale industrial units, public sector units held 78.6% (Ministry of Industry 1985). Thus, the privately owned industrial sector remained small, as compared to the total size of the economy. In addition to its limited space in the Indian economy, the business community itself was plural, heterogeneous, and too insufficiently mobilized to articulate a consistent set of class interests prior to economic liberalization.

Super-imposition of state control to produce socialism[2] in a semi-feudal society empowered the Indian bureaucrats and politicians to exercise control over all business/economic decisions, including investment, production, technology, location, prices, imports, exports, financing, and foreign capital. It also led to a mindset among the political elite that expected and demanded allegiance from the business elite in the form of subservience and political support. Gradually, the system developed an exchange relationship between business and government. In order to attain 'favor', business elites expressed allegiance to the state controllers of the economy by contributing to party funds. Over the years, the two biggest private business houses—Birla and Tata—became the biggest contributors to party funds (Kochanek 1987). The Birla group, based in Calcutta/West Bengal, completely backed the Congress Party as their best insurance against a communist alternative in that radical region. The Tata group was essentially based in Bombay, though they also had business interest in the eastern part of the country. The Tata group contributed to the Congress Party, but also to opposition parties. Business houses set in place elaborate networks of formal and informal mechanisms giving access to government. They learnt not only how to live with the system but also how to use the system to their advantage (Nayar 1971). Indeed the big business groups depended on the system in securing monopoly protection and guaranteed profitability. They grew at a phenomenal rate, especially in the 1970s—the assets of the Tata and Birla industrial houses increased by 44% and 34%, respectively, between 1977 and 1980 (*Eastern Economist* 1982).

According to one informant in this research, the assistant director of the Federation of Indian Chambers of Commerce and Industry (FICCI), "if you keep protecting some of the large business houses, at the end of the day, you are not allowing the rest of the entrepreneurs to grow". FICCI and the Associated Chambers of Commerce and Industry (Assocham) were the two main national civil society groups acting on behalf of big business houses up to the late 1980s. FICCI essentially promoted the interest of the Birla industrial house and Assocham promoted the interest of the Tata industrial house (i.e., lobbied to maintain the dominant status of these business groups). The rapid growth of the manufacturing and service sectors, especially in the 1980s (see Table 2.1), however, led to the entry of many more private entrepreneurs into the Indian market. A larger group of private investors exercised influence on the government of India. Beginning in the 1980s, a more private-capital-friendly government[3] withdrew important constraints on the expansion of big business and encouraged them to enter areas hitherto reserved for the public sector. The Monopolies and Restrictive Trade Practices Act (the MRTP Act), that had effectively limited the growth of big business, was diluted, removing licensing restrictions and allowing big businesses to expand in such core industries as chemicals, drugs, ceramics, and cement (Kohli 2006). The Government also encouraged the private sector to get into electrical power generation. The pro-business policy package included tax concession to private investors which, for the first time, led to pressure on the national budget, forcing the government to restrict public sector investment (Kohli 2006). In the mid-1980s, Rajiv Gandhi, prime minister of India, appointed Manmohan Singh, who had served in the board of governors of the IMF, and Montek Singh Ahluwalia, a former World Bank employee, as economic advisors. Even so, the Indian state was not yet friendly to *global* capital—policy changes essentially benefited the big Indian business groups.

India's smaller private entrepreneurs realized that FICCI and Assocham could not be relied upon to protect their interests. In 1974, the Association of Indian Engineering Industry (AIEI) emerged as a fusion between two organizations representing foreign and Indian engineering companies. In 1986, the AIEI changed its name to Confederation of Engineering Industry (CEI), and in 1992 the organization was renamed Confederation of Indian Industry (CII). The AIEI/CEI/CII emerged as a refuge for business groups unhappy with FICCI and Assocham's overt bias toward big business, especially the Birla and Tata houses. AIEI/CEI/CII also united disgruntled breakaway groups from Assocham, essentially industrialists from the western part of India, with industrialists from the southern part of India who were investing in new industries. These new units were dominated by the engineering industry, which had a stronger than average orientation toward the use of modern technologies, indicated by the almost universal presence of technological collaboration agreements with foreign companies (Confederation of Indian Industry 1992). In the late 1980s and early 1990s, CEI/CII consolidated its position as the main body representing the interest of Indian industries. This change in the power and position of CEI/CII, with respect to FICCI and Assocham, can be interpreted as a change in the convictions and interests of private industry, in a direction different from the traditional outlook of Indian industry. Abid Hussain, one of the architects of India's economic policy regime transformation, observed in an interview in 1988 that "a new breed of entrepreneurs has emerged and it

Table 2.1 Growth Data, 1950–2005 (all figures in percentage per annum)

	1950–1965	*1965–1980*	*1980–1990*	*1990–2005*[4]
GDP	4.1	2.9	5.8	5.9
Manufacturing, construction, electricity, gas, and water	6.8	4.0	6.7	6.1
Agriculture, forestry & fishing, mining, and quarrying	3	1.5	4.7	2.7
Trade, hotels, transportation, and communication	5.7	4.4	5.8	8.5
Finance, insurance, real estate, and business services	3.1	4.0	9.2	8.2
Public administration & defense and other services	4.4	4.2	5.9	6.4

Source: Economic Survey, Government of India, various issues.

is time to support them" (*India Today*, June 30, 1988, p. 55). As the representative of this new breed of entrepreneurs, CEI/CII became a prominent actor exercising influence on the Government of India in a direction that favored domestic capital of all sizes[5], but it was also (and crucially) friendlier toward foreign capital. The stated objective of the CII was to work toward the globalization of Indian industry, with a business philosophy in favor of deregulation, de-control, and de-licensing in all areas (Pedersen 2000). The fact that neoliberal ideologues, Manmohan Singh and Montek Singh Ahluwalia, had become extremely powerful within the Government of India facilitated this transformation[6]. As chief architects of India's New Economic Policy, Manmohan Singh and Montek Singh Ahluwalia received accolades from CII and the privately controlled English language print media. This translated into a general mentality among the English-newspaper-reading urban population that was supportive of the neoliberal New Economic Policy. The transformation of India's policy regime, however, required broader state-society coalitions. The development of this broader coalition is now examined.

For its supporters, economic liberalization has led to a substantial increase in India's economic growth in a transformed society (see Sachs et al. 1995; Friedman 1999; Bhagwati 2004; Sachs 2005). However, an examination of growth data (see Table 2.1) suggests minor differences between the GDP growth rate of pre- (1980–1990) and post- (1990–2005) 'liberalized' India. In fact, the data suggest that India's rapid economic growth started well before the transformation of India's policy regime. An examination of the sectoral composition (see Figure 2.1) and the associated growth rates (see Table 2.1), however, points to the secondary, and more so tertiary, sectors of the economy, assuming positions of increasing dominance within the Indian economy. In addition, since the transformation of India's policy regime, the rate of capital formation in the public sector has been steadily declining at the same time as it has increased in the private sector (i.e., private corporate sector plus household sector; see Table 2.2).

This type of economic growth has provided opportunities for sections of the Indian population with formal education, especially with English as the medium of instruction, to gain employment in the private sector, essentially in large urban areas (i.e., there has been concentration of privatized economic growth in major urban centers). Thus, the government's economic liberalization policy has come to have overwhelming support amongst the educated urbanites working in private companies—this alludes to my earlier argument about neoliberalism being the reassertion of class power in India.

Privatized economic growth has had ramifications on caste-based contestations as well. I pointed out earlier that transformation of a caste-based exploitative social structure to a more egalitarian social order was one of the major problems for the post-colonial Indian state and society.

Table 2.2 Patterns of Capital Formation, by Sector 1970–2005 (percentage of GDP)

Period	*Total Gross Capital Formation*	*Private Corporate Sector*	*Public Sector*	*Household Sector*
1970–1975	18.2	2.8	7.7	7.7
1975–1980	23.3	2.3	11	10
1980–1985	21.9	4.5	10.2	7.2
1985–1990	23.7	4.5	10.5	8.7
1990–1995	23.7	6	9.1	8.6
1995–2000	24.8	8	7	9.8
2000–2005[7]	24.3	6.4	6.6	11.3

Source: Economic Survey, Government of India, various issues; Kohli 2006.

To facilitate this transformation, affirmative action in favor of people classified as outcast in Hindu society (constitutionally classified as scheduled caste) was made mandatory in all government jobs (excluding the military) and in educational institutions[8]. This affirmative action or positive discrimination policy never had the support of the upper-caste population, for the simple reason that it cut into their near-complete control over government jobs and educational institutions, though also it was never opposed in any notably organized and sustained form. At the same time, this policy was essential for the democratic state of India to gain legitimacy among the substantially large scheduled caste population, which was not only socially, but also economically, deprived. The upper-caste population, however, felt that this positive discrimination policy impinged on merit and forced them to share positions in jobs, governance, and educational institutions that were rightfully theirs.

The 1980s saw an upsurge in political assertion by the scheduled caste population. Electoral politics enabled increasing numbers of political leaders from this group to occupy positions of prominence. In addition, a substantially large section of the Indian population that was traditionally allotted the lowest position in the caste hierarchy (who traditionally performed manual labor) started asserting political power. As per the 1931 census data[9], this group traditionally made up 54% of India's total population. The *Other Backward Classes* (OBC) started demanding reservations in government jobs and educational institutions. In 1989, Vishwanath Pratap Singh, prime minister of India, who had substantial political support amongst the OBCs, declared the implementation of an affirmative action policy, which reserved 27% of government jobs and seats in educational institutions for this historically deprived group. This was in addition to the already existing 15% reservation for the scheduled castes and 7.5% reservation for the scheduled tribes. The declaration of this policy drew the wrath of the high-caste population, opposed to sharing jobs and positions that they had literally monopolized over the years. I was in secondary school in India at that time and was witness to the turmoil throughout the country, instantaneous protests broke out in the major cities[10]. At some places, high-caste youths made self-immolation bids. The protests forced the government of India to re-evaluate immediate implementation of the policy. Since the proposed policy had the massive support of OBCs, the government could not completely retract from its policy initiative. Implementation of the policy has become a piecemeal affair. Affirmative action has been implemented in recruiting central/federal government employees, but it continues to face tremendous opposition in elite educational institutions like the Indian Institute of Technology, Indian Institute of Management, All India Institute of Medical Sciences, and so on.

Even as caste-based contestation for share in employment and educational opportunities in government institutions has continued, jobs in the private sector, especially the corporate sector, have been monopolized by the upper-caste population (Louis 2004). The private sector refused to adopt the social responsibility of taking affirmative action in providing jobs to scheduled castes, scheduled tribes, and OBCs. Speaking on behalf of the CII, J. J. Irani stated that "we are against quotas and reservations and if a legislation comes in, it would be unfortunate" (*The Hindu* 2006). Thus, the corporate sector has emerged as the safest haven for the class and caste elite of India. It has emerged as a realm that the caste elite need not share with the scheduled castes, scheduled tribes, and OBCs. The leverage that corporations and corporate money have within the government and the political arena, has allowed them to undercut efforts on the part of sympathetic politicians and civil society activists to move legislation to enforce the affirmative action policy in the private sector. Business corporations, where any effort geared to produce social justice or provide affirmative-action-based jobs to the scheduled castes, scheduled tribes, and OBCs is resisted, are also ideal and advantageous from the point of view of the higher castes. Thus, caste and class elites have been supportive of corporations, and in turn neoliberalism, and this support has been formative/fundamental to India's economic transition.

Thus, the exercise of new forms of elite class power in the 1980s favored India's neoliberal integration into the global free market economy. But it was only in 1991, after a balance of payment crisis, that India embarked on a direct path toward neoliberalization. India was shoved into neoliberalism. Internal social contestations paved the way, but economic shock, in the form of a balance of payment crisis and pressure from the IMF and World Bank, forced the exact move. In explaining this, I turn to the global policy regime literature in the following section.

GLOBAL POLICY REGIMES

At the time that India emerged as an independent nation-state in 1947, Keynesianism was the globally dominant developmental discourse. In his *General Theory of Employment, Interest and Money*, Keynes (1936) argued that real investment in new factories, tools, machines, and greater inventories of goods was the crucial variable in economic growth. Changes in real investment fed growth into other areas of an economy. Investors buying machines channeled income to machine builders. In turn these spent money, further increasing national income, with the multiplier effect[11] varying with the proportion of additional income that was spent rather than saved, and so on; a decrease in real investment had the reverse effect. The government could influence this process through interest rate and other monetary policies, shifting the economy from one equilibrium level to another, generally to higher employment levels. Conservative Keynesian economists have viewed the manipulation of interest rates as a relatively non-bureaucratic, non-intrusive method by which the central bank of a country tries to influence national income and employment; an alternative is tax reduction. Liberal Keynesian economists see government deficit spending as a more effective measure: the *liberal* aspect is that deficit spending improves social services (Peet with Hartwick 1999, 37–40). Keynesian economic theory established the legitimacy of state intervention into market economies with the aim of achieving growth rates decided on the basis of social policy, coupled with objectives of striving for social, economic and political justice, and equality of status and opportunity (Austin 1999). This became the guiding principal for development policies formulated in post-colonial India.

Keynesianism began facing opposition from what has come to be known as neoliberalism beginning in the late 1960s. The main arguments put forth by the alternative neoliberal policy regime are (1) macroeconomic problems like inflation and indebtedness derived from excessive government spending drive up the quantity of money circulating in a society; (2) even dalliance with "socialist ideas" (like Keynesian planning) would lead to disaster, and classical Smithian and Ricardian economic principles should be relied on instead; and (3) laissez-faire and rugged individualism was in general good for all economies and societies (Peet with Hartwick 1999; Chang and Garbel 2004). The neoliberal discourse gained precedence over Keynesianism during the 1970s within the context of a macroeconomic crisis that included stagflation[12] and instability in global commodity markets and business cycles (Peck and Tickell 2002). Neoliberal economic policies were put into effect under the governments of Prime Minister Thatcher in the U.K. and President Reagan in the U.S. in the early 1980s with the rhetoric that "there is no alternative", popularly referred to as the *TINA factor* (Krieger 1986; Toye 1987; Chang and Garbel 2004). The U.S. and U.K. exercise tremendous control over the IMF and World Bank through their voting share of 17.4% and 5%, respectively (International Monetary Fund 2003; Jones and Hardstaff 2005). The

IMF and the World Bank (earlier known as the International Bank for Reconstruction and Development), Keynesian-type global governance institutions created in 1944, were converted into advocates of neoliberal policies during the 1970s (Peet et al. 2003).

However, an overview of economic histories of most developed and newly industrialized countries of the world point to state intervention facilitating their economic growth and development. There is abundant empirical evidence showing that many of the successful examples of 'late' development since mid-nineteenth century, as in Germany, Japan, Korea, or Argentina have occurred with heavy state intervention (Gerschenkron 1962; Girling 1981; Deyo 1990; Amsden 1991; Fukui 1992; Johns 1992; Wade 1996; Bosco 1998; Park 1998). More recently, empirical evidence contradicts the neoliberal argument that East Asia's economic success is due to the existence of freer markets with less state intervention than in other developing countries (Chen 1979; Balassa 1981; Aikman 1986; Kohli 2004). In fact, effective development has often required quite radical steps, like land reform or wage restraint, be taken early in a developmental cycle (Leftwich 1994).

Even so, despite the proven success of state intervention in national economies, neoliberalism become the dominant developmental discourse, globally. Most post-socialist and Third World economies were forced to neoliberalize following some kind of economic and/or social disaster. Neoliberal policies were implemented as post-disaster therapy—Naomi Klein (2007) calls this the "shock doctrine". In the following section, I examine the shock that enabled India to be moved from state-led development to neoliberal New Economic Policy.

SHOCK THERAPY

At the end of the 1980s and in early 1990, India faced a series of social and geopolitical crises. The anti-affirmative action, high-caste uprising across India, discussed earlier, plunged the nation into turmoil. This period was also witness to major political/electoral gains made by the Bharatiya Janta Party (BJP), a Hindu fundamentalist/fascist political party. BJP's electoral gains were based on polarizing Indian society along religious lines to consolidate a Hindu vote-bank. Thus, Hindu-Muslim riots erupted in several parts of India, derailing the social order and communal harmony in the country. Rajiv Gandhi, India's former prime minister, was assassinated on May 21, 1991, while campaigning for the forthcoming general elections. Rajiv Gandhi's assassination was a spectacle—a 'human bomb' belonging to a Sri Lankan separatist group, Liberation Tigers of Tamil Eelam, killed him at an election rally. Rajiv Gandhi's assassination was a massive collective shock for India, producing public disorientation and laying the foundation for rolling out the shock doctrine in the form of New Economic Policies proposed by the IMF and World Bank.

India also suffered geopolitical shocks—the Soviet Union, India's long-time friend and major trading partner—finally collapsed in 1991. And the first Gulf War, which began in August 1990, forced the return of large numbers of (Indian) emigrant workers from Kuwait and Iraq with a decline in foreign remittances. Additionally, India faced rapidly rising international petroleum and gas prices.

Nevertheless, India's socialist goals are enshrined in its Preamble to the Constitution. Abandoning these principles, and adopting elements of the U.S.-backed World Bank and IMF neoliberal policy, took more than higher gas prices. The big push toward neoliberalism came with a balance of payment crisis that India underwent in 1990–1991. India managed to prevent payment default by borrowing from the IMF, the World Bank, and the bilateral donors. Gross drawings from the IMF between January 1991 and January 1992, amounting to $3.0 billion (Government of India 1992, 78), came with the condition that India would ensure macroeconomic stabilization. The IMF's prescription for macroeconomic stabilization involves, among other strategies, reduction of budgetary deficits by reducing expenditures, even if such expenditures are geared to producing local development or promoting strategic and vital industries. Ultimately, macroeconomic stabilization is geared to diminish the role of state and allow the market to take the lead in the day-to-day management of the economy. The World Bank approved a "Structural Adjustment Loan" of $500 million in December 1991 that was tied to industrial and trade policy 'reforms' (Government of India 1992, 75). The Asian Development Bank sanctioned a "Program Loan" of U.S. $250 million so that the Government of India could restructure the Oil and Natural Gas Commission and begin neoliberalizing the energy sector.

The balance of payment crisis in India was used as an opportunity by the World Bank and the IMF to negotiate the terms on which India would be lent money, not only in the present, but also in the future. And the terms of borrowing would be applicable to all sectors of the economy. In other words, loans were not simply conditional upon adherence to the World Bank and IMF dictates in the sector for which loans were sought. It was used by the global governance institutions to gain leverage and push 'reforms' in every sector of the economy. For example, the World Bank, formerly a Keynesian institution, had provided loans supporting several state-led developmental initiatives. India's electricity sector had received around $10 billion from the World Bank over several years prior to the balance of payment crisis. But when India received structural adjustment loans, the World Bank (by now a neoliberal institution) laid down conditions that all further loans to the power sector would be contingent upon the Government of India's ability to attract private investments (Purkayastha and Prasad 2002). Here, "ability" implies the government's proactive adherence to the World Bank's ideas of policy changes and transformation/re-creation of spaces to facilitate privatized profiteering in India. Failure to comply meant that no loans would be provided in the future, even if India repaid its structural adjustment loans. Conditionalities were presented by the global governance institutions, and it's political and class allies in India, under the rhetoric of prescription—that neoliberalization would cure India's ailing economy. Thus, the global governance institutions utilized the crisis in India to push economic deregulation as therapy.

The electric power industry is representative of, and formative in, India's overall development and neoliberal transformation. In the following section I examine India's electric power sector, associated policy changes, and their impact.

POWER POLICY IN INDIA

Before India's independence, electricity was generated and supplied locally by private entrepreneurs, enterprising municipalities, and provincial governments. The emphasis was on supply to large urban concentrations, and there was little coordination or cooperation between different suppliers (Rao 2002). In the colonial economy, the generation and supply of power had clear-cut extractive and profit motives (i.e., making immediate profit was the sole motive of electricity generators and suppliers). The colonial government had no plans for promoting electricity generation and supply to produce the long-term social and infrastructural development of India. The function of policy and legislation[13] was to "regulate the generation, supply and use of electricity . . . and for the protection of person and property, from injury and risks" (The Indian Electricity Act, 1910). The post-colonial Indian state, in sharp contrast, envisaged electricity as a vital input in facilitating India's long-term economic growth and development. Drawing broadly from the United Kingdom's Electricity (Supply) Act of 1926, which had elements of the idea of state intervention in the process of national development, the Government of India passed the Electricity (Supply) Act of 1948. The Electricity (Supply) Act of 1948 reflected the government's vision of development by stating that "the coordinated development of electricity in India on a regional basis was a matter of increasingly urgent importance for the post-war reconstruction and development." State-supported development was envisaged as a strategy to consolidate the national identity. So the goal, stated in the Electricity (Supply) Act was "to facilitate the establishment of regional coordination in the development of electricity transcending the geographical limits of local bodies". The Act provided "for the rationalization of the production and supply of electricity and generally for taking measures conducive to the electrical development of the Provinces of India." This enabled the creation of state electricity boards for promoting the coordinated development of the generation, supply, and distribution of electricity in the Provinces and in other areas of India. The Industrial Policy Resolution of 1956 reserved generation and distribution of electricity almost exclusively for the states, letting existing private licensees, however, continue. In 1976, amendments to the existing acts on electricity enabled power generation companies to be set up, with close coordination between the federal/central and state governments.

In the late 1980s, a "new breed of entrepreneurs," along with a newly sympathetic government was closely observing global trends vis-à-vis the electric-power sector. Massive restructuring and privatization of the power sector was taking place in the U.K. This privatization policy had ramifications for the working class movement in the U.K., where the Scargill-led Coal Miners Union was the backbone of working-class opposition to the conservative agenda of the Conservative government. By privatizing electricity generation, the Conservative government opened the door for the use of any fuel—imported or domestic. This removed British coal form its preeminent position in electricity generation. Oil and imported Australian coal soon replaced expensive British coal and led the entire British coal mining sector into bankruptcy. British coal mines shut one by one, and the power of the Coal Miners' Union was effectively broken (Purkayastha and Prashad 2002). The 'employee problem' was a major issue in the Indian power sectors as well (Upadhyay 2000). The state electricity boards in India were considered notorious for worker strikes—so privatization of this sector began to be looked upon as an effective 'remedy'. In addition, Britain's case demonstrated that private companies could use discriminatory strategies in the supply of electricity, something that public sector units could not (Thomas 2002; 2004). The new breed of Indian entrepreneurs found this possibility attractive. They had the money to pay for uninterrupted power supplies, and they felt that their electricity needs would automatically be prioritized, as was being done in Britain, since private investors would not be burdened with the social responsibility of observing equity and equality in supply of electricity. Further, the discourse of privatized efficiency got entrenched in the imagination of the entrepreneurial class, first, because of the collapse of the Soviet Union and its economy and second because Indians began to look up to the U.S. and the U.K. as models to emulate to ensure rapid economic growth. The entrepreneurial class, along with the policymakers, were now of the opinion that the best way to meet the shortfall in power generation in the country was to promote the free market in this sector.

The demands of and lobbying by the elite and the opinion of a few policymakers were simply not enough to force privatization of this vital industry. But when India accepted conditional loans form the World Bank and the IMF, these global governance institutions, in no uncertain terms, pointed out that the electricity sector had to be restructured. Future loans from the World Bank to this vital sector were tied to or conditional upon structural adjustments and marketization of generation, transmission, and distribution of electricity. As elements of neoliberal policy came in during 1991, amendments to the existing power policies were made. In 1991, electricity generation was opened to private investment, including foreign investment. Further amendments in 1998 opened transmission to private investment, subject to approval by the Central Transmission Utility (a public sector undertaking), with a license issued by the Central Electricity Regulatory Commission.

Neoliberalization of India's electricity policy was also facilitated by a change in the mindset of the urban elite and middle-class population, and in turn, the general discourse about the poor, and nature of development and its relationship with the electricity sector. Rao (2002) has argued that there seem to be certain attitudes that are almost axiomatic in the electricity sector. Prior to the initiation of elements of neoliberal policies in India, electricity was understood virtually as a fundamental right that had to be supplied irrespective of certain sections of the population's inability to pay. The generally accepted discourse was that the lives of a large number of very poor people, and opportunities for their economic advancement, would greatly improved if electricity was available to them and that making electricity available should be the responsibility of the state. Increases in the accessibility to electricity in economically backward regions, and among the poorer sections of the population, were understood as desirable social goals. Thus, state ownership, that gave precedence to social objectives over profit motives, was understood as being good for the society. Generation and supply of electricity were seen as opportunities to expand and create employment opportunities by the Indian state adhering to Keynesian economic policy and socialist goals.

Neoliberal policies, however, are embedded in an elite discourse and mindset dissimilar to this. Proponents of neoliberal policies argue that power generation and distribution should be run on the principles of efficiency and profit, rather than on the basis of social objectives, and that this will ensure the sector's growth. State ownership of this sector is seen, by comparison, as subsidizing and supporting inefficiency. 'Professional management', as opposed to bureaucratic control is epitomized as rational, qualitatively different, and better. The power sector's social objective of creating employment opportunities is criticized for giving rise to inefficiency. Markets, as opposed to the state, are understood as being fair, and the state's effort to ensure accessibility to electricity by backward regions and the poor are criticized as being populist measures put forward to attract votes. The current mindset of the elite and the neoliberal policies steaming out of such a mindset allude to my earlier argument about neoliberalism being the reassertion of class and caste power in India.

I earlier pointed out that the mobilization of the urban elite and middle class was fundamental to India's neoliberalization. In the electricity-power sector too, demands and mindset to the urban elite are fundamental to its policy changes. Urban centers with high foreign direct investments are spaces with relatively high levels of affluence, juxtaposed to squalor and slums. During the last few years, the urban elites have increasingly tried to sanitize their localities of poverty and the poor (Baviskar 2003; Kundu 2004). The desire of the rich to inhabit urban spaces free of poverty, however, is enmeshed in socio-spatial contradictions. The poorer sections of the population, made up largely of the scheduled caste and the OBCs, provide essential services, including cleaning the city, laboring in factories and construction sites, or working as domestic help in the homes of the rich and the middle class. Despite this, the rich often perceive these poor as having characteristics, like vagrancy, ignorance, and the refusal to accept social duties—as if such characteristics were hereditary. Such characterization, in the minds of the city elites, makes the poor undesirable in areas inhabited by the rich. In the city of Delhi, for example, nearly 52% of the population lives in what is classified as squatter clusters, designated slum areas, unauthorized settlements, and/or regularized-unauthorized settlements. The story is no different in terms of the overwhelming presence of slums in other Indian cities. The rich in the cities believe that those living in the slums make unauthorized use of electricity—and it is because of such unauthorized, illegal, and free use of electricity that paying consumers have to suffer long hours of load-shedding or power cuts. They believe that the government's inability to take tough measures against the slum dwellers by cutting off their electricity supply is a reflection of the populist nature of the democratic state. Thus, the city elite has favored privatization of electricity generation and supply—privatization has been accepted as a system that has greater accountability (i.e., a system that will be vigilant about unauthorized leakage of electricity and take the offenders to task). The discourse of electricity theft that is entrenched in the imagination of the elite is now reflected in the law as well. According to one of my interviewees, Mr. Ramakrishnan, member[14] of the Central Electricity Authority, Government of India, who was speaking about the Electricity Act, 2003, "theft of electricity is now a cognizable offence and the government is trying to come up with special courts and special bills to prosecute and dissuade people from doing that—earlier it was not so." On examining the Electricity Act, 2003, I found that sections 135 through 152 lay out, in detail, laws related to electricity theft and corresponding punishments. Mr. Ramakrishna, however, also informed me that "there is some theft of electricity in the slums, but if we look at the quantum and proportion of such theft, it is industry, commercial establishments and the affluent section of the population that are the major culprits". He pointed out that while most homes in the slums might use a single bulb and/or a fan, the industry, commercial establishments and affluent homes use air-conditioners and high electricity-consuming appliances. Mr. Ramakrishnan concluded by pointing out that "It is theft committed by the elite which essentially hurts the system—though people in general, do not recognize that". Despite the disconnect between the discourse and the reality, privatization of one of the most basic socio-economic utilities (i.e., power) was started with India's integration with the neoliberal global economy.

In fact, efforts to privatize the electricity sector and make it dependent on foreign direct investment have proven to be detrimental. The power sector has linkages with all other industries, since they all require electricity, and with the agricultural sector, through farm mechanization. Hence rapid growth in the electricity generation capacity of the country is vital for sustaining and increasing the rate of India's economic growth. An overview of the increase in power-generating capacity in India through the Five-Year Plan periods (see Table 2.3) shows that the rate of increase in capacity has been relatively high. Even more noticeable is the fact that prior to the initiation of neoliberal policies (till the end of the Seventh Plan), the rate of increase in capacity was far higher. Percentage increase in capacity declined from 60.11, 49.69, and 49.43 in the Fifth, Sixth, and Seventh Plan periods respectively to 24.22, 22.28, and 25.70 in the Eighth, Ninth, and Tenth Plan periods (after the onset of neoliberalism) when actual capacity added fell far short of the targeted capacity addition. The decline in the rate of increase of power-generating capacity occurred despite the fact that from 1997–1998 through 2003–2004, energy shortages in India have ranged anywhere between 5.9% and 8.8%, and peak energy shortage have ranged from 11.20% to 13.90% (Government of India 2005). Additionally, only 55.80% of houses in India had electricity connections in the year 2001 (UN-Habitat 2008). Existing shortages are clear pointers to the fact that the power sector is nowhere close to its saturation point, so slowdown in its rate of growth is neither 'natural' nor acceptable from any rational economic perspective. Thus, the neoliberal tendency of the Indian state seems to be adversely affecting the power sector's growth.

CONCLUSION

Most of the literature on the developmental state indicates that, during times when the state was most actively involved in development, their political regimes were relatively non-democratic. This has not been the case with India. Since independence from colonial rule, India has been a democracy, and state intervention in the economy has not involved deprivation of democratic rights. The state functions in collaboration with the society. I understand the state as a political project in a continual process of formation, deformation, and reformation (cf. Painter 2000). I understand the state as being fragmented rather than monolithic, actively engaged with society, with no sharp demarcation between the two, and with social, political, and economic changes forged on the basis of state-society coalitions (Gramsci 1971, 160, 261; Alvarez 1997; Bosco 1998; Young 2000). The nature of state-society coalitions in a democratic country, however, differs from those in non-democratic countries. Unlike the situation in a non-democratic political regime, where state-society coalitions reflect the relatively stable class or clan power of those controlling the means of production (Park 1998), in India, such coalitions are amorphous and in a state of flux; they constantly form and

Table 2.3 Five-Year Plans and Growth of Power-Generating Capacity

Year/Five-Year Plan	*Installed Capacity at the Beginning of the Plan (MW)*	*Target for Capacity Addition (MW)*	*Actual Capacity Added (MW)*	*Percentage increase in Capacity*
1947	1,362			
First Plan (1951–1956)	1,713		1,173	68.48
Second Plan (1956–1961)	2,886		1,767	61.23
Third Plan (1961–1966)	4,653		4,374	94.00
Fourth Plan (1969–194)	12,957		3,707	28.61
Fifth Plan (1974–1979)	16,664		10,016	60.11
Sixth Plan (1980–1985)	28,448		14,137	49.69
Seventh Plan (1985–1990)	42,585	22,245	21,051	49.43
Eighth Plan (1992–1997)	69,065	40,000 (revised to 30.538)	16,730	24.22
Ninth Plan (1997–2002)	85,795	40,245	19,119	22.28
Tenth Plan (2002–2007)	105,046	41,110 (revised to 39,920 in 2004)	27,000	25.70
Eleventh Plan		60,896	Anticipated	

Source: Government of India Five Year Plan, various issues.

re-form based on principles that include the universal adult franchise, in addition to factors like class, caste, and ethnicity. It is in this context of intra-class and inter-class and caste contestation that India's economic and electric-power policy transformations have to be understood. In a situation where the vast majority of the population remains very poor, the state continues to function in collaboration with the society, and the elite continue to exercise power over the government. Pre-neoliberalism, the Indian state focused on producing balanced economic growth and primarily invested in rural development, and also public utility and industry—as in the case of electricity examined earlier. A major focus on agricultural reforms and assistance, and associated utility services helped India tide over chronic hunger, starvation, and famine that had become common during the British rule. Even though rural elites benefited disproportionately, policies were geared to address the concerns of the majority of the population who lived in rural India or migrated to cities in search of jobs in the publicly owned manufacturing industry. But neoliberalism has been accompanied by a disproportionate rise in the political and economic power of the urban elite—disproportionate because the urban elite constitute the numerical minority, yet, neoliberal policies benefit only this small segment of the Indian society and neglect the poor, the vast majority of whom continue to live in villages (Patnaik 2008), and the remainder who live in the slums of the cities. But neither the elite, nor the poor, are monolithic groups. The elite section of the society has fractured along the lines of the industry and economy they control or benefit from, in addition to the region in India from which they principally operate. Further, one's class position within the Indian society, to a large extent, intersects with one's caste position. And higher castes in India have had greater access to education and wealth, and they have benefited most from India's New Economic Policy. This has ramifications for the nature of economic change, as state-society collaboration continuously undergoes formation, deformation, and reformation. This is evident in how "a new breed of entrepreneurs," represented by the Confederation of Indian Industries, matured through the mid and late 1970s and the 1980s to occupy position of prominence in the 1990s—in terms of influence on the state, they surpassed the traditional industrial bourgeoisie, the Tatas and the Birlas. This is also evident in how the urban class and caste elite were able to reassert class and caste power, which had started declining after India gained independence and began affirmative actions/programs to ensure social justice. Even under the constitutional rhetoric of socialism, and prior to liberalization, the class and caste elite continued to have access to superior education in the English language and get better jobs in public institutions. When India started neoliberalizing, the Indian elites were in a position to usurp the advantages accruing out of international technological collaborations, profits, and expansion of employment opportunities in the corporate sector (requiring human-resource conversant in the English language). Reassertion of class and caste power through neoliberalism has been fundamental to the New Economic Policy's continuance in India. Growth of private industries and corporations has led to the creation of 'secure' spaces for the elite where any discussion or action to ensure social justice or affirmative action have been shunned. So even though neoliberalism was thrust on India by the World Bank, the IMF, and the U.S., its continuance has been ensured by a section of the class and caste elite. In other words, the exogenous power of the global governance institutions has worked in tandem with the interest of the local elite to produce what Gramsci calls hegemony or the production of consent through non-physically coercive means.

ACKNOWLEDGMENTS

An abridged version of this paper titled "From Mixed Economy to Neo-Liberalism: Class and Caste in India's Economic Transition" has been published in *Human Geography*.

I thank Dick Peet for intellectual guidance. I am also grateful to Jody Emel, Nancy Ettlinger, Ipsita Chatterjee, and my former professors at the Center for the Study of Regional Development at Jawaharlal Nehru University for their earlier engagement with my ideas that culminated in this chapter. The usual disclaimers apply.

NOTES

1. I have used the term 'semi-feudalism' here to convey that the relations of production had more in common with the classical feudalism of the master-serf type than with industrial capitalism. India's population, which even now remain overwhelmingly rural, had sharecropping; perpetual indebtedness of small tenants; concentration of two modes of exploitation, namely usury and land-ownership in the hands of a certain class which essentially boiled down to the higher castes; and lack of accessibility for the small tenants to the market, as core characteristics (Bhaduri 1973).
2. See Preamble to the Constitution of India.
3. Rajiv Gandhi, son of Indira Gandhi and grandson of Jawaharlal Nehru, headed the private-capital-friendly government. Rajiv Gandhi, at the age of 40, was installed as the prime minister of India by the Congress Party when Prime Minister Indira Gandhi was assassinated in 1984. A sympathy wave, following Indira Gandhi's assassination, ensured a landslide electoral victory for the Congress Party and Rajiv Gandhi in the national general elections (elections held later in 1984). Prior to becoming the prime minister of India, Rajiv Gandhi had remained aloof from politics, and, in turn, from the nitty-gritty of political realities and social basis of political power in India. Upon assuming power, he sought counsel from a group of young men who came from relatively elite and urban backgrounds.
4. Processed data include provisional estimates for the budgetary year 2003–2004 and quick estimates for the budgetary year 2004–2005.
5. More than 84% of the members of CII were classified as small- or medium-scale entrepreneurs in 1992 based on the size of employment in their business units (Confederation of Indian Industry 1992).
6. Manmohan Singh and Montek Singh Ahluwalia had become the union minister and secretary in the Department of Economic Affairs, respectively, in the Ministry of Finance, Government of India.
7. Processed data include provisional estimates for the budgetary year 2003–2004 and quick estimates for the budgetary year 2004–2005.
8. Approximately 15% and 7.5% of all government jobs and seats in educational institutions were reserved for the scheduled caste and scheduled tribe population, respectively. Those traditionally classified as outcaste within the Hindu caste system were referred to as scheduled caste, and those from tribes or civilizations that had developed in relative isolation were referred to as scheduled tribes. The term 'scheduled' referred to the constitutional schedule that classified them as such.

9. Caste-based data in India was generated through the census of India for the last time in 1931.
10. This has been well documented in all Indian newspapers.
11. The degree of economic expansion induced by investment.
12. Economic stagnation accompanied by inflation.
13. Electricity Act of 1887; Indian Electricity Act, 1903; and The Indian Electricity Act, 1910.
14. To be a member of the Central Electricity Authority, Government of India, one has to be a very senior bureaucrat/technocrat. In terms of power hierarchy, this position is just below that of the chairperson of the organization.

REFERENCES

Aikman, D. 1986. *The Pacific Rim: Area of change, area of opportunity*. Boston: Little Brown.

Alvarez, S. E. 1997. Reweaving the fabric of collective action: Social movements and challenges to "actually existing democracy" in Brazil. In *Between resistance and revolution: cultural politics and social protest*, edited by R. G. Fox and O. Starn, 83–117. New Brunswick, NJ: Rutgers University Press.

Ambedkar, B. R., and V. Moon. 1979. *Dr. Babasaheb Ambedkar: Writings and speeches*. Education Dept., Govt. of Maharashtra.

Amsden, A. 1991. *Asia's next giant. South Korea and late industrialization*. New York: Oxford University Press

Austin, G. 1999. *The Indian constitution: Cornerstone of a nation*. New Delhi: Oxford University Press

Balassa, B. 1981. *Newly industrializing countries in the world economy*. Elmsford: Pergamon.

Baviskar, A. 2003. Between violence and desire: Space, power, and identity in the making of metropolitan Delhi, 89–98. Malden, MA: Blackwell Publishing Ltd.

Bhaduri, A. 1973. A study in agricultural backwardness under semi-feudalism. *The Economic Journal* 83(329): 120–137.

Bhagwati, J. N. 2004. *In defense of globalization*. Oxford: Oxford University Press.

Bosco, F. J. 1998. State-society relations and national development: a comparison of Argentina and Taiwan in the1990s. *International Journal of Urban and Regional Research* 22: 625–652.

Chang, H., and I. Garbel. 2004. *Reclaiming development: An economic policy handbook for activists and policymakers*. London: Zed Books.

Chen, E. K. Y. 1979. *Hyper-growth in Asian economics: A comparative study of Hong Kong, Japan, Korea, Singapore and Taiwan*. London: Macmillan.

Confederation of Indian Industry. 1992. *Directory 1992*. New Delhi: CII.

Deyo, F. 1990. Economic policy and the popular sector. In *Manufacturing miracles, paths of industrialization in Latin America and East Asia* edited by G. Gereffi and D. L. Wyman. Princeton, NJ: Princeton University Press.

Dubash, N. K., and S. C. Rajan. 2001. Power politics: Process of power sector reform in India. *Economic and Political Weekly*: 3367–3390. http://www.epw.org.in/showArticles.php?root=2001&leaf=09&filename=3421&filetype=pdf (accessed September 15, 2006).

Dumont, L. 1970. *Homo hierarchicus: The caste system and its implications*. Chicago: University of Chicago Press.

Eastern Economist. p. 102. July 18, 1982.

Friedman, T. L. 1999. *The Lexus and the olive tree.* New York: Farrar, Straus, Giroux.
Fukui, H. 1992. The Japanese state and economic development: A profile of a nationalist paternalist capitalist state. In *State and Development in the Asia Pacific* edited by R. P. Appelbaum and J. Henderson, 199–225. Newbury Park, CA: Sage.
Gerschenkron, A. 1962. *Economic backwardness in historical perspective.* Cambridge, MA: Harvard University Press.
Girling, J. 1981. *Thailand. Society and politics.* Ithaca, NY: Cornell University Press.
Government of India. 1992. *Economic Survey 1991–92. Part I. General Review.* New Delhi: Ministry of Finance.
———. 2005. *Power India.* New Delhi: Ministry of Commerce and Industry, Investment Promotion and Infrastructure Development Cell.
Gramsci, A. 1971. *Selections from the prison notebook.* edited and translated by Quintin Hoare and Geoffrey Nowell Smith. London: Lawrence & Wishart.
Ilaiah, K. 1996. *Why I am not a Hindu: A Sudra critique of Hindutva philosophy, culture and political economy.* Calcutta: Samya.
International Monetary Fund, Finance Department. 2003. *Quota distribution—Selected issues.* http://www.imf.org/external/np/fin/2003/quota/eng/071703.pdf (accessed December 24, 2006).
Johns, M. 1992. Industrial capital and economic development in turn of the century Argentina. *Economic Geography* 68(2): 188–203.
Jones, T., and P. Hardstaff. 2005. *Denying democracy: How the IMF and World Bank take power from people.* London: World Development Movement. http://siteresources.worldbank.org/INTPRS1/Resources/PRSP-Review/WDMPRSPs-doc.pdf (accessed December 24, 2006).
Keynes, J. M. 1936. *The general theory of employment, interest and money.* New York: Harcourt Brace.
Klein, N. 2007. *The shock doctrine: The rise of disaster capitalism.* New York: Metropolitan Books.
Kochanek, S. A. 1987. Briefcase politics in India: The Congress Party and the business elite. *Asian Survey* 27(12): 1278–1301.
Kohli, A. 2004. *State-directed development: Political power and industrialization in the global periphery.* Cambridge: Cambridge University Press.
———. 2006. Politics of economic growth in India, 1980–2005—Part I: The 1980s. *Economic and Political Weekly* (April 1): 1251–1259. http://www.epw.org.in/showArticles.php?root=2006&leaf=04&filename=9908&filetype=pdf (accessed November 14, 2006).
Krieger, J. 1986. *Reagan, Thatcher and the politics of decline.* Cambridge: Polity.
Kundu, A. 2004. Provision of tenurial security for the urban poor in Delhi: Recent trends and future perspectives. *Habitat International* 28: 259–274.
Leftwich, A. 1994. Governance, the state and the politics of development. *Development and Change* 25: 363–386.
Louis, P. 2004. Affirmative action in private sector. *Economic and Political Weekly.* (August 14). http://www.epw.org.in/showArticles.php?root=2004&leaf=08&filename=7553&filetype=html (accessed November 29, 2006).
Ministry of Industry. 1985. *Twenty ninth annual report on the working of the Companies Act, 1956.* New Delhi: Department of Company Affairs.
Namboodiripad, E. M. S. 1977. Castes, classes and parties in modern political development. *Social Scientist* 6(4): 3–25.
———. 1981. Once again on castes and classes. *Social Scientist* 9(12): 12–25.
Nayar, B. R. 1971. Business attitudes towards economic planning in India. *Asian Survey* 11(9): 850–865.

Painter, J. 2000. State and governance. In *A companion to economic geography*, edited by E. Sheppard and T. J. Barnes, 359–376. Malden, MA: Blackwell.
Park, B. 1998. Where do tigers sleep at night? The state's role in housing policy in South Korea and Singapore. *Economic Geography* 74(3): 272–288.
Patnaik, U. 2008. Imperialism, resources and food security, with reference to the Indian experience. *Human Geography* 1(1): 40–53.
Peck, J., and A. Tickell. 2002. Neoliberalizing space. *Antipode*: 380–404.
Pedersen, J. D. 2000. Explaining economic liberalization in India: State and society perspectives. *World Development* 28(2): 265–282.
Peet, R., with E. Hartwick. 1999. *Theories of development*. New York: The Guilford Press.
Peet, R., B. Born, M. Davis, K. Fehrer, S. Feldman, S. R. Khan, M. Labban, K. McArdle, C. Marcano, L. Meierotto, D. Nile, T. Ponniah, M. C. Schmidt, G. Schwarz, J. Shagwert, M. P. Staton, and S. Stratton. 2003. *Unholy trinity—The IMF, World Bank and WTO*. London: Zed Books.
Purkayastha, P., and V. Prashad. 2002. *Enron blowout: Corporate capitalism and theft of the global commons*. New Delhi: LeftWorld Books.
Rao, S. L. 2002. The political economy of power. *Economic and Political Weekly*. http://www.epw.org.in/showArticles.php?root=2002&leaf=08&filename=4806&filetype=html (accessed December 15, 2005).
Rudolph, L. I., and S. H. Rudolph. 1987. *In pursuit of Lakshmi: The political economy of the Indian state*. Chicago: University of Chicago Press.
Sachs, J. D. 2005. *The end of poverty: Economic possibilities of our time*. New York: Penguin Press.
Sachs, J. D., A. Warner, A. Aslund, and S. Fischer. 1995. Economic reform and the process of global integration. *Booking papers on economic activity*, 25th anniversary issue. 1: 1–118.
Seminar. 1985. The Indian economy. Number 316 (December): 41.
Shiva, V. 2005. *India divided: Diversity and democracy under attack*. New York: Seven Stories Press.
Soesastro, M. H. 1989. The political economy of deregulation in Indonesia. *Asian Survey* 29(9): 853–869.
The Hindu. 2006. Corporates oppose law for quota. (November 16). http://www.hindu.com/2006/11/16/stories/2006111605871200.htm (accessed November 29, 2006).
The Electricity (Supply) Act, 1948. (2006; repr., Delhi: Universal Law Publishing Co. Pvt. Ltd.).
The Indian Electricity Act, 1910. (2000; repr., Delhi: Universal Law Publishing Co. Pvt. Ltd.).
Thomas, S. 2002. Why retail electricity competition is bad for small consumers: British experience. Washington, DC: Presentation to the International Conference Restoring Just and Reasonable Electricity Rates. September 28–29.
———. 2004. Evaluating the British model of electricity deregulation. *Annals of Public and Cooperative Economics* 75(3): 367.
Toye, J. 1987. *Dilemmas of development*. Oxford: Blackwell.
UN-Habitat. 2008. *Housing finance mechanisms in India*, The Human Settlements Finance Systems Series. Nairobi: United Nations Human Settlements Program.
Upadhyay, A. K. 2000. Power sector reforms: Indian experience and global trends. *Economic and Political Weekly*: 1023–1028. http://www.epw.org.in/showArticles.php?root=2000&leaf=03&filename=1110&filetype=pdf (accessed December 1, 2006).
Wade, R. 1996. Japan, the World Bank, and the art of paradigm maintenance: The East Asian miracle in political perspective. *New Left Review* 217: 3–36.
Young, I. M. 2000. *Inclusion and democracy*. Oxford: Oxford University Press.

3 Urban System in India

Trends, Economic Base, Governance, and a Perspective of Growth under Globalization

Amitabh Kundu

1. THE DEBATE AND CONVERGENCE OF OPPOSITES

A change in the perspective of urban development in favor of a liberal system of governance and management is clearly discernable in India, as also several other developing countries since the mid-1980s. This high-profile shift has come at a time when most of the cities in these countries were reportedly experiencing some sort of crisis due to demographic explosion and infrastructural deficiency. The incapacity of the state and local governments to make adequate investments to alleviate this has been seen as a manifestation of the structural distortions which forced many of these countries to usher in programs of globalization and 'structural reform'.

Streamlining the system of governance, reducing public expenditure on infrastructure and civic amenities, and opening up labor, land, and capital markets have been perceived as crucial elements in the strategy to meet the challenge of urban crisis. The need to free the market from the regulative framework of the state, facilitate private and joint sector investment in infrastructure, improve management of basic amenities, and empower local governments to take development decisions have been seen as the critical components. Development of capital market for resource mobilization and ensuring appropriate prices for infrastructure and urban amenities through elimination or reduction of subsidies have also emerged as pillars of the new strategy. The simplification of the legislative system, the flexibility to bring about appropriate land use changes, and the location of economic activities have also been advocated as a part of the remedial package.

The proponents of this perspective have explicitly or implicitly argued that this would accelerate rural urban (RU) migration, give boost to the pace of urbanization, promote regional balance, and ensure sustainable development in the country. The critics of this neoliberalism, on the other hand, have pleaded that globalization would jeopardize sustainable development both in rural and urban areas and accelerate exodus from villages and small towns. Research studies that can support the tenets of either of these perspectives are, however, hopelessly inadequate.

Given these alternate perspectives, the present chapter begins by overviewing the urbanization scenario in the post-colonial period in the context of the demographic and economic trends in Asia. This has been done in Section 2. Section 3 critically examines the urban scenarios projected by international and national agencies and assesses these in the context of their methodological predispositions and their implications. Section 4 looks at the trends in employment and unemployment of various types, wages, and so on and analyses their implications for urbanization. A thesis of formalization of informal sector has been proposed in this section wherein the implications of new forms of organization of production and service activities have been from the viewpoint of efficiency and well-being of the workers. The new system of urban governance and empowerment of local bodies brought about through constitutional amendment and other administrative measures is the subject of investigation in Section 5. The changed perspective for preparing and implementing city-level plans and ushering in land market reforms to ensure greater efficiency and flexibility has also been discussed here, highlighting their implications for future migration and urbanization. The policies and programs for urban development launched by the central governments during the past three decades have also been discussed here in some detail. The final section summarizes the results in the context of the problems and possibilities of adopting a proactive strategy for urban growth and build inclusive cities.

2. PATTERNS OF URBANIZATION AND THE THESIS OF URBAN EXPLOSION

It is important to note a point of convergence between the two ideologically opposite perspectives, presented in Section 1. It is the proposition of rapid urbanization and acceleration of demographic growth in large cities, propagated by both the critics and advocates of economic liberalization[1]. This also fits in well with the thesis of rural exodus and over-urbanization which is considered to be a carry over of colonial hang-up in India and other developing countries, weighing heavily on the minds of demographers and urban planners. The proposition has received empirical backing of sorts due to the 'exceptional urban growth' observed in the country in a couple of decades in the post-Independence period. Notwithstanding the exogenous and definitional factors that seem to inflate these rates, all official projections have been made under the shadow of hyper-urbanization and consequently erred on the higher side[2].

An analysis of the contemporary urban scenario and pattern of growth in India casts serious doubts on the perspective of hyper-urbanization or urban explosion. The growth in urban population in India has at best been modest and fluctuated significantly over the past few decades (Table 3.1). The rate was reasonably high in the 1950s, fell sharply during the 1960s, largely due to definitional anomalies, but reached its peak in the 1970s. These were below those of Africa or Latin America all along—even during the 1970s—the figures for sub-Saharan Africa or South America being even higher (Table 3.2). The rate in India fell again during the 1980s and further in the 1990s, but the corresponding fall for Latin American countries was more dramatic so much so that their figures came down to even lower levels. The urban rural growth differential (URGD) for the latest quinquennial period 2000–2005 for India has been estimated by the Population Division of the United Nations as 1% only. This is below all the continents of the world except Europe and Latin America. Further, it is less than most of the countries in Asia except China, the countries coming out of erstwhile Soviet Union, and those undergoing some kind of political instability (United Nations 2008). India's urban growth as also URGD are much below that of the least developed countries or less developed countries in the world during the past six decades. All these tend to confirm the declining trend of urbanization and question the theories of "urban explosion", "over-urbanization", and the like in India that tend to determine the mindset of policymakers.

More important than the general deceleration in urban growth is the change in the structure of urbanization. During the first four census decades after Independence, the pattern of urbanization was characterized by dualism. Urban growth was high in relatively backward states as many among the small and medium towns here experienced rapid urban growth, largely due to government investment in the district and *taluka* headquarters, programs of urban industrial dispersal, and transfer of funds from the states to local

Table 3.1 Number of Towns, Percentage and Growth Rate of Urban Population in India since 1901

Census Year	*No. of Towns/ Urban Agglomerations*	*Percent Urban to Total Population*	*Annual Exponential Growth ofUrban Population*
1901	1827	10.84	—
1911	1815	10.29	0.03
1921	1949	11.18	0.79
1931	2072	11.99	1.75
1941	2250	13.86	2.77
1951	2843	17.29	3.47
1961	2365	17.97	2.34
1971	2590	19.91	3.21
1981	3378	23.34	3.83
1991	3768	25.72	3.09
2001	4368	27.78	2.73

Note: Estimated population has been taken for the states of Assam and Jammu & Kashmir for the years in which Census could not be conducted.

Source: Census of India (2001).

Table 3.2. Annual Exponential Growth Rate of Urban Population for Major Regions of the World and Asia

Period	World	More Developed	North America	Less Developed	Less Developed, Excluding China	Latin America with Caribbean	South America	Africa	Sub-Saharan Africa	Asia	Eastern Asia	South Central Asia	South East Asia	Western Asia	India
1950–1955	2.97	2.33	2.66	3.83	3.9	4.44	4.58	4.66	4.93	3.5	3.66	2.87	3.93	5.06	2.36
1955–1960	3.06	2.27	2.61	4.02	4.04	4.36	4.41	5.01	5.50	3.64	3.81	2.95	4.15	4.96	2.29
1960–1965	3.06	2.08	2	4.15	4.21	4.39	4.4	5.1	5.47	3.76	3.78	3.41	3.98	4.89	2.98
1965–1970	2.75	1.76	1.63	3.73	4.12	4.01	3.94	4.65	5.17	3.44	3.01	3.51	4.02	4.79	3.14
1970–1975	2.62	1.47	0.98	3.67	4.06	3.81	3.75	4.4	4.85	3.37	2.56	3.95	3.96	4.57	3.75
1975–1980	2.73	1.19	1	3.96	3.98	3.53	3.56	4.43	4.84	3.8	3.39	4.18	4	4.1	3.89
1980–1985	2.66	0.93	1.23	3.86	3.72	2.98	3.09	4.3	4.56	3.81	3.57	3.63	4.29	4.9	3.32
1985–1990	2.69	0.94	1.28	3.75	3.42	2.67	2.72	4.16	4.59	3.8	4.05	3.34	4.11	3.88	3.15
1990–1995	2.34	0.74	1.57	3.19	3.03	2.38	2.33	3.87	4.37	3.13	3.09	2.92	3.97	2.78	2.88
1995–2000	2.19	0.56	1.51	2.96	2.8	2.18	2.17	3.52	4.00	2.91	2.84	2.64	3.91	2.57	2.63
2000–2005	2.07	0.61	1.42	2.68	2.56	1.86	1.95	3.38	3.79	2.62	2.53	2.42	3.47	2.35	2.35
2005–2010	1.98	0.54	1.31	2.53	2.48	1.71	1.7	3.31	3.67	2.46	2.23	2.53	3.06	2.19	2.39
2010–2015	1.91	0.52	1.2	2.39	2.4	1.51	1.48	3.23	3.55	2.31	1.99	2.63	2.63	2.12	2.5
2015–2020	1.81	0.49	1.08	2.23	2.3	1.32	1.26	3.12	3.41	2.15	1.72	2.67	2.25	1.99	2.57
2020–2025	1.7	0.46	0.96	2.07	2.19	1.14	1.07	3	3.27	1.97	1.43	2.64	1.95	1.85	2.6
2025–2030	1.6	0.42	0.86	1.91	2.08	0.98	0.91	2.87	3.11	1.79	1.16	2.54	1.73	1.71	2.56

Source: United Nations (2008).

bodies through a need based or what is dubbed as "a gap-filling" approach. A few among the large cities in developed states also attracted migrants and experienced modest urban growth due to industrialization and infrastructural investment. The relationship between urban growth and economic development on the whole was understandably negative[3].

The 1990s, however, made a significant departure from the earlier decades. Despite overall deceleration, the large cities have registered population growth above the national average (Table 3.3). The small and medium-sized towns, particularly those in backward states, on the other hand, have experienced growth much below that of the country. The disparity in growth rates between large and small and medium-sized towns has thus expanded significantly as urbanization process concentrated in large cities and developed regions. This could, at least partly, be attributed to the new system of governance and measures of decentralization, as discussed later. The large municipal bodies, particularly those located in developed states, have experienced high economic and demographic growth. Due to their stronger economic base, these have been able to secure high credit ratings and raise resources through bonds and other innovative credit instruments. With governmental investment in infrastructure and basic amenities becoming less and less in smaller towns, they find it difficult to finance any development project through internal resources or borrowings from capital markets. The fiscal discipline imposed by the government, credit rating agencies, and other financial intermediaries make it impossible for them to undertake infrastructural investment of any kind[4]. In particular, the towns located away from the "emerging global centres of growth" have failed in attracting such investments due to a high infrastructural deficiency which thus has trapped them in a vicious circle. Given these macro trends in most of the Indian states, there is an urgent need to examine the stipulation that the country would experience "unprecedented urbanisation" in the next three decades, with empirical rigor.

3. FUTURE URBAN SCENARIO

The recent trends in urbanization, as discussed earlier, cast serious doubts on the urban projections made by various expert committees set up by the government and international agencies. In early 1980s, Indian Planning Commission (1983)[5] had projected urban population in the country for the years 1991 and 2001, using two alternate variants. The exercise was undertaken under the overwhelming shadow of "urban explosion" observed during 1971–1981 and, consequently, the projected figures were much on the higher side. Other official projections made during the 1980s and 1990s also reflect this "optimism" and give figures for future urban population even larger than those from the Planning Commission. The Expert Committee for Population Projections for the Eighth Plan, for example, had predicted urban growth (annual exponential) rate to be 4.4% during the 1980s and 4.1% during the 1990s.

Table 3.3 Annual Exponential Growth Rates of Urban Population in Different Size Categories

Census Year	*Class I*	*Class II*	*Class III*	*Class IV*	*Class V*	*Class VI*
1901–1911	0.54	–0.73	0.46	–0.55	–0.43	0.72
1911–1921	1.57	0.68	0.50	0.03	0.46	1.47
1921–1931	2.24	2.89	2.28	1.59	0.89	–1.25
1931–1941	4.81	2.59	2.51	1.47	1.50	–2.26
1941–1951	5.02	2.10	3.07	2.01	1.97	3.31
1951–1961	3.72	3.50	3.05	1.65	–4.05	–11.62
1961–1971	4.29	2.93	2.65	1.67	–1.14	–2.32
1971–1981	4.34(3.46)	4.43(3.09)	2.69(3.33)	2.43(3.00)	1.64(3.15)	5.05(3.90)
1981–1991	3.84(2.96)	2.38(2.75)	2.26(2.59)	1.02(2.50)	–0.13(2.62)	–2.45(3.64)
1991–1901	3.42(2.76)	1.76(2.37)	2.15(2.27)	1.64(2.19)	1.93(2.22)	0.80(3.26)

Note: 1. Size class wise figures exclude Assam 1981 and Jammu and Kashmir 1991.
2. All classes exclude six towns in 1941, four each in 1931 and 1921 and two each in 1911 and 1901 of Goa, which could not be assigned to any size class as their population for these years is not available. Total number of towns therefore do not match the figures in Table 3.1.
3. The growth rates for towns in a size category have been computed by taking the population in the category in the base and terminal year, without considering the change in the number of towns therein. The figures in brackets, however, are computed by taking only the population of the towns that belonged to a category, both for base and terminal years.
Source: Census of India(1981, 1991). For 2001, unpublished data from website are used.

The projections of urban growth made by the United Nations Popular Division (UNPD) are on a slightly lower side but yet make errors of "over optimism". The World Urbanisation Prospects (WUP 1995 Revision) had placed the annual growth rate of urban population for 1990–1995 and 1995–2000 at 2.9% and 3.0% (United Nations, 1996), which is about what was recorded by Indian Census during the 1980s. The percentage of urban population was projected to go up from 25.5% in 1990 to 28.6% in 2000. Importantly, these figures were revised downward in the subsequent WUPs. The growth rates for the periods 1990–1995 and 1995–2000 were brought down to 2.75% and 2.80% while the percentage of urban population in 2000 was placed at 28.4% in the WUP Report for 1998. These figures are below those of earlier WUP, possibly because these take into consideration the decline reported in the natural increase in population in Sample Registration System (SRS) in the 1990s. These estimates, all coming out before the availability of 2001 Census results, however, are above what actually came out in the Census (Table 3.4).

The WUP 1995 projection of future urban growth of 3.2% during 2000–2005 is lower than that of the government committees and closer to the recent Census figure. The WUP 2007, however, puts this at 2.35% while WUP 2009

Table 3.4 Annual Exponential Urban Growth and URGD for India as Given in World Urbanization Prospects of UNDP in Different Revisions

	WUP 1995 (1994 Revision)	*WUP 2004 (2003 Revision)*	*WUP 2008 (2007 Revision)*
Urban growth 1990–1995	2.87	2.73	2.88
Urban growth 1995–2000	3.04	2.54	2.63
Urban growth 2000–2005	3.16	2.28	2.35
Urban growth 2020–2025	2.80	2.53	2.60
Urban growth 2045–2050	NA	NA	1.69
URGD 1990–1995	1.30	1.10	1.09
URGD 1995–2000	1.77	1.07	1.08
URGD 2000–2005	2.22	1.07	1.02
URGD 2020–2025	3.25	2.63	2.66
URGD 2045–2050	NA	NA	2.94

Source: United Nations (1995; 2004; 2008)

lowers total urban projected figure of 2030 by 20 million compared to WUP 2007. Revisions implicitly admit that the projection of urban population, placed at 41.3% by the year 2020 in WUP 1995 is much on a higher side[6]. WUP 2007 places this at around 37.5 only. What, however, is surprising is that this gives higher projections of urban growth in future years than that given before four years in WUP 2003[7]. It is not clear what new information became available, excepting that the natural growth rate of population has gone down, that could constitute the basis for the 'optimism'.

It is surprising that despite India's reporting one of the lowest URGD among the developing countries during 2000–2005, the projected URGD for 2025–2030 or 2045–2050 is one of the highest in the world. It is difficult to go with this perspective especially when India has registered a significant deceleration in urban growth and URGD in recent decades. Given these recent trends, all these projections—made by UN agencies as well as various committees of the government—can be considered as overestimates.

The high growth perspective on urbanization could partly be attributed to the methodology adopted by the UNPD and other national and international agencies, which is based on an exponential function, relating the percentage of urban population with URGD. It implicitly assumes that the URGD would increase in developing countries till these have half of their population living in urban areas. Despite several modifications in the methodology, allowing URGD to come down before these countries reach the 50% level, the UNPD gives figures that are distinctly on a higher side. The policy concerns in developing countries urging to control RU migration and slowing down the growth of large cities has possibly motivated their administrators and policymakers to readily accept this perspective as it provides justification for imposing restrictions on population mobility. Furthermore, this allows the urban elites to demand and corner greater share in the total investible resources for infrastructure and civic amenities. Given urban bias in development planning in most of the less developed countries (Lipton 1977), it is no wonder that such projections have largely gone unchallenged in India as well as in many other developing countries.

In is only recently that the policymakers in India have started questioning the alarmist perspective and with that also the measures for discouraging RU migration and decelerating urban growth. The Tenth Plan documents note that "the moderate pace of urbanisation in the country has been a cause of disappointment", and the Eleventh Plan admits that "the degree of urbanization in India is one of the lowest in the world"[8]. An overview of the contemporary development dynamics suggests that the process of urbanization is unlikely to be stepped up sharply over the next few decades. This is partly due to decline in natural growth of population and partly to slowing down of migration. The decline in the demographic growth in small and medium-sized towns would be sharper compared to larger cities. More importantly, fewer rural settlements would transform themselves into urban centers, and consequently the increase in the number of the latter will be marginal. Assuming the urbanization and RU migration trends to continue, the level of urbanization would be around 40% by 2050, less than what has been projected by most national and international organizations.

4. THE DYNAMICS OF INDUSTRIAL DEVELOPMENT AND EMPLOYMENT GENERATION

The macroeconomic processes, particularly since the 1990s, have led to industrial and infrastructural development getting concentrated in and around a few large cites, with the exclusion of small towns and backward regions. This is partly due to the measures of decentralization whereby the responsibilities of resource mobilization and launching infrastructural projects have been passed on, to an extent, to local bodies. Large municipal corporations, particularly those located in developed states have a strong economic base and, enjoy a competitive advantage. This clearly manifests in their higher capacity of resource mobilization. This has been responsible for their relatively higher economic and demographic growth in recent years.

It may however be noted that the industries that are growing rapidly during the past few decades have low employment potential within the organized segment. Even 8% to 9% growth of industries per annum, as recorded during the past several years, have failed to generate large employment. Private corporate sector and other large industries, where growth in output has been significant during the past decade, have high capital intensity and have generated very few jobs. Many of the public sector units, on the other hand, have gone in for rationalization of workforce and thereby brought down their number of formal employees.

A large part of the employment growth in the large cities has taken place through a process of subcontracting, using regular and self-employed workers who are not covered under any social security system. Despite this outsourcing of jobs, the capacity of the informal manufacturing sector to absorb the labor force has been low. Also, several of these workers have been classified under tertiary sector whose share in employment has gone up steeply. The sluggish growth in manufacturing employment in urban areas can also be attributed to the location of large units outside the municipal limits, thanks to the emergence of an environment lobby in big cities. The industrial dispersal has been facilitated by easier availability of land, access to an unorganized labor market, and a diminished awareness and less stringent implementation of environmental regulations in the city periphery. The poor have been pushed to these "degenerated peripheries" and commute to the city for work or find jobs in the industries driven out of the central areas[9]. The entrepreneurs, engineers, executives, and so on, associated with modern industries and business, however, reside within the central city. A few of them commute to the factories in the periphery, but they return to the city through rapid transport corridors. This segmented structure of demographic growth, emerging in different variants in different regions/metropolises, diverts the poor prospective migrants into the peripheries that in any case are absorbing the evicted slum settlements and their informal activities, declared illegal by Master Plan norms.

There are definite empirical evidences suggesting that the characteristics of the informal sector as emerging now are different from that of earlier decades. The sector in recent years has experienced some type of formalization, leading to employing people on a regular basis. The high growth of employment during 1983–1993 in informal sector was characterized by large incidence of subsidiary or casual laborers, most of them being illiterate and unskilled. Employment opportunities during this period came up in the lowest economic strata, and, as a result, its impact on poverty reduction was very high. The growth of informal sector, thus, was a vehicle for bringing about significant reduction in poverty.

The informal sector employment has grown rapidly during 1993–2004 as well, pushing up the overall employment growth in the economy. This can be attributed to near stagnation in employment in public organizations and the organized private sector, as noted previously. Given the nature of industries experiencing rapid growth after launching of the programs of liberalization, it is not surprising that employment in the organized manufacturing (Annual Survey of Industries data) and service (Director General of Employment and Training data) sectors has shown negligible growth. Private industries within this sector, where growth in output has been significant during the past one and a half decades, have low potential for employment generation. The public units, on the other hand, have often registered a negative growth in their workforce, as noted previously. An important question would be whether the spurt in informal employment in this period would have poverty reduction impact similar to that during 1983–1993?

The difference in the character of the informal sector during the two periods emerges in terms of the component of subsidiary employment. The percentage of subsidiary to total (usual status) employment is low in the latter period compared to the previous period, despite some increase in it in recent years (Kundu and Sarangi 2007). The other related development is that there has been high growth in employment by current status, most of them being in the informal sector. Indeed, job opportunities coming up on a weekly or daily basis in recent years have been high while those by usual status have been relatively low. This has resulted in a peculiar situation where there is a high unemployment rate despite a high growth in employment by daily status. One can argue that the poverty reduction impact of this kind of employment generation would be at best modest. These also raise the apprehension that the benefits of globalization and the changes in the character of employment—moving from total informality to semi-formality—is not trickling down from the entrepreneurs to their workers in urban centers.

Interestingly, the growth of casual employment has declined dramatically in recent years, while that for self-employed and regular workers has gone up. This in a way confirms the proposition that there has been some amount of formalization of informal activities, leading to people getting contracted jobs or employment on a regular basis. The economic rationale for this development is fairly evident and easily understandable. Entrepreneurs facing a globally competitive market have come to recognize that they have a greater chance of success if they standardize their products, meet the specifications of the customers, respect the schedules of delivery and organize production and marketing activities on a somewhat formal basis. Indian entrepreneurs appear to have resorted to this model of 'formal informalization' in a big way in order to take advantage of the emerging global market. As a result, many of the rapidly growing sectors including small-scale manufacturing, trade, commerce, and entertainment activities, particularly in urban areas, have tended to employ their workers on a regular basis so that they can effectively meet the challenge of the global market. Employment of domestic help and other supporting services have followed a similar pattern. It is well recognized that total informality can result in uncertainty in production process, failure to meet the specifications of the product, and irregularity in delivery—a major handicap in getting linked to the global market.

The increase in the rates of unemployment can at least partially be attributed to this process of formal informalization. Many of the illiterate rural migrants (dispossessed farmers, rural artisans, etc.), not having the minimum level of conversation skills or market smartness, are not able to put their foothold in the urban job market (Kundu and Sarangi 2007). This reduces the possibility of disguised employment since work is regulated as per certain (mostly unwritten and nonlegal) contracts and specifications. This is the reason why the growth in demand for labor in the informal sector is not commensurate with that in supply. The fact that a larger percentage of people are seeking or available for work on a daily basis reveals that even the high level of employment generation during 1999–2004 does not meet the needs of the poor households for their livelihood support.

A quick overview of the wage data confirms this hypothesis. The fact that women employment is growing rapidly both in rural and urban areas, despite stagnation and even decline in real wages, is a disturbing fact. Clearly, high growth of employment for illiterate women has been possible because they are willing to accept low wages. The fact that non-agricultural workers, mostly in informal activities where they are not able to maintain real wages in the face of high macroeconomic growth, has serious implications for the welfare of the labor as well as sustainability of growth. One must, however, credit the anti-poverty programs of the government like the National Rural Employment Guarantee Programme for the increase in wages among illiterate agricultural workers, but this has been confined only to rural areas. The segment of highly educated workers who have been able to maintain their real wages constitute a small proportion of the labor force. It is also a matter of concern that unemployment rates among the educated are extremely high.

Using the National Sample Survey (NSS) survey data, one can compute the number of jobs in the labor market as opposed to number of workers. This is done by combining the number of employed as per the principal status with that employed by the subsidiary status. This then provides a total count of the jobs performed, taking in to account multiple activities. Table 3.5 gives the annual compound growth rate of jobs in the rural and urban sectors of the economy.

The highest growth in the number of jobs is recorded in domestic services in private households. These jobs—mostly maids, cooks, gardeners, and the like—require a very low level of education and skill but some amount of training. An increasing level of income in the hands of high- and middle-income households is responsible for employment generation in these services. The next in terms of growth rate is real estate, renting, and related businesses that again require only semi-skilled workers. Another labor-intensive sector is construction which has traditionally been a major employer of the illiterate labor force. This too has recorded very high growth rates. The fourth highest is hotels and restaurants that too require low skill levels, their growth being linked to the incremental income in the hands of the urban upper and middle class. It is thus evident that the activities that have absorbed a large segment of the labor force in recent years have a high incidence of low productive employment. Understandably, here the real wages have not increased, and in several activities, these have gone

Table 3.5 Growth Rate of Jobs by Sector of Activity between 1999 and 2004

Sector of activity	*Growth rate (%)*		
	Rural	*Urban*	*All*
Agriculture, forestry	1.4	5.5	1.5
Fishing	3.0	0.7	2.5
Mining	4.3	4.0	4.2
Manufacturing	4.7	6.0	5.3
Electicity, Gas & water supply	1.5	2.7	2.2
Construction	11.5	5.3	9.0
Wholesale and retail trade, repair of motor vehicles etc	7.0	1.6	3.9
Hotel & Restaurants	5.8	6.1	6.0
Transport, storage & communications	6.4	4.1	5.2
Financial intermediation	7.8	7.1	7.3
Real estate, renting and business activities	11.5	13.4	13.0
Public administration and defense	-4.6	-2.2	-3.0
Education	6.0	7.0	6.5
Health & social work	5.6	4.8	5.2
Other community, social and personal services	-4.3	-0.7	-2.8
Private household with employed persons	39.0	19.1	23.5
All sectors	2.4	4.3	2.8

Source: Based on NSS surveys of 1999–2000 and 2004–2005 as reported in Kolli et al. (2008).

down. This explains the low reduction in poverty in urban areas, bringing the poverty levels in rural and urban areas almost at par in recent years.

A parallel process in the Indian economy is the informalization of the formal sector. Informal workers may be defined as those working in the unorganized enterprises or households, excluding regular workers or those with social security benefits. The workers in the formal sector without any employment/social security benefits[10] would also belong to this category. It is important that the proportion of informal workers in the country was over 90% in 1999–2000 which has gone up further in 2004–2005 (Table 3.6). Correspondingly, the share of formal workers has gone down. The figure works out to be 7.6% only in 2004–2005 which includes private sector workers, civil servants, military personnel, and employees of state public sector undertakings. What however is striking is that while the percentage of formal workers in the informal sector has remained at the level of less than 0.5%, the share of informal worker in formal activities has gone up from 38% to 47%. This implies that while the value added by these informal workers gets reflected in the profits of the formal sector, these workers do not have a reasonable share in it or have an access to social security benefits.

In view of all these, the economic growth in the coming decades, even if retained at 7% to 8% per annum, may not generate large formal employment in urban areas. Furthermore, in light of the different skill requirements for subcontracted jobs as well as the low cost support system, the imposition of a cap on the growth of wholly informal employment seriously discounts the proposition that urban growth will accelerate in future years.

5. NEW SYSTEM OF URBAN MANAGEMENT AND ITS IMPACT ON URBAN MORPHOLOGY

The impact of the new system of urban governance on demography and morphology of Indian cities needs to be assessed carefully. Local governments in many of these cities are currently facing two serious problems in attracting foreign and Indian businesses and industrialists as they promote economic growth. One problem is the scarcity of land within the central city and other prime locations, and the second problem is lack of capital. Many of the cities are working on an ingenious method of attracting national and multinational companies to solve this twin problem. They are opting for a high Floor Space Index (FSI) in the central areas of the city permitting multi-storied structures, providing space for business houses, commercial activities, and high-income

Table 3.6 Employment in the Formal and Informal Sector

Sector	*Number of informal workers*	%	*Number of formal workers*	%	*Total*
		1999–2000			
Informal	341.3	99.6	1.4	0.4	342.6
Formal	20.5	37.8	33.7	62.2	54.1
Total	361.7	91.2	35	8.8	396.8
		2004–5			
Informal	393.5	99.6	1.4	0.4	394
Formal	29.1	46.6	33.4	53.4	62.6
Total	422.6	92.4	34.9	7.6	457.5

Source: Based on NSSO data, as analysed in the Report of National Commission for Enterprises in Unorganised Sector (2006).

residential units. The strategy of permitting vertical growth in areas with high land values has enabled the local bodies to find more space and, at the same time, generate resources for infrastructural development by selling the extra FSI. There is an additional incentive for adopting this strategy as sanctioning of loans by many of the international agencies have become contingent on the acceptance of higher FSI in the central city. Although the basic idea is to promote greater efficiency in the use of land, this has helped the process of reorganization of population, often leading to a greater separation between the rich and the poor.

Importantly, the Constitutional Amendment Act has made it possible to provide differential levels of amenities in large cities across wards, based on the willingness of the users to pay. Elitist preference for low density and clean micro environment has built a powerful lobby to ensure quality infrastructural services, limit new construction, and permit no illegal encroachment in core and high-income colonies. Low levels of basic amenities, unhygienic living conditions, and a deteriorating law-and-order situation in low-income colonies, on the other hand, are strong disincentives for further immigration of the poor. A switch over from planning to free market, therefore, has not given any impetus to urban growth, even in the large cities that are attracting phenomenal infrastructural investment. This has only helped institutionalize disparity and strengthen the process of segmentation of the cities into rich and poor colonies.

Given the resource crunch in the government agencies, a number of financial institutions, international donors, and credit rating agencies have come up with various innovative arrangements for resource mobilization that are making significant impact on the urban scenario. Many of the large Urban Local Bodies (ULB) have gone in for privatization, partnership arrangements, and promotion of community-based projects to lessen pressure on their budgetary resources. The projects sub-contracted to private agencies or launched with public private partnership mostly have stipulations of cost recovery that make these financially self-sustaining. However, the low-income colonies find it difficult to meet the stipulations. Similar stipulations are being adopted in public sector projects that are becoming increasingly dependent on institutional borrowings and capital market. Several of the metropolitan cities have gone in for preparation of vision documents replacing the Master Plans. Its preparation is less time consuming, and, more importantly, it only gives a framework, leaving the task of detailing out the schemes and modalities for implementation to stake holders, including private builders and financial intermediaries, among others. The responsibility of preparing the document has often been assigned to the national and global research agencies that bring in the perspective of other countries and global cities and push the agenda of greater engagement of market-based agencies. All these, it is apprehended, are and would in future accentuate the gaps between rich and poor localities within the cities, particularly in the context of water, electricity, and sanitation facilities, resulting in serious problems of health and hygiene for the entire city. A growing disparity in the quality of micro environment has also been responsible for law-and-order problems resulting in individual and group violence.

A massive program for infrastructural investment through Additional Central Assistance, coming to state/city governments as grants, has been launched in the Tenth Plan under the Jawaharlal Nehru National Urban Renewal Mission (JNNURM) which is the major instrument of intervention for transformation of the cities in the Eleventh Plan. The key objective is to get the state and local governments to commit themselves to structural reforms which the central government had failed in getting them to do, despite adopting several carrot-and-stick measures and incentive schemes. An overview of the projects and schemes launched under its infrastructural development component in different cities reveals that most of the projects have been designed to increase the total capacity of services like water supply, sanitation, and sewer treatment, besides of course roads and flyovers at the city level. There is no explicit provision to improve the delivery of the facilities in the deficient areas that have low incomes and cannot afford the services. As such, the apprehension that many of the benefits from this augmented system will be cornered by better-off sections cannot be ruled out. The current Plan document reposes the responsibility of preparing the City Development Plan (CDP) under JNNURM to local and state governments as a vision document. It holds that the CDP should also provide a scope for participation of private actors and community in the planning process and its implementation.

Given the socio-political reality in India, it is difficult for the private sector to bring about the changes in urban land market, land use, investment in infrastructure, and so on, without the state becoming a partner. The changes in the system of governance and urban planning, as recommended by international agencies and endorsed half-heartedly by local planners, envisage the state's role as an active facilitator. The Indian state has indeed responded quite favorably to these recommendations by ushering in the necessary changes, although the democratic structure and pro-poor stance of the government have made the process somewhat slow. The message, however, comes loud and clear, from the Eleventh Plan document and, more specifically, the design of JNNURM that such changes are possible and are forthcoming. It is important to note that JNNURM proposes to improve the living conditions of the poor through integrated housing and infrastructural projects, implemented through state governments and local bodies, but these plans also envisage engagement of private builders on a massive scale. The capacity of state institutions to ensure that the dwelling units and basic services provided under a scheme reach the deserving sections of the population and that the latter are able to hold on to their units is extremely limited. It is evident that the Mission would provide highly subsidized dwelling units to a few administratively or politically connected people in select cities, as units built by public agencies would be less than 10% of the housing shortage. This is bound to increase nepotism and corruption. In an idealistic situation, the units may be allotted to poor households who are being evicted from their encroached land on and around major city-level facilities in prime areas. This initiative of "sanitization", operationalized through JNNURM or the recently proposed Rajiv Awas Yojana (housing scheme) would meet the commercial interests of national and global actors and may increase the overall efficiency of the city system but make no major dent on the housing shortage of the poor. On the other hand, this would diminish the inflow of rural poor into large cities and decelerate the overall urban growth in the country.

6. A SUMMARY OF CONCLUSIONS AND THEIR DEVELOPMENT IMPLICATIONS

An analysis of the contemporary urban scenario shows that the growth in urban population in India has been modest and fluctuating over the past few decades. It casts serious doubts on this perspective that India will be the epicenter of future urbanization in the world or Asian continent. It questions the future urban scenario as projected by various expert committees of the government as well as Population Divisions of United Nations. It argues that the high-growth perspective on urbanization is largely due to the methodology adopted by these bodies and the negative or ambivalent attitude of the policymakers toward RU migration. The high-growth perspective not only provides justification for imposing restrictions on population mobility but also strengthens the demand of the urban elites for larger infrastructural investment.

The process of urbanization in India has continued to be top-heavy or large city oriented. This is because of higher demographic growth in larger cities, in addition to the factor of upward movement of towns. Given the new dynamics of urban industrial development associated with the strategy of globalization, the small and medium-sized towns, located away from the "emerging global centres of growth", particularly those in backward regions, have failed in attracting much private investment. Moreover, there was declassification of many of these during the 1990s. The number of small and medium-sized towns, as identified by the Population Census has for the first time decreased during the 1990s which should be a matter of serious policy concern.

All these could be attributed to the measures of decentralization whereby the responsibilities of management of civic amenities and investment in infrastructural projects have partly shifted from the central and state governments to local bodies. The large cities that are financially in a stronger position have been able to take up public works and infrastructure development projects on their own. These have created enhanced livelihood opportunities and thereby record relatively higher demographic growth. This is not so for smaller towns. Decline in central or state assistance has made it extremely difficult for towns, particularly those in less developed states, to invest in improving infrastructure and basic services. All these have led to accentuation of inequity in the provision of basic services across the states and size categories of urban centers. Understandably, the urbanization process has been concentrated in developed states and large cities that could attract national as well as global investment.

The growth of employment during the 1990s has been low which is often attributed to the programs of structural reform. The present decade has, however, seen a reasonably high growth in employment by usual status. By weekly and daily status, one gets a more satisfying picture, both for men and women. This has been attributed to a phenomenal growth of the informal sector. The character of this sector appears to be somewhat different from that of the 1980s. The informal sector in recent years is exhibiting some amount of formalization, leading to more rapid growth in regular and self-employment. This can be attributed to entrepreneurs standardizing their products, maintaining quality control, respecting the schedules of delivery, and so on in order to link to the global market. Employment of domestic help and other supporting services, too, have followed a similar pattern, as the men and women working in global sectors must have a regular household support system. The recent increase in the rates of unemployment along with high growth in regular employment can also be explained in terms of this process of formal informalization. Many of the illiterate rural migrants (dispossessed farmers, rural artisans, etc.), who do not have the minimum level of conversation skills or market smartness, are not able to put a foothold in the urban job market since work is regulated as per certain (mostly unwritten and non-legal) contracts and specifications.

Under the new system of urban governance, attempts are being made to open up the land and capital market to enable the local bodies, para-statal agencies, and private developers access land at preferred sites and to mobilize resources for their residential, business, and infrastructural activities in "select global centres of future". This is being done by simplifying the legal and administrative procedures for changing land use and by flushing out "low-valued" activities from these sites. Low-income and slum colonies are the obvious candidates for relocation in city peripheries[11]. The removal is often carried out indirectly and discreetly through slum improvement schemes, "rehabilitating" them out in the peripheries. Sometimes it is done directly through eviction of slum dwellers, hawkers, pavement dwellers, and the like as per the court orders, in response to public interest litigations filed by the urban upper and middle class to clear up encroachment of public spaces. Increasing dependence on the institutional resources and market borrowings have ensured that the new infrastructure and civic amenities meet the requirements of this class which can pay and make these self-sustaining. Initiatives to promote participatory planning through preparation of vision documents and encouragement of civil society organizations and other stake holders have resulted in elite capture in urban planning. All these have been responsible for segmenting cities, accentuating intra-city inequality, and strengthening the process of degenerated peripheralization.

NOTES

1. Expert Group on the Commercialisation of Infrastructure Projects (1996) and Rakesh Mohan and Dasgupta (2005).
2. Kundu (2003).
3. Kundu (2006).
4. Kundu et. al. (1999).
5. Planning Commission (1983).
6. The parameters of the model (used for the projection exercise in the UN study), makes the increase in the percentage of urban population in the initial years to be low, going up subsequently (but coming down ultimately, at a high level of urbanization).
7. The annual growth rates of urban population given in WUP 2003 and WUP 2007 for 2025–2030 are 2.5% and 2.6%, respectively.
8. Planning Commission (2008).
9. Kundu (2003).
10. National Commission for Enterprises in the Unorganised Sector (2006).
11. Kundu et al. (2002).

REFERENCES

Census of India. 1991. *Provisional population totals,* Paper 2 of 1991, Chapter 6 and Table 10, New Delhi: Government of India.

———. 1981. *General Population Tables*, New Delhi: Government of the . . .

Expert Group on the Commercialisation of Infrastructure Projects. 1996. *The India infrastructure report: Policy imperatives for growth and welfare.* New Delhi: Ministry of Finance, Government of India.

Kolli, R. et al. 2008. Estimates of Workforce from NSS Round. 2004–5. *The Journal of Income and Wealth.* Vol. 30, No. 1.

Kundu, A. 2003. Urbanisation and urban governance: Search for a perspective beyond neo-liberalism. *Economic and Political Weekly* 38(29).

———. 2006. Trends and pattern of urbanisation and their economic implications. *India Infrastructure Report 2006.* New Delhi: Oxford.

———. 2008. Employment and poverty linkages under globalisation: Changing characteristics of labour market in India. *Proceedings of Indo-China Seminar.* New Delhi: ICSSR.

———, and Sarangi. 2007. Migration, employment status and poverty: An analysis across urban centres in India. *Economic and Political Weekly* (January 27).

———, S. Bagchi, and D. Kundu. 1999. Regional distribution of infrastructure and basic amenities in urban India. *Economic and Political Weekly* 34(28).

———, B. K. Pradhan, and A. Subramanium. 2002. Dichotomy or continuum: Analysis of impact of urban centres on their periphery. *Economic and Political Weekly* 37(14).

Lipton, Michael. 1977. *Why poor people stay poor: Urban bias in world development.* London: Temple Smith.

National Commission for Enterprises in the Unorganised sector 2006. *Report on the conditions of Work and Promotion of Livelihoods in the Unorganised Sector*, NCEUS, New Delhi.

NSSO. 2001. *Employment and unemployment situation in India 1999–2000*. New Delhi: Fifty Fifth Round, Department of Statistics.

Planning Commission. 1983. *Task forces on housing and urban development*, vol. I. New Delhi: Government of India.

———. 2008. *Eleventh Five Year Plan 2007–2012*. New Delhi: Planning Commission, Government of India.

Rakesh Mohan, and S. Dasgupta. 2005. The 21st century: Asia becomes urban. *Economic and Political Weekly* XL(3): 15–21.

United Nations. (1996). *World urbanisation prospects The 1995 Revision*. New York: Population Division.

———. (2004). *World urbanisation prospects The 2003 Revision*. New York: Population Division.

———. (2008). *World urbanisation prospects The 2007 Revision*. New York: Population Division.

4 New Urbanism, Neoliberalism, and Urban Restructuring in Mumbai

Swapna Banerjee-Guha

1. INTRODUCTION

A new spatial order of cities came into being in the post-1970 era, coinciding with the crises of the Fordist-Keynesian accumulation regime, and the breakdown of the Bretton Woods system. In the following decades, the global capitalist system became increasingly neoliberalized, crystallizing into a world-wide disciplinary regime of deregulation and privatization. With the passage of time, the process intensified and took a dominant form, impacting the social and economic spaces of countries across the world, especially those of the Global South, and finally affecting their entire developmental system. It essentially invoked a new order reflecting a multi-faceted, multi-scalar dynamic promoting inter- and intra-urban competition, and an intense interplay of global and local. The pattern varied substantially from country to country, depending on the country's historical process of development, politico-economic structure, and respective status in the international economy. It was associated with a universal backtracking of the welfare state regime, a reduction in social sector budget, a shrinking of organized jobs and public sector employment, a downgrading of workers' and other democratic rights earned through long, drawn-out struggles, and a tremendous increase in economic uncertainty. At the city level, it was characterized by limitations on planning and the political capacity of elected municipal governments, privatization of basic services, withdrawal of the state from urban development, escalating support for public-private partnerships, increasing gentrification and urban restructuring to expand space for elitist consumptions, and a growing exposure to global economic forces and global competition reflecting the power of a disciplinary finance regime and a hegemonistic cultural framework.

The international political economy literature has extensively analyzed the process of the world-wide imposition of the neoliberal regime and its consequences at specific country levels. Extensive analysis has also been done on neoliberal supranational policies embodied in the framework of International Financial Institutions (IFIs) like the World Bank, the International Monetary Fund (IMF), the European Union, and the Asian

Development Bank (ADB), and their impacts on different countries. Few works (fewer in South Asia), however, have focused on the specificities of policies, institutional frameworks, and the consequences of neoliberalism at the urban scale (Brenner and Theodore 2002a, 343) or the increasing imperatives of the IFIs to move from macro to micro (i.e., from 'region' to 'urban') in order to sustain and transmit their ideological perspectives through cities. The latter is directly related to extraordinary urban growth in the countries of the South, on the one hand, and the initiation of a universal process of gentrification and restructuring in cities, on the other, with a close interrelationship between the two.

The post-1980 urban spatiality of cities was considerably determined by this framework that operated largely in the context of territory, locale, and place-specific nuances. Metropolises located in the Global South deserve special mention in this respect, as they show signs of intense conflict due to the imposition of the neoliberal framework, reflecting contestation between global society and segmented localized communities. Characterized by the demand of the global market and its priorities, the state in these countries withdrew from its welfare functions; reconfigured its role into an aggressive interventionist one; dissociated from public accountability and democratic norms; promoted market-mediated competitive relations; switched from urban liberal policies to a market driven aggressive urbanism; and began advocating multi-scalar 'creative destruction' in various politico-economic spaces. In several countries of the Global South, during recent decades, and in India since 1990s, cities have been undergoing a drastic transformation of their urban form and governance to become equipped to function as incubators of neoliberal strategies. With the rescaling of the global in the current era, these cities, caught up in a process of recasting the 'urban' (Smith 2002, 431), have been increasingly expressing the current imperatives of capitalist production through flexibilization and disaggregation of the production system (Banerjee-Guha 1997, 50), reflecting a wider restructuring of their respective national and regional economies. Acting as a link between global capitalist culture and local spatial formations, they have surfaced as the epitome of a unified urban planning vision that is known to be significant for the construction of hegemony (Lefebvre 1991, 187) and a dominant culture, comprising competition, modernity, and exploitation all in a single framework. In India, this reflects the contradictions of state institutions that are essentially a crystallization of uneven development, indicating a process of 'decentralizing', 'localizing', and 'internationalizing'—a unified as well as a larger process of neoliberal restructuring in cotemporary times (Banerjee-Guha 2008, 19). This partly rests on existing inequalities, but also on the reproduction of newer areas of decline and growth, based on the current forms of economic momentum and the regulatory framework. In the case of India, the legacies of colonialism, post-colonialism, post-colonial import substitution policies, and subsequent export-led industrial growth go to form the base of the trajectory.

This chapter examines the role of current urban policies of India in molding the concept of the 'urban' through the imposition of a neoliberal framework and an intensifying uneven inter-urban and intra-urban development. Using Mumbai as an example, it will be shown how the material manifestation of urban neoliberalism rests on a strategy of political economic restructuring of space, using space as a formidable component of capital. Section 2 discusses the recently launched Jawaharlal Nehru National Urban Renewal Mission (NURM) that has been identified as the official carrier of neoliberal urbanism in India. Section 3 examines contemporary restructuring in Mumbai and the associative role of NURM. Section 4, while drawing conclusion, explains the urban neoliberalism imperatives for cities like Mumbai.

2. THE REAL FACE OF NEOLIBERAL URBANISM: JAWAHARLAL NEHRU NATIONAL URBAN RENEWAL MISSION

Indian cities of various sizes have been remodeled in recent times as 'world class cities' to function as nodes of circulation of global finance, high-tech activities, and global tourism of all sorts (including medical tourism). The essential objective, obviously, is to make these cities sufficiently investment friendly and acceptable to the credit rating agencies so that they emerge as geo-strategic points nurturing neoliberalism in the Global South. To achieve this goal, a homogenized planning vision is being floated by the state at the behest of global capital, ushering in a new era of remapping 'urban' by intense gentrification of the urban space. While reconstructing a new geography of centrality and marginality, this unified planning vision intensifies the contradictions of 'concentration' and 'dispersal' in the existing institutional landscape and capitalizes on the relational character of specific locations for new users, for which it initiates a process of reformulation of place-specific valorization and devalorization (Banerjee-Guha 2007, 269). The overall character represents a gradual fragmentation of territories, economic decline of a larger majority, increasing socio-spatial inequality, and a simultaneous emergence of new/ modern activities in specific locales implying an aggravation in the spaces of difference (Banerjee-Guha 2006, 210). To reconstruct space as a part of the material strategy of the current conceptualization of the contemporary 'urban', displacement and dispossession of urban poor have recently surfaced as an integral aspect of urban development in all large and medium cities of India. This is aided by other methods of marginalizing the poor like closure of small-scale manufacturing and retail units; anti-poor legal order; regulations against informal workers, hawkers, and waste pickers; privatization of basic services like water, sanitation, housing, health, education; or even restriction of access to public open spaces or parks to open up more spaces for elites, and the like, for leisure and entertainment. Ideology, armed with power, is found to create patterns of domination and repression by the foregoing process that varies from city to city, depending on their socio-economic and political setup (Banerjee-Guha 2004b, 71).

Since Independence, externally assisted urban sector projects in India have accounted for more than U.S. $ 230 million. In the mid-1990s, following the introduction of the New Economic Policy (NEP) in 1991, the infrastructural facelift of cities was put forth as a major solution for urban decadence by the pro-liberalization forces inside and outside the planning framework. Consequently, in 1996, the Expert Group on Commercialization of Infrastructure estimated a requirement of around Rs. 2,500 billion investment in urban infrastructure for the coming ten years. This made the entry of private capital an imperative in Indian urban development, as the public sector, as announced, lacked funds. To attract private capital, a major overhauling of the administrative and legislative framework of the government was suggested that finally made it possible to justify the involvement of IFIs like the World Bank, ADB, USAID, DFID in Indian urban reforms, thanks to the facilitating role of the state. This was the beginning of a new regime of regulation that cleared the ground for the vigorous implementation of state-sponsored urban neoliberal policy in the country in the following years, impacting diverse sectors like municipal finance, infrastructure, basic services, land and housing market, land use, and urban form.

With an official announcement that the relentless process of urbanization had led to an acute urban crisis in the country, the Central Government of India, in December 2005, launched its largest post-Independence urban planning initiative, entitled 'the Jawaharlal Nehru National Urban Renewal Mission (JNNURM)', popularly known as National Urban Renewal Mission (NURM) 'for a planned development of Indian cities'. The primary evil that was identified by the Mission was the gap between the disproportionately fast pace of urban growth and urban infrastructural development. At the same time, urban poverty was identified as a cause of unregulated growth and environmental damage of cities, and as a source of growing crime rates. The rationale for the Mission was no different from the general assurances of neoliberal policy: that the suggested reforms would lead to high economic growth and a higher rate of urbanization; that cities covered by the Mission would emerge as 'engines of growth' for their respective urban systems. In reality, large and medium-sized Indian cities en bloc joined the race for achieving an homogenous modernity designed by investors and private capital and, in the process, entered into a contradictory competitive landscape.

The total cost of the Mission was estimated at Rs. 500,000 million for a period of seven years beginning in April 2005. The Mission aimed at developing 63 Indian cities into 'world class' sustainable cities. The major thrust was put on infrastructure, such as wide roads, flyovers, tunnels, skyways, airports, mega commercial complexes, real estates, and open spaces for recreation, all aspiring to achieve an international standard. Since the early 1990s, the concept of 'livable Indian cities' disappeared from the Indian planning lexicon and got replaced by 'world class cities'. As mentioned, NURM intends to cover cities of all size classes: 7 from category A or mega cities, 28 from category B or metro cities, and the remaining 25 of the 28 listed in category C are urban agglomerations (UAs) with less than 1 million population (Mahadevia 2006, 3400). The Mission consists of two parts: Sub-mission A, entitled UIG (Urban Infrastructure and Governance), has 65% of the total funds, to be administered by the Ministry of Urban Development. Projects on roads, transport, associated infrastructure, water supply, sanitation, and beautification (read gentrification) have come under this heading. Sub-mission B, having 35% of the total funds, is for providing Basic Services to the Urban Poor (BSUP) which is being administered by the Ministry of Urban Employment and Poverty Alleviation (MUEPA). Slum improvement, rehabilitation, access to basic services, and shelter projects for the urban poor come under this heading.

Drastic reforms in urban governance are mandatory for cities undertaking Mission programs. Urban Local Bodies (ULBs) are to prove financial stability for access to capital market funds (Jamwal 2006, 26). A perfidious precondition for the states to access funds for their cities is that they need to set up para-statal, non-elected nodal agencies that will be made responsible for evaluating projects, releasing funds to ULBs/ para-statal agencies, managing the same funds, and monitoring projects. Projects with private sector participation have been given priority over projects submitted by the ULBs/ para-statal agencies by themselves. A Central government committee headed by a private bank chairman had earlier justified the 'inability' of the public sector to finance infrastructure projects in which subsequently 100% foreign direct investment (FDI) was invited. Proving this was not enough, the government went ahead to provide 'viability gap funding' to the investors, in case they were dissatisfied with the profit rates. Smith (2002, 427) termed similar concessions as 'geobribes' while explaining the fiscal concessions given by the New York City administration to the global corporations to induce the New York Stock Exchange to stay in New York. Public-private partnership models for provision of basic services were projected as the ultimate panacea that went at par with Central government's National Common Minimum Programme (NCMP) aiming to remove all obstructions to land and housing markets. Last but not the least, there is no provision for public debate on any of the projects (Jamwal, 2006, 28).

In order to be eligible, the cities had to prepare City Development Plans, a 25-year vision document defining the direction of development. The Mission's original idea, to have the Plans chalked out with 'active pubic consultation', was in reality a hypothetical myth: the Plans were made ready in a month's time, hurriedly got evaluated by hired bodies following which, within three months, the Central government disbursed Rs. 864.82 billion for 23 infrastructure projects. All previous Central government funding schemes were brought under the Mission.

One by one the cities have been roped into pledging their commitment to private capital. With the Central government retaining the right to assess the progress of each project, the state governments and elected bodies are obliged to hand them over to private capital for bringing in efficiency. Several non-governmental organizations (NGOs) were co-opted, for example, 'Janagraha' of Bangalore, to convince the people about the efficacy of public-private partnerships.

A careful look at NURM proves that it is essentially a reform linked investment program for private capital in Indian cities. The key items are (i) privatization/commercialization of basic services through public-private partnership with an introduction of user fees; (ii) liberalization of land and real estate market through repeal of the Urban Land Ceiling Acts and change in the Rent Control Acts, development of a stronger mortgage market, 100% FDI in housing and real estate, and easier land use conversion norms; (iii) financial and administrative restructuring of municipalities through implementation of 74th amendment of the Constitution, rationalization and outsourcing, and introduction of e-governance, making elected civic bodies accountable to private credit rating agencies for evaluating the formers' performance for future sanction of funds; (iv) co-opting middle class through high flown rules like the right to information, public discloser law, citizen's participation law, and so on; (v) bringing the urban poor in the orbit of pay- and- use framework, for example, user fee for basic services (CASUMM 2006, 5)

I take up two of these clauses in a little more detail to exposit the diverse pathways of neoliberal localization. They reflect, besides the politics of the projects, their contextuality and the interaction with the socioeconomic setup. First, the Urban Land Ceiling and Regulation Act (ULCRA). It was passed in 1976 to restrict the concentration of land in the hands of a few as well as its speculation. A ceiling was introduced on the ownership of the vacant urban land in order to make more land available for the economically weaker section. The Central Act was repealed by the Union government in 1999. NURM made it mandatory to repeal the entire Act in order to access Mission funds and thereby made a huge quantity of urban land available in the market. In and around Kolkata, for example, abolition of the ULCRA has made huge spaces available for upscale activities in 'former' industrial areas as seen in the Calcutta Riverside Project coming up in more than 80% land area of the Bata India shoe factory and Batanagar Industrial Township. In Hyderabad, scrapping of ULCRA has become a formidable means for 're-claiming' lands on which slums were located (Varma 2008). With 100% FDI allowed in real estate in early 2005, FDI in real estate as a percentage of total FDI inflows increased from 4.5% in 2003–2004 to 26.5% in 2006–2007 making slums in large cities exceedingly vulnerable. In Delhi, since late 1990s, more than 100,000 families have been evicted, while in Mumbai during 2004–2005, more than 90,000 slum units were demolished (CASUMM 2006, 7). All these were being planned when a series of studies brought out facts about the shortfall of urban housing. The National Building Organization estimated that 24.7 million people would be rendered homeless in 2006, of which 97% would be the urban poor (Singh 2006, 6). Second, there was a mandatory requirement for the ULBs) to become financially self-reliant, which in reality meant a reduction in their budgetary allocation. The actual purpose was to restrict their political and financial capacity that had been coming through a democratic framework and to force them to raise funds from the capital market that would be inclined more to grandiose anti-poor projects with assured high returns.

It is quite apparent that NURM is more a requirement for IFIs and big capital to invest in cities and make profit. Even three years after the introduction of the Mission, funds for BUSP have not been released in most cities. Even if released, these have remained unutilized. A more important issue, however, is the inherent conflict that exists between the two submissions in the given framework. How far the globally funded large infrastructure projects, that are being artificially injected (Baran 1958, 230) into the existing socioeconomic city structures for the use of a small section of the people, will be beneficial to the entire city population is a big question. Already they are negatively impacting the poor, displacing them from their homes and livelihoods that cannot be compensated by any rehabilitation package. The ominous link between NURM and global capital, as a part of a larger neoliberal capitalist agenda, is evident from the involvement of international institutions along with global consultant firms like McKinsey in formulating the reform measures and running several projects. Key policy-making academic institutions funded by international development organizations have also taken active parts in formulating Mission policies, to make subsequent the process of intervention easier (Herman and Chomsky 1988, 23). For example, Pune's Development Plan (DP) was drafted by the Credit Rating Information Services of India Limited (CRISIL) with technical assistance from the Financial Institutions Reform and Expansion—Debt (FIRE-D) project of the USAID (Banerjee-Guha 2009). The recently formed Municipal Association of West Bengal is a product of the same FIRE-D involvement (Banerjee and Mukherjee 2008). Take another example: Navbharat-Maytas-ItalThai (ITD_Thailand)-Infrastructure Leasing and Financial Services (IL&FS) Consortium, the formulator of the Metro rail project in Hyderabad, was offered huge concessions by the State Government of Andhra Pradesh. As per the corporate group's demand, real estate development (without any burden of local taxes) and rail-related infrastructure were accepted as a part of the rail system development (all to be undertaken by the same corporate group) for which 538 acres have been handed over to the Maytas Group. As if this is not enough, the State Road Transport Corporation, that has been carrying about three million passengers daily at a much lower rate than what Metro would charge, will be barred from modernizing the bus system on the Metro route (Ramachandraiah 2009).

Going by the effects in several cities where NURM has been introduced, a persistent fact about the Mission, matching with the trajectory of unevenness of neoliberalism, is a systematic tendency to increase social inequality, making the disadvantaged sections of the society increasingly vulnerable and marginalized. That this constitutes the fundamental core of neoliberalism and not its byproduct (many argue that NURM and the globalizing cities need to be more inclusive and committed to the poor) is something that needs a thorough exposure (Harvey 2005, 119). When the very purpose of NURM is to facilitate neoliberal capitalist accumulation, it is obvious that the poor, who due to socioeconomic restructuring are already experiencing dispossession in various forms, will further slide down in the remade physical landscapes of cities (Smith 2002, 435). In Bhopal, for example, slums are being shifted to peripheral locations, far away from the city, while high user-charges are levied for the meager infrastructure provided in city slums. Interventions being made by the state and collateral organizations in the consequent contradictory landscape through zoning laws, state regulations, and the like clearly express the abuse of monopoly power. The number of slum people in Bhopal was drastically reduced from 399,000 in 1991 to 126,000 in 2001 in the official statistics of the state government, by which a large number of slum dwellers could be labeled illegal (Varma 2008). The exact mix of private market, monopolistic control, and state intervention, however, varies from city to city to serve the purpose of social reproduction of a specific region that contributes toward making a series of sub-systems (Banerjee-Guha 2002a, 122), separated from each other by the regional competitive barriers and simultaneously interconnected through a wider neoliberal ideology. For example, the speed of establishing gated communities in the metropolitan region of Mumbai, the budding IFC (international financial center) of India, colonizing the urban periphery at the cost of destroying the livelihood of millions in the surrounding areas, is much faster than the pace seen in Bangalore, Hyderabad, or Kolkata. Urban elites in Mumbai are a vociferous group (as will be explained in Section 3 on Mumbai) in contemporary urban planning manipulations in India that has almost become an icon of the elites of other cities: whether it is the Hyderabad Metro rail project that demolishes huge pedestrian markets that are the historical landmarks of the city or upscale commerce and residential complexes coming up in the former industrial areas or municipal market premises in and around Kolkata in Jadavpur, Batanagar, or Hind Motor, they all have a uniform logic of creating economic regeneration by promoting 'dynamic' sectors of culture, leisure, and consumption to serve a miniscule section of the population in each city (Banerjee-Guha 2009).

Against this backdrop, the following section takes a close look at the contemporary restructuring process in Mumbai, the ranking globalized city of India and a major recipient of NURM funds, and examines the fallout.

3. EMERGING SPACES OF NEOLIBERALISM IN MUMBAI

Mumbai, the financial capital of India, has the largest share of the country's commerce and business. Three-quarters of the country's stock exchanges are processed here. It is the home of premier financial institutions, head office of most Indian and foreign banks, merchant banks, and public and private sector finance and housing finance companies. As many as 130 foreign institutional investors are located in the city. In the 1990s, Mumbai's share of the value of all the check clearances in the country rose to more than 50%. The city processes half the country's export and import accounts for 50% of the corporate taxes and 40% of the center's revenue through income tax and excise duties (D'Monte 2002). The southern part of Mumbai is a chosen location for head offices of several global corporations providing vital connection to global financial and information flows. Following NEP, with the reconfiguring of the concept of 'urban' as an expansion inter alia of mega city spaces for an expanded control of private capital, the city's already scarce and contested land has become a formidable component of the contemporary project-oriented, entrepreneurial planning model that has contributed in a number of ways to the formation of Mumbai as a competitive city (Mayer 1995, 111).

Since the wave of liberalization formally swept the country in the early 1990s, efforts became stronger, both by the public and private sectors, to reconstitute a new identity of Mumbai as an international financial and service center, thanks to steady industrial decline since 1980s and the closure of the cotton mills, once the economic backbone of the city providing direct employment to 250,000 workers and indirect jobs to 250,000 more till the early 1980s. Organized industrial employment has persistently declined since then in this foremost industrial hub of the country. The proportion of manufacturing employment in the city's economy fell from 37% in 1980 to 18% in the late 1990s, while that in trade and finance went up from 31% to 42% (Table 4.1).

The industrial decline, however, was not an isolated phenomenon, but an indicator of many other changes that were going to come in the future with the official implantation of neoliberal policy, with its intense flexibilized model of planning. With the changing city image, the elected municipal body started being overpowered by powerful corporate consultant group in terms of shaping the future course of urban development. The earlier planning perspective, with a focus on extending and upgrading basic services, was replaced by competitive strategies that promoted cost competition through fiscal conservation, tax incentives, deregulation of land use planning, growing role of consultant firms, public-private partnerships, and last but not the least, privatization and marketization of the local state (Harvey 1989, 9).

The task of reconstituting the status of Mumbai as a globalized city was initially achieved through the production disaggregation and the flexibilization

Table 4.1 Decline in Manufacturing Employment: Mumbai, 1980–1998

Activity	*Percentage of Workers in Major Activity Groups*			*Variation in Absolute Number of Workers*		
	1980	*1990*	*1998*	*1980*	*1990*	*1998*
Agriculture and allied	1.04	0.43	0.26	23,081	10,491	6,877
Mining and quarrying	0.04	0.01	0.01	920	348	182
Manufacturing	36.73	28.47	17.73	817,718	690,621	468,413
Electricity, gas, and water	0.65	0.45	0.29	14,388	10,997	7,620
Construction	0.63	0.83	0.61	14,028	20,082	16,002
Trade, restaurants, and hotels	24.51	29.07	28.30	545,591	705,127	747,733
Transport and communication, etc.	9.43	5.42	9.97	209,883	131,472	263,504
Finance, insurance, real estate, and business services	6.24	10.25	13.69	138,849	248,541	361,888
Community, social, and personal services	13.64	23.87	28.52	303,557	578,945	753,648
Other (specified) activities	7.10	1.21	0.37	157,996	29,257	9,833
All major activities	100.00	100.00	100.00	2,226,011	2,425,881	2,642,577

Source: Economic Census, Directorate of Economics and Statistics, Government of Maharashtra, 1998.

model of globalization (Banerjee-Guha 2002b, 4507; Sassen 1991, 255), reflecting a wider restructuring of the economy that brought in its wake a reconstructed and a more attractive image of Mumbai as a 'world class' finance center than the erstwhile industrial capital of the country. It is relevant to mention in this context that way back in 1993, McKinsey, an international consultancy firm, in its report, had made a strong case for developing Mumbai as a global financial center, for which it had called for an improvement of the overall business environment by easing restrictions on land acquisition and labor management that would make available high-quality commercial and residential space and discipline labor. Following the same line, an NGO named 'Bombay First' that was set up by the Bombay Chamber of Commerce and Industry in 1995, with directors of big corporate houses as its board members, came up with flamboyant ideas about Mumbai's crucial role in the success of India's liberalization. To help the city emerge as a finance and service center, the organization offered its services as an advocacy group (Bombay

First 1995, 6). Such groups, promoted by finance and business capital, since 1991, have become increasingly instrumental in rewriting urban land development policies in several cities (Banerjee-Guha 2004a, 4). Earlier I discussed (Banerjee-Guha 1995, 108) the nexus of the state machinery, business, and commercial interests in systematically legitimizing anti-poor and anti-people projects in Mumbai, that consistently blocked the implementation of plans beneficial to the disadvantaged and stated further that, with the introduction of NEP, such efforts would become more vigorous. The ten-year Regional Plan of the Mumbai Metropolitan Regional Development Authority (MMRDA) was the manifest reality (Banerjee-Guha 2002a, 123). While officially admitting to poor infrastructure, declining industrial employment, and a high level of environmental pollution, it drastically contradicted its 1970s position (of supporting decentralization of Mumbai) and started projecting the metropolis as the country's financial capital, a center of international trade, services, and high-tech industries (MMRDA 1995, 9). Moreover, it suggested a shift in the financial resourcing and administration from public sector to private sector as the goal could not be achieved through sole reliance on public investment, regulations, and controls and advocated for land use policies responding more to market potential (MMRDA 1995, 12). The Plan had an uncanny resemblance to the vision plan of Bombay First, made public in 2003.

With the introduction of neoliberal policies (read NURM), these politics of contestation in Mumbai assumed a level of criticality leading to fierce struggles among various claimants of city space and resulting in a range of new practices of controlling urban space (Rajagopal 2002, 72). As mentioned, singular identities of various power groups of affluent citizens that earlier had been fluid or fuzzy started taking on a more aggressive public form, as mentioned, leading to debates in urban planning on class lines (Banerjee-Guha 2004b, 67) and place-marketing, such as, demanding eviction of hutments of waste pickers, enforcement of strict zoning laws for hawkers, and efforts to make the city more beautiful. The epitome of the above process is 'Vision Mumbai', a ten-year city plan of 'Bombay First', published in 2003, in which it benchmarked Mumbai with ten other cities, namely London, New York, Singapore, Hong Kong, Sao Paulo, Sydney, Bangkok, Rio de Janeiro, Toronto and finally, Shanghai. In active collaboration with state government organizations like the Municipal Corporation of Greater Mumbai (MCGM), MMRDA, and various departments of the state government, the plan document was prepared by the same McKinsey & Company that had identified Mumbai as a global finance center in 1993, immediately after the NEP was introduced. In its preface the *Vision Mumbai* boasted of "having conducted interviews with more than 30 key stakeholders of Mumbai, holding more than 10 brainstorming workshops with major government institutions, business groups and NGOs, researched and developed case studies of five international and five domestic city transformations . . . and consulted works done by McKinsey in other parts of the world finally to develop a framework and database for benchmarking Mumbai with other international cities" (Bombay First 2003, 5).

Targeting four 'high-end services' for the city, such as, financial services, health care, IT-enabled services, and media/entertainment/telecom for the coming years, the plan advocated either total privatization or public-private partnership for projects in all these services (including transport). The relevant chapters of NURM echoed it after two years! Maintenance of the Mumbai-Pune Expressway readily got privatized for fifteen years in 2004 (Chaware 2004, 9). The vision plan identified job potentiality in construction, hotel/tourism/recreation and modern format retail that would create 500,000 jobs in the next ten years in upgraded museums, multi-purpose indoor stadiums, and convention centers (in line with Madison Square Garden); in cafes and restaurants in western and eastern sea-fronts; in restaurants and bars: and in supermarkets and hypermarkets that can be located inside the city and on highways. Nowhere was there a mention of Mumbai's potential as a strong production center, or the million jobs it had been loosing over years. The basis of 'Vision Mumbai' was a shift of capital from production to built environment. Hence the city was identified as the future consumption center of the country. Growth of the city, targeted at 8% to 10% a year, was envisaged only through some specific sectors. First was the services market. To activate it, financial services would be geared up based on the already-existing network of financial institutions, law firms, investment banks, and the like. More than 100,000 jobs were envisaged to be provided by this sector. The second thrust was on the health sector and entertainment. With its creative class, production houses, financiers, and distributors and with the overseas market accepting the mainstream Indian cinema, Mumbai was designated as the chosen city in India to create 90,000 more jobs in entertainment and healthcare. 'Vision Mumbai' also intended to put the city back to its premier status as the capital of information technology (not industrial!) in India. Upcoming localities of northeast Mumbai near Andheri, emerging as the future IT hub, were the manifest reality (Business World 2003, 45) of such designs (Tables 4.2A, 4.2B, 4.2C). The state government endorsed the vision plan and came out with its own Mumbai Transformation Project in 2003 on the same line.

The entire project was estimated to have a cost of \$40 billion (about Rs. 1,826,000 million) to be spent over ten years, of which 25% would have to be invested by the state government. The 75% private investment in the housing, telecom, and services sector would be based on market demand (Business World 2003, 44). Not without logic, 'Vision Mumbai' in many sections was identical to the 1995 Regional Plan of MMRDA and was almost completely the same as NURM.

The clientele of the vision plan was clearly earmarked. The provision of upgraded infrastructure and entertainment facilities were slotted for a 'high quality talented' population. The new urban programs put considerable thrust on up-gradation of safety operations (an eight-pronged program was chalked out) for the same group "in the face of economic decline, increasing violence, crime and worsening of quality of life due to proliferation of slums" (Bombay First, 2003, 22). The vision plan not only identified

Table 4.2A Mumbai's Growth Potential

Sector	*Potential GDP(Rs. million)*	*Potential Growth (%)*	*Employment Potential ***
Financial services	374,610	9	89,000
Healthcare	19,550	5	15,000
IT/TES	133,110	20	77,000
Media/entertainment/ telecom	117,150	13	73,000
Construction	103,680	15	244,000
Hotel/tourism	67,630	13	46,000
Retail	275,750	12	263,000
Manufacturing	207,710	12	204,0000
Transportation/logistics	19,420	10	4,000
Total *	1,401,860	11.5	807,000

Source: Business World (2003, 44–45).
* Excludes manufacturing in the hinterland and transportation/logistics. Includes other sectors.
** Additional jobs by 2013.

Table 4.2B Funding Mumbai

Total investment required	2,000,000
Private investment	1,500,000
Available funding with municipality	50,000
User charges, better tax collection	300,000
Government equity	150,000

Source: Business World (2003, 44–45).
Figures in Rs. million.

Table 4.2C Boosting Land Supply

Levers	*Land supply (%)*
FSI increase	30–40
Mumbai trans-harbor link	15–20
CRZ II and III relaxation	15–20
Urban Land Ceiling Act/rent control	5–10
Slat pan, NDZ, Port Trust, NTC Mill Lands	3
Total	50–70

Source: Business World (2003, 44–45).

a spatiality of crime but advocated a deeply interventionist agenda in justifying the need for maintaining private police forces for gated communities, welfare reform, community regeneration, and design of public spaces with maximum surveillance. Undoubtedly the decline of jobs and reduction of social reproduction has led to an increase of illegal livelihoods among the city poor in recent times by which low-income and poorer areas have become increasingly vulnerable. The vision plan's objective was to segregate these areas by furthering militarization of the city space.

The primary source of land has been identified in the heart of the city that roughly takes the shape of a triangle. In an earlier (Banerjee-Guha,2004a, 8) article, I named it the 'golden triangle'. Its northern point is located in the emerging IT hub of Andheri (east), the right arm stretches from Andheri to the Dock area in the south and touches its southeastern point, the base goes west and joins the southwestern point in the mill areas of Parel and Matunga, the left arm traverses north to reach Andheri through the (a) sprawling mill lands, now converted into upper-class commercial-residential areas, (b) Dharavi, the huge slum that is getting ready for gentrification, and (c) the expansive Bandra-Kurla commercial complex built on evacuated slum land and the bed of the Mithi River. In order to get to the crux of the urban neoliberal design for Mumbai's restructuring, it is extremely necessary to understand the nature of transformation of these areas inside the triangle. Together, they make a huge capital for the city's redevelopment as evident from the City Development Plan. The sheer quantity of land is enormous: 522 hectares (1,289.89 acres) comes only from the mill lands from which 200,000 workers have been displaced and many await it, with a sprawling working-class area and a low-income neighborhood. The original development control rules had suggested that one-third of each (sold out) mill land would be surrendered to the state government for the use of workers. Subsequently, the clause was deleted. The estimated land in the dock area (three and a half times bigger than the mill lands) is 753 hectares (1,860 acres) out of which 445 hectares is reclaimed. The Bandra-Kurla complex, coming up as an elite commercial area as a 'city within a city' (MMRDA 1995, 15) has 370 hectares located near the international and domestic airports, to the north of the mill lands where office space was sold in 1994 at Rs. 2,800 per square foot, much higher than the prevailing rate. Next comes Dharavi, housing more than 70,000 hutments on 174 hectares. The redevelopment cost of Dharavi has been estimated at Rs. 56,000 million and would convert the entire area into a model township (the plan has been made by a U.S.-based urban designer) with 500 high-rise buildings for free sale in the market and 600 more exclusively for the slum dwellers. The state government has announced a modern sports complex for post redevelopment Dharavi. The second destination of the sports activities is identified in Andheri, the IT hub that is already crowded with IT-enabled service units and real estate companies. Redevelopment projects in all these areas are with the private sector with the state acting as an active abettor.

The transmogrification of Mumbai largely depends on the rate and intensity of the gentrification of these areas. Mill land can be an example. By mid-2008 almost the entire area has been shaped into a modern commercial hub with global chain shops, corporate houses, and hypermarket complexes (D'Monte 2002, 135). Proactive pursuit of real estate mega projects has, however, been a primary component in the contemporary redevelopment endeavors in the area. China Mills with 500,000 square feet of land has been sold to the Dosti Group Builders at a price of Rs. 530 million on which six residential high-rise buildings, each about 20 stories high, will come up. Financial institutions and private banks are the major buyers of the apartments, initiating a fast track gentrification in the so long lower-middle/working-class area (Bharucha 2004, 5). The official planning process has facilitated a speedy conversion of land use resting on a project-oriented entrepreneurial planning model. With growing aesthetization of the urban space and promotion of signature projects, the working-class-oriented local culture of this central Mumbai tract has been reconstructed into a globally oriented homogenized one, similar to what happened in Toronto in the 1980s (Kipfer and Keil 2002, 243) and in hundreds of other cities as a fallout of the neoliberal crack down.

The other example is Dharavi, one of Asia's biggest slums, located to the north of the mill lands, on the left arm of the golden triangle. Covering an area of 174 hectares, with a population of more than 1,000,000 and 9% of the total population of Mumbai, Dharavi is a vibrant economic hub (Sharma 2000, 78) having a large population of informal workers engaged in diverse activities: leather works, pottery, machine part manufacturing, recycling and repairing, garment making, dry food making, to name a few. With more than 2,000 shops, many small workshops, and an annual turnover of Rs. 40,000 million, living conditions in Dharavi have remained inhuman (D'Souza 2002, 2). Currently this slum has become the center of attraction for planners. Over the years as Mumbai expanded northward, Dharavi has come to occupy a significantly central location so that today it has emerged as an extremely profitable source of land for redevelopment. In order to make Mumbai a world class competitive financial investment Center (HPEC, 2007: 11), the Mumbai Transformation Project suggested that the slums and slum population of the city be reduced drastically, the latter from 60% to 10%. Hence it was decided to redevelop under NURM. Municipal Corporation of the city has announced that Dharavi will be soon converted into a vibrant, well-planned urban center, for which global players have been invited by way of international bidding process. The government has offered 220 square feet tenements to each household on the multi-storied buildings that would be constructed in 40% of the existing slum land. The remaining 60% would be sold on the market that would compensate the builders for providing free tenements to slum dwellers. It goes without saying that such tenements will not suit the requirement of the households in terms of the nature of their activity that will finally push them out from Dharavi. They have formed a resistance group, named the 'Save Dharavi Committee' (Dharavi Bachao Andolan Committee) and secured a stay order from the High Court on further implementation of the Project till a proper survey is done on the number of households that merit compensation and legal consent is secured from the residents. In the midst of official incentives for sell-off of public lands, zoning changes, and land use conversion underwriting gentrification, to what extent the claims of Dharavi residents will be recognized by the government is going to come up as a contentious issue.

To preclude social unrest that may result due to dispossession, interventionist ideas thrown up by groups like 'Bombay First' are being implemented in both public and private domains by integrating surveillance in urban planning and by cleansing the material space of pavement dwellers, hawkers, informal workers, and homeless through creating 'special housing zones' in faraway lands. The reckless process disregards social justice, people's history, and even ecological aspects. The state government's recent decision to dispose of extensive salt plans, the organic bulwark of the city acting against nature's fury, is a blatant example.

The contemporary urban restructuring in Mumbai is visibly becoming a part of the neoliberal reconstruction of the very notion of 'urban' at different layers of the society. One of its primary manifestations is the process of legitimization of a unified concept of urban planning with commodification of virtual space at the level of image building, sharing a strong base in the commodification of real urban spaces. The resultant contest over the right to reconvert homogenized urban spaces into lived places and the planning endeavor to recommodify them happens to be the crux of the matter (Banerjee-Guha 2004b, 76). With the increasing intensity of claims and counter-claims over the contested city space that is significant toward the construction of hegemony (Lefebvre 1991, 155), projects recreating a new generation of spaces in the 'slum free' city with heritage architecture, theme parks, IT parks, golf course are plentiful (in adjoining New Mumbai), sprawling commercial areas with permanent exhibition grounds, and water front development promenades, all exuding a one-dimensional vision of Mumbai and undermining the complexity of urban life of the multi-layered interactive city space where 68% of the population live in slums.

4. NEW URBANISM AND URBAN NEOLIBERALISM IN INDIA

In the aggressive vision of redesigning Indian cities discussed in Section 3, one can see embedded the concept of 'new urbanism' that has its central element resting on the alleged shift of capital from the primary circuit of production to the secondary circuit of built environment (Harvey 1985, 22; Sassen 1991, 325), precisely a move toward financial manipulation as a source of profit. The consequences can be seen in the increased focus on hyper forms and mega construction activities, increased speculation and expanded investment in land and real estate (growth of real estate sector in urban India is estimated to go up from $12 billion in 2005 to $90 billion in 2015), service sector, signature projects, and mega cultural events, and a reduced focus on employment-generating production process, affordable housing, and collective sharing of urban space and resources. A larger restructuring of the economic system and a resultant transformation of urban form and the built environment constitute the basis of this new urbanism (Banerjee-Guha 2006, 219).

For understanding the logic of remaking Indian cities in general, and Mumbai, in particular, we need to look at three basic issues. First, the changing position of the Indian economy with the introduction of NEP and the role of 'urban' therein. The National Commission on Urbanization in 1985 had initially paved the way for reconfiguring the concept of 'urban' in India, acting as a precursor to a major shift in the urban policy in terms of advocating concentration and centralization (Kundu 1989, 1186). Simultaneously, it had initiated discussion on aspects like private sector entry in the provision of urban services, cost subsidies, user charges, and, most importantly, efficiency of service provision. The Commission's Report was followed by the passing of the well-known 74th Constitutional Amendment Act in 1992 that materialized the concept of political decentralization and made the urban local bodies more independent but politically weaker and functionally restricted with reduced budgetary allocations and shrunken economic base. Their additional responsibility of raising funds from the capital market also became a debatable issue (Banerjee-Guha 2002c, 25) as it led to compromises on pro-poor projects. The trend of urban growth in 1981–1991 indicated that there was an increasing population concentration in the relatively larger cities. The 300 urban agglomerations with a population of 1,000,000 and above, accounted for more than 65% of the urban population in 1991 when the number of metropolitan cities rose to 23. Six from them (Mumbai, Kolkata, Delhi, Chennai, Hyderabad, Bangalore) with a population between 4 million to 8 million came to be termed as 'mega cities' (United Nations 1993, 7). The earlier objective of strengthening economic base of small and medium towns went to backstage and renewed investment in large cities, and their regions was officially promoted. No anti-monopoly measures were taken (Bagchi 1987, 18) to curb the consequent inter-urban disparity or lack of services and infrastructure in large cities it led to. In the Seventh Plan (1985–1990), as a natural course, thrust went to private investment in urban development. Following NEP, and with the reconfiguration of the concept of 'urban', Mega City Programme of the central government (Banerjee-Guha 2002c, 31) was launched to primarily develop the infrastructural base of such cities, that were identified as GEM (cities generating economic momentum). 'Hype' of large cities that got legitimized in the preceding manner was essentially a part of a larger world order in the same way as urban neoliberalism belongs to a larger process of rescaling of functions, activities, and relations (Smith 2002, 435). Hence the first issue is interconnected with the second, that is the ascendancy of neoliberalism as a capitalist model of accumulation and its influence on the entrepreneurial approach to city management and resultant urban restructuring (Brenner and Theodore 2002b, 352). Its authentic form includes not only economic relations but also the diverse characteristics of a hegemonic structure. Tightening of control of IFIs like the World Bank, Asian Development Bank, and DFID on urban development in India, with a renewed focus on mega cities, explicates the previously discussed design through a complex ensemble of institutional, social, and political relations and practices that regulates a wider process of capital accumulation. The preceding global-local nexus in contemporary urban development and the nature of NURM projects succinctly symbolize a state-supported urban neoliberalism initiated as a market imperative. Its spatial logic is entangled with the need to restructure cities in all fronts: land use, infrastructure and governance, and so on, to enable them to function successfully as well as market themselves in the new geographical axis of global competition that pits cities against cities (Smith 2002, 447). Connected to the previous two issues, comes the third, that essentially is a regional component of the global strategy of the post-Fordist economy operating through fragmentation and distribution of production and services, more importantly financial services, at wider spatial scales in the form of interrelated sub-processes. Several cities are assigned specific roles in this global hierarchical system for making the capital accumulation process work more efficiently. The important point is not only that cities like New York, Chicago, London, or Tokyo that function as financial command centers are important for this system, but also that with the current operational strategy of finance capital, the cities in the Global South in Africa, Asia, and Latin America are considerably, if not equally, important for the functioning of the previously discussed regulatory and competitive regime. Here lies the significance of Mumbai, the financial capital of India that is geared to act as a viable IFC, failing which serious implications are anticipated for the government (HPEC 2007, 19). "India's financial services industry will not become export-oriented, nor derive significant IFS (International financial services) export revenues, if Mumbai fails to become an IFC. . . . For Mumbai to become an IFC, India's policy makers and financial operators need to fully understand the nature of opportunities in the global IFS market, the activities undertaken in global financial centers (GFCs), and the gap in the capabilities that now exists between Mumbai and the established GFCs" (HPEC 2007). It explicates the imperatives of urban restructuring as a universal strategy. Last but not the least, restructuring of the welfare state into a more vociferous, interventionist, and market friendly structure happens to be interconnected with all the three issues.

A proper understanding and theorization of the new urban form and urban neoliberalism would remain superficial if it did not involve a concern for the deepening polarization and disarticulation that the process creates. This is because such cities not only concentrate a disproportionate share of corporate capital to become key sites for their over-valorization, but they also concentrate an increasingly disproportionate share of disadvantaged and marginalized people and become key sites for their continuing devalorization (Sassen 1999, 106). I have discussed elsewhere (Banerjee-Guha 1997, 246) how capital relocation strategy valorizes a region it finds conducive for accumulation, say in terms of flexible labor laws, tax benefits, or loose environmental regulations, and devalorizes another that may be less conducive for the same purpose. In the recent restructuring process of Indian cities, the previously discussed spatial 'see-saw' has systematically led to a greater marginalization of the poor and segregation of the city space that in recent times is getting linked up with an increased entry of unskilled and semi-skilled workers in the labor market, particularly women, decreasing real income of primary earners and cuts in state subsidies (Tardanico and Lungo 1995, 231). The process of marginalization perpetrated in the name of urban planning does not stop at the city level but expands on a wider space to ultimately culminate in a crisis of segmentation affecting the efficiency of the very system.

The issue of local and global is found to intersect at this point whereby the city space is converted into a space of contradiction and flux. Whether it becomes a space for new politics embedded in the claims and counter-claims is an important question. Because even though the claims of the corporate sector and the rich pave the way for a repressive and revanchist urbanism (Smith, 1996, 196) as evident from the consequences of the redevelopment projects, at the other extreme there are claims made by the dispossessed, struggling for entitlement and alternatives. It remains to be seen whether the powerful contradictions inherent in the interaction between the two would lead to a more progressive, radical, and democratic re-appropriation of city space (Brenner and Theodore, 2002b, 366) or whether neoliberalism would sit deeper. Although the patterns of the claims may reflect an over-valorized and a powerful corporate center occupying a smaller terrain and a devalorized periphery with a large number of people evidently marginalized, it is beyond doubt that this new politics of claims and related struggles of the dispossessed will go to form the most solid part of the neoliberal urbanism in the coming days. In several cities and villages in India, depending on the politics, culture and identity of the regions (Banerjee-Guha, 2006, 222), such struggles, organized by the dispossessed, are signifying a radical politics of contestation challenging the current displacement-based development paradigm. Theories and praxis of urban neoliberalism and the enforcement of the regulatory regime over a wider range of social relations in cities and their regions need to be understood in the light of the contradictions generated therefrom.

REFERENCES

Bagchi, Amiya Kumar. 1987. Towards a political economy of planning in India. *Contributions to Political Economy* 3: 15--38.

Banerjee, Kishaloy, and Ashis Mukherjee. 2008. Urban neoliberalism, JNNURM projects and associated impact on the urban poor in and around Kolkata. Paper presented in the International Workshop on Urban Neoliberalism: Restructuring South Asian Cities, Tata Institute of Social Sciences, November 27–28, Mumbai.

Banerjee-Guha, Swapna. 1995. Urban development process in Bombay: Planning for whom? In *Bombay: A Metaphor for Modern India* edited by Sujata Patel and Alice Thorner, 100–120. New Delhi: Oxford University Press.

———. 1997. *Spatial dynamics of international capital*. India: Orient Longman.

———. 2002a. Shifting cities: Urban restructuring in Mumbai. *Economic and Political Weekly* 37(2): 121–128.

———. 2002b. Critical geographical praxis: Globalisation and socio spatial disorders. *Economic and Political Weekly* 37(44 and 45): 4503–4509.

———. 2002c. *Metropolitan dominance and regional disparity in India: Observations from relevant planning measures of Japan*. VRF Series No. 358. Tokyo: Institute of Developing Economies.

———. 2004a. Shifting spaces and changing identities: New urbanism and Mumbai. Inaugural talk, International Conference on Area Studies in the New Empire, City University of New York, April 14–17, 2004, New York.

———. 2004b. Space, society and geography: Investigating the crisis of postmodern urban space. In Space, Society and Geography, edited by Swapna Banerjee-Guha, 61–82. New Delhi: Rawat Publishers.

———. 2006. Post modernism, Post Fordism and flexibilised metropolis: Dialectical images of Mumbai. In Colonial and Polt Colonial Geographies of India, edited by Saraswati Raju et al., 205–222. New Delhi: Sage.

———. 2007. Post Fordist urban space of Mumbai: The saga of contemporary restructuration. In *Indian cities in transition*, edited by Annapurna Shaw. Hyderabad: Orient Longman, pp. 260–282.

———. 2008. Space relations of capital and significance of new economic spaces: SEZs in India. *Economic and Political Weekly* 43(47): 51–60.

———. 2009. Neoliberalising the 'urban': New geographies of power and injustice in Indian cities. *Economic and Political Weekly* 44(22): 95–107.

Baran, Paul. 1958. *Political economy of growth*. New York: Monthly Review Press.

Bharucha, N. Banks, firms are top mill-land buyers, *Times of India* (Mumbai), July 2, 2006.

Bombay First. 2003. Vision Mumbai: Transforming Mumbai into a world class city. A Bombay First-McKinsey Report, Mumbai.

Brenner, Neil, and Theodore Nik. 2002a. From the new localism to the spaces of neoliberalism. *Antipode* 34(3): 341–347.

———. 2002b. Cities and the geography of actually existing neoliberalism. *Antipode* 4(3): 349–379.

Business World (New Delhi). 2003. Plan or panacea. pp. 44–48.

CASUMM (Collaborative for the Advancement of Studies in Urbanism through Mixed Media). 2006. *JNNURM: A Blueprint for unconstitutional, undemocratic governance*. Bangalore.

Chaware, Dilip. Mumbai-Pune Expressway privatised. *Times of India* (Mumbai), February 28, 2004.

D'Monte, Darryl. 2002. Ripping the fabric: The decline of Mumbai and its mills. New Delhi: Oxford University Press.

Harvey, David. 1985. *The urbanisation of capital*. UK: Basil Blackwell.

———. 1989. From managerialism to entrepreneurialism: The transformation in urban governance in late capitalism. *Geographiska Annaler Series B* 71(1): 3–18.

———. 2005. A brief history of neoliberalism. New York: Oxford University Press.

High Powered Expert Committee (HPEC), Ministry of Finance, Government of India. 2007. *Making Mumbai* an *international financial centre*. New Delhi: Sage.

Jamwal, Nidhi. 2006. 'Urban myths', down to earth. 15(7): 26–34.

Kipfer, Stefan, and Keil Roger. 2002. Toronto Inc? Planning the competitive city in the New Toronto? *Antipode* 34(2): 227–264.

Kundu, Amitabh. 1989. National commission on urbanisation, issues and non-issues. *Economic and Political Weekly* 24(2): 1185–1188.

Lefebvre, Henri. 1991. *The production of space*, translated by D. Nicholson-Smith. UK: Blackwell.

Mahadevia, Darshini. 2006. NURM and the poor in globalising mega cities. *Economic and Political Weekly* 41(31): 2299–3403.

MMRDA (Maharashtra Metropolitan Regional Development Authority). 1995. Draft regional plan for Mumbai metropolitan region, 1996–2011. Mumbai.

Rajagopal, Arvind. 2002. Violence of commodity aesthetics. *Economic and Political Weekly* 37(1): 65–76.

Ramachandraiah, C. 2009. Maytas, Hyderabad metro and the politics of real estate. *Economic and Political Weekly* 44(3): 36–40.

Sassen, Saskia. 1991. The global city. Princeton, NJ: Princeton University Press.

———. 1999. Globalisation and the formation of new claims. In *The urban moment*, edited by R. A. Beauregard and S.Body-Gendrot, 99–118. Sage.

Singh, Mahendra. Urban housing bomb ticking, *Times of India* (Mumbai), November 25, 2005.

Smith, N. 1996. The new urban frontier: Gentrification and the revanchist city. New York: Routledge.

Tardanico, T., and M. Lungo. 1995. Local dimensions of global restructuring: Changing labour market contours in urban Costa Rica. *International Journal of Urban and Regional Research*, 223–249.

United Nations. 1993. *World urbanisation prospects*. New York.

Varma, Umesh. 2008. Urban poor and housing in Hyderabad: Reformed out of the system. Paper presented at the International Workshop on Urban Neoliberalism: Restructuring South Asian Cities, Tata Institute of Social Sciences, November 27–28, Mumbai.

5 Economic Liberalization and Urban Governance

Impact on Inclusive Growth

Shipra Maitra

The process of urbanization runs the risk of harboring economic and spatial inequality which is not neutralized automatically through flow of rural-urban migration. The labor force is relatively less mobile, for various sociocultural reasons that are not necessarily guided by economic reasons. Macroeconomic policies that stimulate growth are not sufficiently distributive to neutralize location-specific growth. Cities tend to attract high-value investments and create shortages of common urban resources, like land. As the competitive value of land is beyond the reach of, especially, the vulnerable section of society, direct government intervention is required in terms of demarcation of land for the deprived section and speedy provision of basic services to reduce economic and spatial inequality. The modern urban agenda, followed by the Government of India, emphasizes efficiency and competitiveness for overall economic development. In this chapter, I attempt to analyze whether this is in tune with the concept of inclusive growth.

This chapter is divided into six sections. The major elements of economic liberalization experienced in India are described in Section 1. Urbanization, decentralization initiatives, and urban governance are elaborated upon in Section 2. Concepts of urban deprivation are discussed in Section 3. Reform-based institutional linkages are detailed in Section 4. In Section 5, the challenges of inclusive growth are taken up. A brief conclusion is given in the last section.

1. MAJOR ELEMENTS OF ECONOMIC LIBERALIZATION IN INDIA

Economic liberalization in India since the 1980s is characterized by a loosening of licensing procedure of the post-Independence years. Liberalization began with the growth of the telecommunications and software industries with increasing involvement of the private sector and reduction in public sector domination. This momentum was captured by the New Economic Policy (NEP) of 1991 that was formulated in two parts. The first part was concerned with large and medium-sized industries, while the second part related to small industries. The private enterprises are allowed to make commercial decisions without government control in the case of almost all industries, excepting some core activities. The distinction between the large-scale and small-scale sectors is no longer valid for most of the industrial items in terms of market penetration. The number of industries reserved for the small-scale category has been considerably reduced. The allocation of resources among industries with respect to type of industries, scale, and nature of products are largely determined by market price. The NEP has covered both the domestic and foreign sectors. It is characterised by replacing the Controller of Capital Issues with the Securities and Exchange Board of India (SEBI) and establishment of a National Stock Exchange (NSE) for liberalizing the capital market, reducing import tariffs from 85% to 25% on average, increasing maximum share limit from 40% to 51% in joint ventures with foreign capital, increasing foreign equity participation to 100% in certain priority sectors, and streamlining procedures for approval of foreign direct investment (Acharya 2001). Export subsidies are encouraged. Special Economic Zones (SEZ) have been established in several states with several tax concessions and input for expansion of exports.

In the domestic sector, a number of activities, which were exclusively in the realm of the public sector, are now open to the private sector. The industrial licensing required for the creation of industrial capacities or investment has been abolished for all projects, except for specified areas related to natural security, social disparity, hazardous chemicals, and environmental concerns (Virmani 2004).

Another feature of NEP is related to the location of new industries. The thrust of the policy is to shift industries away from big congested cities to the rural and backward areas. The industrialists are not required to obtain approval from the central government regarding the location of industries, other than in metro cities (population > 1 million), excepting industries subject to compulsory licensing. In metro cities, pollutant industries are not allowed within 25 kilometers of the periphery.

The NEP is significant in ensuring spatial decentralization of industrial activities as well. It has provided incentives to attract industries away from congested areas to villages and backward regions. It favors expansion of agro-based industries near the farming areas. Similar incentives have been provided to small industries to ensure their development in small towns and villages.

The NEP has very significant implications for spatial agglomeration and urban growth. Expansion of foreign direct investment (FDI) has led to the growth of the real estate sector, Information technology (IT) industries and other capital-intensive sectors with increase in demand for high-value land. In metro cities, demand for commercial space has increased manifold with the expansion of non-polluting economic units like information technology enabled services (ITES). This, in consequence, has led to growth of residential demand resulting in a rise in land prices. Creation of SEZ has increased land values in the outskirts of urban areas leading to increase in land values in the periphery as well (Maitra 2008a).

2. URBANIZATION AND URBAN GOVERNANCE

Urbanization is acknowledged as one of the most significant changes taking place within low- and middle-income nations, according to various studies. However, its relationship with economic development is not always clear.

Urban change in all nations is influenced by the structure of government (especially the division of power and resources between different levels of government), the extent and spatial distribution of transport and communications investments, and macroeconomic policies. These in turn influence the spatial distribution of new investment and the locations where employment expands or contracts. The size and rate of change of the population in each of the 50,000 or so urban centers in the world are influenced not only by such international and national factors but also by local factors related to each, very particular, local context—including the site, location, natural resources endowment, demographic structure, existing economy and infrastructure (the legacy of past decisions and investments) and the quality and capacity of public institutions (Chandler 1987; Fay et al., 2000; Satterthwaite 2005).

Most nations have "urbanized" during last century. The proportion of the world's population living in urban areas grew from a minority (15%) in 1900 to 50% by around 2008, with projections suggesting an increasingly urbanized population in the future. The immediate cause is the net movement of people from rural to urban areas. The main underlying cause is the concentration of new investment and economic opportunities in particular urban areas. A nation's urban system (the network of urban centers and their interconnections) is best understood as the "geography" of its non-agricultural economy and government system. It is also, in effect, a map of where profit-seeking enterprises have concentrated and where people working outside agriculture make a living.

In low- and middle-income nations, rural-to-urban migration is overwhelmingly the result of people moving in response to better economic opportunities in the urban areas, or to the lack of prospects in their home farms or villages. The scale and direction of people's movements accord well with changes in the spatial location of economic opportunities. In general, cities, small towns, or rural areas with expanding economies attract most migration (Jones 2004).

Urban centers also concentrate public-service provision. Most secondary schools and higher education institutions are located in urban areas;

so too are most hospitals and higher-order medical services (although not necessarily primary healthcare centers). Over the last 50 years, there has also been considerable growth in the scale and range of public service and bureaucracies in low- and middle-income nations. These are overwhelmingly concentrated in urban areas and are part of the reason for increased urbanization—related not just to education and healthcare but also to local government. When many of these services like secondary schools, hospitals, and government services are located mostly in small market towns and administrative centers, they tend to reduce the level of special disparity and social deprivation and serve both rural and urban populations (Satterthwaite 2005).

The most cost-effective way of providing both rural and urban populations with access to education is to have primary schools (and, where possible, pre-school services) in most villages and urban neighborhoods, secondary schools in urban areas, and universities or other higher education institutes in district or state capitals. Similarly the most cost-effective way of providing both rural and urban populations with access to health care is to have primary healthcare centers in most villages and urban neighborhoods within a hierarchy of health centers, where the more specialized services are in district capitals and larger cities, and these act as the referral centers to which are sent the cases that the primary healthcare centers or the small district hospitals cannot manage. In many nations, especially those without large urban economies, the list of urban centers and their relative sizes usually corresponds quite closely to the hierarchy of administrative centers, from the national capital to the state or provincial capitals to district capitals to sub-district capitals. This is also the case for many relatively little urbanised regions within nations. This has accommodated the need for expanding civic services to various size classes of towns (Zlotonic 2004).

The internationalization of world production and trade (including a very rapid expansion in the value of international trade) has been an important underpinning for the rapid growth of many cities and has influenced urban trends in most nations. Many cities owe their prosperity to their roles within this increasingly internationalized system of production and distribution. International, national, and local tourism has been vital to development of many cities and smaller urban centers.

Cities actually have tremendous potential for ensuring universal provision of infrastructure and services. That cities have economies of scale, proximity, and agglomeration, that bring substantial benefits for most businesses, is well known; less discussed are the economies of scale and proximity for public goods and services or the diseconomies caused by poor urban management (Hall et al., 2006).

Most urban problems reflect not the inherent characteristics of cities but the limitations in their governance structures. However, there are many examples of innovation and better practice from low- and middle-income countries, where the need for improved governance is most evident, which give clues on how current problems can be tackled. Many come from local initiatives that arise from more competent and democratic urban governments in nations where decentralization programs have given more power and resources to such governments. Many others come from innovative local civil-society groups—usually a combination of grassroot ogranisations and local non-governmental organizations—and increasingly from partnerships that these groups form with local governments, which in turn contributes to more competent and democratic local governments.

India's experience with urbanization has not been uniform. The National Commission on Urbanisation (1988) observed that, the skewed pattern of urbanization in India has been determined by macroeconomic factors at the national level and is not strongly linked to development of the rural economy. In-migration into urban areas is not strongly linked to rural poverty or deprivation. The strategy of economic reform has given a boost to the growth of industries and business in a few large cities, attracting inflows of capital from outside the region or country, as well as investment by local entrepreneurs. These pull factors have brought a large number of skilled and semi-skilled personnel from small towns and rural areas into these cities. Demographic and economic growth in these towns, as a result, has gone down drastically in recent years.

Table 5.1 shows the level and growth of urbanization across 14 major states of India. These states accounted for more than 87% of the total urban population in 2001. There are only five states where the level of urbanization is higher than the national average of 2001. The rate of urbanization has continuously declined since 1971, excepting in four states (i.e., Tamil Nadu, Punjab, Kerala, and Haryana). These states have experienced random fluctuations in the growth rate of urban development. Tamil Nadu brought some changes in the definition of "urban" during 2009. The consequent sharp rise in both levels and growth rates is due to definitional changes or administrative reasons. Punjab and Haryana have undertaken significant increase in developmental expenditure that has attracted migration to the cities. The level of urbanization has remained almost stagnant in Kerala, with a significant fall in the growth rate. This is a direct fallout from global recession, where a decline in remittances from the Middle East has restricted movement from rural to urban areas. In general, even though the level of urbanization has continuously increased, the rate of decline in growth rate has been sharper in the less urbanized states like Bihar, Madhya Pradesh, Orissa, Rajasthan, and Uttar Pradesh. The opposite is true for more urbanized states like Gujarat and Maharashtra.

Inadequate development of smaller urban areas has failed to encourage rural–urban migration. There is not much movement within states, while out-migration is continuous. Bihar accounts for a significant proportion (36%) of total migrants in Delhi (Maitra 2006).

Table 5.1 Level and Growth of Urbanization across Major States in India 1971–2001

Sr. No.	*States*	*Level of Urbanization*				*Rate of Urbanization (Per Annum)*		
		1971	*1981*	*1991*	*2001*	*1971–1981*	*1981–1991*	*1991–2001*
01.	Andhra Pradesh	19.3	23.3	26.8	27.1	3.9	3.6	1.4
02.	Bihar	10.0	12.5	13.2	10.5	4.3	2.7	2.6
03.	Gujarat	28.1	31.1	34.4	37.6	3.4	2.9	2.8
04.	Haryana	17.7	22.0	24.8	29.0	4.7	3.6	4.1
05.	Karnataka	24.3	28.9	30.9	34.0	4.1	2.6	2.5
06.	Kerala	16.2	18.8	26.4	26.0	3.2	4.8	0.7
07.	Madhya Pradesh	16.3	20.3	23.2	26.7	4.5	3.7	2.7
08.	Maharashtra	31.2	35.0	38.7	42.4	3.4	3.3	3.0
09.	Orrisa	8.4	11.8	13.4	15.0	5.2	3.1	2.6
10.	Punjab	23.7	27.7	29.7	33.8	3.6	2.6	3.2
11.	Rajasthan	17.6	20.9	22.9	23.4	4.5	3.3	2.7
12.	Tamil Nadu	30.3	33.0	34.2	43.9	2.5	1.8	3.6
13.	Uttar Pradesh	14.0	18.0	19.9	20.8	4.8	3.3	2.8
14.	West Bengal	24.8	26.5	27.4	28.0	2.7	2.5	1.8
15	All India	20.2	23.7	25.7	27.8	3.8	3.1	2.7

Source: Sivaramakrishnan et al. (2005).

This overall slow rate of urbanization is associated with the concept of deprivation as well as regional inequality. Table 5.2 shows the relationship among economic inequality, poverty level, and state income. It shows that the share of consumption expenditures of the top 20% has increased in every state during last 10 years with the exception of Tamil Nadu, where it has remained almost the same.

The share of bottom 20% has uniformly declined in all the major states, excepting Madhya Pradesh, Punjab, and Rajasthan. The states of Kerala and West Bengal, that have egalitarianism as a declared objective of governance, have experienced sharp increases in share of the top 20%, more than the national average, during last decade, while the share of the bottom 20% has declined, indicating significant disparity in overall welfare. Economic liberalization, with an increasing thrust on competitiveness, is likely to increase this disparity without significant governance intervention (Mazubdai and Sarkou 2004).

According to Kundu (1993), decline in income poverty does not always result in decline in urban deprivation, though it varies directly with per capita state domestic product (PCSDP). Scholars have shown that poverty incidence is not equally distributed over space and regions (Shitole 2007). Analysis of various National Sample Survey Organization (NSSO) data shows that poverty has been severe in Bihar (32.9%), Madhya Pradesh (38.4%), Orissa (42.8%), and Uttar Pradesh (30.9%). These four states have accounted for more than 40% of total number of poor in the country. These states have also accounted for 27% of total urban population in the country. Urban poverty is not directly associated with a high level of urbanization as revealed in these minimally urbanized states. On the other hand, highly urbanized states like Gujarat and Punjab have shown declining incidence in urban poverty. Poverty incidence has been found to be low in moderately urbanized states of Andhra Pradesh and Karnataka as well as minimally urbanized states like Himachal Pradesh and Jammu & Kashmir. Hence urbanization and poverty level are weakly, though positively, correlated.

Regional analysis shows a more direct relationship between income growth and level of poverty reduction. The four states mentioned earlier have shown a high level of poverty with a low rate of urbanization and rate of growth of per capita SDP much lower than the national average. Income level and income growth are critical conditions for poverty reduction (Mukherjee and Banerjee 2008).

3. CONCEPT OF URBAN DEPRIVATION, INSTITUTIONS, AND RESOURCES

Urban deprivation is not adequately explained in terms of income poverty only (i.e., low per capita income). Along with the income component, urban poverty is also measured in terms of lack of tenure security, inadequate access to public infrastructure and services, lack of resource-generating assets, and deprivation of social and legal security. Urban deprivation is explained in terms of vulnerability in health and education, lack of protection in work places, increase in crime, and lack of proper forum to raise grievances and be inclusive in the decision-making process. Low per capita income does not reflect total urban deprivation but accentuates its depth and coverage. That is why there is hardly any marked difference in quality of life among people Below Poverty Line (BPL) and those just Above Poverty Line (APL), thereby running the risk of excluding many deserving beneficiaries of poverty alleviation programs, as these programs are focused on BPL groups only (Himanshu 2007).

Urban deprivation is both people-centric and area-centric. The metropolises are often distinct with increasing slum population while smaller urban areas are deprived of proper infrastructure and economic activities. Regional plans and Master plans are busy in calculating such area-centric

Table 5.2 Relative Shares of Urban Households in Consumption Expenditure and State-wise Ranking in Per Capita State Domestic Product and Poverty Level

S. No.	*States*	*Bottom 20% of Urban Household*		*Rank in Level of Urban Poverty **	*Top 20% of Urban Household*		*Rank in PCSDP**
		1993–1994	*2004–2005*	*2004–2005*	*1993–1994*	*2004–2005*	*2004–2005*
1	Andhra Pradesh	7.57	7.24	9	40.31	45.18	11
2	Bihar	7.28	6.60	10	38.77	41.19	16
3	Gujarat	6.81	6.00	2	36.28	43.90	3
4	Haryana	6.64	7.04	4	35.33	43.90	6
6	Karnataka	7.46	7.13	13	39.72	44.46	9
7	Kerala	8.04	7.93	6	42.78	49.44	8
8	Madhya Pradesh	7.73	7.86	15	41.17	49.00	13
9	Maharashtra	8.36	7.31	12	44.52	45.59	4
10	Orissa	7.19	6.83	16	38.26	42.62	14
11	Punjab	6.57	7.77	1	34.95	48.49	5
12	Rajasthan	6.87	7.19	14	36.56	44.85	12
13	Tamil Nadu	8.14	6.94	8	43.34	43.26	7
14	Uttar Pradesh	7.64	7.09	11	40.67	44.23	15
15	West Bengal	7.91	7.42	3	42.13	46.27	10
16	All India	8.04	7.26	—	42.81	45.28	—

Sources: Levels and Patterns of Consumer Expenditure, Report No. 402 (December 1995), National Sample Survey, 50th Round: Report No. 508 (December 2006), National Sample Survey, 61st Round (2006), NSSO, Ministry of Statistics and Programe Implementation, Government of India, New Delhi.
* Hasim (2009).
Note: Ranking is on descending order, top ranked state showing the best performance.

infrastructure deficits. As direct consequences of population growth, urban areas are witnessing massive strain on the labor market and on the availability of shelter, infrastructure and services, leading to large scale marginalization and deprivation (Kundu 2007).

Area wise deprivation can be observed from Table 5.3. It shows that during last five decades, growth rate of class VI towns has been less than one percent and that of class V towns has dropped considerably. Class II and class III towns also have experienced much lower growth rate during the same period while class I towns have shown increasing growth rate in every decade since 1961. Lower growth rates of smaller order towns show weak linkage with villages, implying that villagers have to move to higher order towns for satisfying their non-food needs.

Larger cities are attracting migration both from rural areas and smaller towns, owing to area centric deprivation. Town Planning Institutes have come up both at national and state level to plan for urban areas, but spatial planning has not yet been able to fulfill the objective of balanced regional growth. The objective of India's economic planning has been balanced development but it has not been translated into effective economic and spatial policies (Kundu and Maitra 1999, Maitra 2008c, Mahadevia 2008).

Public interventions in urban issues mainly addressed problems like housing, slum clearance, slum improvement and up gradation, preparation of Master plans, development of small and medium-sized towns, and strengthening of municipal civic administration until the Sixth Five-Year Plan (1980–1985). The Sixth Plan made a new beginning by explicitly recognizing the problems of urban poor not only as spillover of rural poverty but as a link with creation of employment opportunities. It is now being recognized that urban policies can directly contribute to achieve the goals of poverty reduction and removal of unemployment and under-employment. During the last decade, the growth rate of employment in the urban areas averaged around 3.3% per annum, while the growth rate of slum population was around 4%, indicating degradation of living environment.

Table 5.3 Percentage of Urban Population in Different Size Categories of Towns

	Percentage of Urban Population					
Census Year	*Class I*	*Class II*	*Class III*	*Class IV*	*Class V*	*Class VI*
	(>100,000)	*(50,000–99,999)*	*(20,000–49,999)*	*(10,000–19,999)*	*(5,000–9,999)*	*(< 5,000)*
1901	26	11.29	15.64	20.83	20.14	6.1
1911	27.48	10.51	16.4	19.73	19.31	6.57
1921	29.7	10.39	15.92	18.29	18.67	7.03
1931	31.2	11.65	16.8	18	17.14	5.21
1941	38.23	11.42	16.35	15.78	15.08	3.14
1951	44.63	-9.96	15.72	13.63	12.97	3.09
1961	51.42	11.23	16.94	12.77	6.87	0.77
1971	57.24	10.92	16.01	10.94	4.45	0.44
1981	60.37	11.63	14.33	9.54	3.58	0.5
1991	65.2	10.95	13.19	7.77	2.6	0.29
2001	68.67	9.67	12.23	6.84	2.36	0.23

Source: Census of India (2001).

The Seventh Five-Year Plan proposed that planning of urban development should essentially be supportive of the economic development in the country. Throu⌐h strategic industrial location policy, it was designed to promote small and medium-sized towns to check migration of population to the metropolises. The identification of regional urban systems were based on regional characteristics and needs, and functions of each urban system was embedded in particular regional context. More explicitly, the needs of the poor were to be taken into account in all physical planning exercises.

The phenomenon of slums and squatter settlements has been a distinct feature of Indian urban life since Independence. Following the separation of India and Pakistan, the city of Delhi was placed under enormous pressure to accommodate the incoming refugee population. During that period, the refugees had no alternative other than to squat on government colonies planned by the Delhi Development Authority (DDA). The size of the squatter population increased steadily. From time to time, places were identified for resettlement by the DDA in the suburban areas of Delhi. The squatter population living on prime land in the city was relocated to enable this economically valuable land to be utilized for infrastructure development. These relocation spaces often invited criticism as they were away from the work places and had little infrastructural provision. However, as more and more squatter settlers were relocated, the magnetic economic strength of Delhi kept attracting migrants and volume of encroachment piled up. The object of population dispersal through formation of the National Capital Region (NCR) was not fulfilled through Regional Plans for want of suitable institutional framework (Sabir Ali 2003, Papola 2004).

The Census 2001 has revealed that there has been an increased number and percentage of slum population in urban areas (Table 5.4).

The Census 2001 is the first Census to delineating slums for studying their demographic features. It contains data for 640 towns against almost 5,000 Census towns. It excluded towns with populations less than 50,000. It has also excluded slum clusters which are not recognized if the population was 300 or less. Hence it does not provide a comprehensive picture of

Table 5.4 Slum Population in Urban India

Year	*Slum Population*	
	Number (Million)	*% of Urban Population*
1981	28.00	17.5
1991	45.7	21.5
2001	40.6	22.8

Source: Census of India (2001).

the slum population. It also reflects the problems inherent in not having an accepted definition of slums and the absence of proper listings of slum settlements in the urban offices concerned with slum improvement and civic amenities. The Municipal Corporation of Delhi (MCD) had prepared such a list as early as in 1994. The working group on housing for the Tenth Plan has observed that around 90% of housing shortages pertain to the weaker sections that generally belong to slums and squatter settlements.

Financial Resources

Resource allocations in national plans have also been inadequate for urban development as is revealed by Table 5.5.

Expenditure on urban development has remained a small proportion of the total plan budget, excepting in the Fifth Plan when poverty alleviation was taken up in a big way. During the First Plan, expenditures on urban development consisted solely of housing expenditures. Refugee rehabilitation was the primary housing activity taken up by the central government. It shouldered the bulk of expenditures in the urban sector. However, urban development is a state matter. From the Second Plan onward, central government financing in the urban sector was reduced, while that of the states increased. The central government generally finances urban development through centrally sponsored schemes routed through the states. The contribution fluctuates according to the states' ability to utilize central funds.

Total plan expenditures more than doubled during the Ninth Plan. The Tenth Plan outlay was nearly one and half times the previous plan figures. The expenditure on urban development, however, remained nearly the same in proportion. With the increase in urban population and consequent pressure on cities, budgetary resources have become inadequate for the states. India infrastructure Report (1996) has estimated that not more than 10% of required expenditure on urban infrastructure would be available from public sources in the coming decade. From the Eighth Plan onwards financing for urban development has became more market oriented. Centrally sponsored schemes only focus on the vulnerable groups while the states have been directed to raise more finance from market to spend on urban development. Public-Private Participation (PPP) models have been given significant priority in the Eleventh Plan as well.

Institutional Structures

The institutional structure in urban India is a large mix of national, state, and local government departments, public sector corporations, *para-statal* agencies, and autonomous bodies. The following chart helps to explain the structure.

Table 5.5 Investment on Housing and Urban Development during Five-Year Plans (in Crore Rs.) (Rs. 1 Crore = 10 Million)

Category	*First Five-YearPlan (1951–1956)*	*Second Five-Year Plan (1956–1961)*	*Third Five-Year Plan (1961–1966)*	*Fourth Five-Year Plan (1969–1974)*	*Fifth Five-Year Plan (1974–1979)*	*Sixth Five-Year Plan (1980–1985)*	*Seventh Five-Year Plan (1985–1990)*	*Eight Five-Year Plan (1992–1997)*	*Ninth Five-Year Plan (1997–2002)*	*Tenth Five-Year Plan (2002–2007)*
(a) **Total plan**	**2,068.78**	**46,600.00**	**8,093.53**	**15,902**	**37,250**	**97,500.00**	**180,000**	**434,100**	**941,041**	**1,525,639**
Expenditure	(100)	(100)	(100)	(100)	(100)	(100)	(100)	(100)	(100)	(100)
(i) Central Sector	1,240.54	2,557.06	4,076.35	9,296.00	19,577.00	47,250.00	99,302	254,115	547,557	893,183
	(59.96)	(55.58)	(50.36)	(58.45)	(52.55)	(48.46)	(55.16)	(58.53)	(58.18)	(58.54)
(ii) State Sector	828.24	2,042.93	4,022.18	6,606.47	17,673	50,250.00	80,698.0	179,985	393,184	632,456
	(40.03)	(44.41)	(49.69)	(41.45)	(47.44)	(51.53)	(44.83)	(41.46)	(41.81)	(41.45)
(b) Total Expenditure	48.81	80.33	141.96	216.00	2,165.00	1,490.87	6,702.80	15,957.3	30,814.00	54,682.96
On Housing and Urban Development	(100)	(100)	(100)	(100)	(100)	(100)	(100)	(100)	(100)	(100)
(i) Central Sector	38.50	13.56	25.00	48.60	505.00	300.00	350.14	2,896.45	17,119.00	29,719.0
	(78.87)	(16.88)	(17.96)	(22.43)	(23.43)	(20.12)	(5.22)	(18.15)	(20.00)	(16.00)
(ii) State Sector	10.31	66.77	116.96	168.00	1,660.00	1,190.87	6,352.36	13,060.8	136,950	24,963.16
	(21.12)	(83.11)	(82.38)	(77.56)	(76.67)	(97.87)	(94.77)	(81.84)	(80.00)	(84.00)
(c) Percentage of (b) to (a)	**2.35**	**1.74**	**1.75**	**1.36**	**5.81**	**1.52**	**3.72**	**2.67**	**3.00**	**3.00**

Source: Plan documents of different years. *Note:* Figures in parentheses refer to percentage to column total.

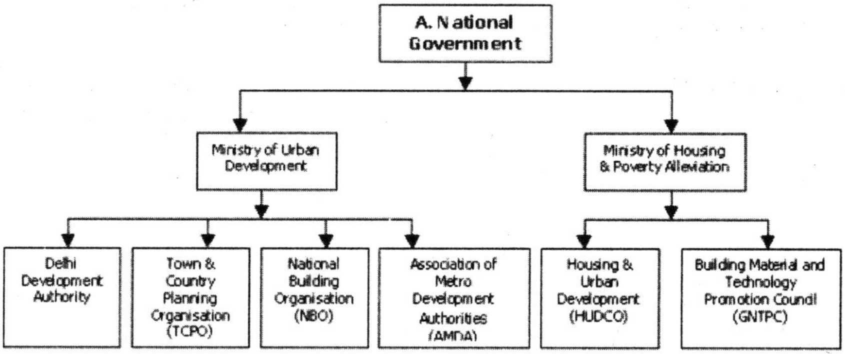

Figure 5.1 Organisational Structure in Urban India—National level.

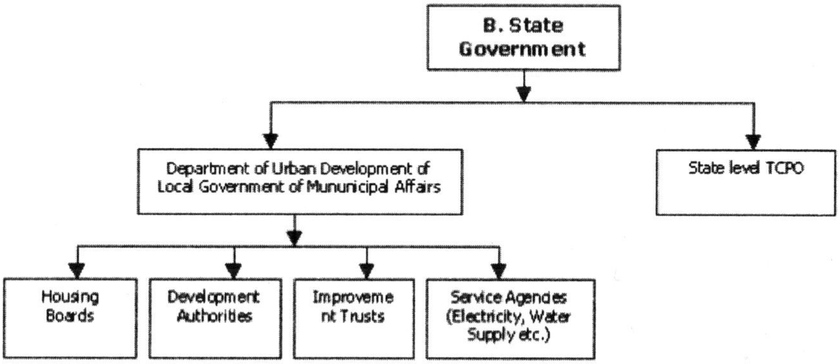

Figure 5.2 Organisational Structure in Urban India—State level.

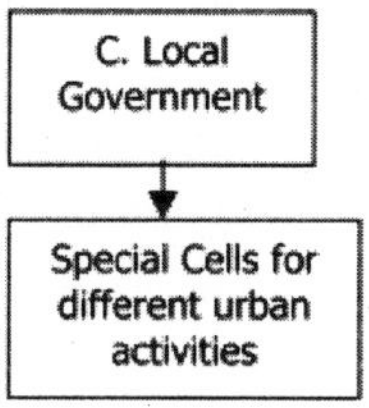

Figure 5.3 Organisational Structure in Urban India—Local level.

The Ministry of Urban Development at the national level is unified or bifurcated from time to time depending more on political considerations than economic issues. Other agencies have different work jurisdictions, though sometimes they do overlap. The major conflict arises in identifying ownership of land in which development is to be implemented. In Delhi, it is not always clear whether the designated land belongs to the local body, development authority, railways, or others. Absence of clear land title is a major hurdle to development (Maitra 2006).

State-level town and country planning organizations (TCPOs) are responsible for monitoring city Master Plans, while city-specific development authorities are responsible for implementing them. Housing boards are engaged in constructing low-cost housing for the economically weaker sections in particular, though they take up other housing projects as well. They do not work at target-oriented projects. Planning targets are loosely set by the planning authorities and loosely monitored. Hence unauthorized developments are mushrooming all over the urban areas, fueled by economic policies. The growth of Multi National Cooperations (MNCs), the industrial lobby and the builders' lobby are influencing physical development, while urban deprivation is increasing, as the vulnerable section of society is loosing its stake in the development process. Planning authorities generally take the advisory role without much regulatory power. Lack of proper monitoring in physical development leads to deepening of urban deprivation.

Along with the TCPOs, several improvement trusts, development authorities, and the like arose in the 1960s to take care of land use planning, while several para-statal agencies were created for provision of basic services. Yet planned spatial development could not take place owing to lack of implementation policies. In all major cities, 50% to 60% of total constructions are unauthorized. The national capital is a glaring example of mismatch between spatial planning and economic planning. Spatial planning could not keep pace with the growing economic strength of the national capital. Though land was preserved for future development, construction lagged behind. Delhi's increased prosperity resulted in an increase in land value, leading to random changes in land use from residential to commercial, while there was no action against violation of Master Plan by the MCD which sanctions building plans and issues completion certificates. DDA, which is the sole implementing authority of Delhi Master Plan, the first step toward planned urban development in the country, does have the power to cancel land allotment against land use violation so long as the land is leasehold. It cannot take action against freehold land.

Decentralization Initiatives

India's experiment with decentralization is more than a decade old. There has been a detailed study on various aspects of decentralization and their effects. Cities have taken various initiatives of local governance in order to create productive environment and eradicate poverty of living conditions. The results have been mixed so far. Service delivery has improved, yet poverty has not declined. The slum population is on the increase. Even in the capital city, the poverty level has increased from 8% to 15% (Economic

Survey of Delhi 2006–2008). All these are indicative of ineffective governance, rather than efficient decentralization. Decentralisation may be necessary, but definitely not sufficient in promoting development.

This point may be further elaborated by looking at the changing characteristics of state intervention. Liberalization is increasingly being characterized by increasing constraints in planning and the political capacity of elected municipal governments, privatization of basic services, withdrawals of state from urban development, escalating support for PPP, especially in infrastructural projects, increasing gentrification to expand space for skewed consumption, and a growing exposure to global competition reflecting the power of the disciplinary financial regime (UNESC 2005).

The changing urban scene, and urban poverty alleviation, are increasingly recognized as a responsibility best addressed by Urban Local Bodies (ULBs) which are closest to people. ULBs have a vital role in delivering the essential urban services and reducing economic and social inequality. The decentralization initiatives are based in the following functions and responsibilities of ULBs.

- First, most urban local authorities control access to land, land-use planning, regulation, and security of tenure. The ease of access, the cost, and the location of land available to the urban poor have a significant impact on their livelihoods and living conditions.
- Second, access to urban infrastructure and basic urban services highlight the linkages between the health costs incurred by the poor due to unsafe water supply, sanitation, and inadequate healthcare.
- Third, the extent of local economic development determines the resources available for investment in areas, such as improved access to land, infrastructure, and urban basis services.
- Fourth, local economic development policies can be supportive of the urban poor by promoting labor-intensive work methods and providing support for micro enterprises and the urban informal sector.
- Fifth, urban local authorities can improve the access of the poor to justice and insist on the enforcement of laws.
- Finally, the capability of the urban poor to influence local decision making to a great extent determines the 'pro-poor ness' of local strategic planning, priority asserting, and investments.

4. REFORM-BASED INSTITUTIONAL LINKAGE—BYPASSING LOCAL PARTICIPATION

The Jawaharlal Nehru National Urban Renewal Mission (JNNURM) was launched in December 2005 as an offshoot of Common Minimum Programme of the national government. It is a reform-linked incentive scheme for providing assistance to state governments and urban local bodies in a selected list of 63 cities, comprising cities with over one million population, state capitals, and cities of religious and tourist importance, for the purpose of reforming urban governance, facilitating urban infrastructure, and providing basic services to the urban poor. With more than Rs. 1,000,000,000,000 at stake for a period of seven years, the mission is the single largest initiative of the central government in the urban sector. This mission is also unique in its emphasis on institutional reform and regulatory framework. The eligible cities will have to prepare a city development

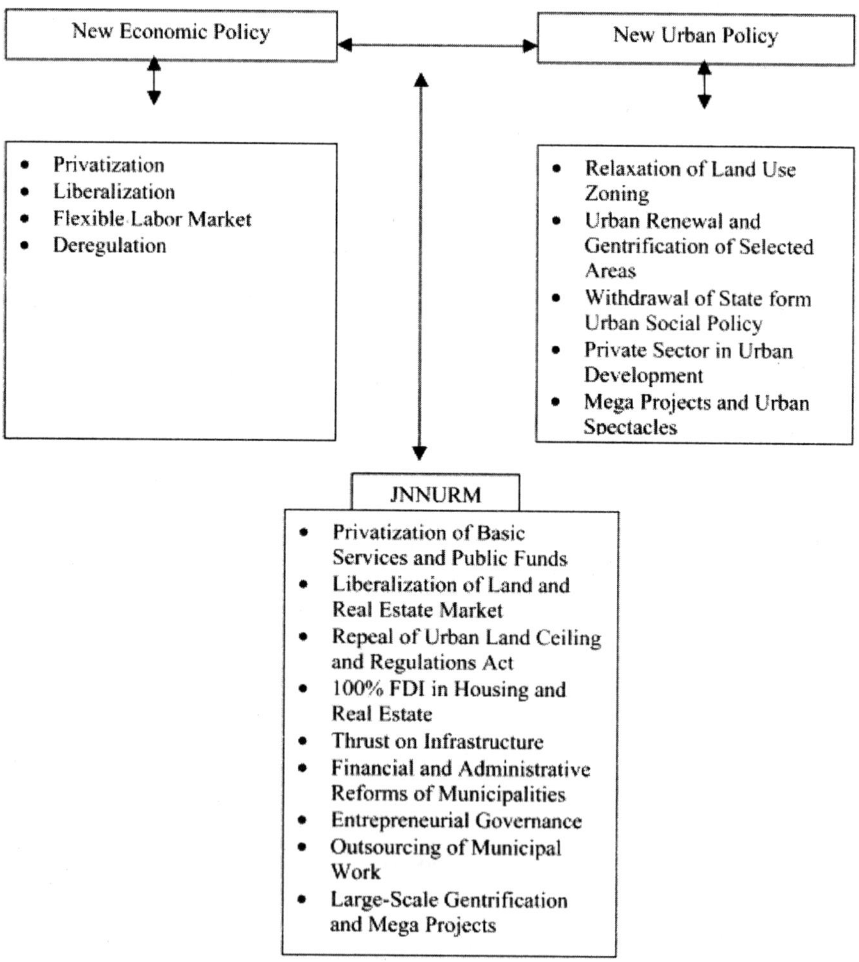

Figure 5.4 Linkage between Economic Policy and Urban Policy. *Source:* Banerjee-Guha (2009).

plan as well as detailed project report for undertaking projects in the identified schemes.

The relationship between the New Economic Policy, New Urban Policy, and the National Urban Renewal Mission may be explained with the chart on p. 113 (Figure 5.4).

This mission is divided into two sub-missions, one focusing on urban infrastructure and governance and the second focusing on basic services for the urban poor (i.e., integrated development of slums through shelter and basic service-related projects).

The distribution of activities under these two sub-missions, however, raises some doubts. The sectors and projects eligible for assistance under these two sub-missions are clearly identified. But financial allocation is not specified in proportion. Projects under the first sub-mission (i.e., for urban infrastructure and governance) are comparatively more commercially viable than those under the second sub-mission (i.e., provision of basic services for the urban poor). The cities may propose more activities under the first than under the second as the obligatory components are not specified. It may be observed that in the local government context, there is clear distinction between obligatory and discretionary services, but services may not be performed in that order. Obligatory services are financed by state, while discretionary services are financed by the ULBs. It is the availability of funds, which determines the priority of service provision. There is no obligation on the state or the local bodies that before taking further developmental activities, the deprived areas must get the basic services on the priority basis.

The central government has initiated poverty alleviation schemes from time to time in the last two decades. The latest scheme (JNNURM) is, however, unique in initiating some institutional reforms linked with availability of finance specified at both the state and local levels. It is directed to address the problems of provisioning of infrastructure and basic services to the poor in the cities and towns in a holistic manner. It envisages reform-driven, fast-track planned development of the identified 63 cities, with a focus on efficiency in urban services delivery mechanism, community participation and accountability of urban local bodies toward citizens. JNNURM is expected to be based on the concept for inclusive cities and pro-poor city development in accordance with the strategy for the Eleventh Five-Year Plan. The Mission is based on the rationale that the reforms would lead to economic growth assisted with a higher rate of urbanization and that cities covered by the Mission would emerge as "engines of growth" for the respective urban systems and would be more livable, secure, and, of course, global in character, materializing the concept of a modern homogenized urban society.

The basic difference between JNNURM and other urban schemes lies in its corporate-type appearance—detailed Memorendum of Understanding

(MoU), detailed Terms of Reference (TOI) for City Development Plan, detailed toolkit for implementation prepared by a professional body like the Infrastructure Leasing and Financial Services (ILFS), and most significantly, the time bound approach which is a distinct feature compared to previous schemes, loosely formed. The amount of money also has been raised significantly, much more than the amounts recommended by both Eleventh and Twelfth Finance Commissions.

The indicative MoU, TOR and five sets of tool kits prepared for the JNNURM refer to several time bound activities and performance criteria which are no doubt very much necessary for raising efficiency and city productivity level. In the MoU itself, financial governance, citizen accountability and service indicators are specified which are undoubtedly important for success of the mission. In this context, the Integrated Development of Small and Medium Towns (IDSMT), a flagship urban project launched during the Sixth Plan may be recalled, where lack of time-bound activity has been a very serious factor hindering the success of the project. There are detailed guidelines of City Development Plan indicating the need for reform, the basic requirements, potential roadblocks, and potential triggers. In the objective of JNNURM, it is observed that the budget process does not include consulting with and building in citizen's input on priority setting. The budget is also not performance based or linked to a system of reporting back to citizens on actual performance. The state-level reform agenda includes implementation of the 74th amendment as mandatory requirement.

All these are positive developments, but some problems reappear when we consider basic rights to infrastructure and shelter. JNNURM touches upon public disclosure laws and community participation laws, but there is no linkage with the Right to Information Act, that has been enacted in the Parliament, yet the states are bringing it into their respective legislations. This is the basic meaningful public right. The Citizens Charter has been launched with much fanfare but public authorities are yet to specify the information that citizens are entitled to obtain, and what can be withheld from them under the Official Secrecy Act. There is concern regarding public-private participation but nothing is mentioned regarding the formation of ward committees as one of the performance criterion for the local bodies. Ward committees, a constitutional obligation, are important platforms, where citizens can voice their concern. Instead, the Mission mentions the formation of Ward Sabha. This is not the same as the former in letter and spirit and may create confusion without any clear statutory background. Public-private participation has emerged in terms of participation of big developers to bag big contracts from the public agency, but not in terms of regular meetings with local bodies and community-based organizations to discuss different aspects of the local budget. Neither is it mentioned in various performance criteria developed in details. There are several examples of institutional reforms with citizens' participation in the decision-making process. For example the U.S. model of municipal bonds is very forcefully cited as an invincible model of raising resources for local bodies. In the U.S., when municipal bonds beyond $1,000 are to be floated, a regular public meeting is compulsory to discuss the reasons and to specify why alternative arrangements are uneconomic. Here, we do not know why the city of Ahmedabad is issuing one set of bonds after another highlighting the status of "without state guarantee". The debt servicing of municipal bond depends on escrowing revenue from Octroi, a state tax imposed on goods entering the municipal areas. However, many states have abolished Octroi as it proved to be a source of corruption. If that happens in case of Gujarat, the municipal resource base will be considerably weakened. Additionally, the citizens are not involved in the decision-making process to determine, for example, the impact on infrastructure supply or the components of infrastructural expenditure that must be reduced in order to meet the liability of debt servicing. Examples of Canadian municipalities also may be quoted where the municipalities may float municipal bonds but annual debt servicing must not be over 5% of revenue expenditure. In a recent survey of Ahmedabad, it is observed that debt-servicing component has increased from 18% to 24% of annual revenue expenditure during 1997–2002 (Maitra 2002). Citizens have a right to take a part in such a decision-making process involving supply of services that directly affect their quality of life. Right to basic services means not only getting the service but also being involved in the process of decision making. The proper inclusive guidelines for assertive rights to services and shelter are not yet chalked out in the Mission.

Non-involvement of people is evident in the preparation of City Development Plans (CDPs) as well. Every city has to submit a CDP for getting financial assistance. A few cities like the Municipal Corporation of Surat have taken a lead with involvement of city councilors. But others have taken help from the professional consultants who emphasize the financial viability of the projects much more than the physical availability of services. Elected city governments are not at the center of activities with reduction of volume of deprivation as the prime objective.

In order to be eligible, municipal corporations are required to prepare CDPs, 25-year vision documents defining the direction of development. The Mission's original idea to have the plans chalked out with "active public consultation" was not carried out in the proper sense as the majority of the plans were ready in a month's time, hurriedly evaluated by hired bodies, following which, within three months, the central government disbursed Rs. 864,829.5 million for 23 infrastructure projects. All previous central government funding and urban development schemes were brought under the Mission. Projects that were given priority were mega infrastructure projects, gigantic commercial complexes, shopping malls, cultural facilities, and urban spectacles. One by one, cities started joining the bandwagon and pledging their commitment to private capital for transforming their physical and institutional landscapes. With the central government retaining the right to assess the progress of the development projects, "efficiency" became the catchword that systematically went to justify the entry of private capital in running the projects. Several non-governmental organizations in different cities were co-opted to sway people about the efficacy of PPP. This has resulted in a shortage of land supply for low-income housing. Local bodies have not earmarked any such area where fast track construction can begin to provide houses to the deprived (Ramahandraih 2003, 2009).

A careful look at JNNURM proves that it is essentially a reform-linked investment program of private capital targeting Indian cities. Based on subtle forms of competition, place-marketing, and regulatory undercutting for attracting investment, it is tangled by a range of conditional ties at state and city government levels. The key items are (i) privatization/commercialization of basic services through PPP with the introduction of user fees; (ii) liberalization of the land and real estate market through repeal of Urban Land Ceiling Acts and changes in Rent Control Acts; (iii) development of a stronger mortgage market alongside 100% FDI in housing and real estate; (iv) easier land use conversion norms; (v) reforms in property tax and reduction in stamp duties; (vi) financial and administrative restructuring of municipalities through implementation of the 74th amendment of the Constitution; (vii) rationalization and outsourcing; (viii) introduction of e-governance; and (ix) dominance of private sector and private credit rating agencies over elected civic bodies. The sweeping transformation of urban governance is meant to create a functional impotence of democratically elected bodies and encroach upon the constitutionally devolved areas of state government jurisdiction.

The urban projects that the JNNURM pursues are a material expression of a developmental logic that views mega projects and place-marketing as means for waging a competitive struggle to attract investment capital. Their impact is felt at all levels—local, regional, national, and international—producing a new articulation of regulatory scales. The associated new urban policy, developing in parallel with the neoliberal economic policy thus squarely revolves around re-centering the city; and replacing old forms, functions, and organizational configurations by a new urbanity and assertive, entrepreneurial urban governance that will stand the tests imposed by a global and neoliberal world order. Simultaneously, the re-imaging of the city space is made keeping in mind the consumption pattern of the investor, the developer, and the rich, depriving the urban poor. In the CDPs, there is no relocation plan for the workers in the unorganized sector, whose livelihood is threatened with construction of roads and flyovers to make way for the big investment. The role of the elected representatives is becoming marginalized.

5. CHALLENGING INCLUSIVE GROWTH

Although a classification of reforms into "optional and mandatory" was theoretically made, in practice, all NURM-prescribed urban governance reforms seem to be mandatory for cities undertaking the Mission programs. In addition, all ULBs need to prove financial stability for accessing capital market funds (Jamwal 2006). Additional precondition for the states to access funds is that they need to set up para-statal, non-elected nodal agencies that will be made responsible for evaluating projects, releasing funds to ULBs/para-statal units, managing the same funds, and monitoring projects. Projects with private sector participation are to be given priority over projects submitted by the ULBs/para-statal units by themselves. A central government committee headed by a private bank chairman had earlier justified the "inability" of the public sector to finance infrastructure projects in which subsequently 100% FDI was invited. At the behest of the World Bank, in the Eleventh Plan draft, PPP had already been accepted as the prime alternative to fund infrastructure projects. From nearly Rs 2,600 million in 2007–2008, the infrastructure budget is expected to increase to a whopping Rs 5,740 million (approximately) in 2011–2012 (Economic Survey, GOI, 2009–10). To woo the private sector and safeguard its profit rates, the government even went ahead in providing "viability gap funding" (i.e., sharing 40% of the capital cost of the projects). Similar concessions were termed as "geo-bribes" by Smith (2002) in his analysis of fiscal concessions provided by the New York City administration to global corporations to induce the New York Stock Exchange to remain in the city. PPP models for provision of basic services were thus projected as the panacea in JNNURM too, which went at par with the central government's National Common Minimum Programme (NCMP), aiming at removing all impediments to the land and housing markets. Interestingly, no provision was kept in the Mission for public debate on any of the projects.

The total cost of the NURM was estimated at Rs 500,000 million for a period of seven years beginning from December 2005. The Mission aimed at developing 63 Indian cities into "world class" sustainable cities. Since the early 1990s, as the concept of "livable Indian cities" has disappeared from the Indian planning lexicon, getting replaced by "world class cities", the major thrust of the Mission went to infrastructure, like wide roads, flyovers, tunnels, skyways, airports, mega commercial complexes, real estates, and open spaces for recreation, all with an aspiration to achieve international standards. Cities of all size classes are targeted: seven from category A or mega cities, 28 from category B or metro cities, and the remaining 25 of the 28 listed in category C are urban agglomerations (UAs) with less than one million population. The Mission is classified into two parts: Submission-A, entitled Urban Infrastructure and Governance (UIG) accounts for 65% of the total funds, to be administered by the Ministry of Urban Development. Projects on roads, transport, associated infrastructure, water supply, sanitation and beautification (read gentrification) have come under this head. Sub-mission B, having 35% of the total funds, has been earmarked for providing Basic Services to the Urban Poor (BSUP), which is being administered by the Ministry of Urban Employment and Poverty Alleviation (MUEPA). Items like slum improvement, rehabilitation of the displaced, access to basic services, and housing projects for the urban poor come under this head.

In the agenda of reforms, JNNURM proposes mandatory reforms at both the state and local levels. These are basically financial, rather than administrative. It mentions provision of basic services to the urban poor as mandatory reform. It is also mentioned that levy of reasonable user charges with the gradual objective of full cost recovery within seven years is mandatory. Does it mean that if cost recovery is not possible, there will be no service in the deprived areas? Cost recovery and services provision in the deprived areas have always remained very difficult objectives to attain, and unfortunately, the new mission, JNNURM till now offers no solution to this problem. Cost recovery must take a back seat if we prioritize basic service rights, and there is no doubt that it requires a huge subsidy from the state. Unfortunately, we equate the subsidy component with inefficiency when it is specified to basic service provision in deprived areas. But this is not so when government offers huge subsidy to Software Technology Parks. In that case, subsidies are regarded as drivers of efficiency, whereas in the former case, it is visualized the other way.

JNNURM has also specified optional reforms common to the states, ULBs, and para-statal agencies. A major optional reform is earmarking at least 20% to 25% of developed land in all housing projects (both private and public) for economically weak sectors (EWS) and low-income groups (LIG) category with a system of cross subsidization. If this component can be categorized as optional, it raises question regarding its seriousness—do we really consider basic services and housing as rights, and again whose right? Gurgaon and Noida—the prominent IT hubs in the National Capital Region—are glaring examples of what happens when EWS housing is optional. During 1992 and 2002 Noida's squatter settlement population increased from 16% to 22% of total population as the real estate boom took place gradually, while housing supply in Gurgaon and Noida actually exceeded its demand for the higher income groups. Even though master plans have demarcated some lands for the EWS, the construction of EWS and LIG dwelling units never started because public agencies do not take construction activities in Gurgaon and Noida. Thus, basic rights cannot be honored simply by demarcating certain areas for EWS and LIG, without specifying institutional responsibilities (Maitra 2008b).

Metro cities are getting ready for globalized investment. These cities must improve water supply, drainage and sewerage, roads, and flyovers to invite global investment. This infrastructure will not automatically include the poverty-stricken areas unless strategized and planned. The Ministry of Urban Development has sanctioned 67 projects till now. Of them 52 are for water supply, drainage, and sewerage; 11 are for improving the transport network likes flyovers and road development; and the remaining are for urban renewal and solid waste management. These do not ensure that the deprived areas are also included in these schemes. Improved infrastructure is likely to lead to fierce competition for urban land for residential and commercial purposes. Existence of slums in the vicinity may reduce land value, which may result in relocation and removal of slums. There are hardly any guidelines to see how and when the evicted slum dwellers receive alternative accommodation. In the environment of increasing land value, the Mission document clearly states that (a) land cost will not be financed and (b) housing for the poor will not be provided free of cost. The objective of the Mission is not clearly reduction of deprivation. Increase in per capita income cannot by itself reduce income inequality. Similarly, increase in basic services cannot reduce spatial inequality unless focused on area-centric deprivation.

A glance at the reform measures of JNNURM reveals that these are potential factors to feed land speculation. The repeal of Urban Land Ceiling and Regulations Act (ULCRA) in 1976 gives a free hand to the developers to drive away the poor from the formal land market. DDA could construct more than 1 million houses for the EWS and LIG in Delhi because it controlled the land supply (Maitra 2008a). The existence of the private sector in other cities of India has not increased the supply of housing of the poor. The ULRCA was never functional earlier as the excess land was consumed by the same landowners by changing land use pattern by turning residences into hotels and the like or sold in the market to worthy buyers. With 100% FDI allowed in real estate in early 2005, FDI in real estate as a percentage of total FDI inflows increased from 4.5% in 2003–2004 to 26.5% in 2006–2007, making slums in large cities exceedingly vulnerable as a future source of land for these activities. National Building Organization estimated that 24.7 million people would be rendered homeless in 2006 of which 97% would be constituted by the urban poor. Repeal of the ULCRA in 1976 in several cities is found to have created havoc by making land of different nature and size readily available for speculation. Second, the mandatory requirement for the ULBs to become financially self-reliant essentially means a reduction in their budgetary allocation and restriction in their political and financial capacity. Moreover without having any role in authoring the CDP, they are obliged to administer its urban development projects, sanctioned by para-statal bodies. For example, the Karnataka Urban Infrastructure Development

Finance Corporation, a para-statal body in Karnataka (entrusted to receive the total central and state government funds for urban development for the state), disbursed the funds among the ULBs for running all related projects. It has also become obligatory for these bodies to raise funds from the capital market that prefers mega projects for funding even if they go against the larger interest of the society. For example, transport projects sanctioned in the first year of the Mission for Hyderabad and Nagpur at a cost of Rs 61,280 million and Rs 86,280 million, respectively, were quite against the National Urban Transport policy with its goal to strengthen the public transport system.

JNNURM reforms are likely to put pressure on the urban land market. Speculative increase in land value also cannot be checked. The developers cannot acquire the land and keep it vacant without construction by Supreme Court order. However, sold houses may remain unoccupied for long in order to reap speculative benefits. In Delhi, the total number of houses exceeds the number of households by 830,000 (Census of India 2001). Further break-down of the 2001 Census data shows there are 3 million occupied houses and 380,000 vacant houses. On the other hand, homelessness in Delhi between 1991 and 2001 increased by 26.89%.

Along with the JNNURM, both the central government and states have direct poverty alleviation programs which fail to reach the target groups owing to lack of proper implementation and monitoring. Without proper time-bound targets, these programs take a back seat with non-utilization of financial assistance piling up.

The National Commission on Urbanisation (1988) identified several National Priority Cities (NPCs) and State Priority Cities (SPC) whose growth were essential for urban development. It is interesting to notice that out of 63 cities identified under JNNURM, 50 cities are NPCs and 12 are SPCs, only Varanasi in Uttar Pradesh is the new addition. The growth potential of these places was identified 15 years ago. Yet no spatial planning was effectively implemented till economic policies to encourage competition changed the priorities. Cities, as preferred locations for investment of private sector and even for foreign investors, have now come under national priority to make them livable, healthy, and safe.

The CDP, to be prepared under the Mission, is both a perspective as well as a vision document for the future development of a city. It defines the potential of the city and reflects its unique attributes in terms of comparative and competitive advantages, value, and preference of the city's residents. The selection of a strategy under CDP is an extremely important constituent and needs to be done with wide-ranging consultations among key stakeholders. A strategy that links the urban poor with service provision may be preferred, as compared to the aims of expansion of service without any reference to its potential beneficiaries or target.

The city Investment Plan under the CDP provides an estimate of the level of investment that will be needed to implement the CDP. It is an estimate and approximation and provides an order of investment arrived at by using financial norms or standards for service provision and up-gradation, or directly estimating the cost of implementing a reform agenda. It considers the options and strategies for financing the vision as contained in the CDPs (i.e., whether it will be financed by the local government by mobilizing resources or in partnership with other tiers of government and financing institutions or by resorting to capital market and so on). All these options need to be systematically examined while preparing the CDP.

The financial profile of the city indicates the state of city finances and its capacity to manage its finances and mobilize resources. The analysis should focus on assessing the current financial status of the city with the objective of examining whether the level of expenditure on services are skewed in favor of certain areas.

Similarly the infrastructure profile under CDP refers to the current state of infrastructure and utility systems in the city, while the physical profile relates to topography, natural drainage systems, and land availability. Hence the focus of CDP is on the development of economic and social infrastructure with strategies that affect urban poor and strengthen municipal governance and finance.

CONCLUSIONS

The new urban agenda of India has not only focused on reducing urban deprivations but has actually shown elements that can intensify it. The improvements in explicit forms, compared to earlier programs, are quite impressive, but as the trend shows till now, market-oriented reforms are likely to ignore both area-based and people-based urban deprivation. There is no evidence that investments will be directed toward reducing spatial inequality. There is an effort to integrate economic and spatial planning through mandatory preparation of CDPs, but states can opt for more competitive environment in attracting infrastructure. The mandatory reforms spelled out by the Mission are more market-based reform oriented rather than welfare-oriented. It offers no assurance to solve the age-old dilemma between growth and development. The national government and the state governments are withdrawing gradually from welfare activities in order to create a competition-enabling environment. JNNURM is directed at attracting global investment at the cost of neglecting local poverty. The financial policies of the national government are also of no help. If the states do not carry over poverty alleviation programs, the central grants are withdrawn. It puts further restrictions on inadequate resources of the states, which lean more on building remunerative assets with public-private co-operation. The strategy should be to restrict the flow of competitive investments to the states that do not carry out poverty alleviation programs and reduce urban deprivation on a priority basis. JNNURM, with its shining and progressive-looking coverage, is silent on these issues. Economic planning defeats the purpose of spatial planning with the objective of preserving land for the poor when open competition in land is encouraged by the former. The new urban initiative has not provided adequate safeguards to the interests of the deprived in urban areas. The urbanization process in the developing countries has led to rural-urban inequality in general and urban-urban inequality in particular. The widely publicized urban reform process in India is unfortunately showing signs of contradictions that fuel this trend.

REFERENCES

Acharya, Shankar. 2001. *India's macro economics management in the nineties.* New Delhi: Indian Council for Research on International Economic Relations.

Census of India 2001.

Economic Survey of Delhi (2006–08), Planning Department, Government of NCT of Delhi, New Delhi.

Economic Survey (2009–10), Government of India, Oxford University Press, New Delhi.

Fay, Marianne, and Charlotte Opal. 2000. *Urbanisation without growth: A not so uncommon phenomenon.* Washington, DC: World Bank.

Banerjee-Guha, Swapna. 2009. Neoliberalising the "urban": New geographics of power and injustice in Indian cities. *Economic and Political Weekly* (May 30). Vol. XLIV No. 22 pp. 95–107.

Hall, Peter, Kathy Pain, and Nick Green. 2006. Anatomy of the polycentric metropolis: Eight mega-city regions in overview. *The polycentric metropolis: Learning from mega city regions in Europe,* edited by Peter Hall and Kathy Pain, 19–64. London: Earthscan Publications.

Himanshu. 2007. Recent trends in poverty and inequality: Some preliminary results. *Economic and Political Weekly* 42(6): 497–508.

Hasim, S. R. 2009. *Economic development and urban poverty in India.* Urban Poverty Report, UNDP. New Delhi: Oxford University Press.

India Infrastructure Report (1996), Thompson Press, New Delhi.

Jamwal (2006). Urban Myths, *Down to Earth,* Vol. 15 (4), pp. 26–34.

Jones, Gravin W. 2004. Urbanisation trends in Asia: The conceptual and definitional challenges. In *New Forms of Urbanisation: Beyond the Urban-Rural Dichotomy,* edited by Tony Champion and Hugo Graeme Hugo, 113–150. Aldershot: Ashgate.

Kundu, A. 1993. *The name of the urban poor: Access to basic amenities.* New Delhi: Sage.

———. 2007. A strategy paper on migration and urbanisation in the context of development dynamics, governmental programmes in evolving institutional structure in India. In collaboration with Harbans Gills Debolina Kundu, and Niroop. Paper commissioned by United Nations Populations Fund (UNFPA).

Kundu, A., and S. Maitra. 1999. Access of urban poor to basic service—An analysis in the changing perspective of urban governance in India. *The challenge of urban governance*, edited by O. P. Mathur. New Delhi: National Institute of Public Finance and Policy.

Maitra, Shipra. 2002. Municipal indebtedness and supply of services: Some thoughts for financial management. *Nagarlok* Vol. 3(July–September), 45–65.

———. 2006. Delhi: The city and the capital. Status report submitted to the Delhi Government by Institute for Human Development, New Delhi.

———. 2008a. "Special economic zones", by passing local government? *Urban India*, XXVIII(182), pp. 30–47.

———. 2008b. Financing urban development in Delhi: Towards inclusive globalisation? In *Inside the transforming urban Asia*, edited by Darshini Mahadevia. New Delhi: Concept Publishing Company.

———. 2008c. Dynamics of high tech urban spaces—Lessons from IT sector expansion in the national capital region. In *Dynamics of high-tech urban spaces—Asian European perspectives*, edited by C. Ramachandraiah, Guus Westen, and Sheela Prasad. New Delhi: Manohar.

Mahadevia, D. 2008. Inclusions and exclusions. *Economic and Political Weekly*, Vol. XL III No. 5 (February 2): 42–44.

Mazumdar, Dipak, and Sandip Sarkar. 2004, Measurement and determinants of poverty in pre and post reform period in India—An analysis for India and major states. Working Paper Series No. 22, Institute for Human Development.

Mukherjee, Ashis, and Kishaloy Banerjee. 2008. The big capital in retail in West Bengal: Stories of space encroachment. Paper presented in the Workshop on Urban Neoliberalism: Restructuring South Asian Cities, Tata Institute of Social Sciences, November 27–28, Mumbai.

National Commission on Urbanisation, India. 1988. *Report of the working group on urban poverty*. New Delhi: Government of India.

Papola, T. S. 2004. *Globalization, employment and social* protection: Emerging perspectives for the Indian workers. *Indian Journal of Labour Economics* 47(3): 891–900.

Ramachandraih, C. 2003. Urbanisation and urban services. In Andhra Pradesh development: Economic reforms and challenges ahead, edited by C. H. Hanumnatha Rao and S. Mahendra Dev. Hyderabad: CESS, pp. 245–265.

———. 2009. Maytas, Hyderabad Metro and the politics of real estate. *Economic and Political Weekly* 44(3): 36–40.

Sabir, Ali. 2003. Magnitude of slum problem in Delhi. CSD working paper (2002/03).

Satterthwaite, David. 2005. Meeting the MDG's in urban areas: The forgotten role of local organization. *Journal of International Affairs* 58(2): 87–112.

Shitole, G. Y. 2007. Urban poverty management in India with special reference to micro finance to urban poor in Mumbai. In *Micro economic politics reforms in India: Pro-poor dimensions—Health, agriculture, services and infrastructure*, edited by Bibhuti Patel and Manisha Karne. UNDP.

Sivaramakrishnan, K. C., A. Kundu, and B. Singh. N. 2005. *Handbook of urbanisation in India: An analysis of trends and process*. New Delhi: Oxford University Press.

Smith (2002). New Globalism, New Urbanism; Gentrification as Global Urban Strategy, Antipode. Vol. 34(3), pp. 427–50.

United Nations Economic and Social Council. 2005. *Policy dialogue: Decentralisation for poverty reduction*. Bangkok: United Nations.

Virmani, Arvind. 2004. Sources of Indian economic growth. Indian Council for International Economic Relations, New Delhi. Working Paper No. 131.

Zlotonik, Hania. 2004. World urbanisation: Trends and prospects. In *New forms of urbanisation: Beyond the urban-rural dichotomy* edited by Tony Champion and Hugo Graeme Hugo, 41–64. Basingstoke: Ashgate.

6 The Right to Waste

Informal Sector Recyclers and Struggles for Social Justice in Post-Reform Urban India

Bharati Chaturvedi and Vinay Gidwani

> Pauperism is the hospital of the active labour-army and the dead weight of the industrial reserve army. Its production is included in that of the relative surplus population, its necessity is implied by their necessity; along with the surplus population, pauperism forms a condition of capitalist production, and of the capitalist development of wealth. It forms part of the *faux frais* ['incidental expenses'] of capitalist production: but capital usually knows how to transfer these from its own shoulders to those of the working class and the petty bourgeoisie. . . . The more extensive . . . the pauperized sections of the working class and the industrial reserve army, the greater is official pauperism. *This is the absolute general law of capitalist accumulation.*
>
> Karl Marx, *Capital*, Vol. 1

> Social needs have an anthropological foundation. Opposed and complimentary, they include the need for security and opening, the need for certainty and adventure, that of organization of work and of play, the needs for the predictable and the unpredictable, of similarity and difference, of isolation and encounter, exchange and investments, of independence (even solitude) and communication, of immediate and long-term prospects. The human being has the need to accumulate energies and to spend them, even waste them in play.
>
> Henri Lefebvre, "The Right to the City"

Ghaziabad, in the state of Uttar Pradesh, is a rapidly growing city that borders metropolitan Delhi. In November 2008 a small band of waste pickers in Ghaziabad began a low-key protest. Their issue? Extortion, under pain of violence. A group of previously unknown people was demanding a payment of Rs. 400–600 per month from each waste picker in exchange for letting them continue their work. According to the waste pickers, they would be approached by 'agents' of a contractor, Chand Qureshi, claiming that he now owned all rights over waste in the area. If anyone wanted to pick waste, they would have to compensate him. Not doing so, he warned, would be tantamount to theft, which he threatened to deal with severely. Waste pickers refusing to comply were beaten up. Fearful, several of them began to pay Qureshi the monthly amount he demanded. With the collapse in global (and subsequently, local) scrap prices, the payment equaled nearly five days' earnings for the average picker.

Qureshi's method of generating income from municipal waste was new, and represented a sharp departure from prevailing arrangements. It was neither a standard work contract with the city to gather waste nor a public-private partnership of the kind municipalities around the world have been furiously creating. Nor too was it a sub-contracting arrangement between a municipality and a private company. It was, in fact, a legal arrangement with the city that allowed Qureshi to claim temporary proprietorship of Ghaziabad's municipal waste and, on that basis, a tax from waste pickers for right of use. Unwittingly or wittingly, the Ghaziabad Municipal Corporation (GMC) created and contracted out the right to tax a source of livelihood for the urban poor in the name of privatization and efficiency. How did this scenario arise?

For several months in early 2009, as the GMC both denied and affirmed the order granting Qureshi the right to collect dues from waste pickers, it became evident that the municipality's actions were far from being arbitrary. In fact, they were the culmination of several autonomous processes, whose concatenation led to the emergence of an institutional arrangement that verged on legalized extortion. What were these processes?

First, Delhi's suburbs, such as Ghaziabad, have witnessed an unprecedented building boom over the past decade. Once considered too far to live and commute from, peri-urban developments like Ghaziabad are now viable, even sought after, addresses for thousands of middle-class Indians who work in Delhi. As property prices in Delhi have skyrocketed, placing rentals and home purchases beyond the reach of many, areas like Ghaziabad have become increasingly attractive residential options. Second, the spurt in residential growth and the pool of middle-class consumers has prompted rapid growth in formal and informal sector retailing—and correspondingly, in the daily volume of municipal waste.[1] The content of everyday garbage has changed too with the increasing use of plastics in consumer packaging, as well as cardboard and paper in mail advertising (Table 6.1).

The global economy was a third contributing factor. China's emergence as "the world's factory" has unleashed explosive demands, at its end, for raw materials for use in production and packaging, with the result that China is now one of the world's leading buyers of scrap and recyclable materials. From Boston to Buenos Aires, recyclers and export agents now ship vast quantities of waste paper, used plastics, scrap metal, and other recyclable items to China. Buoyed by China's economy, world prices for scrap have been rising steadily, touching a historical high in 2008, before receding due to the global recession. Even outsiders to the waste trade have

Table 6.1 Shifts in Physical Composition of Solid Waste in India (%)

Year	*Biodegradable*	*Paper*	*Plastic/ Rubber*	*Metal*	*Glass*	*Rags*	*Other*	*Inerts*
1996	42.21	3.63	0.60	0.49	0.60	—	—	45.13
2005	47.43	8.13	9.22	0.50	1.01	4.49	4.016	25.16

Source: D. Zhu et al., *Improving municipal solid waste management in India: A sourcebook for policy makers and practitioners* (Washington, DC: The World Bank, 2008).

come to recognize it as a lucrative business proposition. With the 1990s adage 'waste to wealth' becoming 'waste *is* wealth' in the new millennium, the taxation of urban waste became a viable prospect for revenue-hungry municipalities like the GMC. Historically, to 'own' the city's garbage—or, to be more legally exact, the garbage deposited in neighborhood municipal bins called *dhalaos*—was a liability for municipalities since, under the municipal charter, it carried the obligation to remove it. Disposal, often costly, was a drain on strapped city budgets. Today, garbage has become an asset (see Sethi, 2006). For Urban Local Bodies (ULBs) that are under increasing pressure to become more financially self-sustaining and responsible in the wake of neoliberal transformations of India's economy, this realization has sparked a rush to capitalize on waste through a variety of new ventures that, in one shape or another, privatize what was earlier a de facto 'urban commons' used free of charge by the city's poor as livelihoods.

The GMC, in this sense, is no different. What is different is the route it chose. For reasons not entirely clear—but quite likely, a combination of staffing limitations, political expedience, and openings for graft—the GMC decided to capture revenue from garbage through a perverse form of privatization: by selling the right to waste, found in municipal bins, to private contractors; in this instance, Chand Qureshi, for an initial period of two years (2008–2009 and 2009–2010). How Qureshi then chose to interpret this as a right to extort a monthly toll from waste pickers is a lesson in both personal ingenuity and municipal apathy. When Ghaziabad's waste recyclers found they were unable to spurn the contractor's demands, some of them—previously residents of Delhi who moved to Ghaziabad after being evicted from squatter settlements in the metropolis—contacted Chintan, a Delhi-based environmental justice group they were associated with and that supports its own incipient waste recyclers' organization, Safai Sena. Based on discussions, the coalition decided to pursue a two-pronged strategy: first, to engage with the GMC; and, second, to treat each case of beating as a criminal act. Soon after, several groups of waste pickers forced their way into a local police station, where two small junk dealers and a Chintan staff member attempted to file an FIR (First

Information Report, a formal police complaint) against Qureshi and his affiliates. Although the police are obligated to accept an FIR, should a citizen wish to file one, in practice this is rarely a straightforward matter for the poor. The police may ask for a bribe, dilute the complaint, or simply refuse to enter an FIR if the person who stands accused is a powerful patron. They may also refuse because an FIR negatively impacts a police district's performance statistics. In the Qureshi case, it took a few weeks of intense pressure to get the Ghaziabad police to relent and finally register an FIR. The complaint, which named several people, alleged: "They stopped me today and said that if you want to work here, then you have to pay me . . . or we will kill you. We somehow escaped them. They have already taken away two of our cycle rickshaws. They have also threatened our colleague, X, that they will have him implicated in some case or the other and jailed." A few of the contractor's henchmen were subsequently detained, but Qureshi himself remained free.

The outcomes of the next few weeks were not surprising. The contractor sent other representatives to threaten the waste pickers. Local junk dealers were threatened as well, and expressed fear for their safety. On one occasion, according to a Chintan staff member, one of Qureshi's representatives warned: "What do you have? I have orchards, three ponds where we cultivate fish. I'm not just anyone. If you trouble me, you've had it." Some suggested these representatives were carrying guns, and things could turn violent. Two people were beaten up, and their rickshaws were seized. Then, one morning, some waste recyclers and Chintan staff received a notice from the Uttar Pradesh High Court. It said nothing about waste, or the right over it. The contractor's detained henchmen were seeking bail, which the court granted.

That was not the end of the matter. Qureshi was furious at being challenged, and used the court hearing as a new ploy to frighten waste pickers. He issued threats that the courts were now planning to have all the waste recyclers arrested and jailed for not paying up, a prospect that genuinely worried many of them. A young 15-year-old claimed that he challenged Qureshi's people forcefully when they caught him. He said he knew from Chintan's legal literacy workshops that a private contractor could only be given the right over waste that was present in *dhalaos* (municipal bins). "I told them I collect waste from houses. Your contract is only for dustbins, so you can't touch me." He was let off, he said, without a beating or payment.

While this was happening, another unlikely order was issued. This order, signed, of all people, *by a health officer* of the GMC stated that the contractor was in fact authorized to collect "dues" from waste pickers (as we will see, the original contract between GMC and Chandbabu Qureshi did *not* sanction collection of money from waste pickers). The police called up the waste pickers and Chintan staff to tell them that they were no longer able to detain the contractor's representatives now that the court had granted them bail and the GMC had issued Qureshi a clean chit of action. The henchmen were released. The extortion started all over again.

Groups of waste pickers and the Chintan staff visited the GMC's office to understand why waste pickers were being forced to accede to these new demands, but were rebuffed, failing to meet even junior officials. They also found it impossible to lay their hands on a copy of the health officer's order authorizing collection of payment from waste pickers. After considerable persistence, Chintan was able to set up a meeting with the municipal commissioner, who in turn summoned his entire staff to the meeting. The meeting was tense, and revealed internal fissures within the GMC. The commissioner denied outright to ever having any knowledge about the order sanctioning collection of money from waste pickers. The health officer who had signed the order was unable to explain how the order was issued. Chintan asked for the legal basis of the order. Ultimately, the order was rescinded. But the original contract with Qureshi stood.

The GMC's original contract with Qureshi, dated 20 November 2008, (Figure 6.1), on the basis of which the health officer issued his subsequent order confirming Qureshi's authority to collect money from waste pickers (Figure 6.2), is significantly different in content. The GMC contract allows M/S Chand Babu Qureshi the right to pick and segregate waste, listed as rags, cardboard, plastics, metals, glass, plastic ropes, plastic bags, and paper, from the Mohan Nagar Zone of Ghaziabad. It also says that should any other people (referred to as workers, or *shramik* in the contract) engage in this work, the contractor is obligated to do the following:

- Ensure they have uniforms and gloves
- Ensure they have insurance
- Ensure that the treatment of such persons is in compliance with the U.P. Labour Department's rules.

Furthermore, the contractor is required to pay the GMC Rs. 180,000 annually, of which, the contract states, he has already paid Rs. 50,000. There is no mention that Qureshi has the right to collect monetary payments of any sort from waste pickers.

What are we to make of the contract? Could it have really been issued, as the municipal commissioner repeatedly emphasized, for the benefit of the waste pickers? Two aspects of the document are striking: first, there is a recorded payment the contractor must make to the GMC, making it a beneficiary in this arrangement; second, there is no means of recording the compliance on other requirements, such as those related to workers' benefits. Notably, the agreement provides no indication how the contractor proposes to generate income from waste. While, strictly speaking, municipalities are not obliged to know the operational details of a private contractor's "business model", due diligence and the fact that municipalities are public entities require that they understand it. Failure to do so, out of deliberate neglect or routine apathy, leaves open an interpretive "gray area"—with potentially adverse consequences for vulnerable populations, as the Ghaziabad case demonstrates.

When Chintan staff met officials of the GMC in April 2009, five months after the contract was approved, the GMC claimed that it did not have any documents related to the compliance of the contract, implying that implementation clauses not related to payments to the GMC were understood to be optional. Such lack of accountability would not have been the case had the waste pickers (described as "workers" [*shramik*] in the contract) been a central consideration for the municipality.

The math offers a third, useful perspective. A survey by Chintan in May 2009 revealed that approximately 7,000 waste pickers work in the Mohan Nagar zone of Ghaziabad. Most of them had been paying the contractor an average of Rs. 400 every month since the end of 2008 (some even claimed they were asked to pay Rs. 600). Based on discussions with waste pickers and scrap dealers, Chintan concluded that up to 20% of them had been able to resist the contractor's demand and had refused to pay, bringing the number of payers to 5,600. If accurate, the payment from this group to the contractor adds up to the tidy sum of Rs. 2,240,000 per month. In effect, contractors like Qureshi were able to mint money without any capital outlay or investment in infrastructure. A responsive municipal partnership is all that was required. Indeed, it was a win-win scenario for the GMC and the contractors. Qureshi, for example, was able to earn more than the entire amount he was obliged to pay to the GMC in a single month! If able to sustain his extortion scheme, Qureshi was in line to make Rs. 2.69 crores a year from waste pickers—or, 149 times the amount he was enjoined to pay the GMC as per the terms of the contract. From the vantage point of a waste picker, Qureshi stood to make over 900 times the annual earning of an average waste picker—for doing absolutely no work, or undertaking any entrepreneurial risk. Indeed, the economics are so absurd that one can only conclude GMC agreed to such a lopsided contract because of the considerable scope for graft (i.e., "under-the-table" payments).

There is little doubt that the GMC had come to realize the considerable market value of recyclable waste and tap it for surplus revenue. On paper at least, it had tried to be legally (and politically) correct in its approach, listing benefits that the contractor was obliged to provide to his "labor". The GMC was also legally correct in assuming that waste that is already in community bins or dumps (*dhalaos*) becomes the property of the municipality, giving it the right to contract out work that helps it meet the solid waste management standards of the country. But as noted earlier, while the GMC was the de jure 'owner' of waste disposed in *dhalaos*, customarily it was waste pickers who sifted recyclable materials from the garbage at considerable cost to themselves in terms of health, family, and foregone life opportunities. Their work was an economic service and ecological subsidy to the city, for which they were not compensated. In peremptorily annexing these customary rights from waste pickers, the GMC both effaced their historical labors and undercut their source of livelihood.

* * *

Every municipality is constituted by a specific legal act that delineates its rights and duties. The Municipal Corporation of Delhi (MCD) was constituted under the *Delhi Municipal Corporation Act, 1957.* The Act authorizes the MCD as the body responsible for daily cleaning of streets and the removal of rubbish and filth (Section 35). This 'rubbish' and 'filth', along with 'polluted and obnoxious matter' from general public latrines, urinals, and cesspools (Section 355) is designated as the 'property' of the corporation (Section 351) and can be stored in receptacles, depots, and places specified by the MCD commissioner (Section 352). It is the duty of owners and occupiers to collect and deposit rubbish and the like from premises in specified depots (Section 353); factories and workshops must obtain written permission to operate and to dispose their waste from the commissioner (Section 356). No rubbish will be allowed to stay for more than 24 hours other than in a receptacle approved by the commissioner (Section 357).

The New Delhi Municipal Council (NDMC) was constituted under a similar act, as was the Ghaziabad Municipal Corporation (GMC). The provisions of these municipal laws are important because they have deep implications for the emergence and viability of the 'informal sector'. Municipal laws operate as boundary markers, demarcating the 'formal' from the 'informal'. More precisely, they stage a continuum of 'informality' that dislodges the conventional tendency to view the 'formal' and 'informal' as substantively different domains or, indeed, the 'informal' as a realm of activities that lies outside the ambit of state legibility (Roy 2005). Effectively, then, municipal laws thrust the informal waste management sector into a gray zone, because, as previously noted, waste is not municipal property *until* it reaches a formal disposal point (such as the municipal bin or dump [*dhalao*]). Customarily, waste pickers have operated at the bin, treating it as a common resource; as well as before the disposal point (e.g., via door-to-door garbage collection), where they can better regulate their claims to waste and demand legality for their work.

Structurally, ongoing urban transformations have prompted the emergence of new forms of rule and resource allocation and sharpened struggles over 'the right to the city'. In India, initiatives such as the Jawaharlal Nehru National Urban Renewal Mission (JNNURM) have become the public face of the New Economic Policy (NEP) in urban areas. While it is too early to assess the net impact of JNNURM, it is increasingly clear that Indian cities have become battlegrounds around questions of 'the right to the city' (Mitchell 2003; Harvey 2008). Like Ghaziabad, contemporary Delhi too offers a window into the stark predicament of waste pickers. Delhi today has a sub-population of 150,000 to 200,000 informal sector waste pickers, who generate livelihoods by laboriously sequestering, sorting, and selling an array of recyclables found in the approximately 7,500 metric tons of garbage that the city generates every day. Their working conditions are often abject. Some, who are able to territorialize work and living spaces by warding off rival efforts to territorialize–either from other waste pickers or, more often, arms of state such as municipal bodies, urban development authorities, courts, and police—are able to store and sell, and occasionally become entrepreneurs who can take risks, make gains from spatial and temporal arbitrage, and accumulate. This line of social and economic mobility is now threatened by the privatization of urban infrastructure and services, a trend in which Delhi is actively participating.

To appreciate the human implications of this, it is necessary to understand how the informal recycling sector in Indian cities is structured. The structure takes the form of a pyramid, with individual waste pickers and scrap collectors at the base and large corporate re-processors perched at the apex. The waste pickers gather garbage from households and roadsides in designated areas, sometimes through internal negotiations of territory and, increasingly, on the basis of institutionalized arrangements with Residents' Welfare Associations (RWAs). They also engage in the "free" collection of scrap from municipal garbage bins and dumps (*dhalaos*), as well as municipal landfills. Between the scrap collectors and the re-processors are various other actors, mostly involved in trading. Marginally above waste pickers in the hierarchy of informal recyclers—and commonly risen from their ranks through small savings and painstaking investment in social infrastructure—are the itinerant buyers who purchase small quantities of scrap from households.

The shop of the middling junk dealer, or *kabari*, as he is locally known, is the cornerstone of the recycling system. Typically, it is a dingy, poorly lit, one-room establishment tucked away in a bylane in an old city neighborhood or in one of Delhi's several "urban villages". Like petty traders lower in the hierarchy, these larger scrap dealers are most often former waste pickers who have scraped their way up the commercial ladder by dint of toil, savings, bribes, opportunity, entrepreneurship, networks, and even violence.[2] It is every waste picker's dream to own a business, however small. The lesson for critics of contemporary urbanization is that the urban poor frequently view capitalist enterprise with a great deal more ambivalence. Waste pickers, for instance, experience capitalism's injustices—drudgery, exploitation, punishment—intimately, everyday. They can deliver razor-sharp critiques of it. Yet they also find, in its solvent energies, opportunities to dislodge sedimented social orders and fabricate a better life. Within this plebeian logic of urbanism, to own a *kabari*'s *dukaan* is to possess an engine of arbitrage: the node where "raw" waste is purchased, segregated, and stored, before being channeled into secondary circuits of value.

Soaring property values and creeping corporatization of waste management in metropolises like Delhi have exacted a toll on precisely this cornerstone of informal recycling. In the early 1990s, a *kabari* in Delhi had more space in which to operate, as well as more clients. And there were more *kabaris* in the center of the city, where the urban elite live and work. Today, most *kabaris* have been evicted from areas in the city's center. Where *kabaris* continue to operate, they do so under severe space constraints and average no more than seven waste pickers as clients. Although this means razor-thin profit margins, they are unable to recruit more clients. *Where is the space to store their goods*? The seductive logic of the 'rent gap' has convinced municipal authorities and real estate developers that land can be put to far more profitable uses. The potential displacement of *kabaris* and waste pickers from their livelihood catchments barely registers in their calculus. A November 2007 interview that the *McKinsey Quarterly* conducted with Rajiv Singh, CEO of DLF Corporation, India's biggest developer, is illustrative:

The Quarterly: Is the government doing enough now?

Rajiv Singh: I don't want to use the word government. Sometimes the government may announce an initiative and it's stayed by the courts. Or it's protested. I do not want to isolate the government or the courts; rather it is the system that just doesn't allow something to happen. The whole system was not and still is not geared to rapid provisioning of infrastructure. There's too much political freedom, too many legal rights, too much media.

By contrast, I was in Shanghai recently and one day passed a bunch of huts beside the road. The next day they were all gone. The third day there were a bunch of guys rolling out sod and planting trees. And on the fourth day they inaugurated a park.

This is Rajiv Singh's utopia. Let us say the obvious: Singh is dead wrong about "too many legal rights". Take Delhi's *kabaris*. In an era of openly partisan judicial activism by the Supreme Court of India, as well as the Delhi High Court, many *kabaris* have been branded as "illegal squatters" or "public nuisances". These legal judgments willfully forget the repeated neglect of Delhi's waste recycling needs in its Master Plan documents. Rather than viewing *kabaris* and waste pickers as political subjects with claims on the city's amenities and spaces, or even as economic service providers, judges and planners have instead come to see them as disruptions to "public order"—a view that is often anchored in the crudest of bourgeois aesthetics, as the minutes of court rulings reveal.[3] In this judicial logic, which complements other, older, tactics of spatial control—namely, municipal ordinances and zoning laws—certain populations and spaces must be, as the writer-activist Dunu Roy puts it, "structurally adjusted" in order to promote the well-being and security of lives that matter.

* * *

In the 1990s, India's urban bourgeoisie began to protest the inadequacy of municipal waste collection and advocate for better waste management with upgraded technologies, more in keeping with a 'modern' city. These protests were registered via a legal device known as Public Interest Litigation (PIL) that allowed citizens to challenge local, state, and federal legislations in court in the name of "public interest".

Many of the early PILs were environmental challenges, and two in 1996 pertained directly to the issue of solid waste—*B. L. Wadhera v. the Union of India and Others* (1996) and *Almitra Patel v. the Union of India and Others* (1996). In *Wadhera v. the Union of India*, the plaintiff, Dr. Wadhera, contended "the MCD and the NDMC had been totally remiss in the performance of their statutory duties to scavenge and clean Delhi city, as it was their mandatory duty to collect and dispose of the garbage/waste generated from various sources in the city." The plaintiff also argued "there were inadequate facilities to dispose of hospital wastes and only a handful of hospitals had incinerators to burn the hospital wastes." Lastly, the plaintiff claimed that his "constitutional rights guaranteed under Articles 21, 48A and 51A(g), which place responsibility on the state to provide for protection and improvement of the environment were also being violated."

Meanwhile, Almitra Patel, a retired U.S.-educated engineer running a family-owned business in Bangalore, explained her decision to go to court as follows:

> Frogs sang in the twilight on our scenic country road until 1991, when Bangalore City Corporation began daily dumping truckloads of city garbage on both sides of the road and into the marshes and stream banks. That led me on a long and lonely path, via 2 years of chasing Govt files to secure dumpsites for Bangalore, and two Clean India Campaigns led by Capt. Velu of EXNORA in 1994 and 1995, during and after which I have personally visited 86 Indian cities to date and their open dumpsites (or lack of them). What we saw, and the urging of fellow INTACH Conveners, led me to file a PIL (Public Interest Litigation) to protect India's peri-urban soil and water and the health of its urban citizens through hygienic practices for waste management, processing and disposal.

The Wadhera petition led to the enactment of the Bio-Medical Waste (Management and Handling) Rules, 1998. It also produced several dramatic moments in court, when top-level functionaries were summoned to explain the non-performance of their municipalities. Such public humiliation of municipal officials had a salutary effect: it drew unwelcome attention to under-performance by public bodies (an issue of persistent concern at a time when India was unrolling its New Economic Policy) and, by the same token, ratcheted pressure on Delhi's municipalities to find new answers to the city's compounding waste. Privatization of waste handling became a real possibility for the first time.

In the meantime, *Almitra Patel v. the Union of India* had resulted in the Solid Waste (Management and Handling) Rules, 2000—the first set of rules ever on solid waste, and the most widely used and important ones to date. The Solid Waste Rules emphasize the need for recycling. However, they do not acknowledge the right to livelihood of informal sector recycling workers anywhere in their mandate. Nor, indeed, did Patel press to acknowledge the informal sector's importance to urban solid waste management, although the conclusion of her Supreme Court hearings and the date when the Rules came into effect were marked by a five-year interregnum. Instead, she, like other well-intended persons in positions of influence, underplayed the relevance of informal sector recyclers relevant to the task of urban waste management. This policy of neglect by state and civil society actors toward informal sector recyclers has resulted in a farcical situation where the latter, having waited years for official recognition of their livelihood rights, were finally granted it—through the National Environment Policy of 2006, under the sub-theme of "soil pollution"! The 2006 policy states: "Give legal recognition to, and strengthen the informal sector systems of collection and recycling of various materials. In particular enhance their access to institutional finance and relevant technologies." The recognition, unfortunately, has amounted to little. Since the legal weight of legislation exceeds that of a policy, it is the law—the Solid Waste Rules, 2000—that has remained etched in municipal memory and become the regulative ideal.

In short, the absence of any reference to the informal recycling sector in the court's judgment in *Almitra Patel v. the Union of India* has had the tragic effect of effacing the contributions of waste pickers to the urban economy and environment and, by extension, consideration in future policy debates. But there was another, more dangerous, outcome that threatened not just the livelihoods of waste pickers, but their access to living space within the city as well. One of the judges in the Almitra Patel PIL, during a hearing that referred to Delhi as India's showpiece, declared that "rewarding an encroacher on public land with a free site is like giving a reward to a pickpocket for stealing." Given Delhi's chronic—and according to some, deliberate—undersupply of low-cost housing (Verma 2003), combined with unaffordable rents in authorized settlements, this often leaves its urban poor, including its army of waste pickers, no option but to squat on public land or rent a sliver of space in unauthorized slums from slumlords. The judge's unwarranted observation in *Almitra Patel v. the Union of India* speaks to the prejudicial workings of judicial activism in advancing an anti-poor agenda in Delhi (Baviskar 2003; Batra 2008; Ghertner 2008).

The process envisions a 'clean and green city' for those propertied citizens who are not squatters. Thus, the 2021 Master Plan for Delhi (hereafter, MPD 2021) calls for a 'slumless' city—as part of a vision to transform Delhi into "a global metropolis and a world-class city, where all the people would be engaged in productive work with a better quality of life, living in a sustainable environment" (Puri 2007, 1). Over 40% of the city's residents, who live in slums, are effectively excluded from this frame of reference. 'Bourgeois environmentalism' criminalizes Delhi's urban poor—its unwanted inhabitants—in the name of cleaning the city of unwanted effluents, industries, and built structures. Within this anti-poor agenda, waste recyclers have been forced to bear the brunt of injustice twice over: first as workers, whose contributions to the city are devalorized; and second, as a lower rung of 'citizens' whose political claims to the city are suppressed in favor of upper-class demands.

This class bias has been reinforced by various judicial and municipal orders that have resulted in multiple episodes of mass demolition from 1990 onward as part of "slum clearance" drives. And although it is estimated that nearly 100,000 houses were destroyed between 1990 and 2007, fewer than 25% of those evicted in the later phases have received alternate plots of land (Bhan 2009). Most of them were 20 to 30 kilometers away from their places of work. This not only made it difficult for relocated persons to stay employed but, in fact, created a perverse incentive to be homeless as a way of remaining in the city and preserving a 'survival niche' that was frequently the culmination of arduous labor and hardship. Waste pickers and itinerant buyers, whose work is strictly territorial, were among those whose livelihoods were most jeopardized by slum demolition and relocation.

To add to the burden of some, the process of relocation has been geographically uneven. Of the 14 relocation sites, at least two—Bhalsawa and Bawana—are sites of an existing and proposed landfill, respectively. Global data show that even the best landfills are engineered to be functional for a finite period, typically 50 years. They leak—producing leachate that severely contaminates the groundwater. The landfill at Bhalsawa is not an engineered one. It is in fact no more than a dump. Studies have shown that the groundwater there is severely contaminated. Bawana, on the other hand, is the main relocation site for a slew of small industries that were forced out of Delhi's residential zones at the *fin de millennium* by judicial orders, on grounds that they posed a pollution hazard to area residents. Such concerns of exposure to pollution have apparently not figured in the decision of municipal authorities to site the slum relocation area near an industrial zone with potentially harmful levels of environmental toxicity—a move that is likely to intensify the health burdens of the resettled poor, and adversely affect their capacities to earn and lead productive lives. Studies investigating morbidity rates and rates of birth defects around landfill sites in Europe indicate that living near landfills may lead to higher incidence of, both, illness among children (sore throats, severe headaches, nose-bleeds, and fatigue), as well as mothers giving birth to babies with serious birth defects such as spina bifida and heart malformations. Proximity of residence to landfills has also been associated with higher miscarriage and cancer rates. In short, relocation can have a profound inter-generational impact. That Delhi's planners are willing to let its poor residents bear a disproportionate share of the city's toxic burden speaks to the differential value of life and hierarchy of citizenship that informs the middle-class urbanism reshaping contemporary Delhi.

* * *

The war against Delhi's poor has been conducted on other fronts as well, and frequently by resort to PILs. Consider, for example, the 2006 order by the Supreme Court of India, sealing a wide range of commercial establishments located in residential areas. The judicial order preempted the 2021 Delhi Master Plan that had not yet come into effect (in part because the previous bi-decadal 2001 Master Plan was belatedly implemented in 1990, instead of 1981 as originally scheduled). The city had changed enormously in the interim, and a combination of new economic forces and large capital inflows had radically transformed the nature of urban consumption. Several shops and commercial enterprises had arisen to cater to the steep increase in disposable income among the city's rich and middle classes. Since they were not anticipated or sanctioned by the existing 2001 Master Plan they were all, technically, illegal. So were many small shops and roadside shacks, set up to cater to the urban poor who serviced these areas. By late 2006, over 13,000 commercial units were sealed. Subsequently, about 1,500 areas and wider roads were declared exempt from demolition. Large shops in de-notified areas were told they could continue to function. To enable predominantly middle-class residents to obtain daily household items in the proximity of their neighborhoods, the MCD exempted a special list of 24 'essential services' (including ATMs) from demolition. Consistent with the anti-poor agenda, *kabari godams* (recycling shops-cum-storage facilities) operating in residential areas were absent from the list of 24. In a punitive move, they were also prohibited from areas designated as 'mixed zone' in the Master Plan.

To return, then, to PILs: one of their most significant effects was to push municipalities to re-examine their delivery mechanisms. Delhi's municipal bodies concluded that only segments of the private sector, with large capital outlays at their disposal, were in a position to meet the delivery goals mandated in judicial orders. Capital requirements that were stipulated in eligibility criteria for municipal waste management contracts sparked a form of capital-intensive privatization that excluded lesser private entrepreneurs from the fiscal concessions granted by Delhi's municipalities as part of Public-Private Partnerships (PPP), an institutional form that has become the dominant vehicle for neoliberal urban reform the world over. Today, three large corporations—Delhi Waste Management (DWM), AG Enviro Infra Projects, and Metro Waste Handling Pvt. Ltd.—have contracts to collect garbage from municipal *dhalaos* and neighborhood collection points for transport to landfills. The implications of privatization are not lost on waste pickers. They have an acute understanding of the altered economic and political landscape. The views of a subset of waste pickers associated with Chintan, who were interviewed in February 2008 as part of an assessment to gauge their most pressing concerns, are instructive:

Krishna Das: "When private companies have entered [the municipal solid waste sector] after using so much money and pull, they aren't simply going to go away. We need to start talking about what we will do to oppose them."

Manwara Begum: "Today private companies have installed two-two [*do-do*] bins for waste [at neighborhood dumps], but they are too large and it's difficult for us to sort *maal* [saleable recyclables] in them. Men can take recyclables out of them, but women can't."

Nazir: "Back in 2000 the police used to beat up, but today we work with freedom. But we aren't able to save any money. Private companies have wreaked damage. There is no benefit [to waste pickers], the waste is neither properly segregated nor can *kabari bhais* extract any *maal* from the waste. Today private companies know that waste pickers are organized, so they don't say anything to us. But tomorrow if [an organization like] Chintan ceases to exist they will physically drive us out. We should not allow this to happen and instead plan ahead. We should call a meeting with MCD, NDMC, NGOs and the government, where we should raise the issue of a place to live . . . tell them how much [money] our work saves them and [ask why] in return you want to drive us out the city? We are constantly threatened [with eviction], and our *jhuggis* [hutments] are demolished. We must have a place to live in Delhi and we will have to raise this demand with the government in large numbers, otherwise no one will listen to us."

Ajmuddin: "Previously households whose waste we collected never gave us money [the reference is to a monthly tipping fee for the service provided], but now even those people have started to give us money. RWAs should provide living space inside their colonies to those who do door-to-door collection [of their daily household waste]."

As we saw, privatization has proceeded differently in neighboring Ghaziabad. The GMC's agreement with contractors like Chand Qureshi has put the city's waste pickers in a tenuous position. The legal contract notes the duties of the contractor to his "workers" (*shramik*), but Qureshi has no workers because he employs none and does nothing with the waste itself. Nevertheless, Qureshi has claimed all waste pickers as his "workers" in order to justify his extortion as collection of welfare dues from employees even as, in practice, he disavows being an employer who is obligated to discharge certain duties toward his workers. This Kafkaesque arrangement works because contractual enforcement by the municipality is (intentionally or unintentionally) lax, and the legal language is gray. Qureshi is spared the cost of contributing to workers' social security, and the effort of managing an enterprise with mandated labor registers.

So, why didn't Qureshi simply open up a recycling warehouse to segregate and store the garbage he paid GMC to own? There may be two reasons. First, although recycling waste in India is profitable, it involves complicated business transactions based on kinship networks, regional alliances, relations of patronage, religion, location in the city, and so on. Second, by setting up an actual business—which would have required an outlay of capital—Qureshi would have been exposed to price fluctuations in the scrap trade, non-payments by other dealers, and several management issues that would have to be routinely confronted.

As mentioned earlier, a typical *kabari* shop has about seven clients (waste pickers) who sell to it regularly. The rental for such a shop, often operated illegally, averages Rs. 8,000 per month. This is in addition to the monthly bribes to police and municipal field staff to look the other way. Payments to laborers who work in the shop can also be substantial: even if a shop has only five workers, one of them a supervisor, the labor bill runs at least Rs. 20,000 per month. Other costs—a few hours of electricity, water, tea, upkeep of the shop, and so on—total roughly Rs. 5,000 each month. In addition, the shop's proprietor must tally the opportunity costs of his time and of participating family members. In short, if Qureshi had used his ownership of the waste to set up a legitimate business enterprise, he would have incurred operating expenses of at least Rs. 33,000 per month. Based on the average turnover at prevailing scrap prices, he would have likely earned a profit of no more than Rs. 12,000 to Rs. 15,000 each month, and less during the monsoon. Compare this to his monthly earning of Rs. 2,240,000 from extortion! Qureshi judged, correctly, that taxing existing recyclers was a more lucrative business proposition than trying to earn by actually collecting, segregating, and trading waste. Like mafiosos elsewhere, he was able to pervert private enterprise in order to make extra-legal, extra-normal income.

The GMC's contract with Chand Qureshi underwrites a privatization model that is substantially different from the model of privatization implemented in adjoining Delhi. There, court rulings driven by PILs set the stage for its municipalities to transfer solid waste management to large corporations rather than to small private contractors. By 2005, 6 of 13 zones in MCD's jurisdiction—accounting for almost 50% of the municipality's jurisdiction—had already converted to privatized collection and transportation of waste. Contracts were handed out, as mentioned, to three companies: Delhi Waste Management, AG Enviro Infra Projects, and

Metro Waste Handling Pvt. Ltd. All are Indian firms, with DWM and AG Enviro created as consortiums. None had substantial prior experience in solid waste management or recycling. But corporate privatization appealed to Delhi's municipal decision makers because it followed dominant practice in Western countries and promised to deliver efficiencies from scale economies. Disregarded, indeed de-valorized, were existing informal recycling enterprises that were cost-effective engines of employment for the urban poor, and remarkably efficient in terms of waste recovery. This disregard was critical in paving the way for corporations to enter waste management.

The municipal contract with large private companies requires them to gather waste from neighborhood collection points and transport it to landfills. Hired after an (ostensibly fair) international bidding process, their contracts also include the Ownership and Control of Recyclable Wastes (Article 5.15 of the Contract) and Control and Rights over the Dhalao Space, including advertising rights. The agreement, in essence, awards corporate contractors three sources of revenue: the waste matter itself, the bin or neighborhood dump space, and municipal payments for collection and transportation of garbage. Delhi's corporate form of privatization has aggravated injustices in numerous ways (in the words of one impacted waste picker, "Privatization is a form of death for us").

Widespread Loss of Livelihoods

Initial assessments indicate widespread displacement of waste pickers and junk-dealers in MCD zones where waste collection has been privatized. For instance, Chintan's survey of informal recyclers in R. K. Puram, a residential area now under Delhi Waste Management's mandate, painted a troubling scenario:

Privatization in the MCD area has resulted in approximately 50% of the waste pickers losing their jobs or experiencing a reduction in income. Many went to nearby areas not yet privatized, but in the process they have impacted the earnings of waste pickers in these areas, often culminating in conflict. The impact on the fabric of community has been no less damaging. Prior to privatization, several waste pickers used both their informally demarcated territory, and the *dhalao* space, to earn a living. While some picked waste in the morning, others would sit at a bin for a fixed number of hours. The privatized system did away with this informal social sharing, replacing it with a hired bin guide who is responsible for maintaining the *dhalao* space. The net result has been that, in any given area, fewer people earn from the same volume of waste. Worse still, because being a bin guide implies inflexible hours, most women are unable to try for this job, as they have to juggle household work with waste picking. Privatization has therefore had added negatively impacts on women waste pickers.

Table 6.2 Impact of Privatization on Informal Recyclers in Delhi's MCD Zones

	Before	*After*
A.	Self-employed waste pickers were able to use waste to sustain livelihoods	Waste pickers no longer have access to dry waste, the primary source of recycling income, resulting in loss of livelihoods
B.	Waste pickers identified as a community and would share waste in the dhalao in order to generate incomes	Only one waste picker gets a lowly paid job from DWM, to guard and clean the dhalao
C.	Work was hazardous	Work continues to be hazardous, and picking waste from dhalaos has been criminalized
D.	Waste pickers used to share the dhalao space to segregate waste	Waste pickers are no longer allowed to use dhalaos for segregation of waste, hence face new conflicts and hardships
E.	Entrepreneurial waste pickers were able to set up shop, become junk dealers, and buy locally from waste pickers—enabling livelihoods for many	Junk dealers' operations have been severely jeopardized

Poorer Segregation

Privatization has also led to poorer segregation of municipal solid waste. Whereas waste pickers gather and segregate 15% to 59% of the waste, depending on their area of operation, municipal contracts allow private companies to segregate at much lower levels. Thus, in the eight year of their contract the private operator is only required to segregate 20% of the waste. Privatization of waste collection has aggravated a long-standing problem faced by Delhi's informal sector waste pickers: a space to efficiently segregate their laboriously gathered waste. Previously, many used the *dhalao* as a space to segregate. Although they were occasionally harassed by municipal field staff and beat cops, the situation appears to have worsened after privatization. Many pickers have begun to complain that the privately employed bin guide, on orders from management, no longer permits them to segregate their own waste in the bin area; nor to throw post-segregation waste remains into the *dhalao*. As such, they are forced to travel longer distances to sift and throw household waste. Furthermore, as private contractors have begun to sell valuable waste directly to the recycling factories or large dealers, a legion of petty scrap dealers now find themselves out of business.

Cost Savings at a Cost

At first glance, privatization appears to be yielding significant savings in transportation costs for the MCD. Estimates indicate that the cost per landfill trip per truck was approximately U.S. $3.78 for private companies, as contrasted to U.S. $12.6 for MCD-operated trucks and U.S. $17.64 for NDMC-operated trucks. Greater efficiency and stricter monitoring are possible reasons for these savings; but so too, it appears, is the ability of waste management companies to exploit workers by paying them below-minimum wages. A recent World Bank study suggests that the cost differential between private and municipal entities is an India-wide phenomenon, and that the difference can be in the range of 20% to 40%.[4] Comparing the costs of waste collection and transportation in 10 towns in the southern Indian state of Karnataka, the report suggests a trend of cost reduction across the board. However, the report also notes that "One of the reasons for the relatively lower costs incurred by the contractor is quoted as differential wages, particularly when private contractors tend to pay lower than minimum wages to their sanitary workers." Local municipal and government authorities, on the other hand, cannot indulge in such labor practices and therefore are likely to incur much higher costs for the same tasks performed by an equal number of workers.

* * *

At the heart of the privatization controversy, then, is a crucial political and legal issue: *Who controls the right to waste?*

Driven by this understanding, advocacy groups across the country are collaborating with impacted waste pickers and junk dealers to produce a charter of demands that seeks to restore control over waste to informal recyclers. The charter stems from a premise that formal ownership of waste is essential to the livelihoods of informal sector workers and that waste pickers must be able to determine what to do with the waste if they are to add value to it. Essential to the stance is the claim that the informal sector has also operated as a conglomeration of private actors, who harnessed their labor, skills, entrepreneurship, and social networks to provide private waste management services to the city, long before Delhi embraced privatization as a paradigm shift. Call it 'informal privatization', 'petty privatization', or 'privatization-from-below'. The basic argument remains unaltered: that what is new about contemporary Delhi is not the idea of privatized waste handling but rather the kind of privatization, requiring large capital outlays, that has found favor with municipal authorities. This 'privatization-from-above', according to the restorative charter of demands, unjustly disqualifies other existing private entities, able to offer different forms of equity (such as knowledge and social networks), from managing Delhi's waste.

A significant element in the opposition to corporate privatization is the risk posed to informal recyclers: in shrinking or outright eliminating their painfully improvised survival niches in the city and transforming them from petty entrepreneurs, with some dignity of work, into daily wagers or, sporadically, into salaried employees of waste management companies, afforded neither independence of work nor meaningful economic security. Tellingly, while Delhi's municipalities have consistently resisted granting the city's *kabaris* designated spaces to segregate and store waste, citing land shortage, the MCD was quick to allocate land to private waste management companies for the purpose of separating and warehousing stocks of recyclable waste. Such policy decisions reveal the institutionalized bias of urban planners against the informal sector, and the reason why they have never bothered to incorporate them in municipal waste-handling solutions.

The competing ideas of control, employment, and entrepreneurship described earlier draw attention to the manner in which the political rights and economic contributions of the poor are slighted by policymakers and affluent residents who have embraced the tenets of 'urban entrepreneurialism'. The MCD's response to these criticisms has been to point out that it has, in fact, tried to be inclusive of the informal sector by inserting a series of clauses in its contracts with private concessionaires:

- Article 5.19t: Endeavour to employ the informal Municipal Solid Waste collectors within the concession area to carry out the work of collection and segregation of MSW, in accordance with this agreement and applicable law.
- Article 6: MCD Obligations: Give all assistance to the concessionaire to employ the existing informal Municipal Solid Waste collectors including rag pickers and assist the concessionaire in solving issues arising from the redeployment and employment of such waste collectors by the concessionaire.

It is reasonable to assume that the MCD is aware of the work—and the specificity of work—of informal recyclers, since it has listed them by name in the contract. Yet, the clauses manage to relegate waste pickers to the status of generic laborers, merely another segment in Delhi's pool of surplus labor, rather than providing ways for informal recyclers to harness their intimate knowledge of materials and thereby add value to waste.

The alternative charter of demands, by contrast, seeks control by informal recyclers over, both, space and the flow of materials. In principle, this could co-exist with privatization of collection from central points for transport to landfills—without requiring transfer of control over materials and bin spaces to corporate entities. The latter could continue to receive payments for waste transported and income from advertisements on the walls of the *dhalaos*. The informal sector has pressed its demands through dialogue with municipal authorities, street protests, and a media campaign. Its main points have been as follows:

A) Renegotiate the contract

- Article 5.15, regarding sale/distribution of recyclable substances must be scrapped. All rights to dry, recyclable waste as enumerate in the list of 40 items in the contract must belong to the city's waste pickers as a matter of right.

- The contractor must not be given the rights over *dhalaos*, but should be able to collect waste at fixed times from it. Waste pickers must be allowed to use *dhalaos* to segregate waste.
- Additionally, large *dhalaos* that are underused must be assigned to junk dealers to carry out their business. A case-by-case decision must be undertaken in every single zone.
- As long as contractors are paid on the basis of low segregation rates and total weight alone, there will be no incentive for them to work with waste pickers. The contractor must be paid on the basis of segregated wet waste alone, and should not have rights over dry waste.

B) Recognize organized waste pickers

- Many waste pickers in Delhi have already organized themselves directly and indirectly. Grant them formal recognition and allow them to handle waste until the stage where it is ready for transportation to landfills.
- Encourage waste transportation efforts by waste pickers and other 'bottom-of-pile' actors by legalizing their forms of transportation.

C) Recognize and facilitate junk dealers

- Junk dealers' contribution to saving waste from landfills should be recognized. They must be given both space and licenses to operate in a formal manner.

D) Incorporate development and social components into waste management

- All solid waste management policies must be examined within the context of poverty reduction. India has 700 million people who live on incomes under U.S. $2 per day and 267 million who live under U.S. $1 per day. Approximately 3 out of every 10 Indians are poor.[5] Unfortunately, privatization of waste in Delhi is threatening to force over 100,000 urban poor into dire poverty.

In short, the alternative model of 'privatization-from-below' proposed by the informal sector recognizes waste as a source of income and wealth, not merely for large corporate entities, but as a means for large-scale poverty alleviation in cities that has the added benefit of building urban environmental sustainability.

* * *

Despite the harm it has inflicted upon informal waste recyclers, and therefore the city, privatization in Delhi had a clear objective: to collect more waste and transport it to landfills. But Delhi is, of course, self-consciously attempting to fabricate itself as a "world class city". By comparison, Ghaziabad's municipal corporation has seemed to be devoid of specific plans. The GMC's decision to privatize was not prompted by an imperative to handle the city's solid waste better. In fact, formal "privatization" did not alter waste collection operations in the city at all, although it further impoverished an already poor population of informal recyclers. Privatization, it appears, was merely a garb for extracting surplus revenue, both, legally and illegally.

Earlier, we noted how formal acknowledgment of the services of waste pickers had to wait until the release of the National Environment Policy in 2006. While such policies do not serve as municipal guidelines, they can nevertheless be valuable in confronting bureaucrats. In the Qureshi case, the policy's endorsement of waste pickers was used in discussions with the GMC to nullify the secondary order endorsing the contractor's authority to collect money from waste pickers. But matters did not end there. Soon after, waste pickers had to organize again to battle another similar contract awarded by GMC, this time in Ghaziabad's City Zone. The repetition of events unexpected, since the Municipal Commissioner had previously claimed that he understood the gravity of the matter and had empathy for the informal sector's place in the law, and that the GMC would support waste pickers to upgrade their livelihoods. Chintan even submitted a proposal on behalf of the waste pickers that would help to improve their prospects. However, the commissioner failed to communicate with waste pickers thereafter and refused all communication with Chintan. Instead, his subordinates met with media investigating the contract to insist that it was Chintan, not the contractors, which was corrupt and demanding money from waste pickers. "You also take money from these people. You are upset that you aren't able to charge the same amounts as these [other] people, that's all," a medical officer employed by GMC accused one of the authors.

The contract for Ghaziabad's City Zone was awarded to someone other than Qureshi, but it is widely believed that he was a relative. This time too, some of the accused were detained after Chintan and the waste pickers lodged complaints with the police. The accused called up officials in the GMC and, by the evening, GMC had dispatched a letter to the police. The letter (translated from Hindi) read: "We wish to inform you that Mohd. Zahid Qureshi . . . has been contracted to pick out the cardboard, plastic etc. from the waste. It may also be mentioned that the contracted firm has full rights to charge external labor money for its own welfare." Upon receipt of this astonishing letter, the police let the accused off. The lawyer for the accused called up one of the authors and insisted on a meeting "to settle the problem." He firmly insisted: "I will come to meet you, why not? I want to honor you [*main aapko sammanit karoonga*]. We must talk." As he was finishing, he let it slip that he was a politician affiliated to a major political party.

For the time being, Ghaziabad's waste pickers are organized and—with the exception of a few who fear being beaten up—are collectively refusing to pay the contractors. The police have summoned the waste pickers and Chintan to make statements, but they have also tried to foist a settlement each time. Ghaziabad's waste privatization strategy veers perilously close to legalized extortion. Instead of instituting policies that could help the poor to emerge from poverty, the city government has instead constructed a scenario where the poor are unable to consolidate their earnings or savings. The fight for a just and sustainable livelihood is ongoing, but it is also an everyday struggle for safety and survival.

Although the informal recycling sector has been disenfranchised by a variety of formal maneuvers all across India, it has tried to defend or recover its spaces of work. In Delhi, waste pickers are learning to tactically represent themselves not just as demanders of rights but also as service providers, as a means of staking their legitimate presence in the city. Although such tactics are consistently able to ensure legitimacy, livelihoods, or a survival space, it is nevertheless emerging as a key approach, because it comports with, and yet adroitly subverts, the new language of the ordered city: the language of 'urban entrepreneuralism'. Ghaziabad's waste pickers, by contrast, are only just learning to organize around issues and preparing for a prolonged battle.

* * *

Waste picking and other informal sector livelihoods such as vending and street hawking are often stigmatized within urban policy. Reluctant to acknowledge these as essential services that enable the urban economy and the lifestyles that the urban elite demand, municipal authorities and urban policymakers often display visceral mistrust of the urban poor who engage in these activities. The global trend toward privatization and formalization of informal sector activities, in which the cities of Delhi and Ghaziabad are active participants, is misguided for a number of reasons, not the least because it (a) fails to confront the issue of employment generation and urban poverty; (b) blithely ignores the fact that the urban poor—despite their precarious access to employment and housing—have equal right to make claims on city resources as the urban elite; and (c) disregards the fact that they are economic actors and entrepreneurs, whose work sustains the urban economy in critical ways.

Take garbage: it is something every city in the world produces everyday. A large portion of this waste is recycled with startling efficiency by the armies of waste collectors who rove city streets. In Delhi alone there are at least 150,000 informal recyclers, some desperately poor. Their working conditions are often abject, but improvement demands that their labor and contributions to urban economy and ecology be recognized and legitimized. Unless policymakers take measures to safeguard their work, they will lose their livelihoods to corporations. They will also continue to work under hazardous conditions, with illness as a hallmark of their work.

Delhi's new Master Plan 2021 foresees Delhi as "a global metropolis and a world-class city."[6] This theme is constantly broadcast in various initiatives undertaken by the Government of Delhi: whether infrastructural development, transportation planning, street and park beautification programs, tree planting, slum demolitions, child welfare schemes, public-private partnerships, or privatization of waste management.[7] Delhi's status as host to the 2010 Commonwealth Games—a project that has sparked enormous changes and disruptions in the city—is the iconic symbol of Delhi's lofty aspirations.

As Delhi pursues these objectives, the focus of government is resolutely on the 'formal' sector economy, and improving the conditions of possibility of its growth. The formal sector is seen as the repository of skills that constitute the city's stock of "human capital"; it is the site of foreign direct investment and innovation; it is the engine of entrepreneurship, productivity, and employment growth; economic transactions in the formal sector are, for the most part, legal and hence taxable; corporate taxes are a source of revenue for the city, as are property taxes on business holdings and private real-estate investments by formal sector employees; the surging incomes of formal sector employees translate into demand for income-elastic goods that generate sales taxes, VAT, and income and employment in the urban retail sector; formal sector employees channel income surpluses into savings and investment. In short, the formal sector commands privilege in urban policy and planning circles as the engine that drives production and consumption and ensures the government its cash flow.

The 'informal' economy—a legal artifact of the state—is treated as a stepchild: sometimes used, often abused. It can't be excised from the city, so it must be restrained. City governments have an built-in prejudice against the informal sector. From the vantage point of government, employers in the informal sector are difficult (sometimes impossible) to identify, and since most transactions within the informal sector occur via verbal arrangement and in cash, they are invisible in government accounts. They yield little or no tax revenues for government coffers. Furthermore, most workers in the informal economy are regarded as formally unskilled. They don't possess recognizable forms of "human capital". They tend to be poor, hence are thought to engage in income-inelastic forms of consumption that contribute little to the urban retail economy. They save little and invest even less. The informal sectoı may underwrite petty rent seeking and corruption by city councilors, lower-level bureaucrats, and police, but it does not generate significant tax income for the city. Most policymakers believe that informal sector activities exhibit low economic productivity and show scant evidence of economic entrepreneurship. Many workers and business owners in the informal sector reside in unauthorized settlements and slums and, in the view of urban planners and municipal authorities, "free ride" on urban infrastructure such as electricity, water, roads, and sanitation services. High incidence of nonpayment for these services burdens the city's ability to adequately provision the formal economy.[8] But rarely do cities acknowledge that chronic undersupply of low-cost housing over several decades has contributed in profound ways to the proliferation of unauthorized dwellings, shanties, and encroachments in urban areas. In short, an array of preconceptions about the informal economy—some partly true, others outright false—color the views of urban policymakers and planners. Such preconceptions make it difficult to convince urban decision makers about the profound economic value of informal sector activities such as waste picking.

Regrettably, there are very few studies that analyze (far less measure) the multi-faceted contributions of informal sectors to city economies. What needs to be reiterated here is not only the significant employment impact of urban informal sector economies but also their dense inter-linkages with formal sector economies within cities. A vast menagerie of production inputs and consumption goods utilized by the formal sector and its employees are manufactured by the informal sector: everything from electric cables and conductors to portable fans, paints, industrial solvents, household and office furniture, storage devices, automobile accessories, carpets, clothing items, leather goods, and so on. The informal sector also provides a compendium of services that enable formal sector employees to enjoy their desired quality of life: the vegetable vendor, a cell-phone call away, who delivers to the door; the store clerk, who mans the local grocery store; the cycle cart puller, who delivers a newly purchased refrigerator or sofa to the buyer's doorstep; the construction laborers, who are hired by contractors to pave roads or build additions to Delhi's posh residences; the plumber, who is ready at hand to clear a clogged drain; the electrician, who repairs damaged electrical fixtures; the grocer, who provides home delivery on bulk orders of foods and toiletries; the maid, who comes to wash clothes; the neighborhood *presswala*, who irons these clothes; and the waste picker, who goes door-to-door everyday to collect household garbage. In short, the well-being of the formal sector economy and its employees is critically dependent on goods and services provided by the informal sector.

Equally though, the well-being of informal economies is positively correlated with the well-being of formal economies. A decline in the consumption power of the formal sector, say due to recession, will negatively impact incomes in the informal economy. But it may also cause the informal economy to *expand* as pinched formal sector employers attempt to avoid taxes and costly regulations by increasingly resorting to unrecorded transactions and unemployed formal sector workers turn to informal forms of work for sustenance.[9] In short, the two parts of the urban economy, although frequently (and unjustifiably) treated as discrete domains by urban policymakers and planners, exist in a relationship of interdependence.[10]

Our chapter has examined the nature of this interdependence between Delhi's informal and formal economies against the backdrop of India's New Economic Policy and the trend toward privatization and formalization of solid waste management—a move that jeopardizes the future livelihoods of Delhi's informal sector waste collectors and foregrounds profound questions of social justice. Rather than strike a defeatist note, we have instead attempted to emphasize the tenacity, and organizational will, of waste pickers, their efforts to recast their labor as an economic service and ecological subsidy to the city, and their struggles over the 'right to ownership of waste' as a way to make broad-ranging claims on the city: from the right to secure habitation, to the right to municipal services, to the right to sustainable livelihoods, to the right of their children to education—in short *the right to the city as right to anticipate a future*, like its more privileged residents.

ACKNOWLEDGMENTS

Our utmost thanks to the many waste recyclers in Bhopura and the following Chintan staff members, who participated in the Ghaziabad events: Prakash Shukla, Dinesh Kumar, Suraj Kumar, Anupama Pandey, Malati Gadgil, Jai Prakash Chaudhury, and Dhanraj. Thanks as well to Dick Peet for his searing comments (no other description for it!) on an earlier version of this chapter.

NOTES

1. In the absence of reliable data from the GMC we must infer this, first, from trends in neighboring Delhi, where the quantity of solid waste generated increased 128% over a 15-year period, from 3,500 tons per day in 1994 to 8000 tons per day in 2009; and second, from the growing population of waste pickers in Ghaziabad.
2. A 2003 in-house survey of *kabariwalas* by Chintan revealed that 78% of them began their careers as waste pickers.
3. Gautam Bhan, a PhD student in urban planning at the University of California, Berkeley, is writing a dissertation on the sources of judicial reasoning by judges in Indian courts. He gave one of the authors of this chapter an example of how such reasoning might proceed (and we paraphrase): "*Mein subah gadi mein jaa raha tha, raste par dekhe yeh kabadi apna maal phelaye huye baithe hain, kisi ki phikar nahin* . . ." ("I was out in my car this morning, I saw a junk-dealer with his stuff spread out on the road, unmindful of the inconvenience he was causing . . .").
4. The World Bank (2006).
5. As per the most recent World Bank and National Poverty Line data.
6. Ministry of Urban Development (Delhi Division), Notification, New Delhi, February 7, 2007, in V. K. Puri, *Master Plan for Delhi 2021* (Delhi: JBA Publishers, 2007), p. 1.
7. See, for example, the collection of papers in *Draft Delhi Master Plan 2021: Blueprint for an Apartheid City* (New Delhi: Hazards Centre, July 2005).
8. See the note by The World Bank Group, 'Concept of the Informal Sector,' available online at: http://lnweb90.worldbank.org/eca/eca.nsf/0/2e4ede5437 87a0c085256a940073f4e4?OpenDocument [last accessed April 30, 2010]
9. Kristina Flodman Becker, *The Informal Economy: Fact finding study* (SIDA, March 2004).
10. See Martha Chen, "Rethinking the Informal Economy," *Seminar* issue # 531 on Footloose Labour (November 2003). Available online at http://www.india-seminar.com/2003/531/531%20martha%20alter%20chen.htm [last accessed April 30, 2010]. Chen extends these ideas in a subsequent paper; cf. "Rethinking the Informal Economy: Linkages with the Formal Economy and the Formal Regulatory Environment," paper for the 2006 UN-ECOSOC Meetings. Available online in PDF format at http://www.un.org/Docs/ecosoc/meetings/2006/forum/Statements/Chen's%20Paper.pdf [last accessed April 30, 2010].

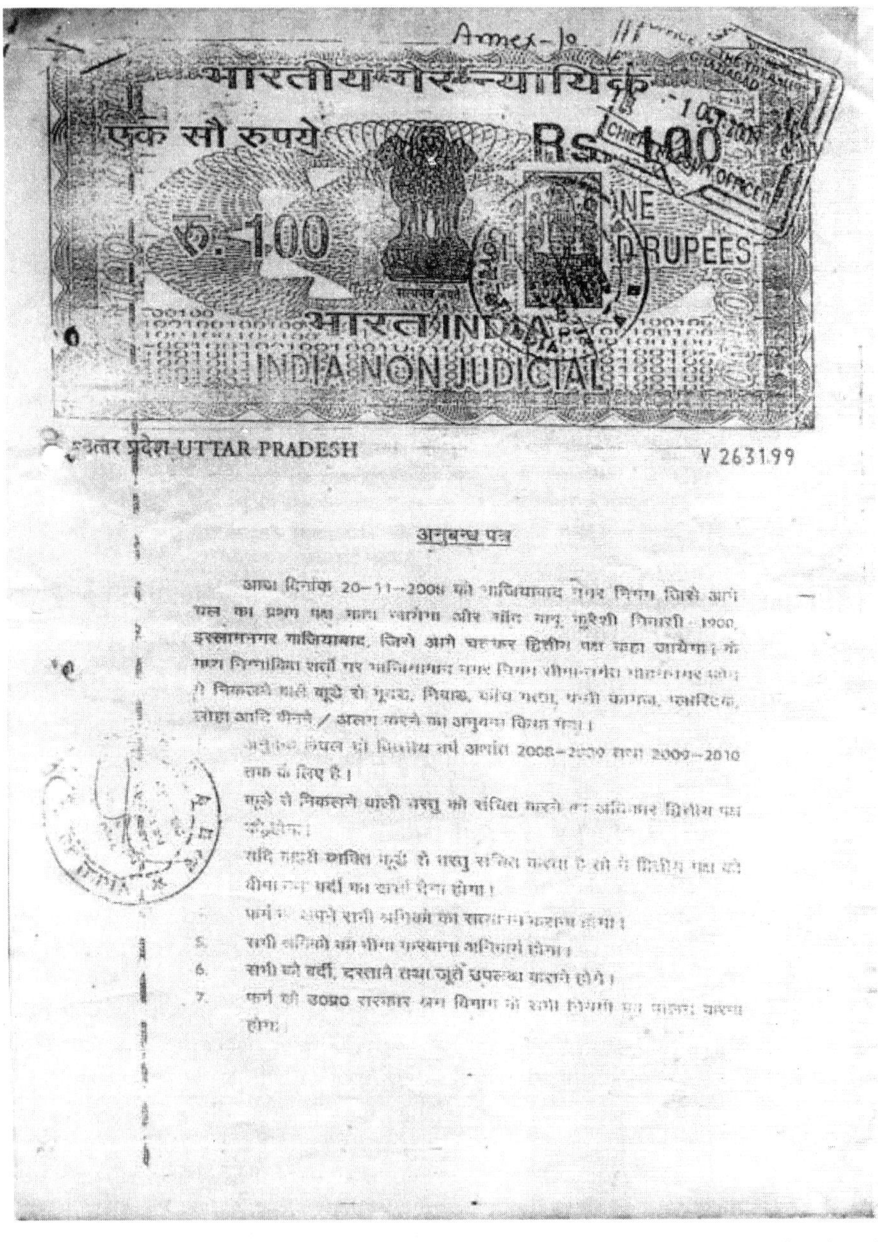
भारतीय गैर न्यायिक
एक सौ रुपये
Rs. 100
रु. 100
ONE HUNDRED RUPEES
भारत INDIA
INDIA NON JUDICIAL
उत्तर प्रदेश UTTAR PRADESH
V 263199
अनुबन्ध पत्र

Figure 6.1a Ghaziabad Municipal Corporation's original contract with Chand Babu Qureshi dated 20 November 2008.

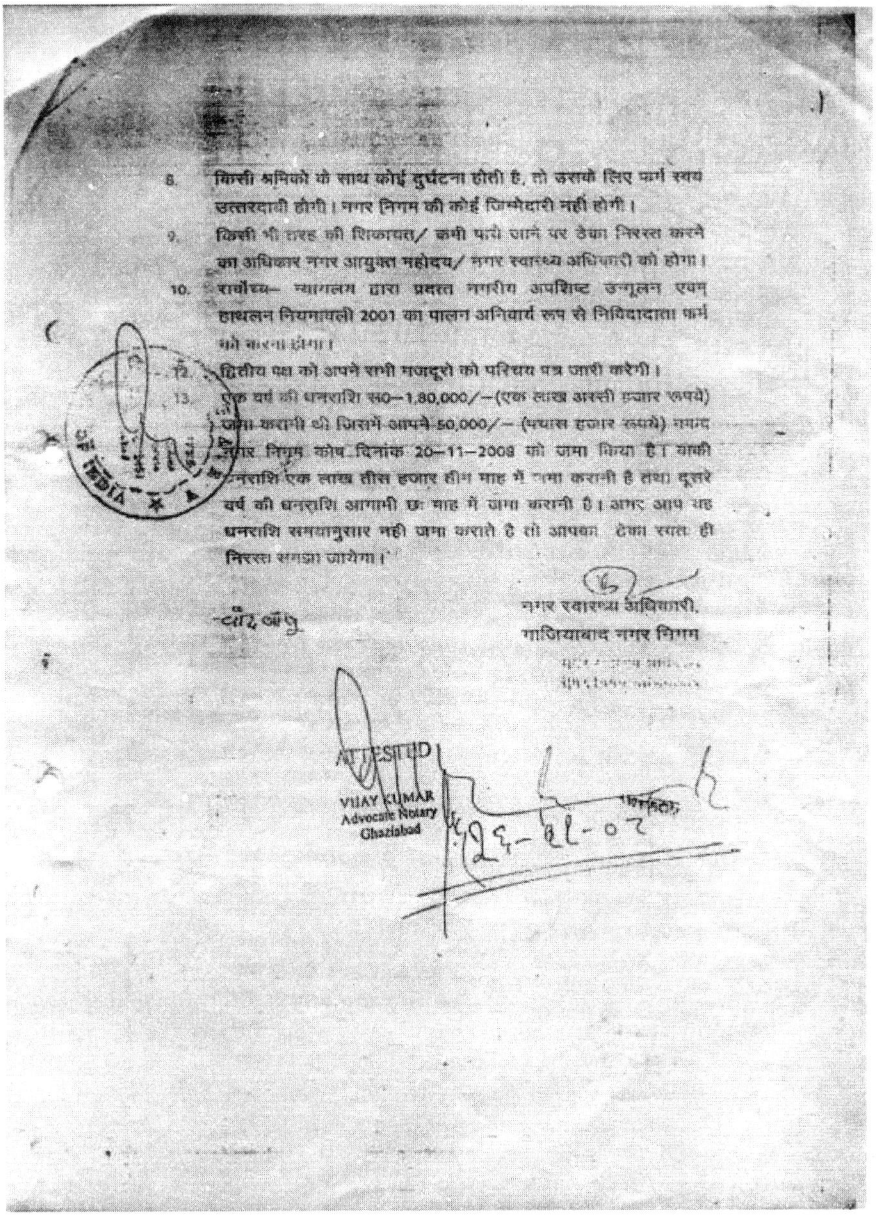

8. किसी श्रमिको के साथ कोई दुर्घटना होती है, तो उसके लिए फर्म स्वयं उत्तरदायी होगी। नगर निगम की कोई जिम्मेदारी नही होगी।

9. किसी भी तरह की शिकायत/ कमी पाये जाने पर ठेका निरस्त करने का अधिकार नगर आयुक्त महोदय/ नगर स्वास्थ्य अधिकारी को होगा।

10. सर्वोच्च– न्यायालय द्वारा प्रदत्त नगरीय अपशिष्ट उन्मूलन एवम् हथलन नियमावली 2001 का पालन अनिवार्य रूप से निविदादाता फर्म को करना होगा।

12. द्वितीय पक्ष को अपने सभी मजदूरो को परिचय पत्र जारी करेगी।

13. एक वर्ष की धनराशि रू0–1,80,000/–(एक लाख अस्सी हजार रूपये) जमा करानी थी जिसमें आपने 50,000/– (पचास हजार रूपये) नगद नगर निगम कोष दिनांक 20–11–2008 को जमा किया है। बाकी धनराशि एक लाख तीस हजार तीन माह में जमा करानी है तथा दूसरे वर्ष की धनराशि आगामी छः माह में जमा करानी है। अगर आप यह धनराशि समयानुसार नही जमा कराते है तो आपका ठेका स्वतः ही निरस्त समझा जायेगा।

नगर स्वास्थ्य अधिकारी,
गाजियाबाद नगर निगम

ATTESTED
VIJAY KUMAR
Advocate Notary
Ghaziabad

Figure 6.1b Ghaziabad Municipal Corporation's original contract with Chand Babu Qureshi dated 20 November 2008.

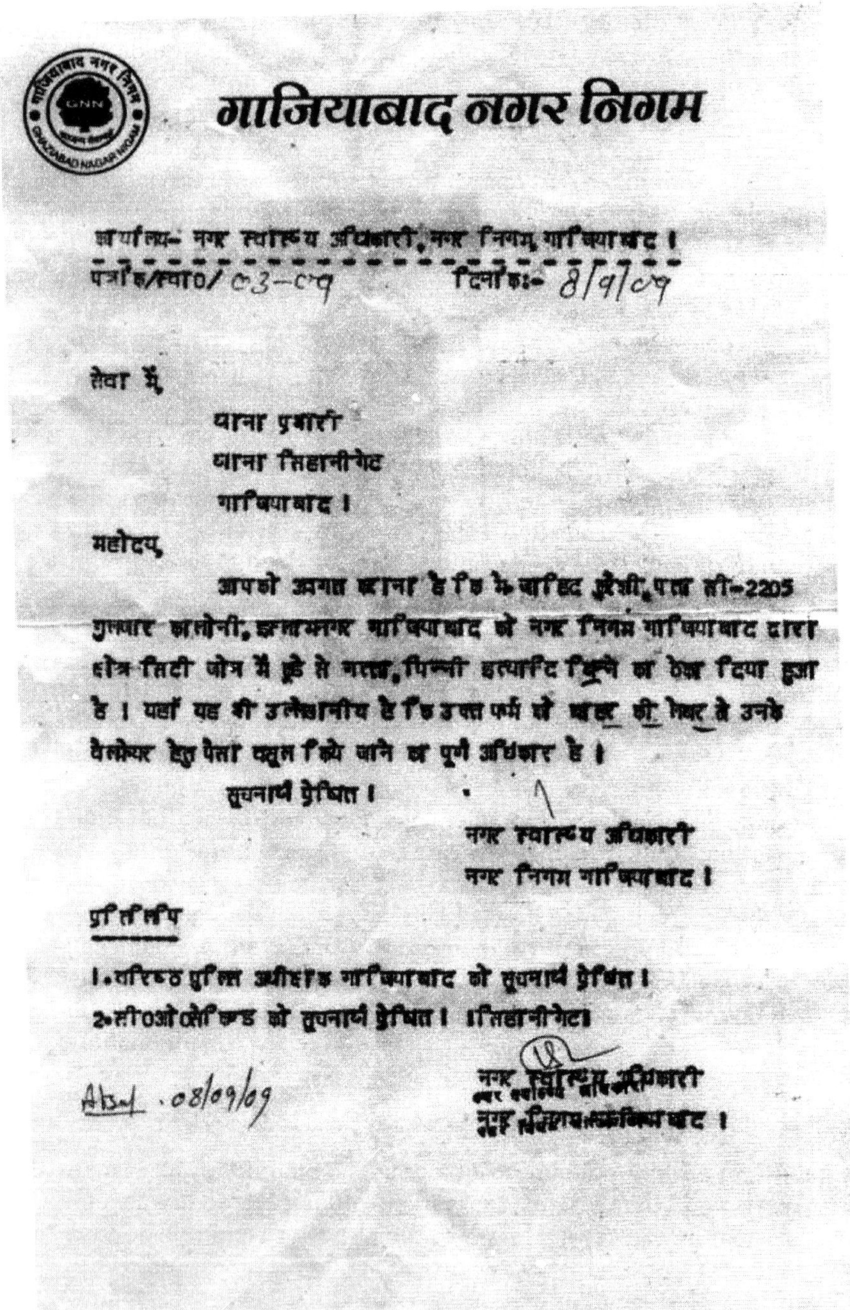

गाजियाबाद नगर निगम

कार्यालय- नगर स्वास्थ्य अधिकारी, नगर निगम, गाजियाबाद।

पत्रांक/स्वा0/ 03-09 दिनांक:- 8/9/09

सेवा में,

थाना प्रभारी
थाना सिहानीगेट
गाजियाबाद।

महोदय,

आपको अवगत कराना है कि मै0 साहिद कुरैशी, पता सी-2205 गुलधार कालोनी, [illegible] गाजियाबाद को नगर निगम गाजियाबाद द्वारा क्षेत्र सिटी जोन में कूड़े से गत्ता, पिन्नी इत्यादि बीनने का ठेका दिया हुआ है। यहाँ यह भी उल्लेखनीय है कि उक्त फर्म को कबाड़ की लेबर से उनके वेलफेयर हेतु पैसा वसूल किये जाने का पूर्ण अधिकार है।

सूचनार्थ प्रेषित।

नगर स्वास्थ्य अधिकारी
नगर निगम गाजियाबाद।

प्रतिलिपि

1. वरिष्ठ पुलिस अधीक्षक गाजियाबाद को सूचनार्थ प्रेषित।
2. सी0ओ0सेकिन्ड को सूचनार्थ प्रेषित। ।सिहानीगेट।

Abd. 08/09/09

नगर स्वास्थ्य अधिकारी
नगर निगम गाजियाबाद।

Figure 6.2 GMC Health Officer's [*Swasthya Adhikari's*] order dated 9 September 2009.

REFERENCES

Batra, Lalit. 2008. Deconstructing the 'world class' city. *Seminar* 582 (February), 47–50.

Baviskar, Amita. 2003. Between violence and desire: Space, power and identity in the making of metropolitan Delhi. *International Social Science Journal* 55(175): 89–98.

Becker, Kristina. 2004. *The Informal Economy: Fact Finding Study* (Stockholm: Swedish International Development Cooperation Agency [SIDA]).

Bhan, Gautam. 2009. "This is no longer the city I once knew": Evictions, the urban poor and the right to the city in millennial Delhi. *Environment and Urbanization* 21(1): 127–142.

Chen, Martha. 2003. Rethinking the informal economy. *Seminar* issue 531 on Footloose Labour (November 2003). Available online at: http://www.india-seminar.com/2003/531/531%20martha%20alter%20chen.htm [last accessed April 30, 2010].

Chintan. 2003. *Space for waste*. New Delhi: Chintan Environmental Research and Action Group.

Ghertner, D. Asher. 2008. Analysis of new legal discourse behind Delhi's slum demolitions. *Economic and Political Weekly* (May 17): 57–66.

Gidwani, Vinay, and Reddy, Rajyashree N. Forthcoming. The afterlives of "waste": Notes from India for a minor history of capitalist surplus. *Antipode*.

Harvey, David. 2008. The right to the city. *New Left Review* 53 (Sept-Oct).

Hazards Centre [Khatra Kendra]. 2005. *Draft Delhi Master Plan 2021: Blueprint for an Apartheid City* (New Delhi: Hazards Centre, July 2005).

Mitchell, Don. 2003. *The Right to the City: Social Justice and the Fight for Public Space* (New York: The Guilford Press).

Puri, V. K. 2007. *Master plan for Delhi 2021*. Delhi: JBA Publishers.

Roy, Ananya. 2005. Urban informality: Toward an epistemology of planning. *Journal of the American Planning Association* (*JAPA*) 71(2): 147-158.

Sethi, Aman. 2006. Waste and wealth. *Frontline* 27(3) (April 8–21). Available online at: http://www.thehindu.com/fline/fl2307/stories/20060421002508600.htm [last accessed April 30, 2010].

The World Bank. 2006. *Improving management of municipal solid waste in India: Overview and challenges*. New Delhi.

Verma, Gita Dewan. 2003. *Slumming India: A chronicle of slums and their saviors*. Delhi: Penguin Books

The World Bank. nd. Concept of informal sector. New Delhi: The World Bank. Available online at: http://lnweb90.worldbank.org/eca/eca.nsf/0/2e4ede543787a0c085256a940073f4e4?OpenDocument [last accessed April 30, 2010]

Zhu, D. et al., 2008. *Improving Municipal Solid Waste Management in India: A Sourcebook for Policy Makers and Practitioners* (Washington, DC: The World Bank).

7 From Red Tape to Red Carpet?
Violent Narratives of Neoliberalizing Ahmedabad

Ipsita Chatterjee

INTRODUCTION

Mainstream analysis of market mechanism and critical analysis of contemporary capitalism occupy opposite sides of the ideological spectrum. Yet they converge in their assessment that markets and states are undergoing re-organization. The free-marketers refer to this re-organization as "market reforms"—a process of liberating (liberalizing) the market from the shackles of an intrusive Keynesian state (in Anglo America) (Brenner and Theodore 2002; Peck and Tickell 2002; Leitner et al. 2007; Peet 2007), or a democratic socialist state (in large parts of the Third World). Those on the left of the ideological spectrum, refer to this re-organization as "neoliberalism"—new and more virulent form of old-style classical and neoclassical liberalism of the nineteenth century, which calls for a rollback of the state as a mechanism for redistribution, relinquishing control over society to the invisible hand (Peet et al. 2003). The critics of neoliberalism argue that relinquishing state power in favor of the market aggravates vulnerability and inequality at all scales, between classes, communities, and nations, in the short as well as in the long run. The problem lies not merely in the nature, pacing, and manner of implementation of (neo)liberalization, but rather liberalization itself is problematic.

No matter what position on the political spectrum one occupies, there is no doubt that since the early 1980s, large parts of the world are undergoing liberalization/globalization/neoliberalization. In the Third World, this process of liberalization has been referred to as globalization, structural adjustment, neo-imperialism—the term 'neoliberalism' being relatively less known. The existing literature theorizes the characteristics (supply-side economics), policy perspectives (trade liberalization, tax reforms, capital market reforms), institutional dimensions (World Bank, International Monetary Fund, World Trade Organization), and sectoral impacts (industrial restructuring, agrarian reforms) of this new socioeconomic re-organization (Jessop 2002; Peck and Tickell 2002; Peet et al. 2003). Peck and Tickell argue that neoliberalism is often attributed a "quasi-climatic" "out there," "disembodied" character (2002, 382–383), so that its variegated nature, as it actually exists, is left un-theorized. Similarly, Brenner and Theodore (2002) argue that the spatially embedded nature of neoliberalism is relatively under-theorized in the developed world.

This argument holds true for India as well. This chapter focuses on the contextual spatial "embeddedness" of neoliberalism in Ahmedabad city, India. It examines how the market and the local state re-organize themselves (W. Ahmed 2007), and how such re-organizations impact class, space, and ethnicity through entrepreneurial urban development. Ahmedabad is a particularly potent example because it represents an outward-looking, vigorously entrepreneurial space, invested in attracting and fixing foreign capital, and simultaneously, inward-looking in its ethnoracism and Islamophobia. The year 2002 was a benchmark in terms of ethnic violence—members of the Hindu community, aided by the local Hindu fundamentalist government, unleashed unprecedented violence against the Muslim minority. This chapter examines how neoliberalism is socio-spatially embedded in Ahmedabad, and why such embedding can be violent.

MARKET-STATE DYNAMICS

The period of the late 1980s is considered to be the era of politicization of neoliberal discourse popularized by Thatcher's "There is no alternative" ("TINA") slogan (W. Ahmed 2007), complemented by Reagan in the U.S. The Bretton Woods institutions (International Monetary Fund and World Bank) were originally created at the end of the Second World War, under the assumption that markets left to themselves often did not work well, resulting in massive unemployment and recession—the depression of the 1930s being a case in point (Stiglitz 2003). The Bretton Woods institutions were therefore quasi-public institutions, that were eventually assigned the responsibility of alleviating poverty, and hence maintaining global economic stability. Keynes pointed out that equilibrium at the market may happen at very low levels of employment of the factors of production (land, labor, and capital), and that unemployment of massive amounts of labor can threaten the market system (Peet et al. 2003). Keynes's influence shaped the objectives of the Bretton Woods institutions and ushered in an era of managed capitalism with controlled markets. The Keynesian welfare state employed monetary and fiscal policies to discipline the market in order to meet its social objectives. State-regulated markets conjoined with Fordism to produce a system of protected domestic markets with demand management in the form of higher wages for workers.

In large parts of the Third World, newly independent countries interested in nation building and self-sufficiency designed welfare states with mixed economies—states managed important sectors that formed the backbone of the national economy (like steel, textiles, infrastructure, power). Import substitution industrialization was pursued—instead of importing, nations attempted to produce substitutes by protecting domestic industries through licensing, quotas, and tariffs. The production of consumer goods was largely left to private entrepreneurs. India adopted a mixed economy approach with the state employing a central planning commission to plan the development of different sectors of the economy, different spaces (urban, rural), and different groups (economically backward, historically backwards, indigenous people) (Rudolf and Rudolf 1987). It was assumed that markets could bring growth, but not development, in the sense that development was viewed as bigger than growth, not necessarily measured in terms of gross domestic product (GDP) and gross national product (GNP), but included larger social objectives of inter-class, inter-regional, and inter-group equality.

The late 1970s oil crisis created new challenges for both the developed and the developing world. Free-market economists, drawing from Hayek's and Friedman's writings, started clamoring for a market that should be liberated from the state. According to the free-marketers, state intervention was perverse and inflationary. The Washington Consensus of the 1980s among the International Monetary Fund (IMF), World Bank (WB), and the U.S. Treasury Department framed policies which could free the market from the shackles of a bureaucratic state (Peet et al. 2003, Stiglitz 2003). The policies included a rollback of state intervention, privatization, trade liberalization, capital market liberalization, reduction of public expenditures (on social objectives like education, health) and encouragement of foreign direct investment (FDI). Third World countries that were unable to afford the more expensive petroleum (due to the oil crisis) went to the IMF for loans—where they were 'asked' to trim their respective states, and free their markets or, in other words, 'integrate' or globalize. The process of integration would involve structural adjustment packages along the lines of the Washington Consensus policies, first pushed on Latin American countries, and then uncritically applied as a 'one size fit all' approach to other Third World countries (Stiglitz 2003). There was little that was contextual, embedded, or locally sensitive about the neoliberal packages imposed on the Third World—during their visits to understand the local situation, IMF officials stayed overnight in five-star hotels, before prescribing the same privatization-liberalization mantra. In that sense there is a quasi-climatic, 'out there' character to neoliberalism, its contextual embeddedness arising from the variegated manner in which local states (national, provincial, municipal) re-organized themselves vis-à-vis the market to survive in the post 1980s world. A process of transition toward a more post-Fordist style flexible production system ensued where, in large parts of the First World, a decentralization of the Fordist assembly line and associated flight of segments of the production process to various parts of the world rendered production processes geographically decentralized and flexible. Centralized factories started losing their protected domestic markets in the developed world and started taking advantage of a 'global' labor force by outsourcing production to sites of lower wages in order to compete with foreign goods intruding their domestic markets. In the developing world, states phased out licensing and quotas, centralized factories started losing their home advantage, and industries that could not restructure closed down (Kundu and Mahadevia 2002).—labor freed from erstwhile formal sectors, previously managed by states, were pushed into the informal sectors, and in some places were picked up by capital for industrial homework and sweatshop-style subcontracting, within a more post-Fordist global economy.

CONTEXTUAL SPACES OF NEOLIBERAL EMBEDDEDNESS

Neoliberalizing states and markets along ideological, sociocultural, economic, and political fronts cannot be done in a day (Peck and Tickell 2002). The process of transition entails several types of state-market negotiation which, in turn, yield diverse imprints on society and space. Since society, and the space it occupies, is not a tabula rasa, neoliberalism-generated state-market re-organization 'works-on' the existing sociogeographical terrain to produce 'new' contextual spaces, which can be emancipatory or violent. Brenner and Theodore (2002, 357–361) argue that the reconfiguration of politico-institutional contexts due to neoliberalization demonstrates "path dependency", in which pre-existing "politico-institutional contexts" determine the direction of change. Change, they say, involves a dialectical give and take between destruction and creation—destruction of existing institutional configuration and creation of new ones.

Cities are important sites for embedding these 'new' configurations of state-market re-organizations. The national state, reconfiguring its own institutional arrangements to accommodate market rule, simultaneously urges local states (city governments) to fend for themselves and survive in the midst of a liberalizing order. Cox and Mair (1988) and Uitermark (2002) believe that this ushers an era of place-place competition for capital. Harvey (1989) refers to this inter-place competition as "urban entrepreneurialism". As with governments at the national scale, city governments must trim public spending, relinquish goals of social equality and justice, and become astute sales persons for their city spaces, beautifying and dressing up the city with waterfronts, parks, fast track corridors to airports, promenades, and so on (Harvey 1989; Swyngedouw et al. 2002). Other forms of place marketing may include demarcating parcels of the city as free-trade zones or special economic zones to lure flexible capital, promising tax breaks, non-unionized super-desperate labor forces, and relaxed environmental standards. Often place marketing results in newer and more entrenched uneven development within the city, where certain areas are purposely left underdeveloped in order to support more 'globalized' parts of the city (Brenner and Theodore 2002).

Neoliberalizing cities are therefore like mega malls offering "buy one, get two free" services, fast-escalators, and shiny spectacles to attract those who can buy. The shops at the mall city must be 'manned' by pretty people where only a selected few can roam. Slums, homelessness, poverty, degenerated factories, people's resistance, and unions reduce the attractiveness factor and must be contextually 'worked upon,' erased by the local entrepreneurial state so as to facilitate the market. Who, or what, is dispensable is decided by an economic cost-benefit analysis. Some cities are more credit-worthy than others, because of pre-existing socio-politico-institutional characteristics, like non-unionized labor, ethnic-immigrant labor, software professionals, and English-speaking college graduates willing to work in back offices. Some cities demonstrate greater willingness to reconfigure local state-market relations. Cities and groups that lack the required marketable 'skills' are likely to be 'losers,' and hence become dispensable. Loser cities are likely to experience stagnation and out-migration, and losing groups within cities will experience abject poverty. Survival of the fittest is the inner immutable logic of the market mechanism—'fitness' under social Darwinism meaning ability to adapt to the environment. The contextual destiny of people and places is therefore supposed to be ordained by the 'scientific' laws of both biology and economics. It is assumed that there are no ideological underpinnings to the 'new' contextual spaces of neoliberal embeddedness, because the free-market rationale necessitates that the market is truly democratic, since no single individual can singularly dominate the laws of demand and supply.

On the other hand, it is generally accepted that states have always been ideological because they are composed of elected/nominated individuals, who have been chosen or appointed with the explicit purpose of realizing certain ideological visions. There are numerous instances of class-, racial-, ethnic-, gender-biased policies of zoning, segregation, immigration, marriage and property, employment, and in extreme circumstances genocides enacted by the institutions of the state. Weber (2002) indicates how a Keynesian welfare state in the U.S. introduced urban renewal policies to fight urban 'blight,' with concentrations of poor black people in inner cities often qualifying as blight. The market, on the other hand, is assumed to be abstract and face-less, studiously rational (never ideological) because it is driven by laws of price that know no class, color, creed, or ethnicity. But such a free market exists only in the theoretical eloquence of neoclassical economics. The market is everywhere contextually embedded by currency systems, exchange rates, finance ministers, chambers of commerce, banks, bonds, shares, cartels, monopolies, and ethnic, racial, gender, age, and class characteristics of consumers, because the market machinery, like the state machinery, is run by people, and not by the mythical "Rational Economic Man." The 'free' market, in the pristine neoclassical sense, is a theoretical aspiration, hardly ever materialized because markets can never be free of politico-social institutions, unless global society is run by disembodied aliens. When Adam Smith and David Ricardo were arguing for a free market liberated from the shackles of the landed aristocracy, they were arguing from a particular class and geopolitical position—a market free from the aristocracy to be worked upon by Britain's new entrepreneurial class (to which Smith and Ricardo belonged)—and what was good for this new class of entrepreneurs was theorized as good for Britain, and for the rest of the world (Peet 2007). The market is not a level playing field; there was no 'good' to be extracted from the market mechanism by the mass of paupers in seventeenth- and eighteenth-century Britain, or the British colonial subjects in the rest of the world. The free-market imparts freedom of profit extraction to those who can take advantage of the existing ideological-institutional setup. Entrepreneurs have a face, color, race, gender, and class, and they occupy a place—their entrepreneurial quest for profit is enabled or disabled not simply by human's insatiable appetite to consume, but through a host of politico-institutional (state being one such institution), sociocultural factors which are contextual.

In that respect, states and market have always cohabited unless of course the state has an explicit ideological aversion to profit accumulation and private property. The Keynesian configuration explicitly declared that its ideological goals were to manage demand to achieve a more equal society because extreme inequality reduces effective demand and jeopardizes the market mechanism through cycles of booms and busts. Neoliberal configurations of states and markets make no such claims because neoliberalism assumes that the market sees no color, class, or gender; hence, any contextual inequality must result from vestiges of the past, which will disappear in the long run, or any new inequality is a result of an "unfit" space, or lazy, un-innovative people, unable to compete, and therefore deserving to be weeded-out. Since states are comprised of people, it is possible, as Weber (2002) indicates, that local Keynesian states misused their regulatory potential to further racial, xenophobic causes, deviating from their goal of reducing inequality, and such biased policies must be criticized. But, what is dangerous and problematic about neoliberalism is that it assumes no social responsibility toward equality or justice, and no accountability toward growing disparity or inequality because it swears by the ideological neutrality of the market principle. Also, since neoliberalism propagates a truncated role for the state, it falsely assumes that ideological interplay will be minimized because the state as the supreme ideological apparatus has been made to take a back seat—red tape of 'corrupt' states can be downsized so that the efficiency of the market can roll out the red carpet of prosperity. I will indicate through the case study of Ahmedabad city, that the local state in its re-organization vis-à-vis the market is not rolled back, rather, it is vigorously present in its new avatar as market-state where the hyphen between state and market is increasingly blurred. Such a market-state depicts ideological biases—anti-poor strategies (class bias) and anti-Muslim xenophobia (cultural bias) to identify its 'unfit,' dispensable population and dispensable spaces. Market rhetoric is fused with bureaucratic rhetoric to envision a 'new' model of development. Since the market-state is no longer accountable for distributive justice, death of the 'unfit' is no longer considered a failure of the state machinery, it is simply a sad, but necessary consequence of a thriving market system. The state, which has a political face, plays the role of a helpless 'good cop,' so that it can keep contesting elections, while the faceless market is the efficient 'bad cop'—the poor and Muslims are depicted as casualties of spontaneous circumstances and not of any systemic logic.

THE TALE OF AHMEDABAD

Ahmedabad city, in the state of Gujarat, was once referred to as the "Manchester of India" (Breman 2002), owing to its large concentration of cotton textile mills owned by indigenous entrepreneurs. The river Sabarmati divides the city into east and west Ahmedabad. The textile mills were concentrated in east Ahmedabad, which was the first to be industrialized and is inhabited predominantly by a poor industrial labor force comprising of 'low caste'[1] Hindus and Muslims. West Ahmedabad is inhabited predominantly by the middle- and upper-middle-class Hindus (Mahadevia 2002). In the late 1980s and early 1990s, neoliberal reforms, referred to as the New Economic Policy (NEP), were adopted by the central government. The licensing and quotas enjoyed by the Ahmedabad mills were slowly phased out, the textile industries needed major restructuring to adapt to the new post-Fordist regime, and most mills which could not restructure closed down (Breman 2002; Mahadevia 2002). A hundred mills, once the backbone of Ahmedabad's economy, have been closed since the mid 1980s. As a result, 100,000 workers lost formal employment and were pushed into the informal sector, competing for low-paid, part-time jobs. Informal work included unorganized manufacturing, hawking, and vending, with incomes 35% to 45% below what had originally been earned in the mills (Kundu 2000; Breman 2002; Mahadevia 2002). Urban poverty has increased (Kundu 2000). Prior to the economic reforms, mill workers from the Hindu and Muslim communities shared common spaces, meeting in the textile mills and in the labor union associations. With the closure of the mills the common spaces for inter-community interaction have disappeared producing insulation and alienation between the two communities.

Since the NEP reforms, urban development plans in Ahmedabad have shifted from providing cheap infrastructural facilities, and employment generation, to neoliberal urban renewal projects, such as the Sabarmati Riverfront Development Project, several other beautification-road-widening and greening programs, and forced evictions of the urban poor from slums to 'ready' the city for foreign investment (Mahadevia 2002). For the urban poor, the urban renewal projects present no prospects of gainful employment. This has created conditions of "social Darwinism" (Breman

2002) among the informalized poor and frustrated youth of Ahmedabad. Muslims form the super-exploited minority because they experience dual exclusion. Like African Americans, they suffer from poverty, and hence a general class exclusion, which is again coupled with a more specific ethno-cultural exclusion (Rudolph and Rudolph 1987). Corbridge and Harriss (2000) and Vanaik (2001) examine the political economic and cultural impetus provided by neoliberalism toward expanding inter-community, inter-class, and inter-regional disparities in local spaces.

In 2002, a Hindu-Muslim riot occurred in Ahmedabad city; it lasted for two and a half months. The conflict was sparked by an incident in nearby Godhra, where two coaches of the Sabarmati express train were burned, killing 58 passengers. Some of these passengers were supporters of the Bharatiya Janata Party (BJP), a political party that contests elections based on a Hindu fundamentalist agenda. Rumors spread, blaming Muslims for torching the coaches (R. Ahmed 2002). Soon, members of the Hindu community in Ahmedabad went on a rampage and, according to official estimates, killed two thousand Muslims (0.3% of the total Muslim population), but, according to un-official estimates, killed five thousand Muslims (0.75% of the total Muslim population). Killing was accompanied by indiscriminate raping, looting, and burning of Muslim property and the displacement and concentration of large sections of the Muslim population in relief camps, while the police and local BJP government remained aloof, and in some cases aided the rioters (Yagnik and Seth 2002).

According to the national media and the fact-finding commissions, the BJP and its affiliates organized the riots against the minority Muslim community (R. Ahmed 2002; Breman 2002; Sarkar 2002). The BJP has always used discourses of cultural nationalism to garner Hindu electoral support. The discourse that all religious minorities, particularly the Muslims, are foreigners and must be 'Hinduized' to be loyal Indians is a major tenet of its Hindutva politics (Hinduism as political ideology). With 9/11, and the subsequent global labeling of Muslims as terrorists, the BJP hoped to reconcile its local discourse of 'othering' with a global discourse of Islamophobia to win U.S. friendship (Vanaik 2001; Balgopal 2002; Shah 2002). In many ways Hindus and Muslims share a contentious relationship in India due to the legacies of the partition and the creation of Pakistan as an Islamic state. Yet it is common for Hindus and Muslims to interact and be co-dependent in the social sphere of the neighborhood, in public spaces like offices, clubs, factories, shops, markets, and universities. Inter-community interaction, peace, and harmony are largely contingent on the density of these public interactions, and on the extent of tolerance and 'openness' of particular places. Ahmedabad city had a peaceful history in the pre-Independence period (prior to 1947), violence becoming prominent only in the 1980s and 1990s (Varshney 2002), with the 2002 conflict being a landmark event because of its intensity and longevity. The inter-community tension and violence is an important contextual particularity that must be considered while analyzing the state-market re-organization in the post 1991 NEP context. While the state (led by the BJP) has generally been considered to be ideologically biased against the minority community, the new age of neoliberal state rollback has not alleviated anti-minority hysteria, nor lessened inter-community tension. In fact the newly reincarnated entrepreneurial state contextually uses market mechanisms to increase ethno-cultural polarization. The free market is hardly free of class and ethnic bias; it cohabits with a biased state to aggravate social polarization. The 2002 violence is, however, generally interpreted as mob reaction—it is assumed that those unable to compete (poor Hindus and poor Muslims) will ultimately learn to be enterprising. In the mean time if they kill each other, the market-state should not be held responsible for 'social-pathologies' of those who fail to be productive.

ROLLING OUT THE RED CARPET—HOW STATE BECOMES A MARKET-STATE?

Swyngedouw et al, (2002) and Brenner and Theodore (2002) argue that neoliberal urban policies may manifest themselves in different forms, but they usually involve a move away from distributive policies and welfare considerations toward city marketing, beautification, creation of privatized spaces for corporate consumption, gated communities, and mega projects created to attract corporate investment and special economic zones. The New Economic Policy in India has deeply impacted urban governance and has veered urban policy toward market fundamentalism. The Ministry of Urban Development in India clarifies the nature of market-state re-organization in its 2001–2002 annual report:

> Government of India is also encouraging citywide reforms and restructuring so as to ensure that cities are managed *efficiently* and become *creditworthy* (*to attract private finance*) . . .
>
> Hitherto Foreign Investment Promotion Board (FIPB) allowed direct investment in providing urban services on a case to case basis. This scenario has changed with the decision of the Central Government *removing restrictions on FDI* in urban infrastructure facilities which are now open both under FIPB and the automatic route as per sector specific guidelines. We propose to accelerate this process by addressing key issues involved . . .
>
> Municipal Bonds were successfully issued by several Municipal Corporations like, Bangalore, Ahmedabad, Ludhiana, Nagpur, Nasik, Madurai for raising resources for urban infrastructure. The Central Government had announced *tax exemption* in case of bonds issued by Municipal / Local Governments . . . Tax free bonds worth Rs. 1 Billion by Ahmedabad Municipal Corporation have been permitted

for improving infrastructure (Ministry of Urban Development, 2001–2002, emphases mine)

The market-state, in its passion to take the reforms to their "logical conclusion" has re-envisioned the city as a site that needs to be "efficiently" managed for capital. Efficient management in turn means removing all possible restrictions on FDI, and also providing tax exemption on municipal bonds, which itself is a novel (post-reform) concept in India, with Ahmedabad city being the first to sell city bonds. This is supposed to increase private investment in the city, enabling it to accumulate profit, and hence grow. Investment in what, where, and for whom, is not a concern. In contrast, the 1991–1992 annual report of the Ministry of Urban Development reflects a different vision with explicit objectives of reducing regional disparities and generating employment. It wants to:

> . . . reduce migration of population from rural areas to major urban areas; to generate employment by creating resource generating ventures in the small and medium towns and also to provide sufficient infrastructure facilities in these towns so that their hinterland is served better (Ministry of Urban Development 1991–1992)

The Urban Land Ceiling and Regulation Act, passed by the federal government in 1976 with the social objective of preventing individual landowners from holding land above a certain size to facilitate housing for urban poor, was repealed in 1999 to make cities credit-worthy. In their determination to prove the credit-worthiness of cities in Gujarat (the state where Ahmedabad city is located), the state government is organizing a series of Global Investor's Summits in Ahmedabad city to showcase Gujarati cities as perfect investment destinations. Two messages were given to prospective investors:

In Gujarat there is only *Red Carpet* and no *Red Tape*.
It is where Investors can sow a rupee and reap a dollar as returns (Global Investor's Summit 2007, emphasis mine).

The idea of the "Red Carpet" free from "Red Tape" is ingenious; it suggests an absence of bureaucratic bottlenecks or, in other words, a haven where the state is willfully absent and is instead in the service of the market. Neoliberalism allows for a government of the market, by the market, for the market, where traditional social responsibilities of growth *with* equity is incompatible with profit making.

The Ahmedabad Municipal Corporation (AMC) is vigorous in its reincarnation of a market-state. In 1996, AMC prepared a five-year capital investment plan for various urban development projects, 60% of the cost of these projects was to be met through municipal bonds and loans from financial institutions (ICLEI 1995–2000). The AMC developed close ties with the United States Agency for International Development (USAID), to develop the bond issue and to also gain access to the international credit market. In the 'true' spirit of urban entrepreneurialism, or place-place competition, the USAID's Financial Institutions Reforms and Expansion (FIRE) program helped the Credit Rating and Information Services of India Limited (CRISIL), an independent rating agency, to develop a methodology for credit-rating local governments in India. Ahmedabad became the first city to request credit rating to boost its municipal bonds. The AMC was initially awarded an "A+" for Ahmedabad's municipal bonds. In the true spirit of entrepreneurship, the AMC would issue bonds to raise money from local credit markets, and would also raise money by borrowing from the U.S. lending market, with the loans guaranteed by the U.S. government. Thus, HUDCO (Housing and Urban Development Corporation) of India borrowed $10 million from the U.S. capital market, and USAID guaranteed these loans under its FIRE program. However, this global-local entrepreneurial fund raising was accompanied by recommendations like:

Keep budgets under control—This implicitly means that city's having large deficits are not credit-worthy; cities often incur deficits by expending in welfare and public works projects, which under entrepreneurial urbanism indicates an aggressive and wasteful state presence.

Implement projects speedily—Investors need to know that their investments are being efficiently put into use.

Invest in revenue-generating activities—"The loans obtained on both local and international markets do not necessarily have to be spent on *anti-poverty policies in order to have an impact on poverty alleviation*. They may in fact be spent on activities that are more likely to raise the revenue needed to pay back the debt" (WACAP 2008, emphasis mine).

The uncanny resemblance of these conditionalities imposed on city governments with the conditionalities imposed by the IMF on debtor nations indicates that neoliberalism does have quasi-atmospheric, meta characteristics that get regularly echoed at all scales. The conditionalities imposed on the city government imply that the local market-state should function as a corporate body to balance its accounts and increase its profits to satisfy its stakeholders, and those who are not part of the corporate family do not count. But, the irreconcilable problem with the market-state re-organization process in a developing country is that there are usually a large number of poor people who are important for electoral politics and must be wooed by the contending parties to win elections and hence capture the state. The governments need their foot soldiers to win elections therefore, even in its metamorphosis as a market-state, the state needs to keep alive the anti-poverty discourse, even when it actually no longer frames policies to combat poverty. The World Alliance of Cities Against Poverty (WACAP 2008) mentions, on its website, that cities should be investing in "revenue generating" activities, further clarifying that the loans need *not* be spent on "anti-poverty policies." The Ministry of Urban Development, which repealed the Land Ceiling and Regulation Act, and has encouraged indiscriminate intrusion of FDI, therefore still calls itself the "Ministry of Urban Development and Poverty Alleviation." Clearly, "poverty" and the poor are visible realities of urban India, and while the state must continue to talk about them, the market-state need do nothing about them, and in fact must not spend on 'wasteful' anti-poverty programs. The market-state's vision assumes, therefore, that cities can fight poverty through a 'rational' free-market logic of becoming richer (cutting losses and accumulating profit). Cutting losses means balancing budgets, generating revenue, and creating a sense of financial stability, so that investments flow in. The market-state's urban strategy is geared not toward eliminating poverty but, rather, eliminating the poor (by squeezing the last drop of distributive justice from urban policy). Cities will become prettier, glossier, cleaner, and richer, but only for those who are 'fit' to compete—a rich city is not necessarily a just city, but then the invisible hand of price never promises inclusivity, justice, or equity. An astute market-state must, therefore, keep alive departments for poverty alleviation, assist anti-poverty NGOs, and mention poverty alleviation in their five-point programs. But to roll out the red carpet means to simultaneously calibrate policies infused with an anti-poverty idiom, but actually, directed at efficiency and profit maximization.

THE EUGENICS OF MARKETING AHMEDABAD CITY

The market-state in Ahmedabad city is proactive in embedding neoliberalism so as to produce spaces of profit, but what is more dangerous is that market fundamentalism manifests as a new world eugenics, which is designed to annihilate the poor as a class, and in many cases the Muslim poor as a community.

Green Partnership Program

The USAID's "Green Partnership Program" (GPP) with the AMC clearly indicates a combination of market fundamentalism and bourgeoisie environmentalism, where green spaces must be sustained or created overnight to allow for un-interrupted circulation of capital. USAID's reason to participate in this program is outlined here:

> Concerns about deteriorating urban environmental conditions and their long-range implications have become a critical component of U.S.

> foreign policy initiatives. Cities in the developing world are growing rapidly. In these burgeoning urban areas, the pace and scale of growth have outstripped the capacity to maintain acceptable standards of public health, environmental safety, and *sustainable economic growth*. Enormous burdens of ill health and reduced quality of life affect citizens in those cities. Further, those conditions exacerbate global environmental problems and pose very real threats to *U.S. national interests*.
>
> These problems are most intense in the cities where they originate, but they also *jeopardize U.S. interests* in a number of different ways. Urban environmental problems undermine *sustainable economic expansion*. Unstable economies can lead to a rising tide of *economic refugees*. Increasingly unlivable cities are more susceptible to *social unrest* and *political instability*. Robust new strains of *"exotic"* diseases that first appeared in the *overcrowded slums of poorly-managed cities* overseas are showing up with increasing frequency in U.S. communities, inadvertently imported by visitors, returning travelers, or the swelling numbers of environmental refugees abandoning their increasingly unlivable cities (Hales 2003, emphasis mine).

The GPP was started in 1997–1998 after USAID enabled an environmental impact assessment in Ahmedabad to come to the conclusion that air pollution and not water is the major problem in the city. The major objective was to plant trees and to create traffic islands, parks, and gardens. The AMC budgeted 15 million rupees ($333,333) in 1997–1998, and 10 million rupees ($222,222) for each of the next four years. The AMC owns 66 gardens, 45 parks, and 64 traffic islands (Dutta 2000).

USAID's mission statement (quoted at the beginning of this section) indicates that the greening is necessary for "sustainable economic expansion" without hampering "US interests." Deteriorating urban environments is not good business for the U.S.; in addition, it creates socio-political 'problems' of refugees carrying "exotic" disease into the U.S. from "overcrowded slums of poorly-managed cities." Economics and environment are intricately imbricated. Green (clean and beautiful) places must be manufactured so that American investors can be induced to expand; however, such expansions should not encourage return flow of migrants—because economic gains accrued abroad will be offset at home if U.S. taxpayers must bear the brunt of "exotic" diseases brought from abroad. Therefore, capital can roam free, but people of certain places, color, and class must stay put. Pure profit accumulation with no social accountability is possible by infusing an environmental consciousness that does not claim to address the root causes of issues like why Third World cities are becoming over-crowded? Neoliberalism called for a place versus place entrepreneurialism under which goals of integrated regional development (generating employment and infrastructure in small and medium towns—1991–1992 Annual Report of the Ministry of Urban Development, quoted earlier) were abandoned, and small towns were 'left behind' allowing massive out-migration to continue unchecked—the market logic that lurks behind over-crowding is not analyzed, instead "miss-managed" slums are taken as 'given' to be rendered livable by planting trees. Green traffic islands will automatically reduce "exotic" diseases and induce people to stay where they are—jobs, medicine, nutrition, and food security are not even considered as possible measures to reduce morbidity and improve quality of life. Employment generation, healthcare, medicine, and food security calls for public spending, which an agent of market (like the USAID) can never prescribe, and a market-state can never implement. Therefore, greening poverty, it can be hoped, will mask the 'ugliness' and produce enclaves of cleanliness where profit maximization can proceed unhindered. Mahadevia and Brar (2006) indicate how the realization of a green landscape occurs on an uneven plane. East Ahmedabad, which houses the poor working-class Muslims and low-caste Hindus, severely lacks in green open spaces and parks. Field observations revealed that all the greening, cleaning, and beautifying is concentrated in west Ahmedabad, which houses the middle- and upper-class Hindu community. Large amounts of investment have been pumped into greening already green and posh localities of Law Gardens and Parimal Gardens in west Ahmedabad. 'Unfit' spaces like slums in east Ahmedabad, and unproductive beings like the poor and the Muslims cannot be factored within the cost-benefit analysis of green fundamentalism, and therefore must be weeded out.

Sabarmati River Front Development

The AMC launched its ambitious Sabarmati River Front Development (SRFD) project in 1993. The project aims to reclaim land on both sides of the river Sabarmati that runs through the heart of the city. The project aims to reclaim 162 hectares of land, fill it, and raise it to ground level. An approximately 11-kilometer stretch on both banks of the river will be 'developed.' Being located in the heart of the city, the reclaimed land is expected to fetch premium value from private developers. Promenades, water parks, public gardens, hotels, and commercial office complexes will also be built to beautify the river front and be a mirror image of swanky Western cities. The district collector (chief bureaucratic executive) states:

> The SRFD is the first of its kind in India, it will raise Ahmedabad to the status of global cities like Sydney, London, New York. Plans have been drawn to convert both banks of river Sabarmati into spectacular urban corridors, ideal for high-speed travel to the airport, lined with trees, water parks, penthouses, malls. SRFD project will make us proud and will draw foreign investment—investors like to see a city that can match-up to world standards.

When asked if the communal tensions between the Hindu and Muslim communities, particularly 2002 violence against the Muslims not very far from the banks of Sabarmati could be a deterrent for investors, Mrs. Thara expressed disbelief:

> Why do outsiders keep mentioning 2002 violence? There was no violence, the media blew things out of proportion, and people like a good story. Outsiders are jealous of Ahmedabad's steady rise to a status of a world class growth engine and business destination, and they bring up the violence issue all the time. People live in harmony here. This is the safest city in the world. Our aim can be summarized in three words Green, clean and beautiful.

Field interviews revealed that both banks of the river Sabarmati at present are inhabited by the urban poor (both Muslims and Scheduled Caste and OBC Hindus[2]), who live in rudimentary huts made of plastic, mud, and sometimes, cement and brick. The urban poor support the informal sector of the city. They are primarily engaged in hawking and vending vegetables, used garments, toys, and street food; some work as domestic help, others work in auto-repair, many drive auto-rickshaws[3]. The women make kites and incense sticks for hawking. Most had fathers, or relatives, who worked in the textile mills when they were up and running and complain that if the mills were functioning, life would be easier. The older folks reminisce about a time when food, clothing, and shelter were assured as formal employment in the mills fetched a decent income and added benefits.

The youth express frustration and dejection with the lack of organized employment and say that each day is a struggle for livelihood, where they are engaged in "*Faltoo kaam*," which literally means 'useless labor,' but is actually the local term for casual work. Informal employment, they complain is transitory, and does not yield steady income. The SRFD now hangs as a scepter. One Hindu slum dweller said:

> They say that they are going to build water parks, hotels and gardens where we now live. The government thinks that our homes are ugly, and the center of the city must be beautiful. Why does the government not find employment? If we have food, if we have bread, we will be beautiful too! They say that they are going to re-settle us, but we doubt it. Corruption will eat away all the resettlement money, and we have heard that they will re-settle us far outside the city, how will we find work then? Commuting will be un-profitable. We are the 'scum,' the government cares only about the rich.

Official estimates state that 15,000 families need to be displaced, while NGOs put the number at well over 40,000 families (Parekh 2004). Eighty percent of the displaced would be Muslim families, and the rest would be

OBC Hindus and SCs (Combat law 2004). The urban poor on the banks of the Sabarmati are not only marginalized but also divided. The 2002 violence has heightened inter-community tensions. Both Hindus and Muslims live in clusters within contiguous slums; during the 2002 riot many Muslim homes were burned (R. Ahmed 2002). Muslim residents claim that local Bajrang Dal (Muscle wing of the Bharatiya Janata Party—BJP) leaders came by truckloads and incited their Hindu neighbors to violence, while the police stood by and even aided the rioters. Muslim homes were burned, and the fire also spread to Hindu homes. While the Hindus were compensated by the government, the Muslims received nothing. The Muslims believe that even if the Hindus were re-settled, the government would do nothing for the Muslims, because ideologically the BJP openly propagates a Hindu fundamentalist agenda, and being poor as well as Muslim, they can expect no compensation. The Hindu poor hope that they will be re-settled in separate places, away from their Muslim neighbors. They also believe that the Muslims only look poor and in reality the Al Qaeda and other Islamic trusts fund them and that the Muslims are terrorists who have swords in their homes, and therefore deserved to be killed in the 2002 riots.

Both Hindus and Muslims, though disapproving of the project, and doubting the possibility of rehabilitation, are culturally divided. Muslims fear that Hindus will kill them at the next opportunity, and the government will do nothing; if evicted, therefore, the Muslims will have to fend for themselves. Hindus feel that the government should keep the Muslims away, one resident claimed: "Muslims are a menace, wherever they are, in whatever part of the world, they always create trouble, what Bush could not do in his 'war on terror' we could do here in 2002. It is a matter of pride that we taught the Miyaas (slang for Muslims), a lesson." For many Hindus therefore, fewer people to re-settle may mean that resettlement may actually happen. The Sabarmati Nagrarik Adhikar Manch, a people's organization, along with a host of other NGOs have filed a Public Interest Litigation in the Gujarat High court, complaining that the slum residents have not been informed about rehabilitation packages and have been successful in extracting a stay-order against the eviction (The Indian Express 2005). In the meantime however, land filling and construction has already started in the fringes of the slums. Members of Sabarmati Nagarik Adhikar Manch claim that the divisiveness, which has aggravated post 2002, is an impediment toward organizing any kind of joint resistance movement. This divisiveness is supremely ironic in the context of the fact that Gandhi lived and worked among the urban poor along this very bank of river Sabarmati. The first labor union in India, Textile Labor Association (TLA), was formed in Ahmedabad through Gandhi's efforts. Both Hindu and Muslim mill workers organized peaceful strikes under Gandhi's tutelage (Desai 1951; Lakha 1988). Class consciousness took precedence over ethno-religious consciousness, and Hindus and Muslims interacted in the public sphere of the factory, the labor union association, and lived as neighbors. With the decline of the textile mills these public spheres evaporated. Varshney (2002), based on his empirical study of Hindu-Muslim violence in different parts of India, came to the conclusion that the degeneration of formal associational contacts (factories, labor unions, clubs) between the two communities is the key factor in promoting alienation and violence in Ahmedabad city.

The contextual particularities of the SRFD project indicate the embedded nature of neoliberalism. The AMC is hardly a rolled-back state, it is proactive as a market-state in formulating projects that can sell the city and ground investment. The officials repeatedly mention a "world-class" city that is "safe", "Green, clean, and beautiful," and hence is marketable as a foreign investment destination for call centers, information technology, hospitality industries, retailing, and other forms of outsourcing. Promoting harmony, employment generation, relief, and rehabilitation, however, have been rolled back—these fall beyond the scope of an astute market-state. Industrial decline in Ahmedabad was not a 'normal' outcome of business cycles—the state in its evolution as the market-state caused industrial decline by adopting an open market policy and phasing out licensing, quotas. Yet, the market-state assumed no responsibility for the retrenched workers in the informalized sector. The city officials studiously adopt a market rationale where the poor and the unemployed are expected to be automatically absorbed in some production process in the long run, with no vision or plan to indicate how and where this may happen. The mills were concentrated in east Ahmedabad (east of river Sabarmati); with their decline, east Ahmedabad inhabited mainly by the now informalized working class face stagnation and neglect. The informalized do not have the requisite skills to find jobs in the information technology, software, e-commerce, and call center industries, yet there is no attempt made to re-think how the "Green, clean, and beautiful city" might accommodate them.

Keynes, in his critique of the free market, once remarked that in the long run we are all dead (Stiglitz 2003). In the short run, the poor and poverty are absent in the development imaginary of the city officials, and in the mean time, industrial decline and associated informalization will breed frustration and desperation, annihilate social cohesion, and generate inter-community alienation. Class cohesion of the past has slowly been replaced by group competition, egged on by an ideological (Hindu fundamentalist) market-state. Neoliberalism not only encourages place-place competition, but also breeds intra-place competition, which may manifest in the form of inter-community violence, or in the form of individualization of the poor due to the disappearance of sites for collective bargaining, or in the form of uneven development where east Ahmedabad stagnates, while the West is hyper-developed. Islamophobia as a politico-cultural ideology combines with free-market fundamentalism to produce a market-state ideological nexus, where the Hindu poor and particularly the Muslim poor, are 'unfit' for survival in the 'new' Ahmedabad. The Hindu poor can be evicted to the city fringes, and the Muslim poor will be eventually weeded out through silence, neglect, and violence. The market-state is very much an ideological apparatus rolling out the red carpet by contextually grounding neoliberalism in accordance with pre-existing ethno-cultural and social biases. The marketization of the state has not erased these biases in favor of any abstract economic logic where every rational, competitive individual has a chance—in the absence of distributive justice, the poor and the Muslims have no chance of economic or sociocultural mobility, but they are certainly going to be less rational and more competitive as the 2002 violence has shown. The general explanation for the mindless violence has been the BJP's political strategy of polarization to win election, where the poor are used as foot soldiers. There is a lot of truth in that interpretation, but it is important to ask why the poor allow themselves to be used, and why like this, and why now? Clearly, the not very old labor history of Ahmedabad indicates that Hindu and Muslim poor were once capable of sharing common spaces of class unity and common struggles. While political agendas of fundamentalism and divisiveness are potent, it is also important to investigate the contextual particularities of a competitive urban entrepreneurialism to understand how the intended and unintended consequences of embedded neoliberalism may make the poor fight amongst themselves. One respondent on the bank of Sabarmati summarizes this effectively: "What can the poor do? We will fight, kill, steal to keep alive; can you find me a job? I will do anything."

Economically Weaker Section Housing

The erstwhile chair of AUDA (Ahmedabad Urban Development Authority), when asked repeatedly about an inclusive vision of development which is pro-poor said:

> You keep asking about the poor, all these remarkable transformations in terms of greening Ahmedabad, regular mechanical sweeping of the roads, SRFD, widening roads, mean nothing to you? You think we do not care about the poor? The poor provide essential services to the rich; a rich city needs its poor. We have built extensive EWS [economically weaker section] housing for the poor, the best of its kind in India. The poor evicted under various new urban development schemes are housed there, and we will continue to expand it.

There are eight such subsidized colonies: Nandavan, Vraj Bihar I, Vraj Bihar II, Gopal Aavas, Gokul Aavas, Ambedkar Awas Yojna, Vrindavan Avas, and Prahlad Nagar (the last under construction in 2006). Together they contain 4,500 homes and are located in the peripheries of west Ahmedabad with the objective of housing the poor who are casualties of urban entrepreneurialism. The public was made aware of the EWS housing project through advertisements in local, vernacular newspapers like the *Gujarat Samachar*. It is interesting to note that the *Gujarat Samachar* is a newspaper that publishes in the Gujarati language, which is largely unfamiliar to the Muslims, who read and speak Urdu. Subsequently, forms were sold and could be purchased at a nominal fee. Upon submission of the forms, the houses were allotted by drawing of lots. The initial down payment (37% of the total cost) was borne by the owner. The rest of the ownership cost was met by AUDA as a loan that had to be returned as monthly rents. I visited each of these colonies, surveyed the registers, and spoke to the superintendents of each colony and the residents. My aim was to understand how the urban poor acquired these homes, and whether both Hindus and Muslims benefited from the EWS project. Table 7.1 indicates the social composition of the EWS colonies.

A total of 4,500 subsidized homes did not house a single Muslim. Registers did not indicate a single Muslim name (Hindus and Muslims have distinct names in India); the common name plates of the buildings also indicated that no Muslim has ever been allotted a EWS home. When asked, one superintendent explained: "Well, one of the homes went to a Muslim, but he never came to claim it. The home is now locked." Conversations with the residents soon revealed that there was never such a home. Other superintendents claimed that the Muslims never applied, or the allocation was by lottery hence there is no scope of representing every community. AUDA officials are handpicked by the local BJP government, and hence it is hardly a matter of surprise that ethno-religious biases play an important role to spatially exclude the ethnic poor. The fact that the project was solely advertised in a Gujarati newspaper and no Urdu newspaper indicates a clear lack of political will to include the Muslims. The names of each colony are selected after popular figures from Hindu mythology (with the exception of Ambedkar Avas Yojna named after B. R. Ambedkar, an Indian social reformer), blatantly explicating an overt Hindu imaginary in public projects, which are expected to be more inclusive since the Constitution of India proclaims a secular nation. Hinduizing city spaces is part of a larger plan of the AMC—Muslim respondents mention that schools, roads, and bridges have been re-named over the years, and attempt has been made to change the name of Ahmedabad (named after Muslim founder Sultan Ahmed Shah) to a more Hindu version "Karnavati." Muslims account for a large segment of poor in Ahmedabad city; the Sachar committee report (2006) indicates that in the state of Gujarat, Muslims account for the poorest—the mean per capita expenditure of urban Muslims in the state of Gujarat is substantially below that of all other socio-religious categories; the level of urban poverty of Muslims in the state of Gujarat is also substantially higher than all other socio-religious categories, including SC Hindus. In spite of being poor, Muslims have been selectively excluded from EWS housing by a biased market-state.

Table 7.1 EWS Housing Profile

Name	*Locality*	*No. of Homes*	*No. of Years Since Constructed*	*Hindu CommunritySocial Structure*	*Whether There Are Any Muslim Inhabitants?*
Nandavan	Ghatlodiya-Nirnay-nagar	624	4	Mainly OBCs and SCs	None. Official comment: Muslims did not fill the form.
Vraj Bihar I	Vejalpur	992	3	OBCs	None
Vraj Bihar II	Vejalpur	400	3	OBCs	None
Gopal Aavas	Jodpur Tekra	824	3	OBCs and SCs	1. Official Comment: The Muslim house remains closed; they did not take possession. Could not give house number.
Gokul Aavas	Jodpur Tekra	660	5	OBCs and SCs. One Brahmin was allotted, but he sublet to a lower caste.	1. Official Comment: The Muslim house remains closed; they did not take possession. Could not give house number.
Ambedkar Aavas Yojna	Vastrapur	100	4	OBCs and SCs	None
Vrindavan Aavas	Bodakdev	300	3	OBCs and SCs	None
Prahladnagar	Prahladnagar	600	Under construction		

Source: Interview of officials and information from office registers.

Conversations with the Hindu residents of the EWS homes revealed that many homes were not originally allotted to them. The homes were allotted by 'lottery' to 'upper' caste Hindus, who are not actually below the stipulated income level required to qualify for this subsidy, having acquired the subsidized homes, these upper-caste and middle-class Hindus rented them to the poor SC and OBC Hindus, who now pay rent to the original owners. According to the residents, the government exercised caste preferences in allotting homes to the 'upper' castes like the Brahmins (priestly caste) and Baniyas (business castes) and marginalized the SCs and OBCs from owning their own homes. The Hindu residents sufficiently influenced by the local anti-Muslim xenophobia are glad that Muslims have been kept out. Muslims believe that the EWS colonies represent social engineering on the part of the local government to socially and spatially exclude the minority community and to spatially concentrate the 'low'-caste Hindus who will probably constitute the civil militia to be mobilized against Muslims in future riots. The Muslim's fear is based on the fact that during the 2002 riot, the rioting mobs were mainly the 'low'-caste poor Hindus, the 'upper'-caste Hindus serving only as ideological gurus (Shah 2002). EWS housing represents an ingenious ideological strategy to simultaneously deny the poor SC, OBC Hindus, and Muslim community the right of ownership to public housing—the fact that the market-state is not only anti-Muslim but also casteist escapes the attention of both communities—the sad social realities of Ahmedabad induce each group to focus on their own victim-hood and in 'othering' the other.

The market-state uses the EWS housing project to balance out its overt market-orientation. The state must ultimately depend on the poor not only to engineer riots but also to win elections, and projects like the EWS housing are used as baits for prospective voters and as a poster child to ward-off irritant reporters and academic criticisms. The EWS housing project represents a negotiation between the market and the state in the emerging market-state coalition, which attempts to contextually embed neoliberalism. In embedding neoliberalism, the state overtly frees the market through projects like GPP and SRFD; it simultaneously socially disciplines the market (albeit minimally) through projects like the EWS housing, so that the state in the market-state equation can ensure its survival while the civil society 'digests' a newly neoliberalizing city. The EWS housing projects theoretically represent the last remnants of distributive justice still resilient in urban development. In practice, however, the casteist and anti-Muslim biases of the market-state diffuses any potential for distributive justice. The ideological biases of exclusion cleverly hidden beneath the actual spatial realization of the project defeats its very purpose. The cultural (caste and ethnic) injustice overlaps with economic (class) injustice to actualize the contextuality of a new urban entrepreneurialism, which is ruthless in its cultural and economic ideology of weeding out the 'unfit.' The 'unfit' groups are not economically unproductive, the urban poor of Ahmedabad are the laboring communities, whose labor produced the city and still continue to sustain it, however, they are identified and normalized as 'unfit' by the state-market because of their ethno-cultural positions as 'others.'

CONCLUSIONS

As harbinger of neoliberalism in India, the New Economic Policy is still unfolding through a process of market-state re-organization. The pre-neoliberal mixed economic setup is under intense pressure. The states in various hierarchies (national, provincial, local) have been pushed to re-envision themselves as 'shrunken', 'reduced', 'rolled back' in an attempt to free the 'un-tapped' potential of the market. All this is supposed to be good news because of the much touted secularizing and democratic potential of an unfettered market. The neutral and abstract laws of demand and supply are expected to transcend biases perpetuated by ideological apparatuses like the state machinery. Every productive and rational being is therefore, likely to have a fair chance irrespective of cast, creed, religion, gender, or color. In practice however, the market has never operated in an ideological vacuum because it is always grounded in place, and enmeshed in the power, ideology, and vested interests of the leading ideologues of that place. Therefore, neoliberal structural adjustment packages, while imposed in an abstract, one-size-fit-all, quasi-climatic manner in large parts of the Third World, are intensely ideological—the classical free-market ideology is rejuvenated this time not for the rising entrepreneurs in Britain but for rich corporations, investing agencies spread out in rich nations, and also for elites positioned in rich as well as poor nations. This political economic ideology, in turn, is filtered through local cultural economic ideological strata to be contextually embedded. This embedding happens, as always, through a state-market give and take. In India, the state reinvents itself as an entrepreneurial market-state in order to better embed neoliberalism. The contextual embedding of neoliberalism by a market-state manifests itself as exclusionary and violent—unleashing violence on those the market-state excludes as 'unfit.' In the market lingo, fitness is measured in terms of efficiency and productivity, citizens and civil societies must redefine themselves, and spaces and labor must become flexible enough to cater to the whims of international investment; if spaces cannot metamorphose overnight into seductive malls, parks, office complexes, and if labor, rudely pushed out of formal employment, cannot 'fit into' out-sourced occupations, they must fend for themselves. These exclusions become stark in the city, which is now the newest site for embedding neoliberalism.

The city government is vigorous in re-organizing itself as a market-state, the purpose being to market the city as a conducive space for embedding foreign investment. The evolution of the city government into a market-state is an interesting phenomena starkly manifested through a rabid new urban entrepreneurialism, which is unabashed in its pursuit of profit and completely unaccountable to people. The Ahmedabad case indicates that the market-state is now comfortably silent on the goals of distributive justice, poverty alleviation, employment generation, and rehabilitation of the displaced. In its haste to ground capital, the market-state in Ahmedabad enacts its new urbanism through projects like GPP, SRFD, EWS housing, which are neither democratic, nor do they offer a fair chance to all. The projects are explicitly biased against the poor, the Muslims, and the SC, OBC Hindus. The poor, the Muslims, and the SC, OBC Hindus are not unproductive; until recently many had formal employments, and even now they devise creative ways of working the market through the informal sector, yet the market-state marginalizes them as 'unfit'. In the dog-eat-dog scenario of the survival of the fittest, the rules of the game are unfairly biased in favor of big capital, foreign business, upper caste and middle- and upper-class Hindus. Embedded neoliberalism is not ideologically neutral or secularizing, but rather it becomes a double-edged sword where pre-existing biases of an ideological state combine with market fundamentalism to exclude. But, what is more dangerous is that the violence and exclusion is hardly interpreted as a systemic outcome of an ideologically astute market-state, it is usually masked as spontaneous outcomes of the poor fighting the poor, or culturally different Hindus and Muslims alienating each other. The GPP, SRFD, EWS housing projects indicate that there exists a systemic logic in excluding the ethnic minority and dividing the class poor, and the spaces in which they live. In embedding neoliberalism, roots of violence are carefully laid out, the result is a ticking time bomb—in the absence of ameliorative measures they will erupt into riots like those in 2002, which will be interpreted as politically motivated. Ethnophobic politics represents only one side of the ideological spectrum—caste ethnic fundamentalism actually couples with market fundamentalism to inscribe the violent narratives of entrepreneurial Ahmedabad.

NOTES

1. The traditional Hindu social order is considered to be hierarchical where individuals are born into castes which initially represented their family occupation. The Brahmins or the priestly class occupy the top rung, followed by the erstwhile ruling class of kings and landlords, followed by the merchants and traders and lastly by the lower castes who carried out menial jobs like agriculture, pottery, weaving and a whole section of outcastes who performed 'polluting professions' like burning the dead.
2. The census of India classifies certain castes (referred to as Scheduled Castes, or SCs) as having historically suffered socioeconomic discrimination and are accorded special status (reservation of seats in government schools, jobs). The Other Backward Classes (or OBCs) in India are a group of castes officially recognized as having been traditionally subject to exclusion. The

Constitution of India traditionally recognizes the need to extend positive discrimination (affirmative action) to this section.

3. An auto-rickshaw is a cheap mode of local transport available for hire on hailing; it is a three-wheeler like a rickshaw but has an engine, runs on gas, and is smaller and more open than a car.

REFERENCES

Ahmed, R. 2002. Gujarat violence: Meaning and implications. *Economic and Political Weekly* (May 18). http://www.epw.org.in/showarticles.php (accessed April 2005).

Ahmed, W. 2007. Neoliberalism and contested policies of the power industry in India. *The Industrial Geographer*, 5(1): 44–57.

Balgopal, K. 2002. Reflections on 'Gujarat Pradesh of 'Hindu Rashtra'. *Economic and Political Weekly* (June 1). http://www.epw.org.in/showarticles.php (accessed April 2005).

Breman, J. 2002. Communal upheaval as resurgence of social Darwinism. *Economic and Political Weekly,* April 20. Available at: http://www.epw.org.in/showarticles.php, accessed on April 2005.

Brenner, N., and N. Theodore. 2002. Cities and geographies of "Actually existing neoliberalism." *Antipode* 34, (3) 349–379.

Combat law. 2004. *Grabbing urban poor habitat: Sabarmati Riverfront Project.* http://www.combatlaw.org/information.php (accessed October 2006).

Corbridge, S., and J. Harriss. 2000. *Reinventing India.* Cambridge: Polity Press.

Cox, K., and A. Mair. 1988. Locality and community in the politics of local economic development. *Annals of the Association of American Geographers* 78: 307–325.

Desai, M. H. 1951. *A righteous struggle: A chronicle of the Ahmedabad textile labourers' fight for justice.* Ahmedavad: Navajivan Publishing House.

Dutta, S. S. 2000. Partnerships in urban development: A review of Ahmedabad's experience. *Environment and Urbanization* 12: 13–26.

Global Investor's Summit. 2007. http://dst.gujarat.gov.in/global_it_investors_summit_07.htm_

Hales, D. 2003. Practical steps toward healthier cities and a cleaner global environment. http://usinfo.state.gov/journals/itgic/0300/ijge/gj-03.htm (accessed July 2008).

Harvey, D. 1989. From managerialism to entrepreneurialism: The transformation of urban governance in late capitalism. *Geografiska Annaler* 71B: 3–17.

ICLEI. 1995–2000. Increasing resources to local government in India. http://www3.iclei.org/localstrategies/summary/ahmedabad2.html (accessed July 2008).

Jessop, B. 2002. Liberalism, neoliberalism, and urban covernance: A state-theoretical perspective. *Antipode* 34: 452–472.

Kundu, A. 2000. Globalizing Gujarat. *Economic and Political Weekly* 35 (volume no. 34 issue 3) (August–September): 3172–3181.

Kundu, A., and D. Mahadevia. 2002. *Poverty and vulnerability in globalizing metropolis Ahmedabad.* New Delhi: Manak.

Lakha, S. 1988. *Capitalism and class in colonial India: A case of Ahmedabad.* New Delhi: Sterling.

Leitner, H., J. Peck, and E. Sheppard. 2007. *Contesting neoliberalism: Urban frontiers.* New York: Guilford Press.

Mahadevia, D. 2002. Communal space over life space. *Economic and Political Weekly* (November 30). http://www.epw.org.in/showarticles.php (accessed April 2005).

Mahadevia, D., and H. S. Brar. 2006. *Changing development priorities in emerging Mega City: Ahmedabad.* Paper presented at the Conference on Tackling Exclusion: Shelter, Basic Services and Citizen's Rights in Globalizing Megacities of Asia, New Delhi.

Ministry of Urban Development Annual Report. 1990–1991. http://urbanindia.nic.in/moud/quickaccess/ann_report/1990–1991/English/4.pdf (accessed July 2008).

———. 2001–2002. http://urbanindia.nic.in/moud/quickaccess/ann_report/2001–2002/English/4.pdf (accessed July 2008).

Peck, J., and A. Tickell. 2002. Neoliberalizing space. *Antipode* 34 (3): 380–404.

Peet, R. 2007. Deconstructing free trade: From epistemic communities to ideological communities in struggle. *Transactions of the Institute of British Geographers* 32: 576–580.

Peet, R., B. Born, M. Davis, K. Fehrer, S. Feldman, S. R. Khan, M. Labban, K. McArdle, C, Marcano, L. Meierotto, D. Niles, T. Ponniah, M. C. Schmidt, G. Schwarz, J. Shagwert, M. P. Staton, and S. Stratton. 2003. *Unholy trinity.* New York: Zed Books.

Parekh, T. 2004. Displacement issue has potential to derail riverfront project. *Times of India* (Ahmedabad), December 8.

Rudolph, L., and S. Rudolph. 1987. *In pursuit of Lakshmi.* Chicago, London: University of Chicago Press.

Sachar, R. 2006. *Social, economic and educational status of the Muslim community of India: A report.* Government of India. New Delhi: Cirrus Graphics.

Sarkar, T. 2002. Semiotics of terror. *Economic and Political Weekly* (July 13). http://www.epw.org.in/showarticles.php (accessed April 2005).

Shah, G. 2002. Caste, Hindutva and hideousness. *Economic and Political Weekly* (April 13). http://www.epw.org.in/showarticles.php (accessed April 2005).

Stiglitz, J. 2003. *Globalization and its discontents.* New York: W. W. Norton.

Swyngedouw, E., F. Moulaert, and A. Rodriguez. 2002. Neoliberal urbanization in Europe: Large-scale urban development projects and the New Urban Policy. *Antipode* 34 (3): 542–577.

The Indian Express. 2005. HC admits PIL against Sabarmati plan. *The Indian Express*, April 9.

Uitermark, J. 2002. Re-scaling, 'scale fragmentation' and the regulation of antagonistic relationships. *Progress in Human Geography* 26(6): 743–765.

Vanaik, A. 2001. The new Indian right. *New Left Review* (May–June).

Varshney, A. 2002. *Ethnic conflict and civic life.* London: Yale University Press.

WACAP (World Alliance of Cities Against Poverty). http://mirror.undp.org/switzerland/wacap/en/experiences/ahme.htm (accessed July 2008).

Weber, R. 2002. Extracting values from the city: Neoliberalism and urban redevelopment. *Antipode* 34 (3): 519–540.

Yagnik, A., and S. Seth. 2002. Wither Gujarat? Violence and after. *Economic and Political Weekly* (March). http://www.epw.org.in/showArticles (accessed April 2005).

8 Neoliberalism, Environmentalism, and Urban Politics in Delhi

Rohit Negi

A bourgeoning literature on the effects of neoliberal policies on cities across the world has emerged in the last two decades. Urban scholars have chronicled the changes, particularly from a critical standpoint, which have accompanied the neoliberal, and what David Harvey (1989) famously termed the 'entrepreneurial turn' in urban governance in various contexts. From New York (Smith 2002) to Chicago (Wilson 2004), and from Glasgow (MacLeod 2002) to São Paulo and Johannesburg (Murray 2004), cities have undergone social-spatial transformations as a result of the emergent neoliberal order, characterized by "the loosening or dismantling of the various institutional constraints upon marketization, commodification, the hyperexploitation of workers, and the discretionary power of private capital that had been established through popular struggles prior to and during the postwar period" (Brenner and Theodore 2002, 342). Note that Brenner and Theodore here are speaking in the North Atlantic context; in much of the post-colonial world, while neoliberalism does signify parallel structural shifts, these have not appeared at the cost of the so-called Fordist regime of accumulation. Neoliberal transformations here have served to undermine state-capitalist production, import substitution, and at least nominally redistributive regimes that were borne of post-colonial nationalism (cf. Saul 2005). Contributions to this volume and elsewhere have analyzed the political economy of these shifts in India; here I am interested in two related issues: first, the imbrications of a certain kind of environmental activism with the neoliberal reordering of urban space; second, the alternative scales and institutions through which those marginalized by these processes stake their claims.

I use the case of the relocation of industries from Delhi as a window into these issues. This followed the Supreme Court order which required the state administration to close down all supposedly hazardous industries operating in the city and to relocate them outside city borders. Developed land was to be made available for this purpose so that workers were not rendered jobless for a protracted length of time. However, governmental apathy, the inability of small-scale industries to relocate, and the decision of several owners to shut shop meant that many workers were quite severely affected, and eventually unemployed.

Many critical analyses of industrial relocation have correctly read it against the emergence of a discourse of globality in millennial Delhi (Nigam 2001; Routray 2006; Padhi 2007; Bhan 2009), which makes the urban poor marginal to the real and imagined urban economy. The argument is that the politics of urban space has turned, during the last two decades, on the need to remake Delhi as a world class city, an ideological imperative within which certain spaces and inhabitants come to be viewed as superfluous at best, and 'encroachers' at worst. These also happen to be precisely the economic activities and populations that are also considered environmentally degrading by the judiciary. This articulation of the neoliberal and the environmental agenda has tilted the conflict between industrial firms and workers on the one hand, and interests tied to a post-industrial future on the other, in favor of the latter. At stake is the attempted rescaling of Delhi from the capital of post-colonial India, which implies a geography rooted in the hinterland, to one part of a global network that includes other such economic and cultural centers (see Smith 2002). The former are resistant to such a change. In the available literature, however, the specific interests on either side of this conflict are less well theorized.

As noted previously, the workers—joined initially by petty capitalists who owned the small-scale factories under threat—did not acquiesce in the face of this challenge to their livelihoods. There were massive protests that were quelled by the police, leading to the deaths of at least three workers. However, and as a result of workers' organization and pressure, the local state had to intervene to mitigate the worst effects of the original court order. In the end, no significant gains were made toward reducing pollution, while industrial workers were left contemplating the insecurity of their fate in the capital city. Not only did this frustrate environmentalists, but it also left social activists increasingly suspicious of environmentalism in India, which is regrettable because environmental issues are undeniably of pressing concern. This chapter therefore, and after describing the case and the articulation of the environmental and the neoliberal agenda, ends with a discussion on the problems of environmentalism and suggests an alternative way forward.

1. THE CASE

To guide the planning of the Indian capital, the central government created the Delhi Development Authority (DDA) in 1957. Soon after, the DDA devised the first Master Plan for Delhi (DMP-62), which came into force in 1962, and was followed by another for the year 2001 in 1990. The latter classified industries into several categories on the basis of the number of workers employed and power consumption. Based on this classification, existing 'Hazardous and noxious industries', and 'Heavy and large industries' were proposed to be relocated to the peripheries of Delhi, and non-conforming industries—that is, those located in predominantly residential areas—of all types were to be closed, even if they were non-polluting. However, the DMP-2001 set itself a hard task, given that of a total of about 125,000 industries in the city, an estimated 98,000 were in non-conforming areas (Ministry of Environment and Forests 2002). Not surprising then that at the end of the first five years of the plan's enforcement, little was done by the DDA to relocate such industries.

It was in this context that a long drawn out case in the Supreme Court (*MC Mehta vs. Union of India* WP13029/1985) first filed in 1985 and initially focusing on the amelioration of vehicular pollution in Delhi, in due course came to engulf industrial pollution. In successive orders starting March 1995, the Supreme Court ordered that the DMP-2001 be strictly enforced, and that all industries deemed illegal be relocated or shut. The Court gave the state government of Delhi five years to do so (*MC Mehta v. Union of India* WP4677/1985/ July 8, 1996). It was in the year 2000, with almost no factory in the second category having followed the order and the state having dragged its feet, that the Court ordered summary closures. As a result, more than 50,000 workers were unemployed, and many more livelihoods were adversely affected (Nigam 2001, 45). Interestingly, at no point during the case were industrial workers directly part of the proceedings of the Court in the way that the state, large industries, and environmentalists were. Workers entered the picture only after the order was cast. According to the judges: "The hazardous industry has been closed, what remains is the plot, superstructure, and the workmen" (*MC Mehta v. Union of India* WP4677/1985/ March 1, 2001). As part of the superstructure of the industry, workers needed to be dealt with like the other means of production. In sum, dealing with air pollution was prioritized by the Court, and the loss of livelihoods came to be seen as an unavoidable consequence. Given this 'trade-off', two key questions emerge: Through what processes has environmental protection become such an overarching priority? And why is industrial production a key site of environmental interventions? To get at this question I first analyze the environmental turn of the judiciary and then situate it within the broader political economic context at the moment that this matter was being debated.

2. THE ENVIRONMENTAL TURN

Judicial activism, or the shift in power within the state from the legislature or executive toward the judiciary, has a long history in India. For the most part courts have been decidedly positivist, merely interpreting the Constitution of India in letter and not in spirit (Sathe 2002, 4–8). But legal scholars concur that there have been two major points of departure from its positivist proclivities. The first was post-Emergency, when the Court "apologized, in word and deed, [to] the people of India for judicial abdication during the 1975–77 Emergency period" (Baxi 2000, 157). This activism mainly involved a liberal and staunch protection of human rights, which had been undermined during the national emergency. Though it did see the Court concern itself with issues of social justice, there was minimal confrontation with other arms of the state, as the post-Emergency administration during that period was itself strongly inclined to make the perpetrators of the Emergency pay.

The second period of judicial activism is more recent and has been in the field of environmental governance. Key to its rise has been the "enforcement of the right to a clean environment as a facet of right to life itself" (Salve 2000, 366) by the Supreme Court since the early 1990s. In contrast to the former period, here the legitimacy for judicial activism stems from the alleged ineffectiveness of the state at various scales to deal with the perceived environmental deterioration. In particular, the latest wave of activism has been fueled by the initiation and proliferation of public interest litigations (PILs) that have fundamentally altered the Court's conception of environmental issues. These were earlier interpreted purely as matters of nuisance to property, that is, litigations were filed only if the petitioner was directly impacted by things like noise and smoke. In contrast, and this statement concerns a case on river pollution, now anyone "interested in protecting the lives of people who lived on the banks of the river and would use the water flowing in the river, had a right to maintain [the] petition" (Salve 2000, 369). As a result, the space created by the Court for issues that may not personally concern a petitioner encouraged environmental activists to approach it, not as the 'last instance', but as a counter to a supposedly intractable executive. Noted lawyer MC Mehta alone has filed numerous petitions in variegated environmental matters, obtaining about 40 judgments from various courts[1].

The Indian judiciary has, in this manner, played an increasingly active role not only in enforcing environmental laws but also in bringing nature into discourses on social life in general. This has led some to conclude that "environment today is the single most important issue shaping Delhi's physical and social life" (Sharan 2001, 33). In a number of judgments ranging from conversion of the bus fleet to Compressed Natural Gas (CNG), phasing out old vehicles, and numerous demolitions of slums (Sharan 2001, 33), the Supreme Court has reordered space in response to environmentalist PILs. As a result, judicial activism has created for environmentalists the opportunity to require the state to enact and enforce stringent environmental laws. This activism in environmental issues has been widely welcomed by those who view the state as largely dysfunctional—as a wall that NGOs and environmental activists repeatedly run up against in their attempts to 'protect' the environment (Upadyay 2001; Narain 2002). The proliferation of PILs and the judiciary's swift action on them has occurred to such an extent that at some point in this case the Supreme Court described itself as "the guardian angel of the society" (*MC Mehta v. Union of* India WP4677/1985/ March 1, 2001).

To be sure, the courts' actions are related to actually existing pollution in India, especially of its rivers and urban air and the widely acknowledged inability or disinterest of the state in dealing with it. Though this materiality is important, actions do not naturally follow its acknowledgment but remain political choices—what should any intervention prioritize, for instance, clean air or clean drinking water? Preventing noise or providing sanitation? It is thus of importance that the environment gets defined in a particular way that eliminates politics and constructs these questions as technical problems to be solved. The environmental movement is culpable in this move. According to noted environmentalist Sunita Narain, "fighting pollution demands scientific expertise. But civil society [in India] as yet, remains weak in its understanding of technical issues" (2002, 16). As for the courts, since judges are legal experts, and not technocrats, they often rely on "expert committees to guide them on technical matters" (Narain 2002, 16). In this context, consider this predicament faced by the judges:

> We were shown some literature and even gadgets which might help reduction of pollution . . . Some of the aspects that came up for discussion were indeed sufficiently technical . . . [in response, the Court formed] a high-powered committee . . . [headed by] Justice K. N. Saikia who has recently retired as a Judge of this Court . . . the Committee would . . . have the power to co-opt experts. (*MC Mehta v. Union of India* WP13029/1985/ March 14, 1991)

These committees' main job is to translate technical discourses into the language of the Court. Varied environmental expertise—particulates in the air and the harm they do to the human bloodstream—can be mobilized only when translated by experts capable of doing so. In most cases, these expert committees are set under the 'writ of mandamus', such that the committees' findings and reports are considered emanating not from their members but from the court (Anant and Singh 2002). Not only does this unequally empower experts, but it also provides gainful post-retirement employment for judges, thereby perpetuating the institution of expert committees. It is through this move that environment becomes a technical arena populated by experts, and the elimination of politics from it is enacted.

The environmental turn in the judiciary and the wider civil society has been further bolstered by the universalization of the discourse of environmental conservation through the 1990s and after; and the increased saliency of ecology in public life (Zizek 2007). In response to the perils of environmental change, most notably global warming, sustainable development has become the mantra as a goal for social policy across contexts (see Lipschutz 2003). In its order on industrial relocation, the Supreme Court cites the report of the well-known World Commission on Environment and

Development (also known as the Brundtland Commission) of the United Nations several times to portray the urgency of the situation and as a set of actions mandated at a larger scale, from above, which need to be ardently followed.

> Brundtland Report called out for adaptation globally of a strategy of sustainable development that meets the need of the present without compromising the ability of future generations to meet their own needs. (*MC Mehta v. Union of India* WP4677/1985/ March 1, 2001)

> [T]he problem of environmental pollution is global in an increasingly small world and concerns all countries irrespective of their size, level of development or ideology. Notwithstanding political division of the world into national units, the oceanic world is an inter-connected whole; the winds that blow over the countries are also one. (*MC Mehta v. Union of India* WP13029/1985/ March 14, 1991)

The broad definition of the fundamental right to life as also the right to an unpolluted environment has led the courts to a seemingly contradictory view of the relationship between nature and society. On the one hand, they conform to the 'modern' view of environment as separate from society (Latour 1993), wherein the latter is seen to cause strain on and degrade a fetishized and hitherto balanced nature (see Véron 2006). On the other hand, however, issues related to 'order', illegality, and urban management are also elaborated as environmental concerns. With the problems thus defined, the solution takes a two-pronged form—to bring nature back into a balanced state *and* to restore a particular notion of social and spatial order. The following statement by the Supreme Court is particularly instructive in this regard for it shows precisely this logic:

> Delhi is recording heavy population growth since 1951. As the city grows, its problems of land, housing, transportation, and management of essential infrastructure like water supply and sewage have become more acute. Delhi is one of the most polluted cities in the world . . . The city has become a vast and unmanageable conglomeration of commercial, industrial, unauthorized colonies, resettlement colonies and unplanned housing. There is a total lack of open spaces and green areas. *Once a beautiful city, Delhi now presents a chaotic picture*. The *only* way to relieve the capital city from the huge additional burden and pressures, is to deconcentrate the population, industries and economic activities in the city and relocate the same . . . [Emphasis added] (*MC Mehta v. Union of India* and others 1996)

With a somewhat Malthusian slant set in the backdrop of a nostalgic picture of a Delhi past, the Court views urban problems as an inevitable consequence of the pressures of population growth, while also presenting chaos and disorder as environmental issues. It is then logical that 'deconcentration'—or the removal of populations and uses from the city—becomes the solution. It is worth remembering that it is *particular* populations that come to be defined as the problem: those who inhabit 'unplanned' spaces and engage in practices at the edge of legality. This explains the spate of court orders that have targeted slums and squatter settlements recently; but what sorts of growth of 'economic activities' become the problem is a question that must be understood through an investigation of the broader political economic shifts that Delhi is undergoing, for they provide the frame for this selective purge.

3. THE NEOLIBERAL TURN

The orientation of the political economy toward the opening-up of markets and free trade has occurred globally during the neoliberal era. What is more specific to Delhi within this general process is that this shift coincides with aspirations to become a 'global city'. This notion is further related to the emergence of the so-called 'post-industrial' city, which is what a world city is, among other things. However, it is striking that one would be talking about post-industrial cities in an Indian context where development is usually seen as depending on industrial development, or at least it was until very recently (Fortun 2001). It highlights the difficulties that India has encountered in industrializing in the classic secondary sector, and compared to China the occupational distribution is tertiary-sector heavy (Joshi 2004; Bosworth and Collins 2008, 46). The case of industrial relocation in Delhi helps shed light on this puzzle by illuminating some of the struggles around two visions of development: one is manufacturing-led and supported by firms and their workers; the other is service-led and supported by property owners who will gain from the conversion of land and wealthier segments of the population keen to improve their 'quality of life' through getting rid of the externalities of industrial production.

What the latter have been able to take advantage of, in effect, are global discourses of environmentalism, technocracy, and the world city. The original plaintiffs in the pollution case were environmentalists, but the court decision was significant for those factions pushing, at the same time, to convert Delhi into a post-industrial city. The contrast with the conditions under which industrialization occurred in the nineteenth and early twentieth centuries is stark. Then there were no such global discourses which could be brought to bear on countering industrialization or furthering some image of the city as other than industrial. A common view of the politics of uneven development on a global scale is that the more developed countries intervene politically in order to slow down industrialization in developing societies, as through tariff protection of industries or through attempts to impose Western labor standards (see Wade 2003). This literature highlights Western pressures to open up economies of the Global South, factors that compromise the latter's ability to develop their respective manufacturing sectors. But this may be only part of the story. They might also be benefiting from global discourses which have appeal to certain factions in developing countries. In other words, the dependency theory-informed view underestimates the influence of internal forces that aim to retool the city within the global division of labor to benefit from tertiary-sector capital flows.

It is instructive here to consider the Delhi government's plans to make Delhi a global city. Consider the first statement to the State Assembly by the government of Delhi, outlining its plans and vision for the next five years. It pivots around the chief minister's "dream of making Delhi a modern, global city" (L-G lays out govt's vision 2003[2]). This document, as reported in the newspaper article, identifies elements on the "road to global city" (L-G lays out govt's vision 2003). These are increased power and water supply, 'quality' roads and flyovers, buses running on new technologies, and e-governance. These changes, however, must be superimposed upon the existing urban economy and space in Delhi.

There is plenty of evidence to suggest that these plans are being implemented. Two decades ago, David Harvey (1989) pointed out several key characteristics of the 'entrepreneurial city', all of which seem to apply to Delhi: A number of 'public-private partnerships' are indeed being materialized to make the city attractive to foreign investors; 'flagship' projects have been initiated to advertise the city's globality; and Delhi has been increasingly marketed to those beyond its borders. For example, the restructuring of the power sector and the privatization of power distribution is an illustration of the public-private model of urban governance, as is the construction of the new \$100 million toll bridge over the river Yamuna (Noida Toll Bridge Company 2006), advertised as the first of many to come. The construction of the Delhi Metro as a flagship project began in 1995, and just the first phase of the Metro has cost about \$2.4 billion (Delhi Metro Rail Corporation 2006); Delhi is set to host the 2010 Commonwealth Games, through which the city hopes to make itself a more global space of consumption. For the purpose of this chapter, it is important to realize that not only are smokestacks and slums not required in a global city, they actually directly detract from its aesthetic requirements. According to Bhan (2009), there has been a profound reformulation in the framing of the poor within the broader context of the shift in urban politics from the state to the courts; the poor are now increasingly criminalized, and were recently termed 'pickpockets' (139; see also Ramanathan 2004) by the courts. While Bhan and others have correctly interpreted these shifts, the analysis thus far lacks theorization of the competing interests that are tied to the transformation. In other words, and with respect to the discursive shifts related to the projection of Delhi as a 'world city', what actors and factions of capital have acted as the growth machine for Delhi's neoliberal turn?

It has been suggested that the state's initial eagerness to enforce the relocation order was on account of the freeing-up of scarce urban resources: "the closure of factories and mass displacement of workers . . . will release 700MW of power and 50 million gallons of water, alongside a reduction of 40 mgd (million gallons per day) of sewage disposal" (Nigam 2001, 42). This massive capacity, Nigam argues, is likely to be used to further the state's attempts to recreate the city as a space of consumption and as a destination for skilled industries like software and outsourced services. There is certainly a grain of truth in this argument, since a third of the population of the city lives in slum settlements, and there has long existed the logic of beautification which requires the removal of slums and their replacement by things like public parks, and which has been accelerated by this recent emphasis on a new division of labor (Baviskar 2003). It also brings maximum results: though industrial production in 1991 contributed about 10% to the state income, it employed about a quarter of the total population of Delhi (Economic Survey of Delhi 2006). Due to their sustenance wages and unaffordable housing, most industrial and informal workers must reside in the numerous slums in Delhi. What better way to cure the problem of slums than to shut down the industries? Indeed following the relocation order, two extra bogeys were added to trains, and special buses were run for workers and their families to return to the villages and towns they were supposed to have come to Delhi from (Delhi Janwadi Adhikar Manch 2006).

More directly, according to the order on relocation, with regards to the land on which industries were located, a third of the plot that was vacated continued to be private property of the owner and in accordance with the zoning in that area, the owner could develop it according to her wishes. The rest of the land was to be utilized by the DDA to create 'open spaces', 'green areas', and even 'amusement parks', so as to enhance 'lung spaces' in the city. The Court anticipated a windfall for the property owners:

> [The plots'] values may be many times more than the yields which are presently being enjoyed by the operation of these industries and even what they might have totally enjoyed from the time of the start of these industries . . . there is little doubt that [owners] see gold mines in them. (*MC Mehta v. Union of India* WP4677/1985/ May 10, 1996)

Since the relocation order was forced on industries, industry owners were given exemption from the tough national labor laws. Workers were to be paid one-year's wages in case either the industry or workers decided not to relocate. Later realizing that many owners simply shut shop, the Court ordered that in such an instance, the workers were to be paid six years wages, in accordance with the Labor Laws (*MC Mehta v. Union of India* WP4677/1985/ December 4, 1996). But since wages in the city are already meager and employers not responsible for housing or health, this amount was a pittance compared to the windfall in store for owners from redevelopment. It is estimated that the larger industries made a killing by selling their land in prime areas of the city or undertaking commercial development of the land, and the government of Delhi benefited substantially from taxes from these more 'intensive' uses of land[3]. Though it is hard to imagine the Court operating with this rather instrumental sense, there is no doubt that in its order the Supreme Court did consider closure of industries to the economic benefit of the industrial capitalists themselves, and by extension, to the benefit of the city.

Note that these two points—the freeing-up of urban space and the retooling of Delhi toward an 'entrepreneurial' model—still do not provide the material grounding to the changes. As a method of doing so, it is instructive to revisit Cox and Mair's (1988) notion of 'local dependence'. In very brief, different factions of capital have uneven stake in place: certain sectors of capital are more closely tied to the fortunes of the place than others. In the case of the U.S. where this concept was formulated, real estate developers, utility companies, and newspapers are among the branches of capital that are intrinsically tied to local markets, and their growth is directly related to the amount of wealth that flows through that particular place. To these we can add the state and workers, who are also—more or less—dependent on specific places for their continued reproduction. Certain other factions of capital, however, may be less interested in particular places, for their market may extend throughout a broader region, nationally, or even globally. The loss of business for them from a particular market may be offset with the rise of another. Strangely enough, there is hardly any work that details the trajectory of Delhi's property development market, and this account can therefore only provide certain clues.

A radical decision like the relocation of industries from Delhi would have been unimaginable three decades back, when as the poster child of national modernization and scientific socialism, industrialization was considered inherently desirable. Over the last few years, however, decline in industrial production[4] (Figure 8.1) and a rise in investment in retail, office, and branch plant outsourcing (BPO) has meant that manufacturing industries do not enjoy the same discursive power as before. In fact, they are, with this case, implicated in the degradation of both the physical and human environment, through air pollution that endangers public health and poor workers who make the city aesthetically unpleasant. On the other hand, marked improvements in transportation do not necessitate the location of industries inside the city; and given the tremendous rise in real estate prices, and heavy interest from multinational corporations to site in and around Delhi, office, commercial, and residential uses are clearly a more 'optimal' utilization of the space. According to the real-asset management consultancy Jones Lang LaSalle, "Multinational contact centre companies and back-office services are shifting focus to Delhi after the perceived saturation of other key markets like Bangalore and Mumbai" (2003). Transnational corporations like IBM, Microsoft, and Nokia had purchased more than 200,000 sq. ft. of office space in the suburbs in the last quarter of 2004 alone (Jones Lang Lasalle 2004; see also Raman 2008). Further, tens of five-stars hotels have been constructed, many on areas that these same plans have designated as 'green spaces', but the courts have mostly turned a blind eye to *these* violations (Bhushan 2009, 35). The upcoming Commonwealth Games have been a major spur for this spurt in hospitality, and one can foresee a further boost, given that a recent Parliamentary sub-committee concluded a major shortfall in the number of rooms needed for that event (MPs worried . . . 2009). Also, the Delhi Metro Rail Corporation has itself emerged as a key property agent, developing properties around the numerous Metro stations to the tune of up to a third of its total revenues (Awasthi and Sharma 2007).

Another sector that is closely related to property development and has also gained immensely in value is retail (Dupont 2008). Though organized retailing accounted for only 2% of the $180 billion market in 2005, it is expected to grow by leaps and bounds as more and more shopping malls and arcades (A view on mall development 2008) continue to be built; the result is that there are more malls in Delhi (96 total) than other Indian city by far (Mumbai is next with 55). Several resourceful interests thus now have a direct stake in Delhi's space. Property and retail are also the sectors that are most directly related to the proliferation of the signs of globality discussed earlier. Seen together, and more than what their actual numbers deserve, these new growth industries carry immense discursive weight, with places like Delhi hoping to carve a place in their global division of labor[5]. The relocation of industries therefore 'made sense' within these changes, even as the factories themselves seemed out of place in the new, global city of Delhi.

4. THE 'REMAINING' MEANS OF PRODUCTION

These changes in the urban economy need to be read alongside the kind of manufacturing prevalent in the city. The average size of a manufacturing unit is 9 to 11 workers, and a vast majority of units employ fewer than six workers (Economic Survey of Delhi 2006). Surplus value in these factories comes from an absolute exploitation of workers, and twelve to sixteen hours of work a day, six days a week is common (Delhi Janwadi Adhikar Manch 2005). For this, many workers earn anywhere between $40 to $70 a month (DJAM 2005), and there is absolutely no obligation on the employers to provide for housing or health. These firms, moreover, are part of a much broader social division of labor, wherein industries operate through a web of sub-contracted production carried out by large and small firms. As a result, the unionization of labor is limited to only the full-time employees of the larger industries, and the absence of unions in a situation of fragmentation of workers is directly related to the latter's inability to articulate opposition. There is no surprise then that as far as the Court case is concerned, workers had little means to compete discursively or materially.

At the same time, there is a gap between the laws and regulations that the state in its various capacities inscribes and their implementation across urban space. This is the site where public interest litigations operate, and the gap itself is believed to result from the state's inefficiency, arising from either the absence of adequate resources (manpower) or the lack of capacity to make use of its resources. One must recall here that the courts in this case did not technically enter into policy making but sought to coerce the state into acting out its own plans and enforcing its regulations. Put another way, the gap between laws and their enforcement has been conceptualized by activists and courts alike as a technical matter, where the courts are considered to be helpful.

The trajectory of the state's relationship to judicial activism, however, contradicts this understanding. The same state that is seen to drag its feet on this—and other—matters miraculously manages to swing into action after court decisions. This hints at the fact that the gap is not technical but *political*: it is so because even though the post-colonial state enacts laws and spatial regulations, it does so with the knowledge that its actions are open to negotiation (Mbembe 2000). That is, while the institutions and procedures of state were inherited from the colonial state, their practice was in some ways democratized. This is what creates room for strategic contracts the state enters into with sections of the population made vulnerable by law in exchange for electoral support or more covert practices that are signified by the term 'corruption'.

In the case of industrial relocation, environmentalism via the judiciary tried to bridge the political gap between abstract regulations and concrete practices. It sought to reformulate it as a technical matter, which fit the vocabulary and logics of the courts nicely but left out the workers. It must be said though that the workers and the urban poor are not the only actors who seek access to the political gap; more affluent residents who live and operate businesses in the so-called 'unauthorized colonies' also inhabit spaces at the edge of legality. The increased clout of the courts in these matters makes the operation of both these groups difficult: the difference is that the former exist without any safety net, having long been at the margins of society.

As for the wider reactions, the local and national press was unequivocally in favor of industrial closure, as was the English-daily reading public. In a *Times of India* poll 92% of respondents supported industrial closure and relocation, and 83% believed that it was 'not a political issue but a civil issue' (For health and livelihood 2004). In fact, in the immediate aftermath of the closure of industries, as workers protested the Supreme Court order, several English-language dailies chose to highlight the inconvenience to middle-class Delhi, rather than delve into the reasons for the protests. Thereafter, coverage was dominated by the local politicians' attempts to co-opt the opposition, something we return to later.

In 1996, the Supreme Court ordered that all industries be closed and gave the government of Delhi almost five years to make available developed land outside the city borders where industries were to be relocated. The state, however, did not do as the Court ordered; when the ill-fated day arrived in November of 2000, thousands of industries had to be shut down. Interestingly, because of their banishment from the courtroom, workers did not mobilize while the matter was within the judicial spaces. But on November 19, 2000, when the court order arrived on the ground through the law enforcement agencies, they erupted in opposition:

> Thousands of angry owners and workers affected by the implementation of . . . Supreme Court order to close polluting industries . . . have brought the city to a standstill . . . At least three persons were killed by police, and more than 100 sustained injuries in the violent clashes . . . Unrelenting, India's highest Court . . . turned down a hasty request by the government of Delhi to allow it to slow down the process of shifting polluting and unauthorized industrial units in view of the chaos and violence. (Three dead in Delhi 2000)

Despite the tremendous human impacts of the order, and protests against it, the Supreme Court remained adamant. The point seemed to be that as the 'guardian angel' of society it had to remain detached from immediate concerns in order to secure the long-term future of Indian cities. But the fact is that no matter what its orders are, they have to be implemented on the ground by the local state. This reliance of the court on both a willing and efficient sovereign is a necessary condition for its orders to translate into material reality. Workers sidelined by the present case, with no means or basis of participation in court had had an alternate space of resistance, resulting from the structure of law itself. Therefore, local politics is the arena where legally marginalized groups can hope to negotiate favorable terms, because it is what happens here that determines whether or not court orders become concrete. Hence, discursive forces that made the initial order possible were now irrelevant when the order was to translate into reality.

After Partha Chatterjee (2004), in post-colonial India claims through the courts and other institutions of *civil society* are made as/by an enlightened citizenry. On the other hand, the poor act not as citizen but as populations, and it is with their collective numbers that the state—in the capacity of a political party—must engage and negotiate. Electoral compulsions place some, though limited, power in the hands of the workers, and so implementation of judicial orders is intricately tied to the vicissitudes of local politics. Both the major political parties in Delhi, the centrist Congress, and the right-wing BJP were in power between the time when the order was passed in 1996 and when the date for its implementation arrived in 2000. Both parties were faced with the ire of the Supreme Court on the one hand and the risk of unpopularity among workers, their families, and factory owners on the other. And both parties tried their hand at stopgap arrangements to delay the proceedings of the Court. As previously discussed, and related to the room created for individual politicians, the implementation of Court orders depends on the "balance of power between representatives of the local government on the one hand and the state or municipal authorities on the other", and that "individual politicians . . . 'protect' settlements or segments of them from demolition in order to maintain significant vote banks" (Tarlo 2003, 12); becoming in the process their 'saviors'. This is why many slums in Delhi and elsewhere are named after well-known local and national politicians, in recognition of when they were 'regularized' or provided with legal recognition.

Following the Court-ordered closure; certain politicians stepped out to support the cause of the industrialists and workers, thus gaining media publicity and support of the affected parties. In time, a cross-class alliance between owners of industries and workers was formed, on the beckoning of the communist parties, which led to anxieties among other political parties, including the ruling Congress Party as seen in this newspaper report: "The fear of the agitation against closure of industries being "hijacked" by the Left parties made the Congress leadership sit up and take note of the scenario and chalk out a new strategy" (Blame it on Dikshit 2001). Through street protests and local political mobilization, workers and factory owners together managed to pressure the Delhi government to intervene on their behalf. The state legislated changes in the Master Plan to allow many industries—earmarked for closure by the Court—to continue operation, thus reaching a compromise. However, all that such ad hoc interventions achieve is to reproduce the fears and insecurities of people working in industries marked for closure. Even so, their limited but definite presence in local politics means that workers, having been excluded from the legal arena, managed to lessen the impact of the Court order. In the end, pollution remained what it was, and workers were made more insecure.

5. CONCLUSION

Political economic changes in India since the early 1990s have taken a distinctly neoliberal form. In addition to the more commonly understood goals of promoting the conditions for free-market capitalism, these hinge around presiding over a remaking of India's larger cities with the purpose of gaining membership in the cluster of the so-called global or world cities. In Delhi, this has translated concretely into the transformation of the city's hitherto manufacturing-heavy economy toward a post-industrial, service-oriented one. The trajectory of this change is, however, contingent. A key role has been played by certain strands of environmentalism, particularly those that have sought the mediation of the Indian judiciary. All of this points to the fact that the history of the universalization of neoliberalism is not simply a story of Western dictates, but one that centrally implicates indigenous interests and actors. In Delhi, this includes actors that are self-avowedly progressive but have come to facilitate neoliberal spatial transformations.

Erik Swyngedouw (2004) has talked about urbanization as social-environmental metabolism, such that there is nothing particularly unsustainable about any city. What is at issue are "urban and environmental processes that negatively affect some social groups while benefiting others" (11). In the case of industrial closure in Delhi, a particular view of the environment, which saw smokestacks and squatters as polluters, found synergy with the neoliberal agenda in Delhi. As a result of this enmeshment, the protests that the implementation of the order spawned cannot be read, as the mainstream press did, like some kind of anti-environmentalism. Rather, the opposition should be viewed as a disagreement with specific aspects of the judiciary-led environmentalism and as opposition to the neoliberal project itself.

The ideological project discussed in this chapter concerns the re-imagination of Delhi as a global or world city, which implies a markedly different geography than it's hitherto position as the political and in many ways economic capital of post-colonial India. Several interests that are tied to this venture have reaped a windfall from the accompanying reordering of space and increased values, among others, of property. This project has by and large been backed by the middle classes of the city. Their new-found affluence has enervated a self-image as members of an imagined global community of consumers, as citizens of the so-called 'flat' world. This view, however, exists uneasily in a city of over ten million where many struggle daily for bare subsistence and are being written out of the dominant narrative of the coming Delhi. For them the post-colonial state is a fundamentally schizophrenic institution: it is the site of claim making but also the institution chiefly responsible for their continued precariousness. The Indian state has pushed the neoliberal agenda since the early 1990s following its structural adjustment. But the state is at the same time populated by politicians who must face voters every election cycle and are forever anxiously looking over their shoulders in fear of other new saviors of the poor. This so-called populism of the post-colonial state is often decried by those interested in its 'reform' (cf. Collier 2007), but creates some room for negotiation that the urban poor and workers seek access to. It is, however, also a space that can as easily shut them out, in light of reconfigured political calculations. At any rate, these are small victories that do little to ease their precarious existence in the city or lessen the perpetual foreboding that the urban poor live in.

It is at this conjuncture that the environmental movement has managed to gain significant victories in judicial spaces from matters ranging from river pollution, to air pollution, and in this case, to closure of industries in Delhi. However, orders can become concrete only through the democratic state, but a state that must balance its duties with respect to the courts with the pressures from the electorate. In this way, expertise-driven, judiciary-based environmentalism is bound to run its limits when faced with interest-driven, number-based local politics. To environmentalists, the Supreme Court, and to middle-class Delhi their apparent defeat in the political arena seemed like an act of pandering by the state. In fact, at some point the Court declared that Delhi was "much better [as] a Commissioner's province" (SC blasts Delhi govt. again 2000), when it was governed by centralized dictates, instead of a democratically run state government; the Court went on to say that if the "government had its way they would abrogate all laws" (SC rejects Delhi plea 2000). Reflecting a widely held view among the middle class, the editor of the popular English daily *The Hindu* believed that the case showed in "the best possible fashion that street vandalism can so easily bring the Government at all levels to its knees"(Giving in to vandalism 2000). In a sense, the frustration of the newspaper editor is shared by the environmental movement in India. Because it is not—at least not yet—a mass movement, numbers dictate that the gains achieved by the Indian environmental interests through legal spaces are susceptible to qualification and even outright defeat in the political arena, where global shifts, discourses, and agendas must negotiate electoral dynamics.

To be sure, environmental pollution is a major problem in contemporary India, which is why my political purpose is not to hurl invectives at a 'bourgeois environmentalism', as some critics have done; rather, it is to bridge the divide between environmentalism and social activism that exists there. Environmentalists should come to grips with spaces of local politics and forge broader alliances. In particular, the large-scale dispossession brought about by neoliberalism in India must be understood, including the ongoing reordering of urban space. The first step toward this is to acknowledge the role of judiciary-driven environmentalism in the advancement of the neoliberal project. This admission in turn allows us to view the judiciary dialectically: organizing around the opportunities opened by it while also recognizing its undemocratic and anti-political tendencies. As for the matter at hand, environmentalists must attempt to organize around the effects of pollution on industrial workers and the exclusions that are underway due to the state-led neoliberal program. Failure to do so would mean that legal spaces will become even more exclusionary, solutions to actually existing environmental problems will be stymied by popular politics, and neoliberalism will continue to articulate with environmentalism to further marginalize workers and the poor in Delhi and elsewhere in India.

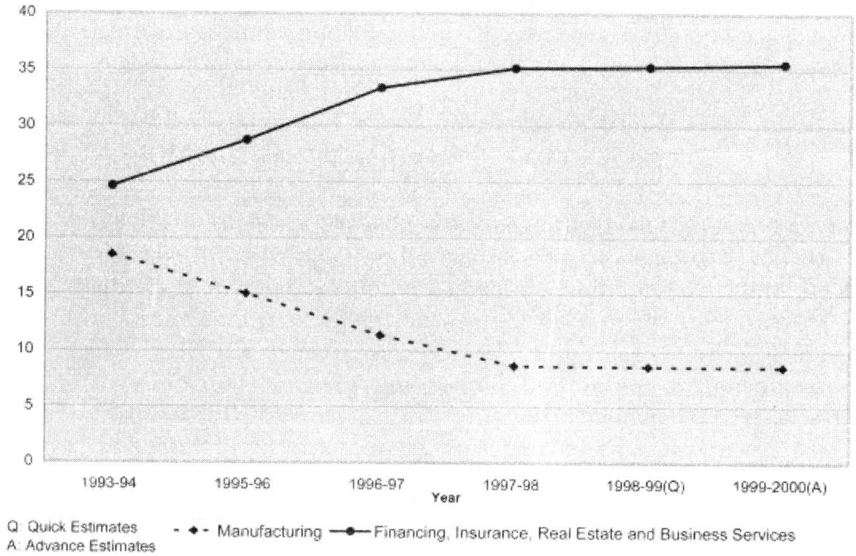

Figure 8.1 Contribution of manufacturing and services to the GDP of Delhi. *Source:* Department of Economics and Statistics, Government of Delhi (2000).

NOTES

1. Number from The Goldman Environmental Prize website. MC Mehta is quoted on the site as saying, "I am not anyone at any time, as I am often perceived to be. I am just for the environment at all times". Available from http://www.goldmanprize.org/node/133 (accessed April 12, 2008).
2. See also interview with Sheila Dikshit, Chief Minister of Delhi, Making Delhi a global city is top priority, available from www.projectsmonitor.com/detailnews.asp?newsid=11154 (accessed October 12, 2007).
3. The DJAM estimates the money generated by Birla Textile by redevelopment to be around Rs. 340 crores ($68 million). "Similarly, Swatantra Bharat Mills and DCM silks were to generate a profit of Rs 700 crores [$140 million] from 441,161 sq. ft and Ayodhya Textile Mills a profit of Rs 225 crores [$45 million] from 10,45,440 sq. ft of land. In these cases, the government share would have come to about Rs 1500 crores [$300 million]" (Delhi Janwadi Adhikar Manch 2006).
4. The recent downswing since 1995 is important as it is, but the fact that even within industrial production, power generation scores much higher and to an extent brings the index up a notch means that manufacturing has done even worse than it appears. For instance, over 1999–2001, with the base index being 1993–1994, the average manufacturing index was 98.2, power scored 108.48 (Government of Delhi 2000).
5. During this period, Delhi Government has put in place a plan to become what it calls, a 'global city', of which development of infrastructure for high-tech industries is a major component (L-G lays out govt's vision 2003).

REFERENCES

A view on mall development in India. *India Realty News*. www.indianrealtynews.com/real-estate-trends/a-view-on-mall-development-in-india.html (accessed April 22, 2009).

Anant, T., and J. Singh. 2002. An economic analysis of judicial activism. *Economic and Political Weekly* (October 26).

Awasthi, R., and S. N. Sharma. 2007. DMRC earns a third from property development. *The Economic Times* (March 5).

Baviskar, A. 2003. Between violence and desire: Space, power and identity in the making of modern Delhi. *International Social Science Journal* 55(175): 89–98.

Baxi, U. 2000. The avatars of Indian judicial activism: Explorations in the geographies of [in]justice. In *Fifty years of the Supreme Court of India: Its grasp and reach*, edited by S. Verma and Kusum, 156–209. New Delhi: Oxford University Press.

Bhan, G. 2009. "This is no longer the city I once knew": Evictions, the urban poor and the right to the city in millennial Delhi. *Environment and Urbanization* 21(1): 127–142.

Bhushan, P. 2009. Misplaced priorities and class bias of the judiciary. *Economic and Political Weekly* Vol. 44 (14) (April 4): 32–37.

Blame it on Dikshit: Dissidents spew venom. *The Times of India*, November 21, 2001.

Bosworth, B., and S. M. Collins. 2008. Accounting for growth: Comparing India and China. *Journal of Economic Perspectives* 22(1): 45–66.

Brenner, N., and N. Theodore, eds. 2002. *Spaces of neoliberalism: Urban restructuring in North America and Europe*. Malden, MA: Blackwell.

Chatterjee, P. 2004. *The politics of the governed: Reflections on popular politics in most of the World*. New York: Columbia University Press.

Collier, P. 2007. *The bottom billion: Why the poorest countries are failing and what can be done about it*. New York: Oxford University Press.

Cox, K. R., and A. Mair. 1988. Locality and community in the politics of local economic development. *Annals of the Association of American Geographers* 78(2): 307–325.

Delhi Janwadi Adhikar Manch. 2006. *How many errors does time have patience for: A report on industrial closures and slum demolitions in Delhi*, http://www.safhr.org/document_2.htm (accessed November 28, 2005).

Delhi Metro Rail Corporation. 2006. www.delhimetrorail.com/corporates/projectupdate/project_cost.html (accessed January5, 2006).

Dupont, V. 2008. Delhi and its 'global city' dream. http://www.reseau-asie.com (accessed March 12, 2009).

Economic Survey of Delhi, Government of Delhi. http://delhiplanning.nic.in/Economic%20Survey/chapter_9.htm (accessed November 28, 2006).

For health and livelihood. *The Times of India*, November 6, 2004.

Fortun, K. 2001. *Advocacy after Bhopal: Environmentalism, disaster, new global orders*. Chicago: University of Chicago Press.

Giving in to vandalism. *The Hindu*, November 23, 2000.

Harvey, D. 1989. From managerialism to entrepreneuralism: The transformation in urban governance in late capitalism. *Geografiska Annaler* 71(B): 3–17.

Jones Lang Lasalle. 2003. Delhi real estate review. http://www.research.joneslanglasalle.com/default.asp?CountryID=85&LanguageID=1 (accessed November 24, 2006).

———. 2004. India property market monitor. http://www.research.joneslanglasalle.com/default.asp?CountryID=85&LanguageID=1 (accessed November 24, 2006).

Joshi, S. 2004. Tertiary sector-driven growth in India: Impact on employment and poverty. *Economic and Political Weekly* Vol. 39 (37) (September 11): 4175–4178.

Latour, B. 1993. *We have never been modern.* Cambridge, MA: Harvard University Press.

Lipschutz, R. 2003. *Global environmental politics: Power, perspectives, and practice.* Washington, DC: CQ Press.

L-G lays out Govt's vision: To make Delhi hi-tech. *The Times of India,* December 23, 2003.

MacLeod, G. 2002. 'From urban entrepreneurial to a 'Revanchist City'? On the spatial injustices of Glasgow's renaissance'. In *Spaces of neoliberalism: Urban restructuring in North America and Europe,* edited by N. Brenner and N. Theodore, 254–276. Malden, MA: Blackwell.

Mbembe, A. 2000. At the edge of the world: Boundaries, territoriality, and sovereignty in Africa. *Public Culture* 12(1): 250–275.

Ministry of Environment and Forests, Government of India. 2002. *White paper on pollution.* http://envfor.nic.in/divisions/cpoll/delpolln.html (accessed March 18, 2006).

MPs worried over slow pace of Games work. *The Hindu,* February 25, 2009.

Murray, M. 2004. The spatial dynamics of postmodern urbanism: Social polarisation and fragmentation in Sao Paulo and Johannesburg. *Journal of Contemporary African Studies* 22(2): 139–164.

Narain, S. 2002. Changing environmentalism. *Seminar* 516: 15–20.

Nigam, A. 2001. Dislocating Delhi: A city in the 1990s. *Sarai Reader 2001: The Public Domain,* vol. 1: 40–46.

Noida Toll Bridge Company. 2006. http://www.ntbcl.com/index.htm (accessed January 12, 2006).

Padhi, R. 2007. Forced evictions and factory closures: Rethinking citizenship and rights of working class women in Delhi. *Indian Journal of Gender Studies* 14(1): 73–92.

Raman, V. 2008. Delhi property one of the hottest real estate destinations in India. www.articlesbase.com/business-opportunities-articles/delhi-property-one-of-the-hottest-real-estate-destination-in-india-600662.html (accessed April 22, 2009).

Ramanathan, U. 2004. Illegality and exclusion: Law in the lives of slum dwellers. Working paper. Geneva: International Environmental Law Resource Centre.

Routray, S. K. 2006. Two kinds of activism: Reflections on citizenship in globalizing Delhi. *International Young Scholars' Seminar Papers on eSS.* www.esocialsciences/com/data/articles/Document13132006410.9377863.pdf (accessed April 23, 2009).

Salve, H. 2000. Justice between generations: Environment and social justice. In *Supreme but not infallible: Essays in the honour of the Supreme Court of India,* edited by B. Kirpal, A. Desai, G. Subramanium, R. Dhavan, and R. Ramachandran, 360–380. New Delhi: Oxford University Press.

Sathe, S. 2002. *Judicial activism in India: Transgressing borders and enforcing limits.* New Delhi: Oxford University Press.

Saul, J. 2005. *The next liberation struggle: Capitalism, socialism, and democracy in Southern Africa.* New York: Monthly Review Press.

SC blasts Delhi Govt again. *Hindustan Times,* November 29, 2000.

SC rejects Delhi plea to 'go slow' on polluting units. *The Indian Express,* November 22, 2000.

Sharan, A. 2001. Claims on cleanliness: Environment and justice in contemporary Delhi. *Sarai Reader 2002: The cities of everyday life,* vol. 2: 31–37.

Smith, N. 2002. New globalism, new urbanism: Gentrification as global urban strategy. *Antipode* 34(3): 427–450.

Swyngedouw, E. 2004. *Social power and the urbanization of water.* London: Oxford University Press.

Tarlo, E. 2003. *Unsettling memories: Narratives of emergency in Delhi.* Berkeley: University of California Press.

Three dead in Delhi protesting closure of polluting industries. *The Indian Express*, November 22, 2000.

Wade, R. 2003. What strategies are viable for developing countries today? The World Trade Organization and the shrinking of 'development space'. *Review of International Political Economy* 10(4): 621–644.

Wilson, D. 2004. Making historic preservation in Chicago: Space, discourse, and neoliberalism. *Polity and Space*, 8(1): 43–59.

Upadyay, V. 2001. Forests, people, and courts: Utilizing legal space. *Economic and Political Weekly* (June 16): vol. 37 (24) : 2131–2134.

Véron, R. 2006. Remaking urban environments: the political ecology of air pollution in Delhi. *Environment and Planning A* 38(11): 2093–2109.

Zizek, S. 2007. Censorship today: Violence, or ecology as a new opium for the masses. www.lacan.com/zizecology1.htm (accessed April 13, 2009).

9 Coping with Challenges to Food Security

Climate Change, Biofuels, and GMOs

Suman Sahai

The current food crisis has emerged from a past of thoughtless domestic policies coupled with an inequitable international situation. A discriminatory framework at the World Trade Organization (WTO) continues to block attempts by developing countries to make agriculture and food production more viable at home. The new 'Buy America' policy promises greater protectionism in one of the largest trading countries in the world and threatens further distortion in global trade. Along with the emergence of climate change and global warming, the US-led biofuel fad and genetic engineering in agriculture have raised new and more immediate challenges for agriculture and food production in India and other developing countries.

THE IMPACT OF CLIMATE CHANGE

Climate change, and its impact on agriculture and food production, has only recently begun to be understood. The climate change issue is global, long-term, and involves complex interactions among climatic, social, environmental, economic, technological, institutional, and political processes. It has significant international and intergenerational implications, and, possibly, its most damaging impact will be on agriculture and food production in the poor regions of the tropics. The developing countries in the tropics are less able to adapt and are more susceptible to climate change damage than the temperate countries, many of which will be beneficiaries of climate change. The least developed countries are the most vulnerable and likely to be hardest hit.

Changes in rainfall patterns and temperature regimes influence local water balances, and this disturbs the optimal cultivation period available for particular crops. Disturbing these periods, known as length of growing period (LGP), can throw food and agricultural production out of gear. According to data derived from global circulation models (GCMs), land with good LGPs (between 120 days and 250 days) will decrease by as much as 51 million hectares world-wide (Fischer et al. 2002).

Adequate LGP is needed to ensure that medium-to-long duration crops are able to grow to maturity. Some crop varieties ripen quickly and are ready for use in a shorter period (short duration varieties). Others, especially among cereals, require a longer period to ripen and become ready for use. A long growing period available in an agro climatic zone means that a variety of crops, from short duration to long duration, can be cultivated there, throughout the growing seasons. This obviously means higher food production. When the LGP contracts, the growing season is shortened, with implications for food production. Most climate change models predict large increases of LGP in the current temperate and arctic regions leading to larger LGPs. This means that temperate regions which are currently one crop zones will become two crop zones, increasing agriculture production and benefiting from climate change.

There is a broad consensus that tropical areas will see an expansion of arid zones. According to climate change models, expansion of arid areas will be accompanied by a contraction of 31 million to 51 million hectares of favorable cultivation areas. This will mean a significant reduction in food production in the most vulnerable areas, where population density is high and food already scarce. Nearly one billion affected people live in these vulnerable environments, dependent on agriculture. These vulnerable populations have limited capacity to protect themselves from the environmental hazards that will accompany climate change, like drought and floods, and will suffer most from climate damage, like land degradation and biodiversity loss.

Coping with changes induced by global warming will require early detection and careful management of factors like land degradation and aridity, diminishing water bodies and water scarcity, reduced forest cover, and biodiversity loss. Policies that reduce pressure on resources, and improve management of environmental risks, will help to improve adaptive capacity and increase the welfare of the poor by developing better coping mechanisms. If climate change impacts can be incorporated in the design and implementation of development programs right away, it will help to reduce vulnerability.

Climate Change: The Polluter gets Paid

As a result of climate change, crop production will be impacted, but this impact will be geographically unevenly distributed. In a perverse irony, the developed (industrialized) countries will experience an increase in agriculture productivity potential as temperate regions get warmer. The regions which because of their industrialization and huge emissions of greenhouse gases (GHGs) are responsible for the climate change phenomenon will actually end up being its beneficiaries with respect to food production. The regions in the developing world in the tropics, that have not contributed to creating this climate hazard, will be its worst victims and will suffer a loss in agriculture productivity, with serious consequences for food availability and hunger. About 40 poor and food-insecure countries, with a projected total population (in 2080) of 1 billion to 3 billion, will lose 10% to 20% of their cereal-production potential. Of these, Africa will be the worst affected, and South Asia will be badly affected. Crop production losses as a result of climate change could further worsen the prevalence and depth of hunger. This burden will fall disproportionately on the poorest and most vulnerable (Fischer et al. 2002). To compound the damage, the overall trend of reduced food production will create market imbalances, which will push up international prices, making it even more difficult for governments of food-scarce countries to access food for their poor.

Cereal consumption in developing countries will decline by about 40 million to 80 million tons. The number of people at risk of hunger will increase. And the extent of malnutrition will increase if proactive steps are not taken to protect the most vulnerable.

According to estimates, almost 40% of the production potential in certain developing countries could be lost. Even if this is on the higher side, the situation should be considered alarming enough. In South Asia, the biggest blow to food production is expected to come from the loss of multiple cropping zones. The worst affected areas are predicted to be the double and triple cropping areas. This means areas where two to three crops are produced in a year and which are predicted to turn into single crop zones, where only one crop can be taken in a year because the rest of the season will be too hot and dry to support cultivation.

Coping with Wheat Loss

For South Asia, particularly India, one of the most serious impacts is anticipated in wheat production. Wheat is the single largest winter crop of North India and states like Punjab, Haryana, and Western Uttar Pradesh produce the surplus wheat that goes into the public distribution system (PDS). The PDS is the government support system which provides subsidized food to poor families. Wheat is a particularly temperature-sensitive crop, and it has been estimated that for every one degree rise in temperature, wheat-producing areas in India and South Asia will lose about four million to five million tons of wheat production. This will have a cascading effect on the supplies to the PDS and food availability for the poor.

The immediate challenge is to find a substitute for wheat as the dominant winter crop for North India and other parts where wheat is cultivated. Tubers like potato can be part of the solution. These could fill the shortfall to some extent, but the cereal deficit will have to be made up by another cereal. Corn could be suitable as a supplementary crop and a partial wheat replacement. Millets are, as yet, an unexplored option in this regard and have not been assessed for their potential. Although millets typically grow during the summer season in Asia, there are also several millet types which are cultivated at high altitude. Such millet germplasm can form the basis of developing new millet varieties suited for cultivation during the winter season of a changed, warmer climate regime.

Millets have good potential. They can grow in a much wider range of soils than wheat can, and they are a more nutritious cereal than either wheat or rice. Millets do not require much water and can grow well under rain-fed conditions, even on fairly poor soils, so their agro climatic adaptability is high. The challenge will be to breed robust new varieties with properties (especially cooking quality) that are more similar to wheat, so that food habits do not have to be radically altered if millets were required to be introduced as a main cereal in the food chain.

The ability of a country to cope with the impact of climate change on agriculture will depend on a number of factors. The total amount of arable land and available water resources will be critical determinants of the ability of regions to adapt to the changes brought by a warming world. Apart from land, the availability of water could become a critical limiting factor. For instance, the impact of global warming on the Tibetan Plateau and Himalayan glaciers will affect the ten or so main rivers like the Indus, the Mekong, the Yangtze, and the Brahmaputra that flow into China, India, Pakistan, Bangladesh, and Myanmar. Harnessing these river waters, as the ice caps and Himalayan glaciers recede, and the water flow in all rivers diminishes, will need skilful diplomatic negotiations so that river waters can be shared in such a manner as to ensure that requirements of agriculture are met in all affected countries.

The ability of agriculture to cope with climate change depends on

- Population growth
- Poverty and hunger
- Arable land
- Water resources
- Farming technology
- Crop varieties adapted to local conditions
- Access to knowledge infrastructure, agricultural extension services
- Marketing and storage systems
- Rural financial markets
- Economic status and wealth and access to inputs

To prepare for climate-altered conditions, practices in agriculture will need to shift from intensive, mechanized, water-demanding agriculture to a more sustainable, conservation agriculture that grows crops using less water. 'More crop per drop of water' is a slogan almost institutionalized in India's plans to tackle drought. The same approach is applicable in a wider sense when addressing the challenges posed by climate change.

The System of Rice Intensification

The System of Rice Intensification (SRI), which is based on a rice cultivation strategy developed in India, was revived and promoted by a Jesuit priest in Madagascar. Instead of flooding paddy fields and leaving standing water as in current rice cultivation, SRI consists of alternately watering and draining the fields in a manner that significantly reduces the amount of water required. SRI is now witnessing a revival and is being tried out in many parts of the world with promising results. Essentially, SRI changes agronomy practices in a manner that enables prolific root formation and tillering that leads to more panicles and hence more grains per plant. This has an obvious impact on increasing crop yields. Similar cultivation practices are now being tried out with other crops like wheat and vegetables to see if the same increments in rooting and tillering will lead to higher yields.

AGRO BIODIVERSITY: KEY TO CLIMATE CHANGE ADAPTATION

In addition to land and water, the other important factor needed in adapting to climate change is biodiversity related to agriculture and crop varieties adapted to local conditions. There is an urgent need to conserve the genetic diversity of crop plants, livestock, forest species, soil micro flora, and marine and aquatic genetic diversity. All the biodiversity related to agriculture is referred to as agro biodiversity and this, according to the FAO, is acknowledged as a key resource to ensure that agriculture in various parts of the world can survive the onslaught of turbulent weather and unpredictable climate. Conserving agro biodiversity means conserving the gene pool and those genes that may come in useful for traits required by crops under changed conditions.

If coastal areas get submerged more inland, then crop varieties will be needed with tolerance to salinity and water logging. If on the other hand inland areas become drier and rain-fed areas face almost drought-like conditions, then crop varieties will have to be bred that are drought tolerant. Turbulence in the weather patterns including moisture and wind could bring new diseases and insect pests, requiring varieties that are resistant to new diseases and pests.

The key to breeding suitable varieties is to have access to genes with desirable traits, like the genes that would confer disease resistance or drought tolerance. Conserving agro biodiversity conserves genes.

GENE CAMPAIGN'S EFFORTS

Recognizing the importance of agro biodiversity to ensuring viable agriculture under difficult situations, like that predicted by global warming and climate change, Gene Campaign began a few years ago to collect, characterize, and conserve the agro biodiversity of local crops like rice, millets, legumes, vegetables, and oilseeds, chiefly in Jharkhand and Uttaranchal. Gene Campaign's conservation exercise is focused on rice, an important staple food. India is the Center of Origin, and the greatest genetic diversity of rice is found here. The Eastern Indian region, consisting of Orissa, Jharkhand, and Chattisgarh, constitute the primary Center of Origin of rice, in other words, its birthplace. This is the region where several thousand years ago, rural and tribal communities bred rice from wild grasses and where large numbers of land races and farmers' varieties are found. Gene Campaign decided that in order to prepare for the challenges that will confront rice cultivation, conservation efforts must be focused in areas where the largest number of genes can be identified and saved for future use.

Our approach to conservation is to set up community-managed, field-level Gene-Seed Banks. These Banks are simple rooms, which are moisture- and light-proof and well aired. The seeds of traditional varieties of rice, and other crops like legumes, oilseeds, and vegetables are collected from the fields of farmers who are still cultivating them, usually in remote areas. At the time of collection, information is recorded about the properties of each variety. This knowledge, held by the farming community, is extensive and detailed, and documenting it faithfully provides a wealth of information about the genetic properties of crop varieties. It is farmers who reveal whether the variety performs well under drought conditions, is resistant to disease, or has a short or long duration to maturity. This valuable information tells the scientists what traits to look for in which varieties.

The seed samples collected from the field are scientifically processed to reduce moisture level and stored in glass jars for medium-term storage and in baskets for short-term storage. The properties of the traditional varieties are characterized, and their genetic features are documented for use by scientists in research institutions. Gene Campaign collaborates with agriculture research institutions to test the agro biodiversity in the Banks for desirable traits, like drought tolerance and disease resistance. So far, five drought-tolerant rice varieties have been identified and are being tested at the Birsa Agriculture University in Ranchi. In addition, two new genes conferring resistance to bacterial leaf blight have been identified in traditional rice varieties being tested in the Indian Agriculture Research Institute in Delhi.

Cold Gene Banks vs. Zero Energy Gene Banks

The international network of Gene Banks consists of cold Gene Banks which are very different from farmer-level, field Gene Banks. The former is an energy intensive bank maintained at low temperature, for long-term storage of genetic material. The latter, a model promoted by Gene Campaign, is a labor-intensive bank with no energy costs. Both are for ex situ conservation of agro biodiversity. The monthly electricity bill of the National Gene Bank in Delhi is over 20 lakh rupees (approximately $45,000) a month. It is not possible to set up many such Gene Banks both for reasons of cost and their large carbon footprint. The Zero Energy Gene-Seed Banks being set up by Gene Campaign have no carbon footprint, and they are located within the community, which administers and uses the bank.

Multiplication and renewal of the seed samples is done by a cycle of growing out each sample every alternate year so that the seed retains its viability. The routine growing out of the seed samples exposes the crop varieties to the prevailing weather and climate conditions, helping them to adjust and adapt. The seed material that is returned to the bank after every grow-out season is adapted to the environment, which includes the climate as well as pests and disease. The material frozen in the cold Gene Bank does not get a chance to adapt to the local climate and when it is taken out at a time of crisis, it may or may not have the adaptive capacity to provide an efficient crop under the prevailing conditions.

Because Gene Campaign's Zero Energy Banks are located in the villages, they are owned by the people. Village youth committees supervised by village elders run the Banks. The seed in the Bank is accessed every season by the farmers who return three times the seed they take when their harvest comes in. The core collection is multiplied in carefully designed plots in farmers' fields, monitored by trained village youth and Gene Campaign staff. The material that is returned to the Bank after renewal is taken from the center of the plot to avoid mixing.

Ultra Desiccation for Long-term Seed Storage

A more scientific approach called ultra desiccation is being tried out for longer duration storage at ambient temperature. Here, following sun drying, the seed samples are dried in a drying chamber at 37°C till the seed moisture is reduced to about 6°C. This is tested with a moisture meter as well as by a more practical test. The seed is cracked between the teeth, if it breaks easily without sticking to the teeth, then it is dry enough to store.

We are conducting a five-year storage experiment with ultra desiccated seed stored at ambient temperature, growing out the seed every year, to test how long the seed remains viable. The season 2008–2009 was the third year of testing, and the seed was still viable. If the method of ultra desiccation proves to be successful, then long-term storage of seed at ambient temperature will become possible, reducing the dependence on high-energy-use Cold Gene Banks for germplasm storage.

BIOFUELS AND FOOD SECURITY

Biofuel Statistics

- Global ethanol production, which account for over 90% of the biofuel production, more than doubled between 2000 and 2005. In contrast, global oil production increased only 7% during the same period.
- Brazil, the pioneer in ethanol production since the mid-1970s, was surpassed by the United States as the largest ethanol producer in 2005.
- Global biodiesel production (much smaller than ethanol production) increased four times between 2000 and 2005.
- The European Union (EU) is the largest producer and consumer of biodiesel.
- Both developed and developing countries are planning enormous increases in biofuel production in the coming years.
- Plans for biofuel expansion have been made with very little analysis of their impact on food and other sectors, yet they have become policy in developed and developing countries.

The biofuel craze was started by the U.S. It is rooted in U.S. politics of keeping corn prices high in the Midwest, and the U.S. refusal to sign the Kyoto Protocol to reduce greenhouse gas emissions. By 'doing something for clean energy', the U.S. tries to deflect global criticism for not agreeing to GHG emission cuts that the Kyoto Protocol tries to regulate and negotiate. With the biofuel strategy, the U.S. has ensured a good price for U.S. corn, which has become the feedstock for ethanol to fuel the ambitious biofuel targets, instead of just an agricultural product to feed cows and pigs and the poultry industry. This process has started a chain of events that has led to spiraling food prices.

U.S. LED BIOFUEL POLICY AND FOOD PRICE RISE

Diverting Maize to Ethanol Production

I

- Maize → Ethanol
- Maize consumers shift to wheat and rice
- Wheat and rice prices rise

II

- Maize → Ethanol
- Maize for animal feed in short supply

- Wheat diverted for animal feed
- Wheat prices rise

III

- Wheat and rice farmers shift to maize cultivation because of ethanol demand
- Wheat and rice production falls
- Wheat and rice prices rise
- Rice shortages, countries ban export
- Global rice supply plummets
- No rice available for food imports and crisis relief
- Spiraling prices and short supply

Following the example of the U.S., we see government policy in many countries propelling the development of biofuels, by providing financial incentives and tax breaks to the private sector. In the U.S., Europe, Brazil, China, and India, government policy has gone a step further and also created a guaranteed market for biofuels by laying down mandatory targets for blending this with petroleum-based fuels in the transportation sector. Legislation on biofuels can be found in many countries. A 2007 study found that of the 50 countries surveyed, 40 had already enacted legislation to promote biofuels, while 27 had mandatory requirements for blending with traditional transportation fuels like petrol and diesel.

India has had a policy on fuel blends dating back to the Indian Power Alcohol Act (1948) when the intention was to harness energy from alternative sources like sugarcane molasses. This law was never implemented and was repealed in 2000 (Indian Power Alcohol (Repeal) Bill 2000, Act No. 32 of 2000), but almost immediately after, in 2002, the Planning Commission established a committee for the development of biofuels, in order to combat rising oil prices. The report of this committee highlights India's position on producing biofuels from non-edible sources. It focuses mainly on the production of ethanol from sugarcane molasses and biodiesel from *Jatropha curcas* (Planning Commission, Government of India 2003).

In accordance with the guidelines of the Committee on Bio Fuels, India does not produce agrofuels from edible crops. The Indian Ethanol Blending Program (EBP) was introduced in 2002 and established a 5% blend mandate in nine states (Goa, Gujarat, Karnataka, Maharashtra, Punjab, UP, Uttaranchal, AP, and Tamil Nadu) and four union territories (Chandigarh, Dadra & Nagarhaveli, Daman & Diu, and Puducherry), taking effect from the beginning of 2003.

To implement the ethanol-blending program, the sugarcane supply needs to be constant, but in India, ethanol production has always depended on the fluctuating availability of sugarcane. This situation is not going to improve, nor is ethanol production certain to increase. There is a shortage of arable land and putting more land under sugarcane means creating a conflict with food production. Also, the cultivation of sugarcane is a water-intensive process and, by and large, rice and wheat farmers have opposed the use of scarce water for growing cash crops. The EBP has reached a dead end because the production of ethanol from molasses and secondary sugar syrup will never be able to meet the requirement for the rising blend mandates of the future. Reliance Industries (RIL) has estimated that in order to achieve a 10% blend mandate, an additional 150 million liters of ethanol is required (Rothkopf,G 2007). This is almost impossible to achieve domestically.

Consequently, recent years have seen a number of deals between India and Brazil, the largest producer of sugarcane-based ethanol, to import ethanol (*The Hindu, Business Line* 2007). In addition to government-level collaboration, private companies have also entered into arrangements for ethanol imports. Reliance Industries and Bajaj-Hindustan have signed similar agreements with Brazilian sugar and oil companies. As a result, India has become the world's largest importer of Brazilian ethanol. In a perverse development, the EBP, which was initiated in order to achieve self-sufficiency in energy, has now created a dependency and necessitated the import of vast quantities of ethanol to satisfy the high blend mandates which have been formulated with no thought given to what the implications of such a policy might be.

Not Self Reliant and Not Economically Viable Either

When India decided to take a page out of the U.S. ethanol book, it did not take into account the high level of subsidies that keep the U.S. ethanol industry afloat. In the U.S., and other large economies like those of Europe, the ethanol industry is artificially buoyed by government subsidies, minimum production levels, and tax credits. High oil prices over the past few years have made ethanol more competitive, but the U.S. government continues to grant large subsidies to corn farmers and ethanol producers. Direct corn subsidies equaled $8.9 billion in 2005, which was paid out over 2006 and 2007. In addition, there is a panoply of tax credits, grants, and government loans included in energy legislation passed in 2005 and the farm bill designed to support ethanol producers. The federal government already grants ethanol blenders a tax allowance of 51 cents per gallon of ethanol they make, and many states pay out additional subsidies (Runge and Senauer 2007).

Biofuels are very expensive to produce, but the adverse economics is neutralized by heavy subsidies. The biofuel policy of the U.S. is a political decision influenced by its need to create markets for Midwest corn farmers. But what about India? With its current pricing, can ethanol or any other agrofuel possibly be implemented without extracting an indefensible price from agricultural production and food security? And in addition to this, there are outstanding questions about its toxicity to animals and the impact this may have on grazing cattle. In Africa and Asia there are serious concerns about *Jatropha*'s environmental and social impacts. Western Australia has banned it because of its toxicity to humans and animals, and because of its capacity to quickly become a hard-to-control, invasive weed.

Land Availability

The fact is that agro fuels, whether produced from edible or non-edible crops, require land. Hence, it is land which is going to become the limiting factor. The question is: will a finite resource like land be diverted to the production of biofuels, even as India remains insecure with respect to food, ranking according to recent studies, as one of the most food-insecure nations in the world, where malnutrition is of crisis proportions.

In its 2008 biofuel policy, India set itself the ambitious target of 20% biofuel-gasoline blending by 2017. To achieve this goal, vast areas of agricultural land must be diverted to produce biofuel. The National Biofuel Development Board of India proposes to establish a self-sustaining *Jatropha* program over 11.2 million hectares. The Indian government has set up a National Biodiesel Mission, with a two-phased approach. Phase I consisting of a Demonstration Project was to be implemented by the year 2006–2007 with an investment of Rs. 1500 crore ($300 million). It involved the cultivation of *Jatropha* on 400,000 hectares and the construction a number of Jatropha oil extraction units and biodiesel plants.

An ambitious Phase II is to follow the Demonstration Project. This will consist of a self-sustaining expansion of the program leading to the production of sufficient biodiesel to meet 20% of the total requirement by 2012. However, the 2008 biofuel policy aims for a total gasoline blending of 20% by 2017. It is not presently clear to what extent these targets are being met. Phase II of the biodiesel program which aims to cultivate 14 million hectares of *Jatropha* has planned for available land as given in Table 9.1. It is clear from this table that arable land has been included in the plans for expanding *Jatropha* cultivation.

The large-scale cultivation of *Jatropha*, with its increasing environmental and health burdens and foreign exchange cost, is being defended from the energy point of view. It is also supported by the Forestry and Rural Development Sector, looking for future income potentials as well as, purportedly, incomes for farmers. Not mentioned in this debate is the likely impact on food security and rural livelihoods of such large-scale diversion of land to non-food purposes. There is no assessment of what such land diversion would do to total agricultural productivity, and whether there were alternative strategies planned to make good any shortfalls in food. There is thus a refusal to acknowledge the potential blow to food security that is likely to result from the skewed and shortsighted move on biofuel

Table 9.1 Land Assessed as 'Available' for Jatropha curcas Plantations (million hectares)

Forest areas	3.0
Agriculture (boundary plantation)	3.0
Agriculture (agriforestry)	2.0
Cultivable fallow lands	2.4
Wastelands under integrated watershed development	2.0
Strip lands such as roads, railways, canal banks	1.0
Total	13.4
Additional wastelands	4.0

Source: http://www.jatrophabiodiesel.org/indianPrograms.php.

production. This is indicative of the official mindset that seems willing to sacrifice the food option for the fuel option.

THE ETHICAL QUESTION

There is an ethical dimension to the biofuel story, a question of equity. Where should limited productive assets, like land and water, be diverted? Should they produce food for the poor or fuel for the rich? Today, instead of investing in technology and research that focuses on rejuvenating the wastelands to meet India's growing food requirements, these wastelands are being used to plant *Jatropha* to provide biodiesel.

Seeing the blatant manner in which land is being apportioned to biofuel production and the fact that this trend is growing, it is perhaps inevitable that in the long term, more and more agricultural land will be converted into biofuel plantations and will pose an even greater threat to India's food security than now. Diversion of land from food to fuel has already started happening in some rural areas. Tribal groups in central India have been dispossessed of their agricultural lands, which have been converted into *Jatropha* plantations, in violation of the law.

The Myth of Wasteland

The first areas being targeted for biofuel production are the so-called "waste lands". This seeks to convey the impression that, with the biofuel program, the country will put to good use something that produces nothing at the moment. But there is no such thing as wasted land in India. All but the most degraded land supports a spectrum of species which varies from region to region. Apart from the special biodiversity that they support, such lands are usually the village commons, which the local community uses in a variety of ways. Foremost is the use for grazing, so 'wastelands' are important for the sustenance of pastoralists. Landless farmers who do share cropping are heavily dependent on livestock for their livelihoods and even small to medium farmers keep cattle for both the extra milk and the organic manure that the cow dung provides. The fodder grasses and plants available on such lands are crucial to the maintenance of livestock. Village communities pick semi-domesticated and wild foods such as seasonal leafy greens and tubers from such wastelands, adding much needed nutrition to rural diets at no cost. These wastelands are home to the many medicinal plants that local communities use for health and veterinary care. It is not as though wastelands are lying around, of no use to any one.

In addition to all these myriad uses, refugees from development projects, displaced persons, jobless laborers, and small farmers facing crop failure often rely on these lands as places where they can put their cattle during an emergency. If these lands are enclosed, the lifelines of many already disadvantaged people will be jeopardized.

What's more, when lands are truly degraded, they can (and should) be reclaimed to grow food, not parceled off for projects that will pose a threat to an already tenuous food security situation. Such lands can be "re-mineralized" and used for the production of food crops as well as for plantations. An initiative of the Indian Institute of Technology at Kharagpur, India, and the University of Western Ontario, Canada, has demonstrated, as part of its Land Restoration through Waste Management Program, that the use of waste material like fly ash generated by thermal plants and sewage sludge, can effectively reclaim degraded lands and make them cultivable.

This reclamation technology has been successfully demonstrated in eight states of India, and about 400 hectares of land has been reclaimed; tree plantations established and edible crop trials conducted in different agro climatic regions with the active participation of the private sector, public sector, and rural communities. For example, in edible crop trials on wastelands in Raichur, in the tribal state of Chattisgarh, sunflower was sown in the Kharif (monsoon planting season) in both red and black soil followed by groundnut in red soil and maize in black soil in the Rabi (winter planting season). The trials were carried out consecutively for three years and the model is available for replication.

Clean Energy or Corporate Takeover?

The story of land and its ownership is getting increasingly murky in India and other parts of the developing world, creating a potential crisis for future food production. Corporate interests in the U.S. and in European countries are buying land in Asia and Africa for biofuel plantations. Apart from that, the corporate sector within countries is appropriating land for real estate in the guise of acquiring land for energy plantations. Like the Special Economic Zones (SEZ) in India, that under the New Economic Policy have been designated for export-led industrial production and have degenerated into corporate land grab, land bids for biofuel plantations are increasingly looking like the corporate take over of so-called wastelands. Such land allotments are creating conflicts with local communities in some cases.

One Indian state, in which biofuels has emerged as a contentious land-use issue, is Rajasthan. There the state government has designed a "green patta" policy (patta being a land title deed), which permits waste land to be leased out to private companies and government enterprises for up to 20 years. (Rajasthan Land Revenue Rules 2007). Though 70% of these "culturable wastelands", as they are called, are to be allotted to farmers' groups and only 30% to companies, there is concern that, in collusion with administrative agencies, companies may take over more than their permitted amount.

There have been other changes that endanger the food and livelihood of local communities, such as abolishing the upper limit on the amount of land that can be held by an individual or company and banning the sale of tribal lands to non-tribals. At the time of Independence, India abolished the feudal system of large land holdings and imposed a limit on the amount of agricultural land that an individual could hold. This program of imposing a land ceiling allowed land to be allotted to landless peasants. As another protective measure, the Indian Constitution grants special rights over land ownership to tribal people. Non-tribal people cannot own such land, and tribal people cannot sell land to non-tribal people, so that land can not be easily alienated from tribal community.

But now in many states, such land ceiling laws and protection of tribal lands is being repealed. For instance, it is now possible for a special government committee to approve up to 1,000 hectares of land to be given to private companies for *Jatropha* plantations. Such easing of the controls makes land investment a far more attractive proposal for large companies like DMC International, a real estate developer.

Activists working on land reform in Rajasthan complain that Sarpanches (village leaders) have very often had their arms twisted not to oppose these changes in government policy. Even so, there is opposition. Part of it results from the violation of deeply held cultural beliefs. *Orans*, or traditional Sacred Groves, are often found in the marginal lands, categorized as "culturable wasteland". *Orans* are places of worship, and the "culturable wasteland" is the lifeline of the 7.5 million pastoralists in Rajasthan. They are now demanding legal recognition of their customary grazing rights on these and *gauchars*—grazing lands.

Despite aggressive promotion by the central and state governments, not many financial institutions have shown interest in financing *Jatropha* cultivation. Bankers appear to be skeptical about the much-heralded high yields, particularly from "barren" lands, and perhaps the authorities share some of the doubts. The Orissa Renewable Energy Development Agency

(OREDA)—the leading government agency handling biofuels—is treating the Orissa draft biofuel policy as a poverty alleviation program. As if this was not bad enough, OREDA is planning *Jatropha* plantations in Kalahandi, Bolangir, and Koraput, the three districts with the greatest food shortages. These districts have become notorious for starvation deaths. Instead of supporting food production in these districts and helping the families to become food secure, the government of Orissa is actively promoting land diversion to biofuel plantations.

Farmers were told that contract-farming deals for *Jatropha* would be an admirable long-term investment and bring them good economic returns, but this does not seem likely. Worse still, with all the emphasis on *Jatropha*, farmers are not being given any support for their biodiversity agriculture, so that agro biodiversity, food, and nutrition, as well as food sovereignty are all in jeopardy.

Embarking on large-scale biofuel production does not make economic sense at this time for all countries. In many developing countries it would make more sense to wait for the emergence of second-generation technologies, and to 'leapfrog' to these technologies later.

Biofuels and Global Food Prices

It is not surprising that the biofuel program has already begun to take its toll on global food security. Although drought-like conditions in 2007 in Australia are credited with contributing to the food crisis, serious analysts recognize the grave outcome of the biofuel policy on the acute shortage of food that led to food riots in many parts of the world.

The World Bank admitted, in a report that it later declined to make public, that biofuels had forced global food prices up by 75%, far more than previously estimated. According to this report, the rising food prices have pushed 100 million people worldwide below the poverty line. Political leaders in the severely affected countries like Bangladesh and Egypt have called the higher food and fuel prices as "the first real economic crisis of globalization". But governments in the U.S. and EU, strong biofuel-promoting countries, appear to be suppressing and ignoring the strong evidence that biofuels are a major factor in recent food price rises.

The projected reduction in calorie availability in various continents by 2010 compared to baseline is given in Figure 9.1. This is calculated for two scenarios: one if biofuel production were to be expanded and the other if it were to be drastically expanded as current plans would seem to suggest.

GMOS AND FOOD SECURITY

Even though the subject of genetically modified organisms (GMOs) has been surrounded by controversy, there has nevertheless been substantial debate on whether or not GMOs have any relation to food security. Despite the propaganda of the Agbiotech industry that GMOs would feed the world, there is little evidence as yet that GMOs have anything to offer to food-insecure countries. There is, in fact, no connection to be seen between GMOs and increasing food production. The causes of hunger are well understood. It is known that people are hungry either because they do not have productive assets like land and water to grow their own food, or because they do not have incomes and money to buy food, if they do not have land.

On the other hand there are fairly well-defined problems that exist in the agriculture and food domain of countries. A number of approaches will have to be used to solve such problems, some of which can be solved more easily than others. GMOs may one day solve one or the other problem in agriculture. But the bulk of high-yielding crops suited to a variety of agro climatic zones and capable of coping with biotic antibiotic stress continue to come from conventional agriculture and plant breeding. This is likely to continue.

Yet countries anxious to jump on to the genetic modification (GM) bandwagon, and this includes almost all countries in the developing world, are diverting ever-diminishing research funds to creating GMOs, whether or not they solve any real-life problems. A third of the GM research in India, for instance, is conducted with the Bt gene, which is owned by Monsanto. So India ends up paying large amounts of money in licensing fees to the Monsanto Company for the use of the Bt gene to produce a range of Bt crops which have no relation either to more food or better nutrition. At the same time, investments in tested agricultural strategies like conventional plant breeding, agronomy, farm management, and extension services

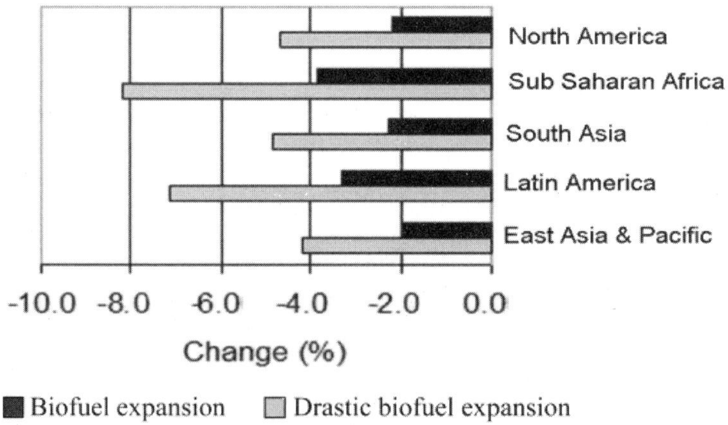

Figure 9.1 Von Braun, J. 2007. When food makes fuel: The promises and challenges of biofuels. Keynote Speech presented at Crawford Fund Annual Conference, "Biofuels, Energy and Agriculture: Powering Towards or Away From Food Security?" August 15, Theatrette, New Parliament House, Canberra. Reproduced with permission from the International Food Policy Research Institute (http://www.ifpri.org). This paper can be found at: http://www.ifpri.org/sites/default/files/2007jvbcrawfordkeynote_0.pdf

are being neglected because research funds are being diverted to GMOs. So along with heavy investment in GMOs, the real agricultural problems remain. Far from contributing to agriculture and food production, the investment in GM research takes away scarce research funds from proven research strategies and poses a new set of challenges to food security rather than contributing anything to support it.

When GMOs like Bt cotton are cultivated, they compete with food crops for scarce resources like land and water. In a situation where food security is already under pressure from climate change, the diversion of land to biofuels and GMOs worsen, not improve the state of affairs. In addition to this, there is scientific evidence showing that the effects of GMOs on the environment and on human and animal health are not always benign. Further, the contamination of native gene pools with foreign genes that escape from GMOs poses a threat to the integrity of genetic resources conserved in centers of origin, with unknown and potentially damaging consequences.

HERBICIDE TOLERANT CROPS

The adoption of herbicide-tolerant (HT) crops is directly against the interest of developing-country farmers, reducing their sources of food and fodder and taking away their opportunities to earn from wage labor. HT, the most pervasive GM technology is designed to destroy weeds chemically, thus obviating the need for manual weeding.

Weeding is an assured avenue for earning casual wages in rural areas, especially for women. Sometimes it is the only source of wages. Farm operations like sowing, weeding, harvesting, and winnowing are important sources of rural employment. The herbicide tolerance trait is essentially a labor-saving and hence a labor-displacing trait and would have economic implications, were it to be introduced in labor-surplus developing countries. In addition, the so-called weeds have several useful functions critical to the well-being of rural communities. They are used as food and fodder and as medicinal plants critical for health and veterinary care.

The biosafety of GMOs remains in question, and their contribution to food security is as yet unclear. The continued adoption of GMOs in developing countries that are already food insecure poses yet another challenge to the ability of these countries to face the future challenges of increasing agricultural and food production for a growing population in an increasingly hostile climate.

CONCLUSION

To answer the question whether the New Economic Policy has been good for the poor in countries like India, one need only look at the current situation. India, today, is home to the largest number of hungry people in the world. The number of poor has increased, not decreased, since economic reforms were introduced in 1991. The Indian data on malnutrition is appalling. States like Jharkhand and Madhya Pradesh now rank below sub-Saharan Africa in terms of the number of children suffering from acute malnutrition.

The situation in the agricultural economy is so adverse that more than half the farmers in India would abandon farming if they had an alternative, according to a survey carried out two years ago by the National Sample Survey Organization. Biofuels are promoted in the name of clean energy at the cost of food security; the poor will get hungrier as common grazing lands are diverted to biofuel production. The supply of agriculture credit has decreased steadily, squeezing institutional credit to farmers and making them dependent on private moneylenders charging usurious interest rates. The resulting indebtedness crushes any prospect of food security for the vulnerable.

REFERENCES

Blyn G., 1966. *Agricultural Trends in India 1891–1947: Output, Availability and Productivity*. Philadelphia: University of Pennsylvania Press.

Braun. J. V. 2007. When food makes fuel: The promises and challenges of biofuels, Biofuels, Energy and Agriculture, International Food Policy Research Institute. http://www.ifpri.org.

Fischer, G., M. Shah, and H. V. Velthuizen. 2002. Climate change and agricultural vulnerability, International Institute for Applied Systems Analysis. http://www.accc.gv.at/pdf/JB-Report.pdf.

Indian Power Alcohol (Repeal) Bill. 2000. Act No. 32 of 2000, Government of India.

Jatropha World. 2009. Centre For Jatropha Promotion & Biodiesel, Rajasthan. www.jatrophabiodiesel.org/indianPrograms.php.

Planning Commission, Government of India. 2003. Report of the Committee on Development of Bio- Fuel, http://planningcommission.gov.in/reports/genrep/cmtt_bio.pdf.

Rajasthan Land Revenue Rules. 2007. Government of India.

Runge C. F., and Senauer. B. 2007. How biofuels could starve the poor. *Foreign Affairs* 86(3), http://www.foreignaffairs.com/issues/2007/86/3.

The Hindu, Business Line. 2007. Brazil's Petrobas enters India with ONGC, June 5. http://www.thehindubusinessonline.com/2007/06/05/stories/2007060505330200.htm

10 Imperialism, Resources, and Food Security, with Reference to the Indian Experience

Utsa Patnaik

1. INTRODUCTION

An objective observer of Indian society and economy today would not be able to avoid a sense of deep unease: on the one hand, there is a visible real estate and share market boom; on the other hand, many thousands of farmers in excess of 'normal' numbers are committing suicide. On the one hand, there is fast burgeoning consumption by the urban middle classes of more varied high-protein diets and of modern consumer durables and electronic goods. On the other hand, foodgrains absorption in rural India has fallen to a level lower than before WWII and the depth of hunger is growing with declining energy intake for the poor majority in villages and more recently in towns as well.

Agriculture and industry, the major material productive sectors supporting together over four-fifths of the population, have gone into stagnation or decline as regards contribution to gross domestic product (GDP) and to employment, with a severe depression in agriculture in particular, marked by falling per head real incomes. Unemployment in both rural and urban India has been rising, and average foodgrains absorption within the country has declined to a historic low comparable to the colonial period, even as grain exports rise, with the brunt of the increased hunger being borne by rural India. There is unprecedented agrarian distress manifesting itself in rising farm indebtedness, loss of assets including land, and many thousands of farmer suicides. Official figures and claims of decline in rural poverty, figures which are reproduced in the World Bank's *World Development Report 2006*, are misleading as they are based on a logically incorrect method of poverty estimation. Correct estimates show poverty to be high and to increase in depth during the period of economic reforms.

Yet, India is widely projected abroad as a shining success story of economic reforms, an important 'emerging market' for Northern goods and services, and an attractive destination for investment, all this in view of the high annual GDP growth rate which has been averaging 6% to 7%, second only to that of China. The portrayal as a dynamic economy is a picture which is indeed partially true, and it carries benefits for a small well-to-do minority, but it is entirely misleading as regards the welfare implications for the majority of the population. A high growth rate by itself conveys no information at all either about the composition of this growth or its income distribution effects.

In fact the only sector of the economy which has registered rapid expansion is the services sector, a small segment being high-income IT-enabled and financial services; the bulk remains low-income personal and catering services for the small minority of rich Indians, a minority which has enjoyed a rapid rise in real incomes under reforms. The real estate, construction, and hospitality sectors also are expanding. There has been a rise in income inequality of a very specific and disturbing kind: an absolute decline of real income for the vast majority of the population and very rapid rise in real incomes for a small minority. This has meant, on the one hand, a real estate and building boom in urban areas and fast growing demand for high-end consumer durables and electronic goods by this minority which is seeking to emulate Northern life styles. On the other hand, for the majority of the population it has meant higher unemployment, indebtedness, land and other asset loss and hunger, in short growing immiseration.

The rapid changes in its economy and society are the direct outcome of adopting neoliberal economic policies and trade liberalization. India started implementing reforms and seriously opening up to free trade from 1991, after taking an Extended Financing Facility from the International Monetary Fund (IMF) of $5 billion following the temporary difficulties created by the first Gulf War. The sum borrowed was small and soon repaid, but it was the entry point for the international financial institutions' agenda pushing for a complete reversal of the strategy followed up to that date, of Nehruvian *dirigiste* planned development, in which the state had been a major investor, banking had been nationalized, and public sector enterprises had been set up in a range of industries.[1] The impact of 15 years of neoliberal economic reforms can be summarized in one phrase: *rural famishment, a new phase of primitive accumulation, and the rapid tertiarization and polarization of Indian economy and society.* The meaning of this will be explored in this chapter with a special focus on the agrarian depression.

The basic question is—why should rapid growth under neoliberal reforms and trade liberalization, advised by the Bretton Woods Institutions (BWI) and under the World Trade Organization (WTO) discipline, be accompanied by agricultural depression and acute distress in particular regions, and why should there be an adverse impact on food security? The answer to this question, at one level is complex but at another level it is quite simple. To understand the background to the present situation, we must start with a brief discussion of the imperialist international division of labor in the production and exchange of primary products.

2. THE INTERNATIONAL DIVISION OF LABOR—HISTORY AND THE PRESENT

The earth, the cradle of all human activity, is not characterized by a homogeneous distribution of resources useful and indispensable for such activity. The primary sector is called 'primary' precisely because it is required to meet all the basic economic requirements of human societies—energy needs, food and raw materials for clothing and shelter. Primary production in the broadest sense—agriculture, forestry and fishing, and mining—together satisfy the entire range of these requirements. But unlike manufacturing which is not limited by location, what crops can be produced is crucially dependent on geography, on specific climate-soil complexes. The major share of the earth's biological and botanic diversity is to be found in the tropical and sub-tropical areas. Minerals and fossil fuels are not evenly distributed but are concentrated in particular regions.

The agricultural output vector in Southern developing countries located in sub-tropical and tropical regions not only contains many more elements, but is a *qualitatively* different output vector compared to that of Northern developed countries located in temperate regions. Confining ourselves to the northern hemisphere to begin with, the matter may be formalized as shown in Table 10.1.

It is obvious that populations located in cold temperate lands—today's advanced countries—would wish to acquire through trade with developing countries not only the typical tropical crops of the B vector, which they could not grow at all, but also the A vector elements, in the winter season when their lands are frozen, in order to avoid seasonal constraints and have a year-round supply. This led to heavy demands on tropical lands in history for the typical tropical crops (sugar, coffee and tea, tobacco, rice, cotton and jute, dyestuffs, and hardwoods being the main items). Even heavier demands on tropical lands have continued into the modern period as rising incomes in the North are leading to even more diversification, and cheap air transport has permitted even highly perishable products, ranging from

Table 10.1 Differing Agricultural Output Vectors in North and South (Northern Hemisphere)

	Winter Season		*Summer/Monsoon Season*
Developing countries	(a1, a2, a3, . . . , an)	+	(b1, b2, b3, . . . , bn)
Advanced countries	(0, 0, 0, . . . , 0)	+	(a1, a2, a3, . . . , an)

Note: The A vector containing the *ai* refer to the typical field crops, tree crops, and root crops cultivated only in summer in cold countries which can also be grown in the winter season in tropical developing countries. The B vector containing the *bi* refer to the typical tropical crops not cultivable at all in advanced countries or cultivable only in small volumes.[2]

fish and fruit to flavorings and flowers, to be accessed by rich Northern populations from distant Southern lands in the three continents.

As Slicher van Bath[3] has documented, the populations of today's advanced countries, in the late feudal period before forcibly acquiring tropical lands, had a very limited and monotonous diet, nor was cotton clothing available for mass wear. The consumption basket of European populations improved and diversified dramatically only after the colonial expansion and forcible acquisition of access to tropical lands. The near-complete elimination of seasonality however is a modern phenomenon: advanced country supermarkets carry the entire range of temperate and tropical products all year round as the giant food business transnational companies have been integrating poor peasant farmers in more and more developing countries through contract systems into a global food chain serving advanced countries.

Trade in primary products is an absolute imperative for the advanced country populations which rely on imports to provide the physical elements of their high living standards entailing highly diversified consumption baskets. It is of little use to be a millionaire in Germany if one cannot ever drink any coffee, wear any cotton clothes, use a teak or mahogany desk, or buy flowers in winter. Such trade is far from essential however for the majority of developing countries which can meet all their primary sector requirements from their own lands. Even such of these latter countries today which are food-import dependent have been brought to that position only owing to the incessant demands on their best lands to grow export crops.

Economic theory has by and large ignored the question of the heterogeneity of primary resources and productive capacities available to different societies. Where it has at all addressed the question, it has said that specialization in production according to the principle of comparative cost, and exchange—always assumed to voluntarily entered into by the trading partners for mutual gain—solves the problem. To this day the Ricardian theory of comparative advantage is invoked by in Northern universities and in fora like the WTO to urge developing countries to open up their economies to freer trade and investment, promising them large gains from doing so. However there is a logical fallacy at the heart of Ricardo's theory with its two-country, two-good model. The conclusion of mutual benefit from trade depends crucially on his assumption that 'both countries produce both goods'. Only if both countries produce both goods can the cost of production of the goods, and hence relative cost in the pre-trade situation, be at all defined. But the assumption itself is incorrect. Germany imports coffee and exports machinery, but we cannot define the cost of production of coffee in Germany; hence, no relative cost is definable, and this trade cannot be explained in terms of 'comparative cost'. Indian economic historians influenced by Ricardo themselves have fallaciously argued that India ceased to export cotton cloth and exported raw cotton instead while importing its cloth from England, because the latter country's 'comparative cost advantage' lay in cloth production and India's in raw cotton. This ignores the fact that England could not produce raw cotton and so the relative cost in the pre-trade situation could not be defined at all for that country. I have discussed the type of fallacy involved in Ricardo's theory in greater detail elsewhere.[4]

The entire argument of necessary mutual benefit from specialization and trade is logically incorrect and an exercise in apologetics, an intellectual rationalization of and justification for what actually happened in history. We know that the history of capitalist accumulation starting from its Western European centers, proceeded in a noticeably less idyllic fashion than that theory of voluntary trade for mutual benefit portrays: it was marked by the forcible colonial subjugation by a handful of Western European nations, of the peoples mainly of tropical and sub-tropical regions, by the promotion of slavery and indentured labor for running vast plantation systems producing tropical consumption goods and raw materials to satisfy the requirements of these European industrializing societies. Where slavery did not exist as in India, the system was marked by heavy taxation of subjugated populations and the use of these tax revenues to purchase export goods in which the country was made to specialize. Costless access to these goods—costless because growing trade deficits with colonies carried no external liability—substantially aided the first industrialization in Britain and that country's rise to dominance as an imperial power. A stable Gold Standard under which this leading imperialist power exported capital to the countries of white settlement despite running current account deficits against these countries, and thus ran up very large balance of payments deficits without incurring any outflow of gold, was only made possible by appropriating the growing exchange earnings from primary products exports of the tropical regions and to thus balancing its payments. The entire imperialist global system of trade and capital flows depended crucially on forced specialization in primary product exports by subjugated populations.[5]

Why was such forcible subjugation and trade at all necessary for capitalist accumulation, why did normal trade between sovereign trading partners not suffice, why did today's ex-colonized developing countries not enter voluntarily into specialization in primary products and their export in exchange for manufactured goods, if indeed it was of great mutual benefit as the standard Ricardian theory argued? The answer lies in the fact that specialization and trade cannot be of mutual benefit, and was not of mutual benefit where primary production is concerned.

First and foremost, an obvious proposition bears repetition for it is never theoretically recognized, at least by the modern discipline of economics. Agricultural land is a resource which is not produced by human labor (though its productivity can be improved by investment), and once the technological limits to productivity within a given social production system is reached, it becomes conceptually on par with non-renewable energy resources. There is a struggle by advanced capitalist countries for control over the productive capacity of limited tropical land resources all over the world, just as there is a struggle for control over fossil energy resources. As a matter of fact, the distinction between agricultural crops and energy resources did not exist in the pre-industrial period. Much of the energy needs in developing Europe and North America right up to the mid-nineteenth century, was met not by fossil fuels, but by agriculture, in the form of cereals used as feed for the army of horses employed for goods and passenger transport.[6] After a century and a half of reliance on fossil fuels, and with currently spiraling oil price approaching $100 a barrel as the world imperialist leader, the U.S., fails to 'pacify' Iraq, the matter is again coming full circle, back to the land. Agriculture is under renewed and strong pressure today to grow biofuels and devote a rising part of grain and sugarcane output to conversion to ethanol for running automobiles. This is a more recent, and very serious addition to the threat to food security already posed by growing external demands by advanced countries for export crops on limited tropical lands of developing countries.

There is ample evidence, some of which I have discussed and summarized elsewhere,[7] that both under colonial systems and in modern times, as primary exports from developing countries grew, there was always a fall in domestic foodgrains availability and declining nutritional standards for the population—no exceptions are to be seen. *In short, there is an inverse relation between agricultural exports and maintaining domestic food security.* In British India during the half century before Independence foodgrains output nearly stagnated while exported commercial crops grew ten times faster (the respective annual compound rates being 0.11% and 1.31%), while per capita foodgrains availability declined about 29% in the inter-War period. Further there were net foodgrains exports as well (Blyn 1966). In Java under Netherlands the main export crops sugarcane and rubber boomed, while per capita rice availability declined by one-fifth over the same period. Colonized Korea was made to export 60% of its rice to Japan by the end-1930s, and the calorie intake of its own population fell substantially. Colonized Ireland experienced the inverse relation with a vengeance, resulting in a massive famine (see note 5). Mexico during the quarter century after the late 1960s, saw the percentage share of its total grain output, which was going as animal feed to meet burgeoning export demand for meat, go up from 5% to 30% while the output per capita of maize and beans, the food staples of the ordinary people, declined. The six largest countries in sub-Saharan Africa, accounting for three-fifths of the region's population, saw a huge one-third decline in per capita cereals output over the decade 1980 to1990 when their primary exports were growing fast, and the decline has continued at a slower rate since then.[8]

The more other societies external to our nations demand the use of our productive and biodiverse tropical lands to underpin their rising living standards and energy needs, the less land is available for meeting the essential requirements of local populations. The entire matter becomes a zero-sum game. More and more foodgrains-growing land is diverted to export crops, and more of the foodgrains, especially the coarse grains, themselves end up as animal feed and biofuel, both of which are mainly consumed by the rich or exported. Even if absolute foodgrains output does not decline or continues to rise, since it rises less fast than the population is rising and its end uses change away from direct consumption to animal feed and industrial consumption, we find that there is a decline in the domestic availability of foodgrains for direct consumption, per head of population. (Availability is defined as net output minus net exports and minus net addition to public stocks). In extreme cases this can become a steep absolute decline in domestic availability.

All this leads to declining nutritional standards of the poor in the country engaging in this type of specialization and increases mass hunger, since foodgrains alone account for seven-tenths of the energy intake of the poor. Any type of shock to the system (severe drought, rapid food price rise) can precipitate visible famine. Even when this extreme outcome may not occur, declining nutrition levels are bad enough. This 'hidden famishment' is the price that poor developing country populations are made to pay as the cost of free trade, but it is a cost which is neither recognized nor therefore addressed by their own governments, which pretend that poverty is declining and continue to follow the same policies increasing mass hunger and malnutrition. Today it is *de rigeur* for international organizations to talk of the problems of child and maternal malnutrition, but the fact that there is increasing undernutrition within the general population as a whole in India including at least 250 million men, is never cognized or mentioned. This strange reverse gender bias is to be seen in the writings of even progressive Indian academics taking their cue from the discourse of the international organizations.

To summarize, the capacity to produce a wide and qualitatively diversified range of primary outputs is concentrated in the poor developing countries endowed with tropical and sub-tropical lands. Global purchasing power, however, is highly concentrated in advanced countries—over 85% of world income is in the hands of less than one-sixth of world population in a handful of rich industrial nations in the temperate regions, which historically have made heavy demands on the diversified production capacity of developing country lands and whose demands are embracing ever new goods as their consumption basket diversifies. Given the nature of tropical land as a limited resource which cannot be augmented by human labor as regards its extent, and whose supply is thus virtually fixed, such external demands lead to a decline in domestic food production for local populations to accommodate rising exports. The economic mechanisms urged by developed countries, through which this is brought about, include trade openness, specialization in export crops, reduction of government's intervention to maintain domestic food security systems, and macroeconomic deflation. These issues are discussed briefly in the following sections in the context of India's experience under neoliberal economic reforms.

3. ELEMENTS OF INVERSE RELATION UNDER IMPERIALISM AND NEO-IMPERIALISM

A severely adverse impact on our food security following adoption of greater trade openness in India, was to be expected on the basis of the past and current experience of present-day developing countries, and I have been warning of this outcome since 1992. That is indeed what has happened: 8 million hectares of land has been diverted away from foodgrains production mainly to export crops within a total gross sown area which is stagnant or somewhat declining, and the end use of grain is also changing with a higher share going as animal feed and industrial use. Yield rise having slowed down has not compensated for area decline, and the growth rate of foodgrains output has halved in the 1990s compared to the 1980s and has becomes virtually zero in the years since 2000 (Table A2). Per capita grain output has been declining more steeply than before and has touched a historic low of 155 kilograms per head annual average in the triennium ending 2004–2005 (Chart 10.1). This is the same level as 50 years ago during the First Plan, and actually lower than the average during 1937–1941 which was 157 kilograms. Forty years of effort in independent India to raise foodgrains output per capita to a peak of 182 kilograms by the early 1990s have been wiped out in the subsequent dozen years of neoliberal reforms.

As Chart 10.1 shows clearly, per capita availability fell even faster than did output between 1998 and 2002. The large gap between the two trends reflects the fact that by July 2002 public foodgrains stocks of 64 million tonne had built up, which was 40 million tonne in excess of the norm of buffer stock for that time of year. The reason was the severe contraction in purchasing power of the mass of the mainly rural population, which we discuss a little later. At the same time private grain exports also rose. Unlike every previous short episode of per head domestic output decline which had been always compensated by net imports and drawing down of stocks to maintain domestic availability, this long period was highly abnormal in seeing the opposite—as per head output declined, more stocks built up and more was exported, reducing availability more and more to a historic low.

The Indian government ignored the real reason for the lower absorption, which was loss of purchasing power and demand deflation, and wrongly argued that the problem was 'over-production'. It put the blame on allegedly 'too high' minimum support price to farmers which gave 'the wrong signals' leading to a higher output than the market demanded. Instead of putting back purchasing power and food into the hands of the poor, which the situation demanded, it proceeded instead to export 22 million tonnes of grain out of stocks during 2002 and 2003, freeze procurement price and reduce public procurement. All these disincentives have led our farmers to cut back on foodgrains output, which became stagnant and hence fell so steeply in per capita terms after 2002 (see Chart 10.1) that imports became necessary to meet the minimum needs of the public welfare programs. There can be few more deplorable stories of incorrect theory and incorrect policies increasing hunger, than the Indian government's handling of the food security question in recent years. By its obtuse attack on the viability of farmers and the purchasing power of the masses, it has succeeded in taking India back to near-stagnant grain output and to deepening undernutrition.

To return to our general argument, there are two further elements to it. First, when public investment rates and public development expenditures in the primary sector are actually declining, there is not the slightest possibility of reconciling an export thrust from farming with maintaining domestic foodgrains availability. The consumption of the mass of the poor is then sacrificed to meet the demands of the external sector. (A similar outcome is seen in China under its internally driven market reforms, where export thrust has entailed declining per capita foodgrains availability for the rural masses.) Second, the argument is incorrect; although it is regularly put forward by economists even to this day, that specialization in export crops need not lead to greater food insecurity because the increased export earnings can be used to purchase foodgrains from the global market. The reality is that unit dollar prices of primary products have shown a secular declining trend, with fluctuations, since the 1960s, and the current value is about one-third compared to then. A doubling, say, of volume exports, can end up in no increase at all exchange earnings if the unit price halves. Further with over 80 developing countries competing with each other to export the same crops under Fund-Bank and WTO-mandated policies, developing countries find themselves in a competitive "race to the bottom" as far as exchange earnings are concerned. Even if a country does obtain increased exchange earnings, these are most unlikely to be devoted to importing food for the poor since the effective market demand of the poor has been reduced by public policy, and governments deny that hunger is increasing. There is no forex constraint in India, but increased exchange earnings are financing imported automobiles and foreign tourism by the well-to-do, not foodgrain imports for the poor.

This brings us to a discussion of the reason why specialization in primary products and their export always leads to an attack on the food security of the poor. The ability to raise productivity (crop yields) and so maintain domestic food availability even with a stronger export thrust, is crucially dependent on more investment in irrigation, high-yielding crop varieties, and extension services. Far from rising, however, all these suffer actual reduction in the present era of neoliberal reforms because the core of such reforms is *deflation*, the reduction in public expenditures advised by the international financial institutions. Public investment in agriculture was already declining in the 1980s but the decline has become steeper in the era of economic reforms after 1991. Plan development expenditures including on irrigation, vital for the primary sector, was nearly 4% of NNP (Net National Product) in the pre-Reform period but halved to 1.9 % by 2000–2001 and continues to be far below the pre-Reform level as Table A3 shows.

Macroeconomic deflationary policies advised by the international financial institutions include reduction in state expenditures, monetary austerity and high real interest rates for producers (but easing of consumer credit), reduction in the ratio of budget deficit to GDP, caps on wages aided by labor retrenchment policies, and currency devaluation. All these together add up to a strongly deflationary package which has been implemented under Fund guidance by successive Indian central governments since 1991 regardless of their political composition. The pattern has been that three years or more of severe contraction immediately after a general election is followed by two years or less, of more expansionary policies as governments try to regain electoral support eroded by the hardships they have inflicted on the people. The main target of the expenditure-deflating policies has been the unorganized sector and the main segment of this sector has been agriculture.

Even though it was the agrarian crisis which propelled the UPA (United Progressive Alliance) government to power in the 2004 general elections, the government, by immediately notifying the Fiscal Responsibility and Budgetary Management Act, reiterated its commitment to a strongly deflationary fiscal stance as advised by the international financial institutions. Under the Act it is mandatory for the government to reduce the fiscal deficit, and this means further expenditure deflation. From around 6% in 2001 the gross fiscal deficit as a percentage of GDP had been reduced to 3.7% by 2007. The irrational policy of expenditure deflation remains the Vedas and the Upanishads for the government; the country is firmly in the grip of the global moneylenders, and their deflationary policies are privileged over the question of livelihoods and food security of the poor, whose worsening situation, if it is to be addressed effectively, requires exactly the opposite policy of a strongly expansionary fiscal stance. While the National Rural Employment Guarantee Act might seem to go against this, it is to be noted that budgetary allocation to this has been paltry, a mere 10% more than was being spent earlier, and even this allocation was cut in the 2007 Budget even though it was announced that the scheme was to be extended to more districts.[9]

The basic reason for such relentless attacks on employment and mass incomes, is that cropping pattern shifts and supply shifts alone will not do the job for the advanced countries wishing to see such specialization on the part of developing countries, for desired supply shifts in modern market economies need corresponding *demand shifts* to succeed. An essential element of the mechanism is to reduce the purchasing power of the masses, generally the unorganized rural population, so that mass demand for basic necessities including foodgrains reduces to release land resources for growing more export crops and for the greater diversion of foodgrains itself toward more commercial and industrial use demanded by the local and foreign well-to-do classes. Under colonial systems where there was direct control, such reduction in purchasing power was directly made through imposing heavy taxes and using a part of taxes to buy up export goods. Under modern conditions where there is no direct control, the same mechanism works through *public expenditure deflation.* All governments in developing countries appear to be in thrall to the dogma of reducing the fiscal deficit and reducing development spending in particular, no matter how high domestic unemployment might be, forgetting that this is a sure recipe for a income-deflating spiral to set in as had happened during the run-up to the great inter-War depression.

Thus the attack comes not only on the supply side reducing output growth through reduced investment but involves a simultaneous attack on mass incomes through expenditure deflation, which sets in motion the reverse multiplier effects of declining development expenditures. Every Rs. 100 less of such public spending, cuts incomes by a multiple of 4 to 5, that is by between Rs. 400 to Rs. 500 (assuming it is reasonable to do that, only one-fifth to one-quarter of every incremental rupee earned is saved and hence three-quarters to four-tenths is spent). Public expenditure deflation has been severe in the primary sector, and it is this which is the main cause of not only lowered levels of activity but also an associated rise in unemployment (including more severe underemployment) and decline in incomes and in purchasing power. Table A2 shows that rise in unemployment under every status (daily, weekly and usual status) has been much greater in rural areas compared to urban areas. The NSS (National Sample Survey) consumption expenditure data clearly indicate fall in real spending on both food and cloth in rural India between 1993–1994 and 2004–2005, and falling energy intake (calorie intake per head per day) in rural India. This lower real spending moreover does not reflect exactly the even greater decline in income since the data also show that in many states net asset change is negative; that is, asset adjustments are being made to maintain even the lowered consumption flow. In short, farmers are selling livestock and land owing to falling incomes and indebtedness.

4. SUBSTANTIAL RISE IN RURAL POVERTY

Not surprisingly, rural poverty has risen steeply although official figures fail to reflect this owing to the faulty official methodology of estimation. The government, under BWI guidance, having implemented policies, which have substantially reduced food security and increased unemployment and hunger, continues to pretend that rural poverty is declining in the face of a mountain of evidence to the contrary. It is clinging to a fallacious method of estimating poverty, which is no longer based on any nutrition norm and which takes the cost of the quantities consumed in 1973–1974, over three decades ago, and simply updates it using a price index. The resulting 'poverty lines' are gross underestimates of the current cost of living and give corresponding underestimates of the population in poverty. A more

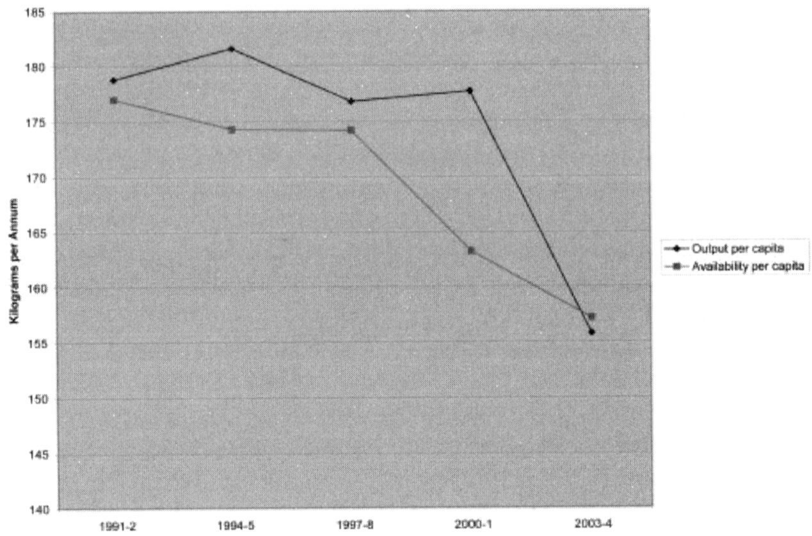

Figure 10.1 Foodgrains output and availability per capita in kilograms per annum, triennial average centered on specified years, 1990–1991 to 2004–2005. *Note :* Output is Net Output = 0.87.5 times Gross Output. *Availability* = Net Output + Net Imports—Net Addition to Public Stocks. Both variables divided by total population for per capita values. Chart updated to 2004–2005 from Patnaik (2007b).

detailed critique, and the basis for my alternative estimates, is available in my other papers [10], while here I give a summary of the actual trends in poverty incorporating the results of the recently released NSS 61st Round consumption expenditure data relating to 2004–2005.

The official rural monthly poverty line expenditure for year 2004–2005, is Rs.356 or Rs11.8 daily, equivalent to 27 U.S. cents at the then prevailing exchange rate. This paltry amount would buy a single one-liter bottle of mineral water, or at most 1 kilogram of the coarsest rice. But it is supposed to cover *all expenditure on food, cooking and lighting fuel, clothing, shelter, transport, health and education*—in short all required daily spending on goods and services for one person! International agencies like the World Bank too have been complicit in promoting equally unrealistic poverty lines: the norm of one-dollar-eight cents a day is deflated to the rupee equivalent of less than one-third dollar a day for India for that year, to adjust for purchasing power parity (PPP), and the national poverty percentage of 35.3 is thereby derived.[11]

The question is, would a dollar a day be a reasonable poverty line for the U.S.—clearly not, for it would have bought at most one bottle of mineral water there, just as the PPP adjusted one dollar in India, could barely buy a single bottle of water. At this very low daily expenditure level, the nutrition norm of 2,400 kilocalories of energy intake per person obviously could not be accessed in India's villages and the actual energy intake at this level is found to be just over 1,800 calories as an All-India average. In six individual states in India, less than 1,675 calories could be accessed at the state level official poverty lines (state poverty lines vary according to the presumed differences in the cost of purchasing the same base-year basket of goods).

It is clearly not difficult to 'reduce' poverty when the consumption level embodied in the poverty line is lowered to such sub-human levels, for few people actually survive long below these levels—those who are there today are on their way to early death. Neither the government nor the individual academics following the same faulty estimation method inform the public that in practice the poverty estimates have been completely de-linked from the nutrition norm and for 1993–1994 and 2004–2005 corresponded to energy intake levels far below the 2,400 calories recommended by the Indian Council for Medical Research, which has been the conceptual basis of poverty studies since the first estimate in 1973–1974.

The main reason the official poverty lines are so low and unable to reflect the actual current cost of accessing the nutrition norm is because the basket of commodities and their quantities consumed in 1973–1974 is held unchanged and its cost is simply updated with a price index, the Consumer Price Index for Agricultural Laborers. There is no logical defense which can be put forward for assuming an unchanged consumption basket when estimating current poverty, since over time the economic environment has changed and consumers face a different set of choices altogether. As the base year of the fixed consumption basket has receded in time, the official poverty line has become cumulatively distant from the true poverty line required for accessing the nutrition norm. The latest 61st Round data for 2004–2005 released recently by the NSS show that at the All-India level the rural consumer required Rs. 790 per month or over Rs. 26.3 per day to access the nutrition norm, more than double the official poverty line of Rs. 356 per month (below Rs. 12 per day).

The initial official poverty lines in the 1970s were not too distant from the cost of accessing minimum nutrition, but became cumulatively distant from the true poverty lines over time, as Chart 10.2a shows. Accordingly at the official poverty lines, lower and lower nutrition levels could be accessed over time as shown in Chart 10.2c. Clearly one cannot make a valid comparison over time when the consumption standard is being lowered, or altered in any way. The official poverty percentages obtained by applying the official poverty lines, increasingly ceased to reflect the true situation of change in poverty. They showed 'declining poverty' solely because they corresponded to a lower and lower consumption standard over time. The decline in poverty claimed by the Planning Commission in India and by individual economists following the same method, and shown in Chart 10.2b, is thus quite spurious and arises from the continuous lowering of the consumption standard inherent in the official estimation method. Charts 10.2a and 10.2b also depict my calculation of the monthly per capita expenditure actually required to access the nutrition norm at each point of time (these can be easily obtained directly from the nutrition data in relation to expenditure levels) and the associated poverty percentages. The percentage of all persons spending below these levels indicate the true extent of poverty, and these are validly comparable over time since the same consumption standard is being applied. These direct poverty estimates show a slow rise in poverty from the late 1970s up to 1993–1994, and then a steeper rise thereafter during the economic reforms period.

In 1993–1994, 74.5% of all persons in poverty spent less than the Rs. 10.8 daily level required for accessing the nutrition norm; by 2004–2005 an all-time record high of 87% of the rural population spent less than Rs. 26.3 per day and could not access enough food to reach the norm. Since the norm itself has been questioned even though it is the official one, I have also estimated and shown the proportion of persons below lower calorie intake levels (2,200 and 1,800), and in every case there is a substantial rise of population below these levels by 2004–2005, indicating increasing poverty depth. By 2004–2005, the proportion of persons consuming less than 2,200 calories has increased in 14 out of the 15 major states in India.[12]

Targeting the food subsidy using the official measures leaves out over 300 million people in rural India who are in reality poor but are not officially recognized as poor. In fact, targeting make no sense where over three-quarters of the rural population is actually in poverty, and targeting the food subsidy since 1998 has amounted in practice to the institutional denial of affordable food to the poor.[13] Faced with an ocean of deprivation, the government and Planning Commission, rather than facing up to hard reality, seem to have chosen the easier path of performing academically indefensible procedures with the statistics to claim poverty reduction. China's current official rural poverty line is also absurdly low at about 800 yuan per year or 2.2 yuan per day (less than one-third of one U.S. dollar) and is identical to the Indian one: its estimates of rural poverty are equally gross underestimates.

Our observations for India are applicable to the other developing countries following reform policies advised by the international financial institutions which have increased poverty and reduced the nutritional levels of populations. But these institutions claim the opposite, namely poverty reduction, because they base their own global dollar poverty lines on the unrealistically low developing country rural poverty lines. Never in the history f economic thought have we seen such wholesale use of illegitimate statistical techniques and such falsification of real trends as we observe today.

5. PRIMITIVE ACCUMULATION: LARGE RISE IN NIL-OPERATED HOLDINGS

Agrarian distress has been manifesting itself in thousands of farmer suicides, underlying which is a step fall in the profitability of production entirely engineered through neoliberal policies. This has led to very striking changes in the distribution of land operated—the actual units in which land is cultivated. As Table 8.3 shows, at the All-India level the percentage of households operating

Table 10.2 The Rural Poor as Percentage of Rural Population in India

	1973–1974	*1993–1994*	*2004–2005*
NSS Round:	*28th*	*50th*	*61st*
RURAL			
Direct Estimate			
MPCE, Rs. required for			
1. 2,400 calories	56	325	790
2. 2,200 calories	49	260	695
Percent of persons below			
3. 2,400 calories	72.0	74.5	87
4. 2,200 calories	56.4	58.5	69.5
Official Estimate			
5. Official poverty line, MPCE, Rs.	49	206	356
6. Poverty percentage	56.4	37.3	28.3
7. Calorie intake at OPL	2200	1970	1820

Source: Simplified from Patnaik (2007b). MPCE is monthly per capita expenditure. Note that the official poverty line (OPL) takes a 1973–1974 base-year poverty line and updates by a price index, without reference to current data on actual cost of reaching the nutrition norm, and so these poverty lines correspond to increasingly lowered calorie intake over time, rendering the associated poverty ratios non-comparable. Not the official norm of 2,400 calories, but a lower one of 2,200 calories was applied in the base year.

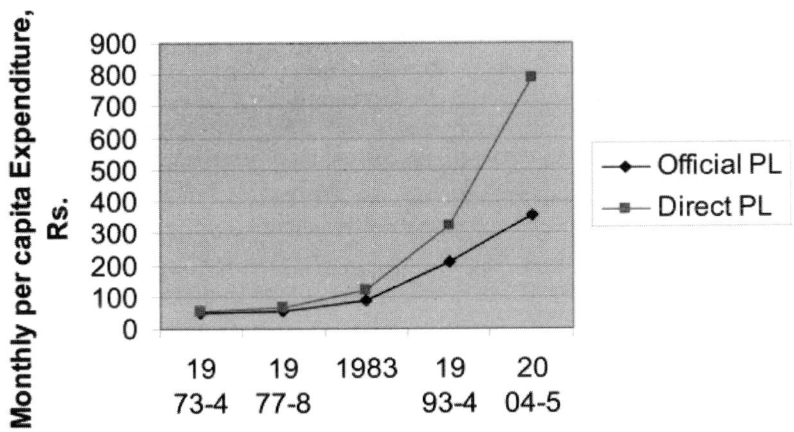

Figure 10.2a Official and directly estimated poverty lines, All-India rural, 1973–1974 to 2004–2005. Source: Table 2 lines 1 and 5.

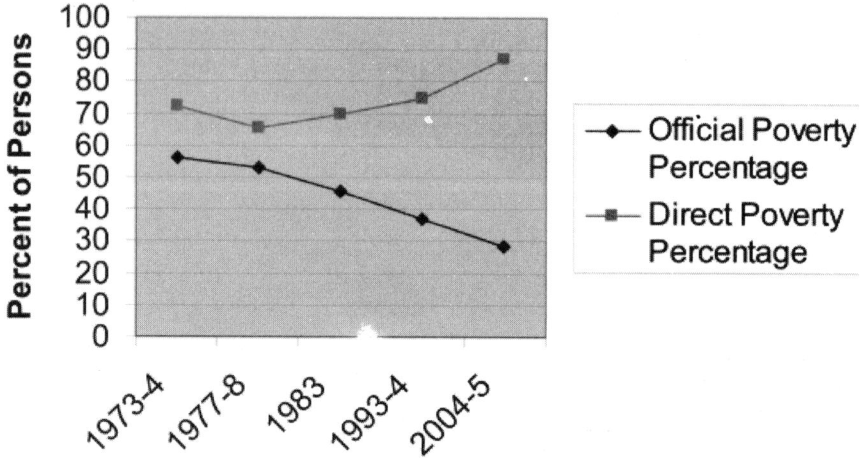

Figure 10.2b Official and directly estimated percentage of persons in poverty, All-India rural, 1973–1974 to 2004–2005, obtained by applying the respective poverty lines. Source: Table 2, lines 3 and 6. 1974 to 2004–2005. Source: Table 2 lines 1 and 5.

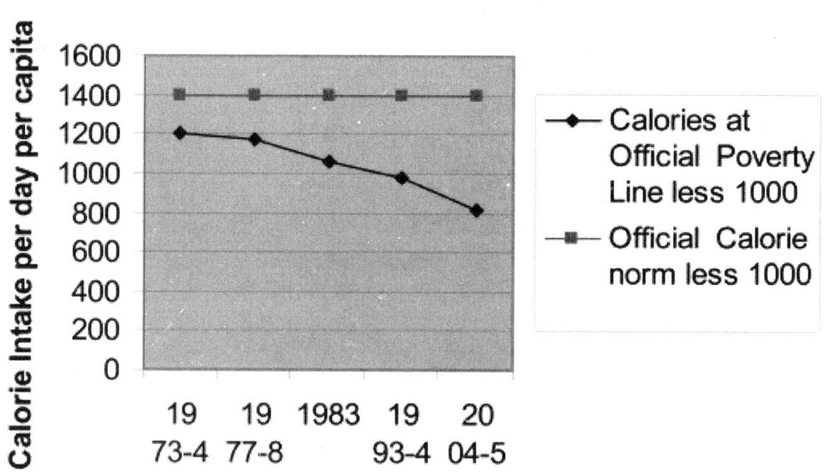

Figure 10.2c Declining caloric intake accessible at official poverty lines, All-India rural 1973–1974 to 2004–2005. Source: Table 2 line 7.

nil land has risen markedly from 19.8% to 31.2%. The state-wise data show a sharper than average rise in all states specially affected by acute farmer distress, including Andhra Pradesh, Kerala, and Punjab. In Kerala the rural households with nil operational holdings have risen from only 5.8% to a record 38.6%. The number of landless households in operational terms (with nil-operated area) has doubled from 23 million to 46 million over the decade of reforms.

The latest data on the profitability of cultivation are available for 2002–2003 from the NSS Report No. 497 *Income, Expenditure and Productive Assets of Farmer Households, 2003*. This shows that the monthly income from all sources—cultivation, animal farming, wage income, non-farm business—taken together, failed to meet the monthly consumption expenditure of a record 96% of farming families at the All-India level. Only the top 4% of all households generated a surplus over-consumption, and the overall position was that the farming sector was in deficit to the tune of Rs. 655 per month. When initial levels of consumption are already very low, there is a limit to further reduction in consumption, and increased borrowing followed ultimately by asset transfer to finance the deficit is the result. Admittedly 2002–2003 was a bad drought year, but the 96% in deficit would be reduced by at most 10 points in a more normal year. Only about 12% of all holdings had productive investment worth mentioning, while on the rest it was so paltry that the overall average figure of productive investment was only Rs. 124 per month.

In addition to all its existing travails, the peasantry in most developing countries, and of late in India too, is facing the onslaught of a new phase of primitive accumulation of capital which involves acquisition of peasant land and pressure on water resources by corporations engaging in agribusiness, retailing and real estate speculation, and more rarely, manufacturing production. The central government as well as local governments in India are facilitating the acquisition of farmland by corporations, a process which contains two distinct components—first, the entry of foreign corporations into agriculture and allied activities through contract systems or setting up farms, and the entry of domestic corporations into urban food retailing by sourcing from agriculture through setting up hundreds of collection points, all of which requires land. These processes will clearly aggravate the problems of declining foodgrains availability discussed at length earlier by shifting even more land to the products demanded by advanced country supermarkets, while corporate retailing will introduce the problem of unemployment among the petty traders and handcart sellers of agricultural produce. The tertiary sector, the only one growing in terms of employment, is also thus coming under the threat of employment reduction. Second, land is sought to be acquired for setting up Special Economic Zones which in practice are turning out to be used mainly for real estate development and land speculation, with very little new manufacturing enterprise.

Against a background of pervasive agrarian crisis and loss of peasant lands against debt, further attempts to take over farm land for SEZs and for corporations, is bound to be bitterly resisted, and this phase of peasant resistance in India has begun. Those who argue that if agricultural

Table 10.3 Comparative Distribution of Rural Households by Land Holdings Operated, 1992 and 2002–2003

	All-India			
Size Class	***1992, 48th Round*** *Percent of*		***2002–2003, 59th Round*** *Percent of*	
Operated Area (hectares)	*Total HH*	*Area Operated*	*Total HH*	*Area Operated*
Nil	19.8	0.0	31.2	0.00
< 0.002	2.1	0.0	0.8	0.00
Subtotal	***21.9***	***0.0***	***32.0***	***0.00***
0.002–0.2	20.3	1.2		
0.2–0.4	7.9	2.1	9.8	0.2
0.4–1.0	20.0	12.2	37.3	22.0
1.0–5.0	26.0	51.4	18.8	50.9
5.0 +	3.9	33.0	2.1	26.9
All	100	100	100	100
Total No. of HHs, lakhs		1,164.173	1,478.376	
No. of Landless HH, lakhs		**230.506**	**461.253**	

Source: NSS 48th Round, NSS Report 408, Land and Livestock Survey 1992; and 59th Round, Report 493, Livestock Ownership across Operational Landholding classes in India, 2002–03. For the latter year the combined figure is given for the two area groups between 0.002 and 0.4 hectares.

production on a peasant basis is so unprofitable the peasantry would be better off by giving it up, forget that 30 million families comprising the very poor, have nowhere to go to, and no prospect of gainful employment given the very low current elasticities of employment with respect to output in all non-agricultural sectors except construction and hotels. To argue that 30 million families can be shifted out of agriculture by non-agricultural growth is a mirage and ignores the hard realities revealed by the employment data. However little their land today yields—and this is directly owing to neoliberal policies—possession of land provides a guarantee of minimum income and security, and its loss cannot be monetarily compensated.

As long as the fact is not explicitly recognized that increasing unemployment, income loss, and hunger have been created by the reduction in rural aggregate demand owing to the expenditure deflating fiscal stance of the government combined with the removal of price support (and this in turn has reduced investment), the importance of seriously implementing the employment guarantee will not be appreciated, it will continue be subverted, and there will be further 'slide into the abyss' of agrarian depression and unemployment. The official 'solution' of the corporatization of agriculture and contract farming, which is aimed at integrating India into the global food chain for filling supermarket shelves abroad and supplying corporate retail outlets meant for the local urban well-to-do, will not rescue 140 million rural families in depression. On the contrary, it will simply further severely undermine food security for the rural poor as more land is diverted away from foodgrains, reduce employment for petty retailers, and lead to no net employment generation as cropping patterns will shift simply by substituting existing crops by new ones within a constant sown area.

What is the solution to the problem of rural depression, falling incomes and food insecurity? First, the revival of agricultural production is essential for reviving employment and incomes. For this a large-scale revival of foodgrains and other crops procurement at realistic support prices giving an adequate return to farmers is essential. Without price support, the millions of farming households in deficit will have no possibility of regaining viability and resuming investment to raise productivity which is required to bring the growth rate back on track. The revival of agricultural production is essential for reviving food security via reviving employment and aggregate demand. Second, to improve the unemployment and incomes problem, a strongly expansionary fiscal policy with much higher rural development expenditures amounting to at least 4% of NNP (Net National Product) and a genuine commitment to implementing the National Rural Employment Guarantee Act is required. Combined with restoring a universal Public Distribution System, this would be sufficient to lift the agrarian economy out of depression and set in motion a virtuous cycle of employment and income generation. Finally, acquisition of farmland for 'development' should be approached in a highly cautious and circumspect manner by the government. The logic if any of establishing large SEZs with substantial tax and other concessions to corporations, is not clear and needs re-examination.

The government and the planners have neither analyzed the employment and livelihoods depression correctly, nor will their proposals to make Indian agriculture a mere supply source for foreign and local supermarkets do anything but worsen the problem. It is intellectually infantile to say that this is a 'depressing scenario' and build up a false picture of positive outcomes. The practical result of the official refusal to face up to the reality revealed by every data source we have is likely to be failure to undertake any measures to check the worsening of income distribution, while a regressive use of demand management is the logical corollary, in order to curtail further the purchasing power of the unorganized poor so as to accommodate the consumption demands of the well-to-do. The proposal to remove the so-called 'above poverty line' persons—who are actually poor—altogether from the ambit of the public distribution system, in line with the self-serving advice of the international financial institutions, is one indicator of this regressive strategy.

ACKNOWLEDGMENTS

This chapter was published in *Human Geography*, volume 1, issue 1.

APPENDIX

Table A1 Percentage Contribution of the Economic sectors to GDP at Factor Cost, 1980–1981 to 2003–2004 (constant values at 1993–1994 prices)

Three-Year Average Centered on the Year	Agriculture, Forestry, Fishing, Mining, and Quarrying	Manufacturing, Construction, Utilities	Trade, Hotels, Transport, and Communication	Finance, Real Estate, and Business Services	All Services
1981–1982	41.34	21.77	18.52	6.78	36.89
1984–1985	39.84	22.33	18.53	7.62	37.83
1987–1988	36.44	23.24	19.18	8.81	40.32
1999–2000	27.49	24.59	22.28	12.49	47.92
1993–1994	33.55	23.93	19.37	11.22	42.52
1996–1997	30.16	25.37	21.12	11.62	44.47
1999–2000	27.49	24.59	22.28	12.49	47.92
2002–2003	24.72	24.64	24.61	12.76	50.63

Source: Govt. of India, Ministry of Finance, Economic Survey 2005–06.

Table A2 Reduction in Rural Development Expenditures under Economic Reforms, Selected Years 1985–1990 to 2000–2001

	1985–1990 Average	*1993–1994*	*1995–1996*	*1997–1998*	*2000–2001*	*2004–2005RE*
1.Rural development expenditures as percentage of NNP	3.8	2.8	2.6	2.3	1.9	2.1
2.Above plus infrastructure	11.1	8.4	6.9	6.4	5.8	6.2

Source: Government of India, Ministry of Finance, annual *Economic Survey,* for years 2001–2002 to 2005–2006, Appendix Table S-44 (actual expenditures). 'Rural development expenditures' here include the plan outlays of Centre and states under the five heads—agriculture, rural development, irrigation and flood control, special areas programs, and village and small-scale industry. Infrastructure includes all energy and transport. Calculated from current values of expenditure and of NNP at factor cost. RE is Revised Estimate.

Table A3 Decelerating Growth Rates of Agricultural Output

Period	*Foodgrains*	*Non-foodgrains*	*All Crops*	*Population*
1980–1981 to 1989–1990	2.85	3.77	3.19	2.1
1990-1991 to 2000–2001	1.66	1.86	1.73	1.9
2000–2001 to 2005–2006	0.14	n.a.	n.a.	1.8

Source: Govt of India, Ministry of Finance, *Economic Survey, 2001–02,* p. 189 for first two lines. Last line calculated taking initial 2000–2001 and terminal (advance estimate) 2005–2006 food grains output figures from *Economic Survey 2005–06* (both were near-normal rainfall years). Note that slowing down of output growth is much steeper than slowing down of population growth entailing fast falling per head output.

Table A4 Rising Unemployment Rates in India

	Males			*Females*		
	Usual Status	*Current Weekly Status*	*Current Daily Status*	*Usual Status*	*Current Weekly Status*	*Current Daily Status*
Rural						
2004	24	47	90	22	45	93
1993–1994	20	30	56	14	30	56
Urban						
2004	46	57	81	89	90	117
1993–1994	45	52	67	83	84	105

Source: Govt. of India, Ministry of Finance, *Economic Survey 2005–06,* Table 10.5. Primary source NSS Reports, 50th Round 1993–4 and 60th Round 2004. Unemployment rate is number of persons or person-days unemployed per 1,000 persons or person-days. Data relate to all economic sectors taken together.

NOTES

1. See P. Patnaik and Chandrasekhar (1995).
2. Cold temperate lands can produce cereals, root crops like turnips and potatoes, vegetables like cabbage and carrot, and fruits like apple and pear—all of these can also be produced in winter in India and in most tropical countries with land at varying elevations. Only tropical and sub-tropical regions, however, produce sugarcane, cotton, jute, tea and coffee, coconut, spices, bananas and mangoes, bamboo and tropical hardwoods prized for furniture, and so on.
3. B. H. Slicher van Bath, 1963. *The Agrarian History of Western Europe A.D. 1600–1850* London: Mathew Arnold.

4. U. Patnaik (2005).
5. There is a large literature. An analysis and some references are available in U. Patnaik (2006).
6. The only temperate land which was colonially subjugated, Ireland under England, was made to export foodgrains and livestock products to England to make good the latter's failure to meet its own needs of energy and food during industrialization. The pauperized Irish peasant population was made to subsist on potatoes and eventually over one-eighth of the total population perished in the great famine of 1846–1947—a larger mortality than in any Third World country under colonialism.
7. U. Patnaik (2003a). Some of these data and discussion also available in U. Patnaik (2007a).
8. Many of these cases have been discussed in U. Patnaik (2007a),
9. Only Rs.10, 900 crores, one-tenth more than already spent under various preceding employment generation programs, was the allocated sum for NREG (National Rural Employment Guarantee) under the budget, and this was cut to Rs.10,000 crores in February 2007.
10. Patnaik (2007b).
11. See World Bank (2006, Table A1, p. 278, cols. 9 and 10). The problem arises because the Bank's global poverty line is based on the unrealistically low national poverty lines of developing countries derived from the median value of the poorest 10 countries' rural poverty lines and this happens to be India.
12. See Patnaik (2007b) for a detailed discussion. See Swaminathan (2002).

REFERENCES

Blyn, G., 1966 *Agricultural Trends in India 1891–1947. Output, Availability and Productivity* Philadelphia: University of Pennsylvania Press.

Ministry of Finance, Government of India. *Economic Survey* (annual publication) for the years from 2001–2 to 2005–6.

National Sample Survey Organization.

Report No. 408, *Livestock and Implements in Household Operational Holdings199–92.*

Report No. 493, *Livestock ownership across Operational landholding classes in India 2002–03.*

Report No. 401, *Key Results on Household Consumer Expenditure, 1993–94.*

Report No. 402, *Level and Pattern of Consumer Expenditure 1993–94.*

Report No. 405, *Nutritional Intake in India 1993–94.*

Report No.457, *Level and Pattern of Consumer Expenditure in India 1999–2000.*

Report No.471, *Nutritional Intake in India, 1999–2000.*

Report No.497, *Income, Expenditure and Productive Assets of Farmer Households, 2003.*

Report No. 504, *Household Capital Expenditure in India during 1.7.2002 to 30.6.2003.*

Report No. 508, *Level and Pattern of Consumer Expenditure 2004–05.*

Report No. 513, *Nutritional Intake in India 2004–05.* Available on www.mospi.nic.in.

Patnaik, P., and Chandrasekhar, C. P. 1995. The Indian economy under structural adjustment. *Economic and Political Weekly* (November 25) Vol. 30, 47, pp. 3001–3013.

Patnaik, U. 1996. Export-oriented agriculture and food security in developing countries and India. *Economic and Political Weekly* 31: 35–37 (1999; Sp. Number 1996; repr. in *The long transition—Essays on political economy,* Delhi: Tulika).

———. 2003a. On the inverse relation between primary exports and domestic food absorption under liberalized trade regimes. In *Work and welfare in the age of finance*, edited by J. Ghosh and C. P. Chandrasekhar. Delhi: Tulika. pp. 256–286.

———. 2003b. Global capitalism, deflation and agrarian crisis in developing countries. Social Policy and Development Programme Paper Number 13. United Nations Research Institute for Social Development (UNRISD), October.

———. 2005. Ricardo's fallacy. In *The pioneers of development economics*, edited by Jomo K.S. Delhi: Tulika. pp. 31–41.

———. 2006. The free lunch—Transfers from the tropical colonies and their role in capital formation in Britain during industrial revolution. In *Globalization under hegemony*, edited by Jomo KS. Delhi: Oxford University Press. pp. 30–70.

———. 2007a. *The republic of hunger and other essays.* Delhi: Three Essays Collective.

———. 2007b. Neo-liberalism and rural poverty in India. *Economic and Political Weekly* (July 28–August 3). pp. 3132–3150.

Slicher van Bath, B.H. 1963, *The Agrarian History of Western Europe AD 1500–1850.* London: Mathew Arnold.

Swaminathan, M. 2002. Excluding the needy—The public provisioning of food in India. *Social Scientist* 30(3–4). pp. 34–58.

World Bank. 2006. *World development report.* New York: World Bank and Oxford University Press.

11 Special Economic Zones
Space, Law, and Dispossession

Rupal Oza

INTRODUCTION

On March 14, 2007, the West Bengal police opened fire on a group of peasants and villagers, killing 14 people. The group was protesting against the CPI-M (Communist Party of India—Marxist)-led government's attempt to acquire the villagers' land for a chemical hub[1] in Nandigram, a cluster of villages 60 miles south of Calcutta. Since 2002 disputes such as this have emerged across the country in response to the appropriation of land for the creation of Special Economic Zones (SEZ). SEZs are spaces acquired for private capital to set up industrial enclaves at low cost. The controversy escalated into a confrontation between Bhumi Uchhed Pratirodh Committee (BUPC or the committee to resist eviction from land) and CPI-M cadre in November 2007, leading to further violence, culminating in what became known as 'operation reconquest' of Nandigram (Bandyopadhya 2007). State repression of the protesters drew widespread criticism from people around the world, leading the chief minister Bhattacharjee to relocate the project to Nayachar.

The controversy in Nandigram came to symbolize the large-scale acquisition of land for Special Economic Zones (SEZs)[2]. Covering hundreds of acres, SEZs fundamentally alter the discursive and material geography of places and the people who live on, and from, the land. Predominantly taking over farmland, SEZs in India have drawn the ire of peasant and farmer groups for the dismal compensation and inadequate rehabilitation measures provided by the state.

There are currently 578 SEZs approved by the Ministry of Commerce and Industry.[3]According to the 2005 SEZ Act, these zones exist separately from the surrounding area and, for the purposes of trade and tariffs, are designated as 'foreign territories.' SEZs are governed and protected by a set of rules and provisions that make them exceptions to a series of local juridical statutes governing labor, industry, environmental assessments, and taxes. I follow the political intent of private capital in India, which is taking over large tracks of lands for SEZs and cordoning them off into enclaves beyond the reach of Indian jurisdiction. My intent is to understand why SEZs emerge at the beginning of the new millennium and what political and economic concerns motivate their support.

I argue first that a crisis of over-accumulation compels the large-scale capture of land and the displacement of people (Harvey 2003). Second, the production of enclaves has required crafting juridical exceptions to existing laws that are justified through discourses of necessity and 'public good'. Lastly, social movements across the country have strongly opposed the massive land grab. In response, the state has instituted a series of security measures that is indicative of the contemporary merging of neoliberalism with the security state (Duffield 2007).[4]

I begin with a brief narrative of the establishment of SEZs in India. Tracing the discourse of necessity, justified in terms of the urgent need for development, I argue that SEZs are an attempt to deal with accumulation surpluses. I then elaborate on the juridical maneuvers by which these zones are crafted into discrete enclaves. I conclude with an account of the vibrant opposition movements against SEZs that have emerged across the country.

BRIEF HISTORY OF SPECIAL ECONOMIC ZONES

In an earlier incarnation, SEZs were called export-processing zones (EPZ). These were popularized in the 1970s and 1980s as a way to catalyze export-oriented growth. According to the International Labor Organization ILO database, there were over 3,500 EPZ across 130 countries in 2003.[5] India's first EPZ was established in Kandla in 1965, followed by a second in Santacruz in 1973. The period between 1964 and 1985 constituted an 'initial phase' according to Aradhna Aggarwal (2004, 4), following which, between 1985 and 1991, on the recommendations of the Tondon committee appointed by the government, four to five more zones were established. Subsequently, some of the more restrictive laws on imports and tariffs were further relaxed to aid in EPZ-led export. However it was only after 2001 that the most rapid expansion of zones occurred. According to current data from the Ministry of Commerce and Industry, there are now 353 SEZs notified under the Act and 574 approved.

This dramatic expansion of the zones, from a handful, to over 500, is part of the trajectory of capital accumulation facilitated by the neoliberal reforms implemented in 1991. In order to understand the political economic conditions that generated the growth of SEZs we need to go back to 1989–1990, when a crisis in the balance of payments initiated the new economic policy (NEP). Guided by the World Bank and the International Monetary Fund (IMF), the NEP set out to implement structural changes in the Indian economy. These changes were based on broadly defined principles that have come to be understood as the 'Washington Consensus' and have become synonymous with neoliberal economic policies implemented in several countries around the world. John Williamson, who originally coined the term, elaborated a set of ten conditions directed at Latin America in 1989 to liberalize their economies including liberalizing trade, redirecting public expenditures, and lowering interest rates among others (Williamson 2000). India's liberalization policy has followed a similar path with cutbacks on state spending, privatization of public enterprises, and a focus on improving import and export capacities.

"The theology of liberalization," C. P. Chandrasekhar and Jayati Ghosh (2000) explain, "is based on the presumption that one of the features of globalization is the emergence of large volumes of footloose capital in search of appropriate locations for the world production market." By lowering tariffs and other restrictions and generating a flexible system, one of the central aims of the NEP is that some of the 'footloose capital' will use India as their production base. For India, in turn, this would generate foreign direct investment (FDI). Increased FDI, the economic policy hopes, will generate higher productivity and development. As Chandarsekhar and Ghosh (2002) further elaborate, "The explicit goals of the economic reform strategy with respect to the external sector, were to create a major shift in the momentum of export growth, and to attract very large inflows of foreign capital (particularly in the form of export-oriented FDI) to augment domestic savings and therefore allow much higher rates of domestic investment."

Since the 1990s successive governments have attempted to achieve the goal of $10 billion annual FDI. However, each government has fallen far short of the objective, with a peak in 1997–1998 of $3.6 billion and falling thereafter. Combined with low FDI, India's trade deficit also widened during the decade since economic reforms, reaching $5.5 billion by 2002. By comparison, China's exports, whose growth model India wishes to emulate, has risen from $2 billion in 1970 to $183.4 billion by 1998 compared to India's dismal $32.9 billion (Chadha 2000).

It is in this context of weak investment performance, that SEZs make an appearance as part of India's export import (Exim) policy. The policy aims to use SEZs as a way to significantly increase India's export earning capacity. On announcing the 2000 Exim policy Murasoli Maran, the minister for Commerce, explained: "Our trade policy reforms are aimed at creating an environment for achieving rapid increase in exports, raise India's share in world exports and make exports an engine for achieving higher economic growth."[6] Since the implementation of the NEP in 1991, increased Exim capacity has been a cornerstone of the reform process and a benchmark by which India measures its rise in the global market.

Thus, with the focus on exports, the 2000 Exim policy sought to implement two major changes. First, it planned to dismantle all remaining quantitative restrictions (QRs) on imports. QRs are limits set up on domestic products the government wishes to protect from international competition. The removal of these limits is of grave concern to those most vulnerable, such as poultry farmers or textile manufacturers, as international firms will dramatically undermine their products by flooding the market with lower priced commodities. Yet this is one of the conditions of neoliberalism set in place by the World Trade Organization's governing rules that argue for the creation of open and flexible market regimes. In fact, the aid from the World Bank and the IMF that averted the crisis in 1991 was predicated on opening India's market. The second major initiative relates directly to expanding exports with the introduction of special enclaves subject to duty-free imports and extensive tax concessions. The intention of these quasi-autonomous SEZs is to attract foreign direct investment to set up manufacturing and other enterprises for the international market.

As a consequence of these initiatives in the Exim policy, hundreds of SEZs began to emerge across the country, classified as commercial (processing) or residential (non-processing). Already over 15,000 hectares of land have been acquired for SEZs raising concerns about the transfer of productive agricultural land into the hands of developers and industry. In addition to the transfer of land, issues around compensation, resettlement, and rehabilitation of those displaced from their lands has drawn extensive criticism of the policy.

Despite the glaring social and economic costs SEZs will incur, the government's insistence on the strategy is based on emulating other Asian countries, especially China, to propel accelerated growth. As one Member of Parliament, during the debate on the SEZ Act argued: "China is a shining example of a country which has developed through its special economic zones. Various facilities given have attracted foreign direct investment and they have done a great extent in developing their economy" (quoted in Gopalakrishnan 2007b: 1492). Yet, as other commentators have pointed out, China's success with SEZs is at best partial, with Shenzhen as the only real success story. Shenzhen's success, of course, is measured only in terms of the profit it generated, ignoring the human cost of extensive suppression of labor rights, and super exploitation of young women. This is a model India would be ill advised to follow. Additionally, India's attempt to emulate China's SEZs ignores the political economic landscape that supported it. Chinese SEZs were driven by an influx of capital from Hong Kong and Macao, and by a political body just transitioning to market socialism.

As Hooshang Amirahmadi and Weiping Wu (1995, 836) point out, the success of such zones in Asia was due to them "take[ing] advantage of the industrial relocation of firms from developed countries in the late 1960s and 1970s . . . [where as now] they are competing for limited flows of foreign investment and the industrialized countries have tightened their markets." India, by contrast, cannot guarantee an influx of capital. It is entering into the SEZ model of development at a different time in the global economy (Gopalakrishnan 2007a, 34)[7]. India's first SEZ, Kandla, was completely dependent on the USSR for its export market under bilateral trade agreements (Aggarwal 2004, 16). Now it must compete on the global marketplace with other countries for its share of export earnings.

Additionally, Aggarwal (2004, 18) shows that "while the value of net foreign exchange in absolute terms increased phenomenally after the mid 1980s, the rate at which it grew remained stagnated and in fact started declining after 1998."

Yet, the zones are justified as necessary structures for optimizing growth and development in the country. Kamal Nath, union minister for commerce and industry, says: "the reason is simple: stable investment needs a stable regulatory regime" (quoted in Gopalakrishnan and Srivastava 2008, 20). The effort to achieve this stable regulatory regime is through the creation of a secluded zone within which a different set of tariff and taxes apply, in effect creating a jurisdiction within a jurisdiction.

CONCEPTUAL BACKGROUND: NECESSITY AND DISPOSSESSION

While the previous section traced how SEZs emerged as a consequence of prioritizing export-oriented growth, here I want to develop a different set of arguments. First, I suggest that SEZs emerge in an effort to avert a crisis of over-accumulation (Harvey 2003). Second, the large-scale displacement of people emulates what Harvey (2003) calls 'accumulation by dispossession.' Yet, for the state, dispossession is justified through a discourse of necessity and public good.

While increasing foreign direct investment offers one explanation for SEZs, I believe a different set of circumstances are revealed by following the trajectory of domestic capital, beginning with the NEP in 1991. Stuart Corbridge and John Harriss (2000, 146) explain: "The crisis of 1989–91 offered a window of opportunity for those amongst India's business and financial elites who wanted to renegotiate the state's relationship to private capital and the process of accumulation." As a consequence of the renegotiation of controls between the state and domestic capital, several policy changes were put in place, including lifting restrictions on key imports and creating flexibility within the system. Chandrashekar and Ghosh (2007) elaborate: "The increase in corporate profitability [was not] a sui generis phenomenon, arising simply out of the growth process itself. Rather, it is the outcome of government policies. It can be explained by the combination of the low interest rates and numerous tax concessions and implicit subsidies that have significantly increased profits over this period."

These shifts in the policies of the state, generated burgeoning growth and huge corporate surpluses and salaries. One of the indicators of the increase in profits is the growth of private corporate savings. Again, as Chandrasekhar and Ghosh (2007) explain: "This very large increase in private corporate savings—a doubling of the rate in around five years—reflects the dramatic increase in profitability over this same period . . . It reiterates the conclusion . . . that the private corporate sector has been the chief beneficiary of the economic boom." The high corporate surpluses,

12% to 16% by some estimates, had by the beginning of 2001 begun to create their own crisis of accumulation (Gopalakrishnan 2007c). By the beginning of the new millennium, the venues and opportunities generated by the NEP to absorb the surplus profits began to saturate. It is this accumulation of surplus, I argue, that sought other places for investment and returns and finds in SEZs a profitable venture.

David Harvey (2003, 149) explains: "overaccumulation . . . is a condition where surpluses of capital lie idle with no profitable outlets in sight". Drawn from his reading of Luxemburg and Marx, Harvey proposes a theory of spatio-temporal fix to capital's chronic tendency of overaccumulation. The two parts include, a geographic reorganization, whereby new markets and reorganizations of space provide profitable outlets for capital to be absorbed and accumulation to occur. And second a temporal dimension in which "surplus capital gets displaced into long-term projects that take many years to return their value to circulation through the productive activity they support" (Harvey 2003, 88). With SEZs both the spatial and temporal dimensions coalesce (for the larger framework of space-capital relations in India, see Banerjee-Guha 2009). Spatially, they offer sites at which surpluses can be invested in the appropriation of valuable land and for the creation of enterprises that in turn will generate profit. And temporally, the SEZ policy prioritizes investment in infrastructure, which will absorb the profits with a promise of future returns.

Prabhat Patnaik (2005), who also theorizes capital crisis, suggests similarly to Harvey that capital 'encroaches' on assets and raw materials to open them up to accumulation. In what he calls 'accumulation through encroachment,' private capital acquires raw materials at low or no cost. In the past this was done by seizing publicly held assets and privatizing them. Accumulation through encroachment occurs whereby public utilities such as water, energy, education, and health become privatized. Capital 'encroaches' onto productive agriculture and primary commodity producers to open them up to the province of private capital accumulation. For Harvey this process is termed 'accumulation by dispossession', where vast amounts of productive land are taken over, often by coercion, expelling the resident population to make them into a landless proletariat.

In an effort to facilitate this 'accumulation by dispossession' the overall state policy toward land acquisition for setting up SEZ has been exceptionally liberal, allowing companies to decide where to build the zones rather than authorizing the state to designate an area (Gopalakrishnan and Srivastava 2008, 20). Thus, prime locations—those closer to infrastructure, urban centers, and ports—are rapidly being acquired by private capital. These areas are often also densely populated and cultivated. Large-scale displacement of people from their land and means of livelihood, the state claims, is necessary for development and growth. Illicit land acquisition then becomes licit when justified as a necessity by the state. However, justification only in terms of necessity is not sufficient grounds for the appropriation of land at this scale. In order for the state to get juridical sanction it had to appeal to moral argument. Thus, need and necessity came to be codified in law through the appeal to a 'public benefit'. That is acquiring the land would be for the benefit of the 'public' fulfilling a 'public good'.

The mandate for 'public purpose' is a central condition of the Land Acquisition Act. But the term is extremely vague. Kannan Kasturi (2008) reveals that in the late 1950s the Law Commission demanded that 'public purpose' in the Act be clearly defined (33). Yet, the term was deliberately kept elastic and, by 1962, even included a clause that the setting up of private industry could now be justified as public purpose. The creation of jobs, boost to industry, and overall development were all encompassed in the term 'public benefit'. This is why over the years state acquisition of land for projects as diverse as student housing to a sugar factory were all justified within the broad mandate of public benefit.

Consequently, a convenient discursive slide was sanctioned, whereby private enterprise came to be defined as public benefit. For Patnaik (2005) the discourse of public purpose is part of the 'accumulation by encroachment strategy' whereby the resources such as mineral wealth, forests, and farmlands are wrested away from the public into the hands of private capital interests. Capital is able to grow or expand therefore by encroaching, through coercion or state sanction, onto public resources. It is this 'accumulation by encroachment' feature in late capital that marks for Patnaik a key strategy of the new phase of imperialism. Facilitated by the state, forcible encroachment is justified through juridical and politico-economic maneuvers to craft it as necessary.

Forcible eviction from land by the state is not a recent phenomenon in India. It is in fact codified in a law that dates back to the 1894 colonial Land Acquisition Act. "The British Colonial state in the 19th century [sought to] progressively claim as state property all land without identified private ownership" (Kasturi 2008, 32). This claim by the colonial state was based in the principle of 'eminent domain', by which any land could be acquired for 'public purpose'. This colonial law has been modified over the years, the latest being under Indira Gandhi's regime in 1984, but has for the most part remained unchanged in its original mandate. The Act states, "Whenever it appears to the [appropriate Government] that the land in any locality (is needed or) is likely to be needed for any public purpose (or for a company), a notification to that effect shall be published in the Official Gazette (and in two daily newspapers circulating in that locality of which at least one shall be in the regional language), and the Collector shall cause public notice of the substance of such notification to be given at convenient places in the said locality."[8]

The significant modification in the law appears in parentheses where land may be acquired "for a company". Facilitating the creation of companies is justified as an economic development mandate, in effect conflating resource allocation for public needs with those of private capital. Since independence, and guided by Nehru's modernizing vision, large tracks of land were needed for infrastructural development projects, such as dams, steel plants, mines, and power grids as well as for private companies. In the 60 years of state acquisition of land for public purpose, over 40 million people have been displaced. Yet despite the vast numbers of people displaced, and those now facing the threat of displacement, the Rehabilitation and Resettlement Bill is yet to be passed by Parliament (Sampat 2008).

Need and necessity, justified through a history of state acquisition for public purpose, form the discursive framework within which the SEZ Act is crafted. Since the creation of SEZs requires the acquisition of land from those who occupy and use it, several laws protecting the rights of peasants, farmers, and forest dwellers need to be navigated. Harvey (2003, 90–91) suggests that capital does not absolutely require infrastructure arrangements such as laws and the like to facilitate accumulation, "but without it faces greater risks." As a result, Harvey continues, "the preferred condition for capitalist activity is a bourgeois state in which market institutions and rules of contract are legally guaranteed, and where frameworks of regulation are constructed to contain class conflicts and to arbitrate between claims of different factions of capital." In India, these frameworks were explicit in the juridical sanction of SEZs to which I now turn.

ACCUMULATION BY JURIDICAL SANCTION

In this section I draw on work that examines the relationship between law, space, and accumulation to demonstrate how the state has twisted juridical statutes to justify dispossession. As spatially demarcated zones, examining SEZs offers an ideal opportunity to understand the spatial manifestations of accumulation in neoliberal India.

In the introduction to *A Civilian Occupation: The Politics of Israeli Architecture* Rafi Segal and Eyal Weizman (2003, 25) write: "Settlements are . . . nothing but the final gesture in the urbanization of enclaves. Perfecting the politics of separation, seclusion and visual control, they can be seen as the end condition of contemporary urban and architectural formations such as enclave suburban neighborhoods and gated communities". Segal and Weizman refer to the segregated landscape of Israeli occupation, but other landscapes, while not motivated by similar policies, can still be understood in terms of the political and economic grids they reveal. Organizing space through urban planning, architectural models, and surveys are profound political and economic gestures. Nicholas Blomley (2003, 127) observes that the organization of space through surveys demarcates land into parcels and units that " . . . helps make a world that exists, not as a set of social practices, but as a binary order: individuals and their practices set against an inert structure. Space is marked and divided into places where people are put. In the process space is desocialized and depoliticized". The policy frameworks that determine the terms of land acquisition and compensation measures hide behind instruments of state coercion that compel peasants and farmers to sell their land and the repercussions that dispossession at such a large scale entails.

SEZs are part of a broader pattern of segregated landscapes, such as gated residential complexes in urban centers, farm houses bought by the wealthy to get away from the urban congestion, health retreats catering to foreign tourists, industrial enclaves, and entertainment parks. Land is cordoned off, and the economic circuits generated circulate among the upper-middle and elite classes. SEZs represent the clearest articulation of this segregated landscape revealing the collusion between domestic capital, individual state governments, and the central governing bodies. Justified through a broad range of juridical maneuvers, SEZs will ultimately capture 200,000 hectares of land across the nation, transferring it for the most part from the hands of farmers and landless peasants to large corporations.

This large-scale transfer of resources is facilitated at different scales. As central government policy, SEZs are motivated by a neoliberal agenda to increase FDI by liberalizing export and import policies. Under India's federal system, state governments control resources such as land, water, and electrical power, and they are responsible for its allocation. In the context of flexible accumulation, much of the resource allocation is directed at private capital. States are motivated to invest in SEZs not only as important revenue and employment generation schemes but also to garner influence and political position within the federation. Individual states therefore have created their own SEZ Acts tailored to the needs of the state. Gujarat, for instance, projects that exports from its SEZs will account for 35% of the total export earnings in the country by the end of the decade (Raghu 2009). Such large contribution to the central government's mandate to improve India's exports solidifies Gujarat's influence and strength. Within individual states, urban and regional development authorities are eager to participate in the massive resource allocation as a way in which to garner influence with state and capital interests. For instance, in Mumbai, the City and Industrial Development Corporation (CIDCO)—the city authority responsible for development in New Bombay—offered Reliance, one of the largest corporate houses in India, 1,000 hectares of CIDCO land to build a SEZ.[9] CIDCO's intent was to cash in on the massive land deal that Reliance was attempting to broker with the farmers in Raigarh district to build India's biggest SEZ. While I will refer to other scales, here my concern is with how juridical justifications are drafted at the national scale to designate space for capital.

The 2005 Special Economic Zone Act, clearly articulates the cordoning off of space for capital: "A Special Economic Zone shall . . . be deemed to be a territory outside the customs territory of India for the purposes of undertaking the authorized operations" (Section 53). The reason behind designating SEZs as 'territory outside of India' is that it is not subject to customs and import duties. While 'outside' the state for customs and duties, they are, for the purposes of other jurisdictions, part of sovereign territory, where some rules apply, while others are suspended. Similarly, writing about Guantanámo Bay, Derek Gregory (2006, 414) elaborates the convoluted maneuverings whereby the United States could exercise complete jurisdiction within Guantanámo, while at the same time not consider it a part of U.S. territory. Guantanámo occupies an indeterminate location, "an ambiguous space—a grey zone over which the United States claims jurisdiction but not sovereignty . . .".

Efforts to distinguish SEZs as foreign territory require mechanisms to spatially demarcate them from the surrounding area. Here the Rules are instructive. Contemporary SEZs are governed by the 2005 Special Economic Zone Act as well as detailed set of Rules set up to enable the government to carry out the objectives of the Act. While legislation can only be modified by the Parliament, Rules can be changed through notifications by central or state governments. As a result, while Rules have authority, they are not subject to the same scrutiny and may often contradict other legal statutes.

An earlier iteration of the Rules explained, in extraordinary detail, the creation of a zone of security around the perimeter of a SEZ. "The processing area and Free Trade and Warehousing Zone shall be fully secured by boundary wall or wire mesh fencing having a height of at least two meters and forty centimeters above plinth level with top sixty centimeters being barbed wire fencing with mild steel angle with specified entry and exit points" (SEZ Rules 2006, Section 11(2)). While this Rule is now modified, the Act also makes clear that people allowed access to the area are to be strictly monitored and that: "Every person, whether employed or residing or required to be present in a Special Economic Zone, shall be provided an identity card by every development commissioner of such Special Economic Zone, in such form and containing such particulars as may be prescribed" (SEZ Act 2005, Section 46).

In the development commissioner are concentrated an extraordinary array of powers. He (and in most cases it is male) will "be the authority for demarcating the areas falling within the Special Economic Zone" (SEZ Rules 2006, Section 11). To him are accorded the delegation of authority of how the Industrial Disputes Act, and other Acts, are to function within the SEZ; the authority to decide on who is hired; and perhaps most egregiously the development commissioner may also be given the authority of the labor commissioner, whose mandate is to resolve industrial disputes between workers and management. The development commissioner's position involves working on behalf of the management of the SEZ, and as such will not be able to fairly arbitrate and represent workers grievances. To appoint him in the position to decide disputes is in essence to nullify the recourse workers may have to bring their grievances to management and expect a fair hearing.

Additionally, all search and seizure activity can only be done with the 'prior approval' of the development commissioner (SEZ Act 2005, Section 22). In effect, the ruling prohibits any other authority to enter the zone without the commissioner's approval, sealing it off from the outside. Akin again to the special courts set up for trail of the detainees at Guantanámo Bay, the Act states that "No court, other than the court designated under sub-section (1), shall try any suit or conduct the trial of any notified offence referred to in that sub-section" (SEZ Act 2005, Section 23(2)). Not only are juridical instruments molded to suit the creation, sanctions, and workings of SEZs, but an alternative court system is set up to adjudicate on cases that may emerge within the enclaves.

The Industrial Disputes Act (IDA) is one of the most prolifically altered laws to accommodate SEZs (Gonsalves and Mehrotra 2007, 14). In her detailed study, Aradhana Aggarwal (2004, 34) found that a majority of corporate houses claimed that the Industrial Disputes Act and Factories Act was most 'constraining for their business'. The corporations claim that the clauses written into the IDA set too many limits on their business ambitions. Consequently, the IDA has been modified, whereby industries within SEZs are now defined as 'public utility services'. The discursive slide where land acquired for private industry is justified as a public purpose and then industries classified as 'public utilities' is deliberate. Defining companies as public utilities severely curtails the rights of workers. For instance, employees have to give 14 day's notice to strike, state governments may ban strikes altogether, and a series of compensatory mechanisms for getting laid off are suspended (Gonsalves and Mehrotra 2007, 14). So the law is not suspended in SEZs, rather, parts of it are exempt from their application to SEZ because of its classification as a 'public utility'.

In addition to the laws such as those in the IDA that are attenuated, one of the most significant suspensions relates to taxation. Companies within SEZs will be exempt from customs and income and sales taxes. SEZs will get a 100% tax break for the first five years, a 50% break for the next five, and a five-year extension on the 50% break if they reinvest the profits back into the SEZ. According to the Finance Ministry the loss to exchequer will be Rs. 1,60,000 crore (approximately $33 billion) by 2010.The fiscal incentives along with the withdrawing of juridical protections are all in an effort to what Don Mitchell (1997, 305) describes as 'annihilation of space by law.' Mitchell is interested in tracking the manner in which cities are made attractive for capital investment by efforts to 'clean up' the city by enacting anti-homeless laws. In either case, laws enacted and withdrawn in cities or SEZs are sanction by the state for the purposes of accumulation.

Labor rights are also not spared so that several states with SEZs have suspended application of the 1970 Contract Labor Act. This Act protects those workers who work as contract labor to appeal to the contract labor board for permanency in their conditions of service. While states such as Utter Pradesh have given SEZs in their state complete exemption from being subject to the law, others limit the application of the law (Gonsalves and Mehrotra 2007, 15). Other laws that have either been suspended or limited in their application are the Minimum Wages Act, weekly hours in the Factories Act, and parts of the Trade Unions Act; all have been modified in violation of ILO conventions. For the peasants and farmers who will be out of work after their land has been confiscated, the laws that earlier accorded them some protections, will no longer apply within these enclaves.

While how the zone will be demarcated and secured, the taxation regulations and labor laws that would apply to it are all modified; they refer to zones that have already been acquired. But the state also has to sanction the conversion of public land for private enterprise. It is here that that peculiar perversions of law occur. Don Mitchell (2005, 582) in examining rights of citizens to be in a public space, observed that the Virginia Supreme Court "endorsed a world in which public property can be made 'private'".

A spectacular instantiation of the perverse twisting of legal statutes for accumulation is in the case of the Pohang Steel Co. (POSCO) in Orissa. Covering nearly 4,004 acres in the Jagatsinghpur district of Orissa, POSCO is India's largest foreign direct investment at nearly $12 billion. The South Korean Steel giant Pohang signed a memorandum of understanding (MoU) with the Orissa government for building a 12 million tonnes per annum integrated steel plant at Ersamma block of Jagatsinghpur. Pohang had initially signed an MoU with Brazil, which rejected the plant because the company proposed to extract ore at below market price. When the deal with Brazil fell through, the Orissa government accepted it in 2005. Navin Patnaik, the chief minister of Orissa, has signed 43 MoUs in the iron and steel sector capitalizing on the state's rich ore reserves[10].

The POSCO SEZ will affect 7 revenue villages and 11 hamlets 'officially' affecting 400 families. In reality, Manshi Asher and Kanchi Kohli (2007) conclude, the total population to be affected is closer to 22,000, because of displacement. The area is rich with thriving betel leaf and paddy cultivation. In addition, cashew nut and pisciculture also generate income for the residents in the area. For the past three years, farmers and peasants in the area have organized to protest the project in one of the most vibrant oppositions against SEZs in the country under the banner of POSCO Pratirodh Sangram Samiti. They claim that taking over their land deprives them of their means of livelihood. In response the state claims that the plant will generate 45,000 jobs and revenue. Orissa has one of the poorest state development indicators in the country. Therefore, the state argues, efforts to improve its development index 'necessitates' an influx of projects that will bring prosperity. In addition, the majority of the land, about 3,566 acres, the state claims are under the jurisdiction of the forest department. Consequently, three gram panchayats, whose lands fall under the area marked for the POSCO project, and the landless farmers who make their living from growing betel leaf and cashew nuts, have no claim on the land.

Yet, the state's denial of the forest dwellers rights to the land directly contradicts existing laws. K. Balagopal (2007, 3906–3907) argues that the farmers living off the land are "entitled to have their rights officially recognized under the Orissa Prevention of Land Encroachment Act, 1972 which permits regularization of occupation of revenue by landless poor up to one acre per family." In addition, the recently passed Scheduled Tribes and Other Traditional Forest Dwellers (Recognition of Forest Rights) Act, 2006 also entitles forest dwellers to cultivate, occupy, and use the protected areas within which they were residing prior to December 31, 2005. Thus, while the farmers are entitled to the land through a series of laws in place, Balagopal continues, "the government of Orissa will not tell them they have these rights. Instead, it treats the land in their occupation as its own unused and unusable property, which can be assigned to factories at will" (3907). The erasure of peasants and farmers entitlement to the land is facilitated by refusing to acknowledge them as subjects to whom the laws apply. And the state is able to deploy its extensive coercive apparatus to forcibly evict them from their land.

Writing specifically about the POSCO project, Manshi Asher (2008) comments that for those who live in Jagatsinghpur, are labeled "encroachers" and "illegal occupants" by the government. The irony is unmistakable; the residents of the area in fact do have rights under the Scheduled Tribes and Other Traditional Forest Dwellers (Recognition of Forest Rights) Act, 2006, yet those who are 'encroaching' (the POSCO project and the Orissa state) claim eminent domain over the land. Akin to the way in which the residents of Jagatsinghpur are erased or labeled illegal, Nicholas Blomley (2003) in examining the link between law, property, and violence, demonstrates that mechanisms such as surveys or the drawing of land grids are important ideological tools in Western private property regimes. For the colonial regime, these tools served to appropriate property. Blomley says, "If colonial possession was dependent upon dispossession, the survey served as a form of organized forgetting" (128). While Jagatsinghpur is not part of a colonial regime, it is nevertheless subject to a paternalistic and coercive state apparatus that can decree the residents as illegal encroachers, erasing their rights to the land. Commenting on colonial appropriation of native lands, Blomley observes that "native space—dense with meaning, stories, and tenurial relations—could thus be conceptually remapped as vacant land" (129). At work then is a kind of perversion that first expels people from land to which they have legal claim, then makes this land into exclusive zones, and finally claims that the people who live there are now illegal occupiers.

Despite the violence that the state unleashes, organized groups across the country have challenged the dispossession of their lands. Through a variety of mechanisms these groups have questioned the state's development policies, drawing attention to the manner in which the state has caste them as disposable and invisible to India's neoliberal mandate.

SPACES OF RESISTANCE

SEZs have been criticized for displacing farmers and peasants from their lands and usurping their means of survival. State collusion with domestic capital in facilitating this land grab has further drawn the ire of citizen groups across the country. This systematic taking over of land, according to David Harvey (2003, 145), is indicative of primitive accumulation which involves "the commodification and privatization of land and the forceful expulsion of peasant populations; the conversion of various forms of property rights (common, collective, state, etc) into exclusive private rights . . .". While emblematically represented by SEZs, forceful eviction from land has occurred throughout Independent India in the name of development and progress. Yet, despite the over 80 million people who have being evicted in the name of development (75% of whom still await resettlement), the current Resettlement and Rehabilitation Bill, according to civil society groups, is a deeply flawed policy initiative that leaves few, if any, measures of redressal for those affected (Asher and Mumtaz 2007).

The lack of serious measures by the state to address the needs of those displaced, as well as the apparent collusion between domestic capital and the state, has spurred vibrant and vocal protests across the country. Generating tremendous media attention, places such as Nandigram, Singur, POSCO, and MMSEZ have become synonymous with the struggle of the disenfranchised against corporate might. Kamal Nath, union minister for commerce and industry, dismisses these agitations as efforts of an uninformed few who reject industrialization and progress for the country, repeating that SEZs will generate 30 lakh jobs (Citizen's Research Collective 2008, 5). However, those jobs, according to the Citizen's Research Collective (2008, 15), have not been created since the implementation of reforms in 1991. Besides many protesting groups claim that even the promise of jobs is false, as companies in SEZs are not legally bound to hire those they make landless within the zones. The lands on which the zones are built are wrested away from the poor to be given over to industry, with the argument that the overall benefits will ultimately trickle down to them. After decades of development policies, these arguments have begun to ring distinctly hollow.

Some of the early efforts to challenge state development policies found redress in the court system. Smita Narula (2008, 13) documents the political shift in the Indian Supreme Court from 1970 that gave hope to the 'disempowered and dispossessed'. The juridical process was used to redress the injustices of development, with many groups seeking intervention from the courts.[11] Then, in the mid-1990s, the Court's attitude toward social justice organizations shifted dramatically reflecting a distinct bias toward privatization and liberalization.[12] These shifts in juridical and state abdication of even basic responsibility toward its most disenfranchised citizens foretold in some ways the structural changes that were to facilitate the creation of SEZs. The shrinking of places from which to get redress for injustices, therefore, gave birth to people's movements across the country. Many of the groups involved in protesting SEZs found their genesis from within movements that have challenged state priorities and violence for decades. Thus, with the state and private capital's efforts in the early 2000s to acquire farmer and peasant land for SEZs, the scope of these movements expanded to include this latest maneuver.

Savahara Jan Andolan, a grassroots organization of farmers and peasants in Raigad district of Maharashtra, has been organizing against political economic policies of the state for over a decade. When Reliance acquired the Maha Mumbai SEZ, Savahara Jan Andolan mobilized a series of protests against it. In 2007 several farmers went on an indefinite hunger strike, and hundreds of others gathered for a massive 'rasta roko' (road blockade). As the largest proposed project, the MMSEZ will affect between 400,000 and 5000,000 people living in 45 villages across the area that rely on the land for agriculture and its costal proximity for fishing. The local revenue department in its report on the land available for industrial development wrote that the land was 'unproductive' (Asher 2007). In fact just the opposite is true, Raigad is a rice-cultivating area. As Anosh Malekar (2008a) reports, "Between 1960–61 and 2001–02, rice constituted 90.51% and 95.07% respectively of the food crop grown. Per hectare yield of rice in 1960–61 was 1,487 kg, which rose to 2,669 kg in 2001–02." The state department claims that the land is unproductive because of saline water contamination. Yet, a vast expanse of paddy fields contradicts this assessment.

The people of Raigad have had a long history of confronting the state. Since the late 1980s they have been agitating about access to irrigation water from the Hetawane Dam. By the time the villages won the fight to get irrigation water from the dam, 22 villages that could benefit from the water supply were earmarked for acquisition for the MMSEZ (Malekar 2008b). Consequently the struggle to get access to water from the dam, the forcible land acquisition from the SEZ, and the loss of livelihood, all emerged as part of the protests by a coalition of peasant and farmers groups against MMSEZ. After a three-year battle against state and corporate interests, and as a result of collective mobilizing by the groups, the state decided to conduct a landmark referendum in the area on the SEZ. On September 21, 2008, in Pen Tehsil 22 villages participated in the referendum. By the end of the day, the verdict was in. It clearly stated that the villagers did not want the Reliance SEZ in the area. "'We don't want Reliance here. Instead the government should take responsibility for irrigating our agriculture land and help us set up income generation activities like poultry and fish farming,' says Sadashiv Mhatre and his young son Ganesh" (Malekar 2008b).

Not all such struggles around SEZ culminate in success against powerful corporate and state interests. Efforts to secure the enclaves against farmers who refuse to give up their lands have in many cases been met with violence. For instance, since 2005 when the project was announced, the POSCO Prairodh Sangharsh Samiti (PPSS) has been in direct confrontation with the state. On April 15, 2007, 20,000 people boycotted the Environmental Clearance public hearing partly in response to the state's deployment of several platoons of the Orissa Military Police. Later that year, on November 29, a peaceful demonstration of POSCO protesters was violently attacked by the police. Despite the attack, the protesters remained determined, and the state eventually imposed Section 144 of the Code of Criminal Procedure in the area, placing a ban on public activity. The ban was specifically imposed on April 1, 2008, in Balitutha—the site of the November police attack. Disregarding the ban, hundreds of people from different groups came to hear Abhay Sahu, president of the Prairodh Sangharsh Samiti. Sahu said the agitation against POSCO is in an effort to "protect our motherland from the onslaught of multinationals and uphold the movement's pledge to control our homeland and its resources" (quoted in Abeson 2008). Hailed as an inspiring leader, Sahu has, for the past three years, dedicated himself to contesting the POSCO project much to the distress of the state. In a blatant display of coercive force the police arrested Sahu on October 12, 2008. His bail plea was rejected on November 4, 2008.

The public ban on gatherings, the arrest of Sahu, and the multiple other coercive tactics used against the people organizing against SEZs are instances of Giorgio Agamben's (1998) exploration of a relationship between law and life. He says, "The relation of exception is a relation of ban. He who has been banned is not, in fact, simply set outside the law and made indifferent to it but rather *abandoned* by it, that is, exposed and threatened on the threshold in which life and law, outside and inside, become indistinguishable" (28). Recall that those residing in the forests around the POSCO project are in fact entitled to reside there according to the Scheduled Tribes and Other Traditional Forest Dwellers (Recognition of Forest Rights) Act, 2006. However, the Orissa state's efforts to supersede the Act are under its claim of dominion over the land. The attack on protestors and the attenuation of civic protections applicable to them are exemplary of the creation of exception.

State repression of the protestors has, in multiple instances, led to killings by the police and the Rapid Action Force in places such as Nandigram, Singur, and Kalinganagar. In each instance, peasant groups mobilizing against forcible eviction have stood against the state and have been beaten up and had their homes ransacked and their paddy fields burned. Examining the relations between resistance, sacrifice, and terror, Achille Mbembe (2003: 39) is concerned with the "subjugation of life to the power of death." In what he calls 'necropolitics' Mbembe suggests that contemporary political life in response to the 'war on terror,' has resulted in a social existence governed by death. He suggests that the governance of death requires cordoning off land into zones. Speaking specifically of the war on colonies, Mbembe (2003, 24) writes, "The colonies are the location par excellence where the controls and guarantees of judicial order can be suspended—the zone where the violence of the state of exception is deemed to operate in the service of 'civilization'". For those disenfranchised from colonial occupation and violent development policies of the post-colonial state, the argument of civilizational progress through enclave economics holds little merit.

CONCLUSION

This essay examined India's recent neoliberal turn by looking specifically at Special Economic Zones. Understanding SEZs as an outcome of capitals' efforts to forestall a crisis of overaccumulation offers a way of examining the geography of enclave economics. Drawing on examples from the 2005 SEZ Act and the 2006 Rules, I demonstrated the ways in which the state through a series of juridical maneuvers secures private capital accumulation. Despite facing tremendous violence from the state and elaborate security measures, SEZs have been vociferously opposed. People's movements, civil society organizations, and citizen's collectives have expressed solidarity with the movements, documenting violent repression as well as challenging the state for its collusion with capital. In response, the state has unleashed a repressive regime that manifests itself in the production of exceptions. Through, structural measures such as fencing off areas, deploying paramilitary forces, and conducting elaborate juridical maneuvers, as well as discursive measures such as constructing those opposing the SEZs as anti-development and unpatriotic and, more broadly, denying them protections and rights as citizens, space is fragmented into enclaves. Urban and rural India emerge through this disjointed geography as selected enclaves of wealth, infrastructure, and privilege cordoned off against a hostile, poor, and impoverished outside.

SEZs, however, are not the only kinds of enclaves under construction in contemporary India. Neoliberalism is spatially manifested in the fragmentation of space at multiple scales, from the body to international borders. In addition to SEZs, smaller enclaves for housing, recreation, and health are mushrooming all over the country. For instance, one of the largest real estate companies in India, the Ambuja Group has entered into a join venture with Elbit Medical Imaging to create a 24-acre private health facility with 1,000 beds outside Calcutta. The venture called Neotia Elbit Health Citi is to be completed by 2010. The private health city will be accessible only to those who can pay its no-doubt astronomical fees. It will become a medical destination for foreigners unable to pay for medical treatment due to rising healthcare costs in their own countries.

If the Neotia Health Citi is at the smaller end of the scale of spatial enclaves, then at the other are international borders and efforts to secure them. Interestingly, Elbit Medical Imaging, which is building the Neotia

Health Citi, is a subsidiary of Elbit, an Israeli transnational company that is commissioned to build the security fence between India and Pakistan in Kashmir. Elbit has experience in securing borders, having been commissioned to build the security wall between Israel and Palestine, as well as working on the border between the U.S. and Mexico. These transnational collaborations are reported devoid of their geopolitical implications.[13] With the increasing violence by the state against people who challenge state policies, measures such as security borders and walls are increasingly part of the fragmented landscape. My effort here in looking at SEZs is to track this labyrinth of spatial enclaves and reveal the political and economic geographies they generate.

ACKNOWLEDGMENTS

I'd like to thank the editors of the collection for comments on prior drafts. I'd also like to thank the anonymous reviewer for extremely helpful suggestions for revision. I am grateful to Beverley Mullings and Vijay Prashad for reading and commenting on earlier versions.

NOTES

1. In Nandigram, the project had added import as the chemical plant being courted by the state was Dow Chemicals infamous for buying Union Carbide, which was responsible for killing more than 5,000 people in 1984 because of a gas leak leading to the worst industrial catastrophe due to negligence.
2. I want to thank Vijay Prashad for reminding me that Nandigram was also about the state's dispute with Maoists, the alienation of peasants from the local party cadre as well as a host of other issues that coalesced around the acquisition of the land for the chemical hub.
3. For a full list of approved and notified industries see http://www.sezindia.nic.in/
4. My larger project tracks the ways in which development imperatives by states are informed by draconian security discourses, particularly legitimized in a post September 11th world. Here I specifically examine SEZs, but there is a broader spatial pattern of disenfranchisement in contemporary India that emerges in the collaboration between development and security.
5. ILO Database on Export Processing Zones. http://www.ilo.org/public/english/dialoge/sector/themes/epz.htm.
6. http://www.rediff.com/business/2000/mar/31eximsp.htm.
7. Countries in Latin America and the Caribbean that created these zones in the 1970s were able to attract FDI through incentives of a large domestic market or by serving as gateways to other markets. I thank Beverley Mullings for alerting me to this point.
8. The Land Acquisition Act, 1984, Government of India Part II 4(1). Emphasis added.
9. The project for which CIDCO offered up its land to Reliance for the SEZ was initially owned by Sea King Infrastructure Limited (SKIL), a company involved in railways, ports, and urban infrastructure. SKIL soon after

acquiring the land sold it to Reliance. The project will be India's largest SEZ acquiring 14,000 hectares of productive agricultural land. The transfer of land from farmers into the hands of one of the largest business houses in India has drawn vibrant and successful protests that I detail in the next section. The project called Maha Mumbai SEZ (MMSEZ) proposed to create high-end residential colonies, financial and business services, and non-polluting industrial units (Sharma 2008). In his detailed study as a member of the team responsible of conducting a Social Impact Assessment of the area, R. N. Sharma, a faculty member of the Tata Institute of Social Sciences, found that several former employees of CIDCO, upon leaving their jobs at CIDCO, were hired for the MMSEZ for significant salary incentives (9).

10. I have drawn on Manshi Asher's exceptionally detailed work on the POSCO project.
11. Narula (2008, 13) documents that the Supreme Court "invoked Article 32 of the Indian Constitution and took radical steps to 'make basic human rights meaningful to the disadvantaged sections of the community and to assure them distributive justice'". One of the groups that sought court intervention in a famous case was the Narmada Bachao Andolan.
12. The shift of the courts was exemplified by its judgment against the Narmada Bachao Andolan (Narula 2008, 16).
13. Elsewhere I have written on the geopolitical alliance between India, Israel, and the U.S. on the figure of the Muslim male as terrorist; see Oza (2007).

REFERENCES

Abeson, Elisabeth. 2008. Profiteers vs the People. *Combat Law* 7(3): 10.

Agamben, Giorgio. 1998. *Homo Sacer*. Trans. Daniel Heller-Roazen. Stanford, CA: Stanford University Press.

Aggarwal, Aradhna. 2004. Export Processing Zones in India: Analysis of the Export Performance. Indian Council for Research on International Economic Relations. Working Paper no. 148.

Amirahmadi, Hooshang, and Weiping Wu. 1995. Export processing zones in Asia. *Asian Survey* 35(9): 828–849.

Asher, Manshi. 2007. Struggle against Reliance SEZ intensifies. *Infochange* (April). http://www.infochangeindia.org/IPRItop.jsp?section_idv=23.

———. 2008. Yesterday's 'encroachers' are today's rights-holders. *Infochange.org*. http://infochangeindia.org/200804127051/Agenda/Battles-Over-Land/Yesterday's-'encroachers'-are-today's-rights-holders.html (accessed October 30, 2008).

Asher, Manshi, and Kanchi Kohli. 2007. Uneasy quiet on the POSCO front. *India Together* (October). www.indiatogether.org/2007/oct/eco-posco.htm (accessed October 23, 2008).

Asher, Manshi, and Rifat Mumtaz. 2007. Displacement in the time of development. *Infochange* (October). http://infochangeindia.org/analysis143.jsp (accessed October 30, 2008).

Balagopal, K. 2007. Land unrest in Andhra Pradesh—II: Impact of grants to industries. *Economic and Political Weekly* XL 11(39): 3906–3911.

Banerjee-Guha, Swapna. 2009. Contradictions of enclave development in contemporary times: Special Economic Zones in India. *Human Geography*. 2(1): 1–16.

Bandyopadhyay, D. 2007. Buddha's killing fields of Nandigram. *Mainstream* XLV(50). http://www.mainstreamweekly.net/article464.html (accessed November 10, 2008).

Chadha, R. 2000. Exim policy changes. *Economic and Political Weekly* 35(16): 1343–1346.

Chandrasekhar, C. P. 2007. Unraveling India's growth transition. *Macroscan* (November 2). Available at http://www.macroscan.org/cur/nov07/cur021107Transition.htm (accessed October 23, 2008).

Chandrasekhar, C. P., and Jayati Ghosh. 2000. FDI and the balance of payments during the 1990s. *Macroscan*. http://www.macroscan.org/the/trade/jun00/print/prnt270600FDI_1990s.htm (accessed June 18, 2009).

———. 2007. Who is doing the saving and investing? *Marcoscan* (May 11). http://www.macroscan.org/fet/may07/fet110507Saving_Investing.htm (accessed October 23, 2008).

Citizen's Research Collective. 2008. Factfile SEZs: Frequently asked questions. *Seminar* 582: 15.

Corbridge, Stuart, and John Harriss. 2000. *Reinventing India: Liberalization, Hindu nationalism, and Popular democracy*. New Delhi: Oxford University Press.

Duffield, Mark. 2007. *Development, security and unending war: governing the world of peoples*. Cambridge University Press.

Gonsalves, Colin, and Pragya Freya Mehrotra. 2007. SEZs spell doom for workers. *Combat Law* 6(2): 14–16.

Gopalakrishnan, Shankar, and Aseem Srivastava. 2008. SEZs have nothing to do with land acquisition. Interview with union minister for commerce and industry. *Seminar* 582: 20–22.

Gopalakrishnan, Shankar. 2007a. In the name of growth: The politics and economic of India's Special Economic Zones. A Study for the Council for Social Development.

———. 2007b. Negative aspects of Special Economic Zones in China. *Economic and Political Weekly* (April 28): 1492–1494.

Gregory, Derek. 2006. The black flag: Guantanamo Bay and the space of exception. *Geogr. Ann.* 88B(4): 405–427.

Harvey, D. 2003. *The new imperialism*. Oxford: Oxford University Press.

Kasturi, Kannan. 2008. Of public purpose and private profit. *Seminar* 582: 32–35.

Malekar, Anosh. 2008a. We do not want to become landless beggars. *Commodity Online* (October 23). http://www.commodityonline.com/news/"We-do-not-want-to-become-landless-beggars"-12335–3-1.html.

———. 2008b. A dam swallowed by SEZ. *Commodity Online* (October 24). http://www.commodityonline.com/news/A-dam-swallowed-by-SEZ-12337–2-1.html.

Mbembe, Achille. 2003. 'Necropolitics.' *Public Culture* 15(1): 11–40.

Mitchell, Don. 1997. The annihilation of space by law: The roots and implications of anti-homeless laws in the United States. *Antipode* 29(3): 303–335.

———. 2005. Property rights, the first amendment, and judicial anti-urbanism: The strange case of *Virginia V. Hicks*.' *Urban Geography* 26(7): 565–586.

Narula, Smita. 2008. Displacement and disruption of livelihoods: Transparency, accountability and civil society in the governance of development projects. NYU Centre for Policy Research Workshop on Global Governance. Working Paper.

Oza, Rupal. 2007. Contrapuntal geographies of threat and security: US, India, and Israel. *Environment and Planning: Society and Space* 25(1): 9–32.

Patnaik, P. 2005. The economic of a new phase of imperialism. *Macroscan* (August 26). http://www.macroscan.org/anl/aug05/pdf/Economics_New_Phase.pdf (accessed November 12, 2008)

Raghu, Sunil. 2009. Gujarat set for big gains as SEZs gather steam. http://www.livemint.com/2008/03/21000424/Gujarat-set-for-big-gains-as-S.html (accessed July 9, 2009).

Sampat, Preeti. 2008. Special Economic Zones in India. *Economic and Political Weekly* 43(28): 25–30.

Segal, Rafi, and Eyal Weizman. 2003. *A civilian occupation: The politics of Israeli architecture*. London and New York: Verso.

Sharma, R. N. 2008. Special Economic Zones (SEZs): Towards Business in Real Estate? Unpublished manuscript.

Williamson, J. 2000. What should the World Bank think of the Washington consensus? *The World Bank Research Observer* 15(2): 251–264.

12 Thinking Militant Particularisms Politically

Resistances to Neoliberalism in India

David Featherstone

INTRODUCTION

In the conclusion to *The Making of Neo-liberal India*, Rupal Oza asks: "When the nation is defended against the global, what form of local resistance is generated? [. . .] Which dominant narratives are solidified in the uncritical coupling of the local as national? Which publics are evoked in the defence of the local?" (Oza 2006, 140). By foregrounding such questions, Oza makes an important theoretical intervention in accounts of the political identities generated through local and national resistances to globalization. She argues, by examining a range of sites, that "middle class and Hindu constructions of the nation dominate the discourse" on globalization (Oza 2006,140). Oza tells stories about the political geographies through which exclusionary forms of the local and national are rendered in opposition to forms of the global. She develops a strong sense of the spatial practices through which such domination works. This opens up a politically prescient set of questions about struggles over how local resistances are envisioned.

This chapter also interrogates the politics of local resistances to neoliberalism in India. However, whereas Oza's work focuses predominantly on the relations between middle-class politics and globalization, this chapter engages with the formation of subaltern political identities. It explores diverse place-based struggles that have emerged in relation to neoliberalization in India which, following Raymond Williams, I term 'militant particularisms' (R. Williams 1989). Drawing on Partha Chatterjee's (2004) work, the chapter emphasizes the importance of understanding militant particularisms politically. It then explores some ways in which militant particularisms have contested neoliberalization and the practices through which militant particularist struggles have been articulated and networked. The engagement with such struggles here is necessarily partial and limited. I seek to outline some significant aspects of the political geographies of resistance, and emphasize what is at stake for left political strategies.

THINKING MILITANT PARTICULARISMS POLITICALLY

Neoliberalization in India has been contested through diverse militant place-based protests. These range from struggles against Coca-Cola in Plachimada in Kerala to struggles against the Tata group in West Bengal and Orissa. These struggles have important histories and geographies. There have been longstanding protests against the neoliberalization of agriculture stretching back to protests against the Dunkel Draft of the General Agreement on Tariffs and Trade (GATT) in 1993. These protests raise important questions about how to theorize the formation of place-based politics, and the forms of political identities, solidarities, and interventions they generate. Raymond Williams's account of militant place-based struggles as forms of 'militant particularism' provides useful ideas in this regard.

R. Williams (1989) used a focus on militant particularist struggles as a way of incorporating place directly into socialist theorizing. These ideas were powerfully developed by David Harvey in his classic essay, "Militant Particularism and Global Ambition" (1996). Williams insisted that there was a "decisive difference between militant particularism and militant socialism". He argued that militant socialism 'necessarily' depended on uniting different local struggles through "a broad strategic aim to transform society" (R. Williams 1979, 380). He celebrated this move as the "unique and extraordinary character of working class self-organisation" through which militant particularist struggles and identities were connected "to a general struggle" (R. Williams 1989, 115). This work foregrounds a set of key political questions about the practices through which militant place-based struggles constitute broader political alliances and movements.

There are important resonances between Williams's arguments and Partha Chatterjee's (2004) interventions on the politics of governmentality in India. Chatterjee addresses the role of subaltern groups in cities such as Calcutta in the formation and construction of place, often in extremely marginal conditions. His essay, "The Politics of the Governed", begins with a discussion of squatters living for more than 50 years alongside railway tracks in Calcutta. Chatterjee addresses the relations through which marginal communities are produced and reproduced and in turn produce the space of their community. Communities such as these negotiate with 'political society' to find some degree of permanence and access to particular goods and services, frequently through the brokerage of particular key individuals.

For Chatterjee 'most' of the inhabitants of India "are tenuously, and even then ambiguously and contextually, rights-bearing citizens in the sense inspired by the constitution". They are not "therefore proper members of civil society and are not regarded as such by the institutions of the state" (Chatterjee 2004, 38; see also Corbridge et al. 2005, 189). Chatterjee explicitly rejects the notion of a fundamental split between elite and subaltern domains that structured the early work of the subaltern studies collective (see esp. Guha 1982). As an alternative, he suggests using the term 'political society' to engage with "the relatively recent forms of the entanglement of elite and subaltern politics" (Chatterjee 2004, 39–40). This asserts the significant presence of subaltern groups in Indian society who have frequently been excluded from the dominant accounts and practices of 'the political'.

Chatterjee's account of place strongly echoes Williams's concerns with the agency of subaltern groups in the formation of communities. It also adds something else inadequately developed in Williams's writings on militant particularism, and Harvey's powerful re-working of them: an explicit concern with the political. Through engaging with the way that marginal groups make their presence felt through 'political society', Chatterjee's work focuses on the relations between the construction of militant particularism and the political. This allows space for thinking militant particularisms politically.

This is significant. Too often, accounts of militant particularism have theorized the political identities constituted through such struggles merely as defensive responses to the actions of dominant groups. David Harvey, for example, argues that dispersed struggles can either remain within 'the confines of their own particularist militancies—fighting an incinerator here, a toxic waste dump there, a World Bank dam project somewhere else, and commercial logging in yet another place or they can treat the contradictions as a fecund nexus to create a more transcendent and universal politics' (Harvey, 1996: 400). In Harvey's account militant particularisms become political only when struggles move beyond their 'particular place based confines' to be articulated as part of broader left political strategies. This obscures the ways in which the very formation of militant particularist action is constitutive of different and contested political identities. These are not 'pre-political' struggles that become political only through being part of 'broader' left imaginaries. Rather, the terms on which militant particularisms are negotiated and produced are, from the outset, political. This formulation permits a focus on the contested and plural characters of militant particularisms, rather than their functioning as components of unitary struggles. Engaging with the terms on which militant particularisms are constructed, as well as the ways in which they are negotiated and networked, is crucial to the formation of left political imaginaries.

This concern with thinking militant particularism politically has the following implications for understanding oppositions to neoliberalization. First, following Chatterjee's arguments, understanding how subaltern political activity engages with spatially stretched power relations is necessary for understanding the political construction of militant particularisms. Militant particularist activity is generated via interventions in cross-cutting relations of power, and through contesting unequal geographies of power. The way neoliberalization works in relation to geographies of unequal caste, gender, and class relations has had effects on the formation of militant particularist struggles. This has shaped the identities produced through resistances to neoliberalization in significant ways.

Second, interrogating the formation of militant particularisms involves unsettling the rather bounded constructions of place that inform the work of both Williams and Chatterjee. Militant particularisms are not necessarily bounded, but can be constituted through ongoing connections between different struggles and routes of subaltern political activity (Featherstone 2005; 2008). Such struggles are not necessarily formed in particular places and then networked, but can have more relational geographies. Subaltern politics in India has been formed in relation to significant histories and geographies of connection. The links between the dalit leader B. R. Ambedkar and the American civil rights leader and intellectual W. E. B. Du Bois or the histories of subaltern groups such as lascars and indentured laborers, defined by forms of mobility which were often forced, are important examples in this regard (Kapoor 2003; Sakar 2007). Contemporary militant particularist struggles in India have also formed in relation to various geographies of connection: between rural and urban movements; and through transnational support networks generated by major struggles, such as those over the Narmada dam (Routledge, 2003; 2008, 343–346). Engaging with these connections can foreground forms of subaltern political identities and agency which would be marginalized by adopting bounded accounts of militant particularism.

Thirdly, foregrounding the relations formed through militant particularist struggles allows a focus on the practices through which they are articulated. Eschewing a pure, autonomous space of subaltern politics permits a focus on the alliances, connections, and relations which constitute militant particularisms, and shape forms of political identities. The Bharatiya Janta Party (BJP), for example, has proven adept at co-opting aspects of popular struggles, such as those against Enron (Ahmed 2007a). Resistances to liberalization in the countryside have connected landless laborers and richer 'middle' peasants, often on unequal terms (see Assadi 1997; Bhalla 1999). This signals the importance of examining the different outcomes of such forms of political activity. These activities can produce exclusionary spaces of politics through the ways they negotiate relations, as well as more open and plural forms of identity.

Fourthly, and related to the previous point, is the significance of engaging with the political practices through which constructions of place are mobilized through militant particularist struggles. Some forms of militant particularist political action have mobilized deeply exclusionary forms of politics of place. Farmers' movements, such as the KRRS and BKU, have often mobilized around particular constructions of 'the village'. They have presented their political demands as being in the interests of the village as a whole. Yet their mobilization has tended to marginalize the grievances of landless laborers and people from lower castes, even at times being actively hostile toward them (see Assadi 1995b; Brass 1995; D. Gupta 1997; Lerche 1999). Similar constructions of the village have also been mobilized by activist intellectuals such as Vandana Shiva (see Shiva et al. 1997; Mawdsley 2006). The constructions of place generated through militant particularist struggles can be exclusionary and open to contestation.

Fifthly, militant particularist struggles opposing neoliberalization in India have been subject to political violence by dominant groups and the state. Diverse struggles like those against the Tata group or Special Economic Zones, or strikes in Honda factories in Delhi, have been subject to violent repression. Communist Party of India (Marxist) (CPI(M)) sanctioned violence in Nandigram, where its cadres targeted women through rape and other forms of sexual violence, which emphasizes the significance of gendered violence. Such violence is not outside the terrain of the political, but relate to histories of intimidation by CPI(M) cadres. SinghaRoy's work in West-Bengal, for example, illustrates how peasant identities are formed in relation to state-building processes through which the gap between 'civil society' institutions and party cadres are minimized, and where there is frequent resort to violence (SinghaRoy 2004, 142–145; see also G. O. Williams 2001).

These relations between violence and neoliberalization are significant. Cases like these bring in to question Chatterjee's characterization of a 'political society' largely unmarked by violence. As Ghosh (2006, 525–256) argues, Chatterjee lays "out a terrain of governmentality that seems to always operate through recognition, negotiation and dialogue, mutually agreed on settlements and inclusion." Ghosh contends that "if we look at development from the perspective of subaltern populations, including adivasis, in India, it is much more deeply marked by coercion and violence than the negotiated platform that Chatterjee sketches". Ghosh's arguments emphasize the significance of violence in constituting the political in diverse ways. This presents an important set of challenges to thinking about the militant particularist struggles formed in relation to neoliberalization in India.

This section has argued for the significance of thinking militant particularisms politically. I argued for the importance of engaging with the ways in which militant particularist struggles bring unequal geographies of power into contestation. The spatial practices and imaginaries produced through these practices shape the political identities generated through opposition to neoliberalization. The next section foregrounds such questions through engaging with the 'maps of grievance' formed through opposition to neoliberalization. I use the term 'maps of grievance' to refer to the practices through which power relations become known, generated, and contested through political activity (see Featherstone 2003).

SHIFTING MAPS OF GRIEVANCE

In Bangalore, on October 2, 1993, the Karnataka State Farmer's Union (KRRS) organized a mass mobilization, known as the 'seed satyagraha', attended by a hundred thousand farmers. Speakers argued that the proposals of the Dunkel Draft round of the GATT to allow private companies to patent seeds "would have devastating effects on their livelihoods in general and on their control of seeds in particular" (Rane 1993, 2391). A declaration, read, stated:

> We do not recognise intellectual property rights on biological materials being granted to companies for their private profits. The knowledge on which crops to plant and on which seeds to use was evolved by generations of farmers and not by the corporations. Therefore we do not accept that they have a right to profit from our knowledge and our experience. Instead, we adhere to the concept of common property rights, where the right to seeds cannot be owned by private companies. Seeds should be allowed to be exchanged freely among farmers in the country and the world, as has been the practice till now. (cited by Rane 1993, 2391).

The declaration emphasizes how farmers' politics contested the generating of seeds in relation to neoliberal conventions and practices. Such politics constructed different ways of generating seeds in antagonistic ways. Neoliberalism is constituted through generating 'heterogeneous associations' of humans and non-humans through neoliberal conventions and practices (Braun 2005, 839). The terms and relations through which seeds have been configured through processes of neoliberalization have been the sites of significant contestation.

Opposition to the Dunkel Draft, produced through events such as the seed satyagraha, were part of an explicit attempt by the KRRS to contest the neoliberalization of Indian agriculture, and to relate this to a broader contestation of neoliberal globalization. Such political activity was an intervention in the political identities and imaginations of power of the Indian New Farmers' Movements. These movements came to prominence in the 1970s and 1980s. The KRRS, for example, was founded in 1980. They emerged through attempts to redraw the lines of political antagonism in rural India by mobilizing a distinction between the countryside and a corrupt and exploitative urban India (Brass 1995; Bentall and Corbridge, 1996). They have constructed this antagonism through denoting the countryside as 'Bharat', or India, and in doing so have produced an exclusionary elision between the nation and the countryside. These movements have drawn on the practices and idioms of Gandhian mass action, and on constructions of an authentic Gandhian Indian countryside where the village is the appropriate unit of political organization. As Omvedt argues, '[r]ather than organising wage-earners against property owning employers they have organised entire village communities against the state' (Omvedt, 1995: 126). Nanjundaswamy referred to the movement as a 'village movement' and as 'a movement for independence' (cited by Krishnarajulu 1986, 31).

Targeting key neoliberal political projects, particularly the Dunkel Draft of the Uruguay round of GATT, represented a significant shift in the 'maps of grievance' of farmers' movements from antagonisms based around countryside versus city, to antagonisms around the unequal and unjust effects of liberalization. This also contested neoliberal globalization and institutions that stretched beyond India, such as the World Trade Organization (WTO) or the Monsanto Corporation. The KRRS-led opposition to the Dunkel Draft of the GATT formed alliances with Mahendra Singh Tikait of the BKU Uttar Pradesh and the BKU Punjab (Assadi 1995a, 194). It targeted key symbols of globalization, as with non-violent direct action on a Kentucky Fried Chicken outlet in Bangalore in 1996. Other farmer's leaders like Sharad Joshi, leader of the Maharashtra-based Shetkari Sanghatana, however, supported the Dunkel Draft arguing that "the interests of the Multi-National Corporations and the farmers coincide" (Bentall 1995, 298). This emphasizes how the strategies of movements like the KRRS were, then, a significant intervention in trying to shape farmer's politics in ways which explicitly contested liberalization of agriculture.

Particularly significant in this regard have been ongoing protests in relation to seeds. Teltumbde argues that liberalization of the Indian seed sector has far-reaching consequences. In 1998, "the World Bank's structural adjustment policies forced India to open up its seed sector to global corporations like Cargill, Monsanto, Sygenta. It has changed the input economy of agriculture overnight. Farm saved seeds were replaced by corporate seeds, which needed optimised inputs of irrigation, fertilizers and pesticides" (Teltumbde 2006, 18; see also Sahai 2000). Contestation of the relations of seeds, including contestation of genetically modified seeds, has continued to be central to farmers' protests. Thus the KRRS-led 'Operation Cremate Monsanto', where activists burned a crop of genetically modified cotton, placed the KRRS at the center of transnational opposition to genetically modified seeds (for critiques of this action, see Omvedt 1998; Herring 2006).

One pernicious effect of neoliberalization on agriculture is the shift from the cultivation of rice to the cultivation of export crops (Patnaik 2007). Such shifts in cultivation practices have been contested. In early August 1997, scores of agricultural laborers belonging to the CPI(M)-aligned Kerala State Agricultural Workers Union, "gate crashed into lands converted from rice to other crops and destroyed the new crops as a protest against the farmers' decision to move out of rice cultivation" (Kannan 1999, 174–175). This emphasizes how subaltern groups have contested the spatial and social relations through which cultivation is produced.

Arguably, one of the most significant ways in which different social and farmers' movements have intervened in debates around the effects of liberalization has been in relation to farmer suicides. More than "five thousand indebted farmers have committed suicide in Andhra Pradesh alone since 1998", with significant additional numbers of suicides in the Punjab, Maharashtra, Karnataka, and Kerala (Patnaik 2007, 221). Suicides are the most severe symptoms of the agrarian crisis accompanying liberalization (see Mohanty 2005; Patnaik 2007). Farmers' and other social movements have been significant in bringing such suicides into the public domain, articulating them directly as part of a politics which questions the 'dark sides of liberalisation' in India. This contests the silence of state governments about suicides and attempts to blame the suicides on the farmers themselves. Thus, Martin argues that the problem of farmer suicide has been 'buried' in the regional pages of English-language newspapers in Karnataka (Martin 2006, 83). He argues that Krishna and the government in Karnataka were unwilling to explore the 'dark underside' of economic reform.

Official reports systematically ignore the broader causes and contexts of farmer suicide. They have focused on issues like alcohol-related problems of farmers, individualizing the problem. A report by Professor Veeresh commissioned by the Karnataka state government was widely criticized by the media, the opposition, and farmers groups for "not squarely addressing the root causes of farmers' distress, including the anti-poor policies of the state government" (Martin 2006, 84). Farmers' movements have sought instead to make suicides visible, emphasizing the links between suicides and policies of liberalization. The KRRS organized a 'Seed Tribunal' in 2000 "which focused on the suicides of farmers in different parts of India in the backdrop of globalisation." This documented "the testimonies of farmers of those areas wherein globalisation has provided the space for committing suicide, and has also adversely affected the economy of peasants" (Assadi 2000). Assadi adds that "although the specific stories of debt trap differed from one region to another the larger picture was the same".

Such response to farmer suicides attempts to make the 'dark side' and inequalities of economic liberalization part of the terrain of democratic contestation in India. Movements contesting the role of foreign and Indian multi-national capital have similarly sought to make visible the unequal relations of power that shape liberalization. Major campaigns against Coca-Cola in India stress the corporation's role in exacerbating water shortages, as with the ongoing campaign in Plachimada in the state of Kerala. Here a diverse coalition has accused the multinational of "creating severe water shortage, of polluting its groundwater and soil, and also of distributing toxic waste as fertiliser to farmers in the area" (Raman 2005, 2481; see also Bijoy 2006). The company has been subject to mounting pressure from local communities, in particular among adivasis and dalits. These struggles against Coca-Cola intersected with a decade-long struggle of adivasis in Kerala for "restoration of land rights guaranteed under various clauses of the Indian constitution" (Aiyer 2007, 642).

On December 16, 2003, in a landmark verdict, the single bench of the Kerala High Court upheld the position of the Perumatty panchayat which "refused to renew Coca-Cola's licence for further production" and directed the company to seek alternative sources of water for its bottling plant in Plachimada. The bench maintained that groundwater belonged to the people and that the government did not have the right to allow a private party to extract water in huge quantities, groundwater being "a property held by it in trust". Coca-Cola, the bench ruled, should be allowed "to use only that quantity of groundwater equal to the amount normally used for irrigating crops in a 34-acre plot, the actual area occupied by the company" (Raman 2005, 2481). Coca-Cola was forced to stop production in March 2004. Legal battles continue over their attempts to resume production in Plachimada (Raman 2005; Bijoy 2006). The National Alliance of People's Movements has been influential in this regard, mobilizing through sites such as the World Social Forum (Drew and Levien 2006: see also Raman 2005, 2484). These protests have led to further contestations of Coca-Cola. Prompted partly by the protests in Plachimada, the Centre for Science and Environment in Delhi conducted studies in 2003 which found that 12 brands of soft drink manufactured by PepsiCo and Coca-Cola contained toxic pesticides residues, a situation which remained unchanged in 2006 (Centre for Science and Environment 2006).

Contesting the effects of economic liberalization has been subject to significant state repression. A central feature of militant particularist struggles against foreign and Indian multi-national capital has been the use of state-sanctioned violence. Jha (2008, 76) argues that "physical repression by the state apparatus" aimed at circumscribing "the right to organize, the right to collective bargaining, right to form trade unions" and "right to strike" has "increased in recent years". During a strike at a Honda Motorcycle and Scooter Private Ltd plant in New Delhi in 2005 3,000 workers corralled into a garden by police were subject to a lathi charge, the violence of which shocked even seasoned trade union activists. Eight hundred people were arrested "60 of those forcibly removed from the local hospital which treated 400 workers that afternoon" (Mason 2006, 182). Indian multi-nationals, such as the Tatas, have also been defended by state repression. In January 2006, for example, when "the tribals of Kalinganagar in Orissa protested against the acquisition of their lands for a steel plant owned by the Tatas [. . .] the state police opened fire, leading to the instant death of sixteen people, four also dying later on the way to hospital" (Menon and Nigam, 2007, 64). This emphasizes how significant the role of violence and state repression are in shaping processes of neo-liberalization. It suggests, contrary to Chatterjee's understanding of political society, making such repression central to accounts of the politics of neo-liberalization.

This section has foregrounded the diverse ways in which militant particularist struggles have contested the effects of neo-liberalization. I have noted the strategic use of state violence to prevent neo-liberalization being brought into the terrain of democratic contestation. The section signaled the diverse forms of identity and agency generated through militant particularist resistances. The next section engages in more depth with the formation of political identities through such resistances.

ARTICULATING MILITANT PARTICULARISMS

A central political issue, in relation to the formation of militant particularisms, is how grievances are articulated, and the relations envisioned through such politics. These are particularly significant issues in relation to the current conjuncture in contemporary India. As Oza has argued, the local and national have frequently been constructed in chauvinistic and exclusionary ways in opposition to globalization, especially by those associated with the Hindu nationalist right (Oza 2006; see also Gidwani 2007). A central task for left political movements in India is to find ways of articulating resistance in progressive and solidaristic ways. This section interrogates some of the practices through which such resistances have been articulated.

A tension in Williams's formulation of 'militant particularism' is the privileging of male-centered forms of bonding in working class communities (see Massey, 2000). As a result, his account is inattentive to differences within place, especially within subaltern groups, such as tensions over gender relations. Engaging with the militant particularisms formed through opposition to neo-liberalization necessitates foregrounding such differences and tensions. As the last section noted, farmer's movements, like the BKU or KRRS, have tended to prioritize the 'interests' of particular caste groups, especially 'middle' peasants who are comparatively rich in relation to landless laborers.

Support for some movements, such as the Bharatia Kisan Union in Uttar Pradesh, is drawn predominantly from particular caste constituencies, such as the Jat caste (Bentall and Corbridge 1996, 34; D. Gupta 1997, 60–61). Their forms of mobilization have tended to ignore differences within the village. Assadi argues that although "there was a strong influence of socialist ideology" on the leaders of the KRRS, they believed that the interests of the rural poor could "be best served in organising the peasantry and not by splitting it into its various sections" (Assadi 1997, 41). Gupta contends that it is easier for Tikait, leader of the BKU, "to stand shoulder-to-shoulder with the Muslims of West U.P. than with the Scheduled Castes of the village, such as the Harijans and the Valmikis." He notes that the BKU has not said anything "about uplifting the ex-untouchables or even the landless labourers" (D. Gupta 1997, 60).

These movements have articulated grievances around neoliberalization in ways that prioritize particular groups while marginalizing others. Alliances have been configured, however, which cut across significant divisions in Indian society. Routledge (2008, 346) has noted the significance of cross-caste alliances in the Narmada movement, but argues that adivasi identities within the Narmada Bachao Andolan tended to become strategically essentialized and homogenized. Sheila Bhalla (1999, 57) engages with alliances between left-led peasants and workers' organizations allied with new farmer's movements in Haryana. These have produced commonalities of interests in relation to specific issues with common rallying points around the "insensitivity of elected political leaders" and "police highhandedness and brutality". Bhalla suggests, however, that the tendency of left-led peasant unions, such as the CPI(M) affiliated All India Kisan Sabha, to "get drawn into agitations mounted by medium and large scale farmers and focussed on issues of particular interest to this class, to the relative neglect of the problems of poor peasants and landless workers" threatens the effectiveness of these alliances (Bhalla 1999, 57).

Utsa Patnaik has argued that the agrarian crisis precipitated by liberalization needs to be met by a "fighting unity of all the peasant classes and workers" (Patnaik 2007, 230). While such unity is clearly desirable, the differentiation of rural society matters in the construction of resistance. This cannot be ignored, as Patnaik does by downplaying the importance of caste politics (see Patnaik 2007, 229). The existing differentiation shapes the conduct and possibilities of organizing in significant ways. A further tension with the New Farmers' Movements has been the 'unambiguous nationalist rhetoric' that has structured the opposition of the KRRS and BKU to neoliberal globalization, the Dunkel Draft, and companies like Monsanto. This draws on the idioms of Gandhian nationalism (Brass 1995, 56n41; see also Assadi, 1995a, 221; Gupta 1999, 292, 313). Nanjundaswamy argued, for example, that the Indian government's acceptance of liberalization has rendered India 'impotent' and that 'genetic resources are our national property' (*Economic Times* May 24, 1999; Gupta, 1999: 292). The maps of grievance mobilized by the KRRS refigured nationalist identities through pitting rural India against hostile foreign forces.

This nationalist articulation of resistance to globalization has been a significant tension in the politics produced in opposition to liberalization. Oza has argued that in the resistance to the Miss World Pageant in Bangalore in 1996, "local opposition was spatially manifested as preserving the nation against the larger forces of globalization" (Oza 2001, 1068). Opposition was comprised of diverse groups including "students, farmers, unions, the Hindu Right and a number of women's organizations that formed a loosely defined progressive coalition" (Oza 2006, 89). Although there were significant differences among their rhetoric "there were several instances in which the progressive group's rhetoric came surprisingly close to the views expressed by the Hindu Right". The left mobilized a strong critique of the linkages between the state and global and domestic capital through the pageant. It did not, however, contest the conservative narrative of the Hindu Right which counterposed globalization with a "threatened Indian culture" (Oza 2006, 91). She argues that both left and right tended to view the nation as "ideologically and symbolically fixed and immutable" (Oza 2006, 101). The implications of these nationalist identities for the formation of solidarities in opposition to neoliberal globalization will be drawn out in the next section. The importance of Oza's arguments about the different political identities articulated in relation to globalization can be further illustrated through Waquar Ahmed's work on opposition to Enron.

In 1992 the Maharashtra State Electricity Board signed a memorandum of understanding with Enron, setting in motion the Dabhol Power Project (DPC), the largest corporate-led commercial venture in Indian history, that also involved Bechtel and General Electric as venture partners (Ahmed 2007a). This was part of a shift from a broadly Keynesian to a liberalized model of electricity supply (Ahmed 2007b). This major neoliberal project was the site of significant resistance, even before the project gained official clearance. The Bharatiya Janta Party, however, proved successful in co-opting and colonizing such opposition. Ahmed details how an alliance of Shiv Sena with the BJP, the state level and the national level right-wing Hindu fundamentalist parties respectively, directed anger at the Congress state government which was seen as "corrupt and supportive of Enron". Despite the BJP's favorable attitude to neoliberalism, though with a "nationalist, and often jingoist, slant", their antagonism to Enron was such "that a large section of the population accepted the Shiv Sena–BJP combine as political leader of the movement. They felt [. . .] that the best way to defeat Enron was to use democracy by voting for a party that would revoke the DPC contract. This in turn, allowed the Shiv Sena–BJP combine to expand their support base" (Ahmed 2007a).

The Shiv Sena–BJP alliance came to power in Maharashtra partly through the support they had won through the anti-Enron struggles. Yet the alliance subsequently reneged on their pledge to renegotiate the contract. Left and secular democratic groups, sidelined through the BJP's co-opting of the resistance to Enron, were left in a marginal position. Their attempts to continue resistance were subject to police harassment. This raises important questions about the co-option of resistance to neoliberal globalization by the Hindu right. The failure of the left to provide an alternative way of articulating resistance to Enron raises difficult questions about left political strategies in response to neoliberalization. As I argued in the opening section the practices through which such militant particularisms are generated, produced, and articulated are central to the formation of left political strategies. Through ceding the articulation of such resistance to the BJP, 'the left' was marginalized, in terms of framing the opposition and more generally as it allowed the electoral success of the BJP. This situation, as Oza's discussion of the Miss World pageant also indicates, is symptomatic of a broader set of tensions in the political strategies adopted by the Indian left in relation to neoliberalization.

There are two key tensions here. First, the left, especially the organized left, has tended to adopt a rather 'contradictory' approach to liberalization. As RoyChowdhury argues, the left in India

> has demonstrated a highly variable approach to liberalisation, marked by criticism at the level of rhetoric and substantial accommodation to the climate of liberalisation at the level of politics and policies. This has certainly not provided the organised left with a great deal of space,

> ideologically or politically, to articulate and alternative development model [. . .]. (RoyChowdhury 2003, 5283)

This lack of political space has closed possibilities that would be garnered by articulating militant particularist struggles in more progressive directions and through more consistent opposition to neoliberalization. In states where the left is in power, as with West Bengal and Kerala, the left has directly adopted neoliberal industrial policies, often subjecting militant particularist struggles protesting against such policies to severe repression (see Banerjee 2008). The violence used by CPI(M) cadres in Nandigram is the most visible manifestation of such repression (see Amnesty International 2007; Report of the People's Tribunal on Nandigram 2007; Harvey 2008). The poor showing of the left in the 2009 elections also suggests the failure of the left to engage successfully with the political conjuncture shaped by neoliberalization (Basu 2009). Some Indian left organizations and social movements have sought to transcend such political impasses through the construction of transnational solidarity networks. The next section engages with the possibilities and tensions of such strategies for left political imaginaries.

NETWORKING MILITANT PARTICULARISMS

Ananthakrishnan Aiyer argues that "Plachimada's struggle against the Coca Cola Company" "is important in having raised serious issues about the role of transnational corporations and globalization in India. It is now firmly tied in the hearts and minds of many activists to the struggles against the Coca Cola Company in Colombia [. . .] or the victory against Bechtel in Cochabamba, Bolivia". Further "their struggle has been inspirational and played a significant role in generating opposition to The Coca Cola Company and PepsiCo in other rural communities in India" (Aiyer 2007, 652). This demonstrates the productive spatial practices through which militant particularist actions like the struggles against Coca-Cola in Plachimada, can be networked. Thus Aiyer notes how the struggles in Plachimada have become 'iconic' in India and beyond, through boycotts against Coca-Cola in U.S. campuses and elsewhere (see Higginbottom 2007; Featherstone 2008, 128–132). Such networking places the Plachimada resistance in relation to broader political mobilization against Coca-Cola and inspires other struggles in India.

Ayier also makes a more cautionary note suggesting that a focus on the transnational can elide the importance of other geographies (see McFarlane 2004). There is a related tendency to construct transnational networking as something of a panacea for alternative political strategies. This section engages with the transnational networking of various militant particularist struggles. It examines the contested spatial practices and political identities constituted through such organizing.

The contestation of Coca-Cola demonstrates that transnational organizing can be productive. It brings together different movements contesting the multi-national on different terms, and in different places. The National Alliance of People's Movements has been influential in this regard, mobilizing through sites like the World Social Forum (Drew and Levien 2006; see also Raman 2005, 2484). Transnational networking has foregrounded the multiple grievances through which Coca-Cola has been contested. This produces a diverse political imaginary through connecting different place-based struggles. This has linked different campaigns against Coca-Cola on issues such as the company's poor record on labor rights and its environmental effects. These campaigns have contested aspects of the power relations of globalization that are placed outside the limits of the political consensus defined by support for liberalization.

Alliances and struggles against neoliberal globalization, however, rarely perform the 'smooth' spaces and alliances envisioned by Hardt and Negri (2004) in their account of the multitude. Rather, these connections and networking practices tend to be striated, contested, and riven (see Featherstone 2008; Routledge and Cumbers 2009). The terms on which 'militant particularist' identities are constituted can exert pressure and set limits, as well as open up possibilities, for the articulation of solidarities. The involvement of farmers' movements, particularly the KRRS, in transnational resistance networks illustrates this.

The contestation of the transnational geographies of power associated with liberalization opened up possibilities for the KRRS in transnational organizing. In the 1990s the KRRS became a key organization involved in various forms of transnational mobilization, including People's Global Action (PGA) and Via Campesina. What is significant about this involvement in transnational mobilization, however, is the limited extent to which it has dislocated the nationalist framings of resistance associated with the farmers' movements. Thus Akhil Gupta has argued that the 'nationalist rhetoric' of Tikait and Nanjundaswamy is "mixed with a shrewd recognition of the current global historical conjuncture and of the importance of forging coalitions with similar groups in other parts of the world" (A. Gupta 1998, 323). Transnational networks, then, are sites of co-existence of different forms of identities, rather than a plane that transcends differences and geographies.

A major PGA/KRRS instigated project, the Inter-Continental Caravan (ICC), demonstrates the significance of the negotiation of political identities and solidarities through such networks. The Caravan was an ambitious project, uniting activists from the Indian New Farmers Movements, with West European green activists, in contesting neoliberal institutions and biotechnology (see Featherstone 2003). The Caravan shaped alliances that were defined by collective mobilization and joint actions against transnational capital and agribusiness. The nationalist 'maps of grievance' that have shaped the political identities of the farmers' movements, however, exerted contradictory pressures and possibilities on the solidarities conducted through the ICC. Nanjundaswamy's insistence that a minimum of 400 activists from Indian farmers' movements would form the core of the project, alongside other activists from India, and other parts of the global South, meant that a very particular Indian-nationalist story was the focus of the Caravan's activity. This tone and style of action made other activists uncomfortable, leading to accusations that at times it felt like an 'Indian Nationalist Caravan'.[1] The Caravan was conceived as a process that would institute solidarities between different struggles against globalization. Some of the particularistic ways that resistance to globalization was envisioned, however, closed down the potential productiveness of these solidarities.

Not only was the Caravan contested through the solidarities it generated, but it also was mobilized as part of internal dissension in the KRRS. Nanjundaswamy's hierarchical organizational style was contested in Karnataka as well as by activists in Western Europe (Madsen 2001; 2005). Disillusionment with Nanjundasawmy's leadership has been directly related to his lack of democratic conduct. Kadidal Shamanna, another prominent figure in the KRRS, argued after Nanjundaswamy's death in 2004 that it was "the refusal of the late Prof Nanjundaswamy to act in a democratic manner which led to dissatisfaction. [. . .] as the movement grew and became a pressure group he seemed averse to taking suggestions from the others" (Kadidal Shamanna cited in *Deccan Herald*, February 10, 2004). The KRRS split in November 1999, primarily relating to tensions over Nanjundaswamy's conduct, especially in relation to the Caravan. Transnational articulations of resistance then can be contested and fragile, intersecting with power struggles and internal rivalries in place-based movements.

Despite such tensions the involvement of Indian social and political movements in transnational networks and organizing has been significant. Through participation in various transnational organizing networks, and through hosting the 2004 World Social Forum in Mumbai, Indian movements have been influential in shaping the terms on which transnational resistance to neoliberal globalization is shaped (Vanaik 2004). Such mobilization has also produced new spaces for articulation of 'new left' political identities. An account of the 2003 Asian Social Forum in Mumbai quotes a feminist and ex-member of the Communist Party of India (Marxist-Leninist) (CPI(ML)) as celebrating the way that, in contrast to forms of left politics, where discipline had been forced, it "gave the space to form new alliances, shape new formulations, design new approaches, and maybe even new theories to underpin all the alternatives" (Jain 2003). The New Trade Union Initiative "an alliance of independent trade unions in India that arose in the mid-1990s and became formally constituted as a federation in 2006" has also been significant (Jha 2008, 78). This initiative has challenged the subordination of trade union strategies to the interests of particular left parties, and forged alternative agendas. These emerging sites of political association have opened space for political identities and practices which were previously marginalized.

CONCLUSIONS

This chapter has sought to foreground the productive spatial practices through which militant particularist struggles have contested neoliberalization in India. I have engaged with the diverse ways in which such militant particularisms have been constituted. This necessitates thinking about the formation of militant particularisms in explicitly political ways. Echoing Rupal Oza's work I argued that the terms on which processes of globalization and liberalization are brought into contestation matter for the formation of progressive alternatives. Indeed, transcending some of the exclusionary nationalist framings of such opposition is arguably a pre-condition for developing left political strategies in the current conjuncture.

A central aim of the chapter was to engage with some of the tensions of left strategies in relation to articulating resistances to liberalization in ways that counter the rhetoric of the Hindu nationalist right. There can clearly be no easy answers here. I have sought to argue for the importance of challenging official left political strategies which have denounced liberalization in theory yet have embraced liberalization and meted out severe repression to militant particularist struggles in practice. As Deepankar Basu has argued important possibilities could be opened up by left parties engaging directly with struggles against neoliberalization rather than focusing solely on electoral politics (Basu 2009, 14). I have also argued for the importance of generating and articulating militant particularist struggles in expansive and solidaristic ways. In this sense transnational networking whilst offering no panacea for left political organizing remains significant as part of articulating resistance to globalization in internationalist and progressive ways.

ACKNOWLEDGMENTS

Thanks to Waquar Ahmed, Andy Davies, Mo Hume, Colin McFarlane, and Paul Routledge for various forms of assistance during the writing of this chapter and/or comments on an earlier draft of this chapter. Finally, thanks to Dick Peet for his very useful editorial comments.

NOTE

1. ICC/Discussions—June 20, 1999.

REFERENCES

Ahmed, W. 2007a. *Spaces of power: Foreign direct investment in India*. PhD Thesis, Clark University.

Ahmed, W. 2007b. Neoliberalism and contested policies of the power industry in India. *Industrial Geographer* 5(1): 44–52.

Aiyer, A. 2007. The allure of the transnational: Notes on some aspects of the political economy of water in India. *Cultural Anthropology* 22: 4, 640–658.

Amnesty International. 2008. Document—India: Concern over human rights violations during 'recapture' of Nandigram by ruling CPI(M) supporters in West Bengal. AI Index: ASA 20/001/2008 January 15, 2008.

Assadi, M. 1995a. Dunkelism and peasant protest in Karnataka: A view from within. *Social Action* 45 (April–June): 191–205.

———. 1995b. "Khadi Curtain", "Weak Capitalism" and "Operation Ryot": Some ambiguities in farmer's discourse, Karnataka and Maharashtra 1980–93. In *New Farmers Movements in India*, edited by T. Brass, 212–227. Ilford: Frank Cass.

———. 1996. Attack on multinationals: Re-enactment of Gandhian violence. *Economic and Political Weekly* (May 18, 1996): 1184–1186.

———. 1997. *Peasant movement in Karnataka*. Delhi: Shipra Publications.

———. 2000. Karnataka: Seed tribunal: Interrogating farmers' suicides. *Economic and Political Weekly* (October 28).

Banerjee, S. 2008. A Political Cul-de-sac: CPI(M)'s Tragic Denouement. *Economic and Political Weekly* (October 18): 12–14.

Basu, D. 2009. The left and the 15th Lok Sabha elections. *Economic and Political Weekly* (May 30): 10–15.

Bentall, J. 1996. *Bharat vs India*. Unpublished PhD thesis, University of Cambridge.

Bentall, J., and S. Corbridge 1996. Urban-rural relations, demand politics and the 'new agrarianism' in northwest India: The Bharatiya Kisan union. *Transactions of the Institute of British Geographers* 21(1): 27–48.

Bhalla, S. 1999. Liberalisation, rural labour markets and the mobilisation of farm workers: The Haryana story in an all-India context. *Rural Labour Relations in India,* edited by T. Byres, K. Kapadia, and J. Lerche, 25–70. Ilford: Frank Cass.

Bijoy, C. R. 2006. Kerala's Plachimada struggle: A narrative on water and governance rights. *Economic and Political Weekly* (October 14): 4332–4339.

Brass, T. 1995. Introduction. In *New Farmers' Movements in India*, T. Brass, 3–26. Ilford: Frank Cass.

Braun, B. 2005. Writing geographies of hope. *Antipode* 37: 4, 834–841.

Centre for Science and Environment. 2006. Soft drinks still unsafe. . . . http://www.cseindia.org/misc/cola-indepth/cola2006/cola_press2006.htm (accessed July 17, 2007).

Chatterjee, P. 2004. *The politics of the governed: Reflections on popular politics in most of the world*. New York: Colombia University Press.

Corbridge, S., G. Williams, M. Srivastava, and R. Veron 2005. *Seeing the state: Governance and governmentality in India*. Cambridge: Cambridge University Press.

Cumbers, A., P. Routledge, and C. Nativel 2008. The entangled geographies of global justice networks. *Progress in Human Geography* 32(2): 183–202.

Drew, G., and M. Levien 2006. The opposition to Coca Cola and water privatization: Activists in Medhiganj, India rise up. **http://www.zmag.org/content/showarticle.cfm?ItemID=10641** (accessed July 2, 2007).

Featherstone, D. J. 2003. Spatialities of trans-national resistance to globalisation: The maps of grievance of the Inter-Continental Caravan. *Transactions of the Institute of British Geographers* 28: 404–421.

———. 2005. Towards the relational construction of militant particularisms: or why the geographies of past struggles matter for resistance to neo-liberal globalisation. *Antipode* 37(2): 250–271.

———. 2008. *Resistance, space and political identities: The making of counter-global networks.* Oxford: Wiley-Blackwells.

Ghosh, K. 2006. Between global flows and local dams: Indigenousness, locality and the transnational sphere in Jarkhand, India. *Cultural Anthropology* 21(4): 501–534.

Gidwani, V. K. 2008. *Capital interrupted: Agrarian development and the politics of work in India.* Minneapolis: University of Minnesota Press.

Guha, R. 1982. On some aspects of the historiography of colonial India. In *Subaltern Studies* I, edited by R. Guha, 1–7. New Delhi: Oxford University Press.

Gupta, A. 1998. *Postcolonial developments: Agriculture in the making of modern India.* Oxford: Oxford University Press.

Gupta, D. 1997. *Rivalry and brotherhood: Politics in the life of farmers in northern India.* New Delhi: Oxford University Press.

Hardt, M., and A. Negri. 2004. *Multitude.* New York: Penguin.

Harvey, D. 1996. *Justice, nature and the geography of difference.* Oxford: Blackwell.

———. 2008. The right to the city. *New Left Review* 53: 23–40.

Herring, R. 2006. Why did 'Operation Cremate Monsanto' fail?: Science and class in India's great terminator-technology hoax. *Critical Asian Studies* 38(4): 467–493.

Higginbottom, A. 2007. Killer Coke. In *Thinker, Faker, Spinner, Spy: Corporate PR and the Assault on Democracy*, edited by W. Dinan and D. Miller, 278–294. London: Pluto Press.

Jain, D. 2003. The empire strikes back: A report on the Asian Social Forum. *Economic and Political Weekly* (January 11): 99–100.

Jha, P. 2008. Globalization and labour in India: Emerging challenges and responses. In *Labour and the challenges of globalization: What prospects for transnational solidarity?* edited by A. Bieler, I. Lindber, and D. Pillay, 65–80. London: Pluto Press.

Kannan, K. P. 1999. Rural labour relations and development dilemmas in Kerala: Reflections on the dilemmas of a socially transforming labour force in a slowly growing economy. In *Rural labour relations in India*, edited by T. Byres, K. Kapadia, and J. Lerche, 182–243. London: Frank Cass.

Kapoor, S. 2003. B R Ambedkar, W E B DuBois and the process of liberation. *Economic and Political Weekly* (December 27): 5344–5349.

Krishnarajulu, B. 1986. The Karnataka peasant movement: It's role in 'identity' formation. In *The peasant movement today*, edited by S. Shahasrabudhey, 30–39. New Delhi: Ashish.

Lerche, J. 1999. Politics of the poor: Agricultural labourers and political transformations in Uttar Pradesh. In *Rural labour relations in India* edited by T. Byres, K. Kapadia, and J. Lerche, 182–243. London: Frank Cass.

McFarlane, C. 2004. Geographical imaginations and spaces of political engagement: Examples from the Indian Alliance. *Antipode* 36(5): 890–916.

Madsen, S. T. 2001. The view from Vevey. *Economic and Political Weekly* (September 29): 3733–3742.

———. 2005. Coconut toddy, chewing tobacco and genetically modified cotton: Moral choices for a farmer's association in India. *The Eastern Anthropologist* 58(3–4): 471–486.

Martin, M. 2006. Farmers' suicides in Kerala: Widowed in Wayanad. In *From debt trap to death trap: An enquiry into farmers suicide* edited by M. Martin and S. Kakde, 31–50. Mumbai: Vikas Adhyayan Kendra.

Mason, P. 2006. *Live working or die fighting: How the working class went global*. London: Harvill Secker.

Massey, D. 2000. Travelling thoughts. In *Without guarantees: In honour of Stuart Hall*, edited by P. Gilroy, L. Grossberg, and A. McRobbie, 225–232. London: Verso.

Mawdsley, E. 2006. Hindu nationalism, postcolonialism and environmental discourses in India. *Geoforum* 37(3): 380–390.

Mohanty, B. B. 2005. 'We are like the living dead': Farmer suicides in Maharahstra, Western India. *Journal of Peasant Studies* 32(2): 243–276.

Omvedt, G. 1998. Terminating choice. http://www.saxakali.com/southasia/iniaenv2.html (accessed February 12, 1998).

Omvedt, G. 1995. "We want the return for our sweat": The formation of a national agricultural policy. In *New Farmers' Movements in India*, edited by T. Brass, 126–164. Ilford: Frank Cass.

Oza, R. 2001. Showcasing India: Gender, geography and globalization. *Signs: Journal of Women in Culture*, 26(4): 1067–1095.

———. 2007. *The making of neo-liberal India*. London: Routledge.

Panini, M. 1999. Trends in cultural globalisation: From agriculture to agribusiness in Karnataka. *Economic and Political Weekly* (July 31): 2168–2173.

Patnaik, U. 2007. *The republic of hunger and other essays* Monmouth: Merlin Press.

Raman, R. 2005. Corporate violence, legal nuances and political ecology: Cola war in Plachimada. 2005. *Economic and Political Weekly* (June 18): 2481–2485.

Rane, W. 1993. Farmers' rally against GATT proposals. *Economic and Political Weekly* (October 30): 2391.

Report of the People's Tribunal on Nandigram. 2007. *Nandigram: What really happened?* Delhi: Daanish Books.

Routledge, P. 2003. Voices of the dammed: Discursive resistance amidst erasure in the Naramada Valley, India. *Political Geography* 22(3): 243–270.

———. 2007. Transnational political movements. In *The Handbook of Political Geography*, edited by K. Cox, M. Low, and J. Robinson, 335–350. London: Sage.

Routledge, P., and A. Cumbers. 2009. *Global justice networks: Geographies of transnational solidarity*. Manchester: Manchester University Press.

RoyChowdhury, S. 2003. Old classes and new spaces: Urban poverty, unorganised labour and new unions. *Economic and Political Weekly* 50 (December 13): 5277–5284.

Sahai, S. 2000. Farmers' rights and food security. *Economic and Political Weekly* (March 11): 878–880.

Sakar, S. 2007. Labour history in India and South Africa: Some affinities and contrasts. *African Studies* 66(2&3): 181–200.

Shiva, V., A. H. Jafri, G. Beli, and R. Holla-Bhar. 1997. *The enclosure and recovery of the commons: Biodiversity, indigeneous knowledge and intellectual property rights*. New Delhi: Research Foundation for Science, Technology and Ecology.

SinghaRoy, D. K. 2004. *Peasant movements in post-colonial India: Dynamics of mobilization and identity*. New Delhi: Sage.

Stone, G. D. 2007. Agricultural deskilling and the spread of genetically modified cotton in Warrangal. *Current Anthropology* 48(1): 67–103.

Teltumbde, A. 2006. Introduction. In *From debt trap to death trap: An enquiry into farmers suicide*, edited by M. Martin and S. Kakde, 15–30. Mumbai: Vikas Adhyayan Kendra.

Vanaik, A. 2004. Rendezvous at Mumbai. *New Left Review* 26: 53–65.
Williams, G. O. 2001. Understanding 'political stability': Party action and political discourse in West Bengal. *Third World Quarterly* 22: 603–622.
Williams, R. 1979. *Politics and letters*. London: New Left Books.
———. 1989. *Resources of hope*. London: Verso.

13 Radical Peasant Movements and Rural Distress in India

A Study of the Naxalite Movement

Raju J. Das

1. INTRODUCTION

The history and geography of all hitherto existing society, to amend an oft-quoted line from the *Communist Manifesto*, is the history and geography of class struggle (Marx and Engels 1977, 108). Peasants have often been important protagonists in the class struggles occurring in the newer post-colonial societies of Asia, as well as the older ones in Latin America. In India, the Naxalite movement, so called because it started in the Naxalbari region of West Bengal province, is one such peasant struggle. Since its inception in the late 1960s, the Naxalite movement has undergone scalar transformation: from a local flare-up to a regional, and some would say, national-scale, movement. It exists, to some degree of intensity, in a quarter of India's 600 districts, covering 40% of the country's geographical area. The prime minister recently called the Naxalites the single biggest national security threat.

This chapter looks at the causes behind the continued existence of the Naxalite movement. In many ways, the Naxalite movement, including its geography, is a window on an Indian countryside in perpetual developmental distress. Distress has only been worsened by the neoliberal New Economic Policy emphasizing 'free' markets, legitimizing the state's withdrawal from pro-poor and pro-peasant activities, and advocating free export and import of commodities, including farm products. Much of my discussion is organized around development, therefore, in the economic and social-political senses of the term. I relate the emergence and continuation of the Naxalite movement to two developmental failures[1]: the basic failure of capitalist development and the failure of the post-colonial state to bring significant benefits to the broad mass of the (rural) population. I then briefly pose a much neglected, but larger, question of the Naxalite movement itself as a potential alternative agent of development.[2] The movement continues not just because of the existence of long-lasting contradictions in Indian society, but rather the contradictions have sharpened under neoliberalism because, on the one hand, capital becomes increasingly more exploitative, and on the other hand, the state is increasingly withdrawing from the provision of welfare to the masses. The continuation of the movement is due also to the Naxalites addressing, albeit to a limited extent, these contradictions by providing some relief to the suffering masses and by helping them stand up for their rights (e.g., rights to land), which are being trampled on by neoliberal capital, especially in areas rich in natural resources. I then turn my attention to major limitations in the movement itself. Acknowledging that it has a considerable following, and already covers a large area, I claim that its limitations are due, first, to the movement as a whole being strategically/ideologically deficient (and this deficiency is stark especially under neoliberalism) and, second, to the extent that part of the movement exclusively focuses on armed struggle, to the fact that it is also tactically faulty.[3]

The chapter is divided into six sections. In Section 2, I provide a brief overview of the origin of the Naxalite movement, its initial suppression by the state, and its later appearance as a powerful movement, split into several major groups. In the next two sections, I look at the causes behind the continuation of the movement. In section 3, I relate the movement to rural distress and the state's failure to address this. I deal with rural distress as caused by class exploitation, that intensifies under neoliberalism, as well as by longer lasting social relations of oppression. Next, I examine the state's failure to significantly mitigate the effects of class exploitation and caste- and gender-based oppression. In Section 4, I look at the ability of the Naxalite movement to offer some help to poor people. This includes helping them, especially in tribal areas, to protest against the neoliberal land grab. Section 5 discusses the movement's limitations. A final section, Section 6, concludes the chapter.

2. BEGINNINGS OF THE NAXALITE MOVEMENT

The northern parts of India's West Bengal province[4] have a long history of peasant and worker struggles. Although short-lived, the first peasant organization in the country was formed in north Bengal as the All Bengal Peasant Conference of 1925 (Samanta 1984, 21). From the early 1950s, a radical section of the Communist Party of India (CPI) organized tribal peasants, most of whom were sharecroppers, in the Naxalbari area of West Bengal's Darjeeling district. In the period 1958–1962, the movement entered a militant phase, when local peasants' associations, led by the Communists such as Charu Mazumdar, called for the harvesting of crops by peasants, arming them to protect their crops, and defending themselves against police attacks (Banerjee 1984). The landlords responded by evicting sharecroppers.

Such peasant activities in Naxalbari coincided with simmering troubles within the then-undivided Communist Party. In 1964, the party split into the pro-Soviet CPI and the pro-China Communist Party of India (Marxist) or the CPI(M). In 1967, these parties formed a United Front government in

Bengal in coalition with some bourgeois parties. The peasant movements in Bengal enhanced the communists' popularity, which helped them form a government. The formation of a communist-led state government increased the peasants' expectations for immediate relief. When this did not occur, the peasants were propelled into more militant action.

On March 2, 1967, in Naxalbari, a sharecropper, Bigul Kishan, armed with a court order, had gone to till his land. The landlord and his hired hoodlums attacked the sharecropper. The police did not take any action against them. The fact that the incident occurred just a month after the formation of the United Front government was seen as indicative of the futility of the hope that a left-oriented government would help the peasants. This perception fueled further militancy. Fifteen to twenty thousand poor peasants, in about two thousand villages, were enrolled as full-time activists, supported by the urban educated youth (Jalal 1995). Peasants' committees were formed in every village. They were transformed into armed guards, possessing traditional weapons, like bows, arrows, and spears. They soon occupied land in the name of peasants' committees, seized the crops from landlords' land, burned all land records which had been used to cheat them, passed death sentences on oppressive landlords, looted guns from them, and set up a parallel administration in the villages. They canceled debts owed to usurious moneylenders and asked them to return the mortgaged properties to the original peasant owners. They fixed daily wages for farm laborers (at five kilos of rice). Prices of essential commodities were also fixed in the big shops (Banerjee 1984). For three months (March to May 1967), feudalism was driven out of a 300-square-mile area. Revolutionary mass organization of peasants held political power. Peasants' control over the area was so complete that no outsider could enter without their permission. The exercise of political power, and control over territory, went hand in hand.

The peasant movement turned violent when landlords resisted the peasant seizure of their land and crops. Police action followed clashes between landlords and peasants. Following the killing of a policeman on May 23, 1967, a major police action was launched on July 12 by the state government, with full support from the central government. The police killed nine people, including two children, as well as six (tribal) women, who played an important role in the movement (Damas 1991, 84). The government's military campaign took back political power from the masses. The Naxalbari movement was defeated.

But the Naxalbari uprising sparked radical movements in many places. According to government reports, 5424 agrarian agitations occurred between 1967 and 1970 (Shah 1991, 291). A Coordinating Committee, and later a party, called the CPI (ML) (Communist Party of India (Marxist-Leninist)) was formed on April 22, 1969 by dissidents from the CPI(M), to coordinate localized struggles into a mass movement. Thus, the CPI(M) was split into the CPI(M) and the CPI(ML). Naxalism came to be associated with the latter, CPI(ML). Government repression continued. By 1973, nearly 40,000 members or sympathizers were in jail.

The CPI(ML) itself split many times into multiple factions, each claiming to be the true party. In post-Naxalbari times, the movement split into some 40 CPI(ML) groups in perpetual territorial fraternal fight for the expansion of their areas of influence. This has now consolidated into three main M-L streams, although a large number of other groups still remain outside. All M-L groups owe their origin to events in Naxalbari and are guided by their interpretation(s) of Maoism (which they find to be an advance in Marxism). They all view Indian society as semi-colonial (i.e., as under clutches of imperialism) and semi-feudal and agree on the need for a democratic revolution to destroy feudal economic and social-cultural relations. The M-L movement is divided mainly on the basis of their tactical approach to parliamentary/extra-electoral politics. Some (e.g., CPI (Maoist)) almost exclusively focus on armed struggle and are underground[5]; while others, such as Kanu Sanyal's group, use mainly overground methods and run mass organizations. There are other groups such as CPI(ML) Liberation using a combination of both underground and overground methods and even participating in elections (Banerjee 1996, 203–204).[6]

3. RURAL DISTRESS, STATE FAILURE, AND THE NAXALITE MOVEMENT

In terms of its original occurrence, and its continued existence, the Naxalite movement must be explained in terms of multiple causes. I focus on three issues, two of which will be discussed in this section: class exploitation and social oppression, and the state's developmental failure. The success of the Naxalite movement as a development actor will be discussed in the next section. These three issues are discussed with respect to the country as a whole as well as the geographical areas of influence of the Naxalites.

Class Exploitation and Social Oppression

The Naxalite movement is founded on unequal land distribution. In the 1960s, about 40% of India's land was owned by 5% of rural households, who did not till their plots personally. Pauperized small holders began selling plots of land to meet their subsistence expenditures. Inequality in the ownership/control over land continues: in 1995–1996, approximately 7% of families operated 66% of the land (GOI 2007, 109), and in 2003, less than 10% of families owned more than 56% of land (Bhalla 2006, 34).[7] Unequal land distribution has become a burning issue since the neoliberal economic reforms began. Under neoliberalism, land reform legislation by the state is considered to be an institutional constraint on the flow of agribusiness investment to rural areas, or on acquiring agricultural, homestead, and forestlands for a variety of non-agricultural purposes including export-oriented industrialization (Special Economic Zones, or SEZs) in the corporate sector (Pushpendra 2000). The existing land reform legislation is being diluted to facilitate the transfer of land from peasants to big business. This partly explains the relevance, under neoliberalism, of the Naxalites' emphasis on the land question, especially in relatively under-developed rural areas. The significance of the Naxalite movement in relation to the land issues is in no small measure due to two failures of the traditional left parties: not only have they generally not developed sustained and militant struggles on these issues (in the last 30 years or so),[8] but also these parties themselves have failed to protect peasants from the pressure of the neoliberal land grab in the states where they are in power. For example, in West Bengal, the left government acquired cultivable land from unwilling peasants for SEZs, which has been a major reason for the left electoral debacle in the 2009 national election (Das 2009).

Associated with an unequal distribution of land is the presence of rental and usurious exploitation. In the 1960s, in Naxalbari and elsewhere, many landlords cultivated their land by leasing it to tenant farmers. Tenants paid at least half of what they produced in rent. Landowners would impose levies on tenants to bear the cost of ceremonies in their landlord's house on special occasions. Peasants performed free forced work on landlords land. They were also forced to do landlord's private chores for free. Many of these practices still exist, although on a relatively smaller scale. There are at least 40 million bonded laborers in India, and close to 90% of them are *dalits* or tribals (Human Rights Watch 1999). These laborers do not have the right to choose for whom they work, for how long, and for how much.

Landowners also had their land cultivated by hired laborers, paying below-subsistence wages. Hired labor is now occurring on a much larger scale than in the 1960s. Minimum wage laws have hardly been implemented. In 1989, in the Jehanabad district of Bihar, a hotspot of the Naxalite movement, minimum wages were paid in only 16% of the 933 villages (Louis 2005, 5372). In addition, agricultural laborers rarely have paid employment for more than 200 days in a year. Poor agricultural wages, and lack of extra avenues of non-farm employment, drove the landless workers to borrow money from private agencies. The rate of interest charged by moneylenders amounted to 50% a year, even more in some cases. According to the Second Agricultural Commission, "of the estimated total number of 16.3 million agricultural labour households . . . 63.9% were indebted" (Banerjee 1984). In 2003, the figure was still 49%; an average farmer's debt was equal to her/his household's total spending in two years (GOI 2007, 73). Since 1983, the percentage of the total debt incurred from private moneylenders, who charge very high rates, has been increasing (Bhalla 2007, 317). Under neoliberalism, institutional sources of credit are drying up, and private moneylenders are a more important source of credit than in the 1960s, when Naxalism started. Apart from large landowners, traders are another class, on which the poor people's lives are dependent, especially in tribal areas where the traders buy forest products from tribals at a cheap rate and sell them their daily necessaries at an expensive rate.

Class relations are experienced through, and reproduced by, caste (or race), ethnicity and gender relations (McIntyre 2002; Giminez 2005; McDowell 2008) that compound the injurious effects of class. There is no perfect one-to-one overlap between the axis of class and that of social oppression: not all dalits, tribals, and women are landless laborers. But when there *is* an overlap (i.e., when someone is a dalit, a woman, and a landless laborer or a petty producer from an economically backward and politically neglected region), the economic and social situation is particularly stark. In addition to suffering class-based exploitation and dispossession from the land, poor women, tribals, and low-caste people, including dalits, are also subjected to social discrimination, political marginalization, and educational as well as medical deprivation. Poor people live under constant threat to their dignity (*izzat*) and political rights. Until recently, low-caste people, even if they had the money, could not buy the clothes they want. They cannot walk in upper-caste neighborhoods wearing footwear or carrying an umbrella. They cannot sit on a cot in the presence of upper castes. Neither can they take upper-caste surnames, nor can students of lower castes sit on front benches in classrooms (Nathan 1999, 162). Recently (July 2009), upper-caste people in a village near Patna beat up a dalit woman for listening to popular Hindi songs on a mobile phone. Caste influences the division of labor and access to assets, as seen in the "continuing confinement of lower castes to the ranks of agricultural labourers and the virtual exclusion of upper castes from the ranks of middle and poor peasants and agricultural labourers" (Nathan 1999, 162).[9] India remains a caste society (or a class-caste society). Mainstream left parties have not emphasized social oppression and extra-economic coercion (human right violation)[10], creating a void partly filled by the Naxalite groups.

Being a low-caste person, and especially being a low-caste woman of the laboring or poor peasantry class (in India's peripheral areas), continues to be probably the worst thing that can happen to an Indian. In many villages, in spite of the availability of water locally, low-caste women have to trudge far to fetch water, for they are not allowed by the upper-caste people to take water from the public ponds or wells near their huts. More importantly, they have little control over their own bodies. Their body is a means for the cheap production of wealth for the landed, and also a means for their sexual enjoyment.

Their body is also a means/weapon of class struggle in the hands of the landlords. Given the ways in which class and caste (and gender) relations are inter-locked, peasants often rebel against social oppression first and then economic exploitation later, says *Liberation*, organ of the Naxalite group, CPI(ML) Liberation (Frankel 1990, 120–121). A fundamental component of the dalit identity in many places is the fact that they are showing resentment against social oppression or demanding the payment of minimum wages (Louis 2000). When low-caste laborers demand higher wages from higher-caste landlords, the latter feel "threatened that a 'low man' [is] . . . challenging their privileged position" (Frankel 1990, 122). In Bihar, the response of upper-caste landlords has taken the extreme form of private landlord armies that ruthlessly suppress the low-caste poor fighting for their legitimate rights.[11] Massacres of the lower classes of low castes by landowners of upper (and sometimes middle) castes are highly gendered, showing how class, caste, and gender are interconnected (see Cockburn 1998 on gender violence during political conflict). For example, the landlord armies (e.g., Ranvir Sena) target low-caste women for the most horrendous mutilation and murder, because they would "give birth to Naxalites" and their children would "grow up to be Naxalites" (*Liberation* 2003). The Savarna Liberation Army's 'mass rape' campaign, conducted between March and July 1992 in Gaya and Jehanabad districts, was, says the Sena, a 'lesson' to the dalits, that if they tried to take on the landlords, the women of their communities would be humiliated (Ramakrishnan 1999). Gender oppression, relatively autonomous of feudal and capitalist exploitation in its origin, is a means of waging class struggle against peasants and laborers. This is part of the landlords' broader strategy of fighting the class war by using force. In some places, landlords shouted: "what is the remedy for getting rid of Naxalites?" "Shorten them by six inches?' (Frankel 1990, 122). Mobilizing extra-economic power (e.g., caste and gender-based oppression), landlords have prompted retaliatory Naxalite activity (Tornquist 1991).

FAILURE OF STATE INTERVENTIONS

How is the state addressing problems of the economic and social-political insecurity of its poorer citizens from whom it demands allegiance to the law? In spite of some achievements, like increasing life expectancy and higher literacy levels, for broader masses, conditions have not improved much in absolute or relative terms.

The post-colonial Indian state has sought to intervene in four major areas in addressing problems of rural distress. These are: land reforms (1950s–), the green revolution (1960s–), cheap credit to poor people (1970s–), and job creation under neoliberalism (2006–). In no small measure have these policies been prompted by the need to deal with, and/or pre-empt, rural class struggles (including the Naxalite movement) (Das 2007). Yet, having raised and then frustrated their expectations, such policies have in turn fueled the Naxalite movement.

Land reforms laws aim at imposing ceilings on land ownership, and distributing to poorer people the ceiling-surplus land (i.e., land held by landowners above the ceiling). Ceilings were kept at very high levels to protect the landlords' interests. For example, the ceiling for a family in Andhra

Pradesh, now a hot bed of Naxalism, was 877 acres. This was the case when about 80% of rural families owned less than 5 acres, or were landless. Ceilings were lowered in the 1970s in part as a response to the Naxalite movement. But the state made little attempt at finding the ceiling-surplus lands and distributing the vested land. Landlords were able to hide surplus land by transferring it illegally into their relatives' and friends' names. In Darjeeling, at the time of initial Naxalite activity, at least 65,000 acres of surplus land owned by tea estates, and about 19,000 acres of private land of landlords, could have been redistributed to poor people. But this did not occur, leading to the violence of 1967 in the area (Duyker 1981). In Bihar, one of the first states to enact land redistribution laws, and where various Naxalite groups continue to fight against landowners, as late as 1993, Maharaja Kumar Singh of Bhojpur and the Tilauthu estate of Rohtas owned more than 700 acres of land each (Louis 2005). This is in gross violation of the land ceiling law, which limits family landownership to 15 acres of land (Louis 2005). In nearly all provinces, landowners were able to retain their large holdings intact. As a result, if we take the land owned by owners with more than 10 acres as a potential pool of surplus land, the land distributed to poor people by 2005 is less than 5% of this potential (and is 1.5% of the total net sown area of the country).[12] The land reforms laws also aimed at regulating rents and providing tenurial security to tenants. Overwhelmingly dependent on landlords for their living, tenants did not even dare to record their names as tenants, and hence could not seek protection from the new laws. Even those registered as tenants could not afford the money necessary to fight a case and wait indefinitely for the judgment. They also did not have the money to buy the land by paying compensation to the landlords.

The abysmal failure of the land reforms legislation can be attributed to two major factors (Das 1999). First, large landowners share state power along with the bourgeoisie. They perform the important role of controlling the rural masses, whose anger against landlordism could be potentially directed at the bourgeoisie itself. So, the bourgeoisie, and the state on its behalf, could not afford to hurt the landowners' interest too much by implementing land reforms. Promises of land reforms on paper were used to quell the resentment of the masses. Second, those who were directly or indirectly responsible for the implementation of the legislation, including judges, came from the landed class or represented their interests. In other words, the state itself, especially at the sub-national scales, was used as an 'instrument' by the landed to thwart land reforms.

Following the failure in the late 1960s of the land reform measures, which were expected to increase land productivity by protecting small-scale peasant farming and tenurial security, the state launched a second rural development policy, the green revolution. This policy aimed at increased food production through technological change. There was a limited improvement in the productive forces, leading to an increase in farm productivity and profitability. Associated with this, the relations of production changed in two ways. Attracted by greater profitability, in many areas landlords evicted their tenants and started direct cultivation by using hired workers some of whom were erstwhile tenants. Thus, capitalist cultivation was given a boost. Initially, laborers obtained some employment at increased wages, but a subsequent increase in the use of machinery threatened to displace a large number of agricultural workers and slowed down/stopped the tendency toward any gain in wages (Das 2002). The state did not, and still does not do much, to make sure landowners pay workers the minimum wages. Thus, while landowners gained, workers did not benefit as much. Chester Bowles, former U.S. Ambassador to India, said on October 30, 1967, when the peasant uprising at Naxalbari had just been crushed: "Landless laborers may accept their wages of two or three rupees a day without much complaint as long as they know that everyone in their village is poor. However, when they see the landowners' incomes rising rapidly while their own rises much more slowly if at all, they become restless and resentful" (in Banerjee 1984).[13] Indeed some of the green revolution areas of central Bihar have become a stronghold of CPI(ML) Liberation (Wilson 1999, 340).

Tenants, who came from middle and poor peasant classes, and who were still used by landowners to cultivate the land, had to pay higher rents because, with increased productivity, land values increased. In many areas, landlords also rotated tenants, leading to enhanced tenurial insecurity, as in the Darjeeling area. The technology itself was expensive. It was generally monopolized by upper-caste owners who control local state apparatuses providing credit and/or subsidized inputs. So, smaller owners, who could not invest as much as larger owners, did not benefit much. Many leased out their land to larger owners because they could not profitably invest in the technology. This is the phenomenon of reverse tenancy. In the specific context of West Bengal, although the green revolution resulted in an overall increase in yields, the tribals of Darjeeling, who had less land and limited access to credit, hardly benefited from the technology (Duyker 1987). Indeed because the technology made it possible to make profits from direct cultivation (as elsewhere), and because the provincial State government sought to (bureaucratically) protect tenants against arbitrary eviction through legislation, landowners started evicting and/or rotating sharecroppers, leading to tribals and poor peasants losing control over land. Finally, the benefits from the green revolution technology were geographically concentrated as a result of a deliberate strategy by the state to concentrate resources in specially endowed areas (e.g., areas with irrigation facilities) to get quick results (Shiva 1991). This meant that vast areas continued to be deprived of public investment, resulting in a low level of development of productive forces and hence poverty.

The green revolution, representing a technological fix to India's rural distress, came to be associated with multiple forms or layers of inequality:

inequality between employers and laborers, between larger and smaller owners, between landlords and tenants, and between peasants in green revolution areas and those in non-green revolution areas. It is these different forms of inequality that led to resentment, which created an ideological climate in the nation for radical action. In this climate, in some areas, including a few districts of the Punjab, a bastion of the green revolution, Naxalism was launched. The green revolution, in a sense, represented a continuity with the earlier program, the land reforms, revealing the class character of the state: while the land reform legislation protected the class interests of the propertied families (landlords, capitalist farmers, rich peasants), who were allowed to possess land beyond the ceiling limit, the green revolution placed new means of production (e.g., the new technological package; credit) precisely in the hands of these families.

As the green revolution could not reduce poverty, in the late 1970s to early 1980s, the state launched the Integrated Rural Development Policy (IRDP). This aimed at giving small loans to poor people to start income-generating activities—setting up small shops, starting dairy businesses, improving farm implements, and the like. This policy, more or less, was also a failure. The overall capitalist system itself, where the use of a nation's resources must be justified mainly on the basis of the profit-logic, put severe limits on the amount of money the capitalist state could commit in the form of pro-poor policies, such as the IRDP,[14] *relative* to the massive need of the tens of millions of the poor whom the system marginalizes (e.g., peasants increasingly losing access to land; people without secure employment for a living wage). And, even the limited money that the state could commit did not reach the intended beneficiaries. A former prime minister was candid enough to say that hardly 10% of the money meant for the poor reached them. It is widely known that officials and politicians work in an utterly undemocratic manner and have unscrupulous links to traders (who were, in many areas, closely connected with the landed class). Therefore, much of the IRDP money ended up in the pockets of the local officials, or with the traders supplying the assets needed for the income-generating activities (e.g., animals; farm implements) (Das 2000). Also, better-off sections, including members of the landed class, received help, although they were ineligible, thus siphoning of the limited money meant for the economically marginalized.

Partly due to the pressure from the parliamentary left, the state started, in 2006, a new policy of employment creation, known as National Rural Employment Guarantee Scheme or NREGS, as many as 15 years after the neoliberal policy was begun.[15] Its aim is to provide at least 100 days of guaranteed waged employment a year to every household whose adult members volunteer to do unskilled manual work at the legislated minimum wage. Early reports suggest that, like the IRDP, a large part of the money meant for this policy has gone to the politicians, officials and property owners (e.g., contractors), except in those few areas where the poor people are able to exercise constant vigilance over the implementation of the scheme (Khera 2008; Liberation 2008; Rai 2007).

In the neoliberal phase, the newly introduced government programs for the poor have largely failed (as earlier), but also earlier programs have been diluted (in several states). This is certainly the case with the land reforms laws mentioned earlier. There is also a dilution of an overall emphasis on state-promoted rural development under neoliberalism, one of the (contradictory)[16] aims of which is to shrink mass income and consumption at home in order to enable cheap exports and repayment of debt to imperialist finance capital (see Patnaik 1999).[17] Since the inception of neoliberal reforms, rural development expenditures as a ratio of the net national product have dropped from 2.8% in 1993–1994 to 2.6% in 1995–1996 to 1.9% in 2000–2001 (Patnaik 2007, 155). The little help available from the government in the name of the economic reforms with a *human* face[18] has not been enough to counter the inhumane effects of neoliberalism (on rural income, employment, and access to land). This has disastrous outcomes, such as declining food availability for the poor,[19] land alienation (especially in tribal areas), and farmers' suicide[20] (whose incidence in Andhra Pradesh is one of the highest in many of the districts most associated with Naxalism).

In discussing the state two issues arise: state form and state policy. Correspondingly, the failure of the state has two aspects: the problematic nature of the *form* of the state and the failure of state's various policies (discussed earlier). In terms of state form, bureaucracy is the characteristic form of the modern state. Bureaucracy insulates the state's everyday activities from democratic influence of the popular masses and makes its everyday operations undemocratic (Das 1996, 50). The formally liberal-democratic Indian state, embedded in a developing capitalist economy, is an exemplar in this regard (Das 2007). Without the popular participation of the poor in the everyday workings of the state, including ways in which pro-poor policies are implemented, government funds meant for the poor are squeezed on their way from the national- and provincial-scale state apparatuses, to the local-scale government officials/politicians. Typically tyrannical, like traditional landlords, government officials and politicians are utterly insensitive to the problems of poor people and generally not accountable to them (Subramanian 1998; Corbridge and Harriss 2000, 201–202). This is seen, for example, in the autocratic management of forests by state officials, guarded by corrupt politicians, and supported by traders, creating serious alienation amongst the forest-dependent tribals, one of the most oppressed subaltern groups in the country (Guha 2007). Officials use administrative coercion, resorting to complex rules that the poor do not understand, and naked physical coercion to oppress and exploit the poor. The bureaucratic state form signifies a serious contradiction: between the state's *formal* democratic appearance and its *actual* functioning at the local scale. Like pro-poor *policies*, the liberal-democratic *form* raises expectation of democratic functioning by the masses, but frustrates that expectation, prompting Naxalite-type anti-state activity.

Apart from the bureaucratic form, the state also has a spatial form. State spatial form refers to two things. First, there is the scale division of labor (Cox and Mair 1991) within the state: the idea that state apparatuses work at local, provincial, and national scales. Decentralization of state power—creation of smaller states and smaller districts—is supposed to be good for the poor in terms of expediting implementation of pro-poor policies. This did not happen. And failure has given rise to resentment against the nation-state, especially in areas occupied by tribals, who in practice are not considered parts of the nation (see Stiefel and Wolfe 1994, 71). Peasant armed insurgency has tended to take place in such areas (Dhanagare 1991, 226; Brass 1994, 325). Exploited through caste structures (by upper castes coming from outside of tribal areas), class structures (by landlords/traders, etc.), and the state structure (by bureaucrats), tribal people have a deep-rooted sense of neglect. Prior to the creation of the new State of Jharkhand, out of the undivided State of Bihar, for example, the feeling was that the region was backward because of the political and bureaucratic establishment, which was dominated by officials from 'non-tribal' areas of Bihar. But problems remained even after the new state was created. This is the case in Uttarakhand (another new state created out of a larger State, Uttar Pradesh), and also in Orissa where new smaller districts were carved out of bigger ones. Not surprisingly, state institutions in both Orissa and Jharkhand worry about the Naxalite threat.

Second, an additional aspect of the spatial form of the state is its geographically fragmentary nature. The state is 'absent' from parts of the territory supposedly under its jurisdiction. Many parts of India (as many parts of the Global South in general) are characterized by the lack of penetration of the state into society, physically as well as institutionally (Migdal 1988). Physically outlying regions of the state may not have been integrated strongly into the state apparatus, partly as a consequence of the uneven economic development characteristic of capitalism. To the extent that the state can and does deliver limited benefits to the poor to gain legitimacy for itself and the ruling classes (albeit in a corrupt and undemocratic manner), lack of state penetration contributes to the lack of development relative to 'core' areas. This has led to people's resentment. In some areas, the administrative systems have collapsed, with no government doctors, teachers, or officials present (Chaudhuri 2001). Law enforcement authorities are virtually absent from these areas. The laws enacted by the state are hardly heard of; and life for the poor is nasty, brutish, and short (Chaudhuri 2001). This situation symbolizes the process of the state being hollowed out, a process intensified when the neoliberal state's commitment to the welfare of the poor is being diluted. It has also created a void that is partly filled by the Naxalite movement.

The ways the private sector has worked and the state's failure to provide adequate help to the poor have produced a situation where millions have not had enough to eat. The official poverty line is based on "inadequate absolute standards" which do not reflect "norms of dignified human living" (Mehta 2002, 34). Even so, the percentage of poor people in the total population went from 38% in 1960–1961 to 54% in 1968–1969, years of the original launch of the Naxalite activity. Many people died from starvation. In terms of the incidence of the movement (in relation to rural developmental distress) in more recent times, available statistical data shed light on important aspects of the agrarian distress. These can be summarized as follows: (1) In 1999–2000, there were 260 million people including 190 million rural poor, living below the official poverty line (which is in fact a kind of 'hunger line'): this means that more than one in every four Indians, and nearly a third of its rural population, was in official poverty (GOI 2001). If we use the minimum calorie intake necessary for survival (2,400 calories a day) as a criterion, 75% of the rural population cannot meet this level and therefore are in caloric poverty (Patnaik 2007, 189). Thus, the potential support base of Naxalite-type movements among poor people is simply huge. (2) Geographically, a person living in villages is more likely to be poor than an urban person.[21] This matches with the Naxalite ideological stress on rural class-struggle. (3) The percentage of the rural population that is poor in the states affected by moderate or heavy Naxalism is generally above the all-India average (Table13. 1, columns 3).[22] (4) The average monthly per capita expenditure of rural poor households and the overall level of rural development tend to be lower in all major Naxal-affected states than the all-India average (Table 13.2). (5) The official poverty level for dalits and tribes, the groups Naxalites are most closely associated with, tend to be higher than for others; this is the case both at the all-India level and in the major Naxal-affected states (Table 13.1, columns 1–2).[23]

Table 13.1 Naxalism and Rural Poverty (1999–2000) among Most Oppressed Groups

% of poor among	*Dalits*	*Scheduled Tribes*	*All groups*
Andhra Pradesh	16.5	23.1	11.05
Bihar[1]	59.1	58.7	44.03
Madhya Pradesh[2]	41.2	57.1	37.06
Orissa	—	73.0	48.01
West Bengal	34.9	50.1	31.85
All States[3]	35.3	44.2	
All-India (rural)[4]	26.5		

Source: Radhakrishnan et al. 2004 in GOI 2005. (1) Includes Jharkhand. (2) Includes Chhattisgarh. (3) All states = percentage of poverty among scheduled castes or among tribes in rural India as a whole. (4) Poverty ratio for rural India as a whole (note that the figure of 26.5 is a little different from the more widely accepted figure of 27.09).

Table 13.2 Incidence of Naxalism and Monthly Average Per Capita Expenditure of Poor People (Rupees) in 1999–2000

	Poor	*Composite Index of Rural Development*
Andhra Pradesh	215	99.3
Bihar[1]	269	70.1
Madhya Pradesh[2]	250	86.8
Orissa	248	93.2
West Bengal	281	103.2
All India	282	115.8 (un-weighted average of all states)

Source: GOI 2005. (1) Includes Jharkhand. (2) Includes Chhattisgarh.

4. NAXALITE INTERVENTIONS

Thus, vast areas, and a large proportion of the national population, have not enjoyed a life of economic security and dignity since independence. The objective conditions exist for a radical movement for justice. The ideological emphasis of the Naxalite movement on agrarian distress and mobilization of peasants is rooted in, and reflects, these conditions. But these two factors—Naxalite *ideology* and the *objective* conditions—do not fully explain the continuation of the movement. One must also consider the possibility that, unless the Naxalites are able to provide some help to the poor in the short and medium term, their appeal will diminish in the context of ruthless repression by the state.

In terms of ideology, the Naxalites have tirelessly pointed out the existence of feudal exploitation and oppression in rural India. Considering the Indian society to be "semi-colonial", the movement is critical of imperialist globalization during the neoliberal era which has hurt millions. The Naxalite groups see the Indian capitalist class as subservient to imperialist powers. According to them the fast rate of economic growth under neoliberalism is mainly identified with India's monopoly houses, whereas agriculture, small-scale industries, and much of the manufacturing sector lag behind miserably (Mohanty 2006, 3164). They have also developed a caste-class theory of Indian society: class and caste relations are seen as interacting in significant ways, with immensely adverse consequences for the poor. One segment of the movement (People's War Group or PWG which is now a part of the CPI(Maoist)), has rearticulated Marx to read "all hitherto history of India is a history of class and caste struggles" (Gudavarthy 2005, 5414). That most Naxalites come from lower-middle-class backgrounds, and choose to live in poverty among the poor, including the tribals (Guha 2007, 3309), is an additional ideological factor appealing to sections of the oppressed.

The Naxalites have also delivered some relief. State agencies ignore or violate the (welfare-oriented) laws in their own interests and in the interests of propertied classes, while the laws are enforced by those, like Naxalites, whom they consider lawless 'extremists' (Banerjee 2008). The Naxalites have tried to ensure justice through direct means. The history of the Naxalite movement is in many ways the history of "courageous battles against a vicious state machinery followed by self-sacrifice by thousands of guerrillas, and patient efforts by dedicated cadres to initiate land reforms and social changes in their areas of control" (Banerjee 2006, 3159). For instance, the granaries of landlords were ransacked in Naxalbari and elsewhere, and records of people's debts to the moneylenders were burned. The Naxalite groups have taken land from landlords and given it to poor peasants and landless laborers, something the state should have done long ago.

In the tribal belts, the Naxalites are widely popular because they give protection to the forest-dwellers for cultivation in 'reserve' forests, and confer various other economic and social benefits on them (Balagopal 2006, 2185–2186). They have taken up issues of fixing prices for forest produce, the most important being raising of prices of "tendu patta" from Rs. 2 for 100 bundles (of 100 leaves each) in the early 1980s to Rs. 80 by the mid-1990s. Fearful of the Naxalites, traders now pay a better price. The Naxalites have provided some protection to tribals from harassment by the police and the forest and revenue department officials (Guha,2007, 3182). Under neoliberalism, which emphasizes export-oriented capitalist development, domestic and foreign big business seeks to take control of the natural resources (e.g., minerals; land) existing in many tribal territories. Along with others, including progressive civil society groups, the Naxalites are a major force mobilizing the tribals both against land alienation (e.g., in Kalinga Nagar and Orissa) and against the destruction of their environment by neoliberal capitalist development in these territories (see Kujur 2006).

In non-tribal areas as well, where attempts have been made to trample on the land and water rights of poorer people to promote neoliberal development, Naxalites have fought, in their areas of influence, against such attempts (e.g., the SEZ cases in West Bengal). In my own research I have seen the CPI(ML) Liberation mobilizing the fishermen castes around the lake Chilika in Orissa, where traditional fishing rights are being violated by rich investors of non-fishermen caste, encouraged by the policy of neoliberalism.[24] Naxalites run schools, health systems, rural credit and seed banks, small irrigation projects, and the like for the rural poor (Navlakha 2006, 2188). They have ensured more equitable access to village commons. In some areas, even government officials admit, Naxalite organizations have successfully protested the non-payment of minimum wages (e.g., green revolution areas in Bihar) (Wilson, 1999, 340; Louis 2005). During the 1960s, and after, their influence generated a 'competitive leftism'; this is a situation where parliamentary left parties also mobilized peasants to expand their spheres of influence, in competition with the Naxalites. Thus, the Naxalites have had a positive 'externality' effect in development.

The Naxalites have pushed gender-sensitive reforms within the *adivasi* (tribal) society, including inside families, and have curbed feudal practices and social oppression (Bhatia 2006). The social basis of CPI(ML) Liberation in Bihar has been very much centred on the dalits' struggle for land, wages, and dignity. In some places, they have organized separate anti-caste mass organizations and fought for legal and socio-economic benefits, including reservation of jobs in the private sector (Gudavarthy 2005). In Andhra Pradesh, because of the influence of Naxalites, the dalit movement introduced a novel combinatory language such as "dalit communists" struggling against a "Hindu feudal order" for a "new dalit democratic revolution" (Gudavarthy 2005, 5418)

Politically, they have tried to "help the adivasi peasantry or dalit labouring classes in some very backward regions to emerge as an independent political force" freed from the influence of landlords and traders, and this "does represent a step forward in democratising Indian society" (Gupta 2006, 3173). If the battles of the rural poor in Bihar or Telengana target both class exploitation and caste oppression, and if struggles in the forests of Dandakaranya or Jharkhand seek to combine class demands with that of self-identity, dignity, and autonomy, Naxalites have played important roles (Gupta 2006). They have actually forced the traditional left and the state to recognize that the poor—poor peasants, laborers, and tribals—cannot always and everywhere be taken for granted, and that they, will not always accept the gap between 'development proper' and 'paper development'.[25]

5. LIMITATIONS OF THE NAXALITE MOVEMENT

The Naxalite movement has a large following because of the three factors, discussed previously: failure of capitalist development; failure of the capitalist state; and pro-poor political-economic interventions of the Naxalites. But could it have a *larger* following, socially and geographically? Banerjee (1996, 222), a sympathetic commentator, says, "[I]n terms of spatial growth", the Naxalite groups have "virtually lost their original pockets in West Bengal", and "have failed to extend their influence beyond their traditional bases" mainly located in the eastern half of the country. The movement has produced some definitely positive effects on the conditions of the poor, the sections of the population often ignored by the traditional left. But could it be *more* effective in addressing their daily problems? In other words, what are the limitations—and indeed limits—to the Naxalite movement, including that segment which exclusively focuses on the armed struggle against the state?

The movement is not particularly powerful in the areas of strong agrarian capitalism, in spite of wage struggles in some green revolution areas. It is generally confined to areas where the development of capitalist relations of exploitation is relatively stunted. A certain segment of the Naxalite movement (CPI(Maoist)) is almost totally confined to the areas demographically dominated by tribals (who constitute less than 10% of the total population of the country). This strategy is not sufficiently sensitive to class differentiation in the tribal population (Brass 2000). It also leaves out vast sections of distressed people, especially the non-tribal poor peasantry and laborers. The Naxalite mobilization is also generally absent from urban areas, which are growing everyday, with the influx of rural people displaced by neoliberal policies (Sagar 2006, 3178). This means that the movement is weakly integrated into the class struggle of the non-agrarian working class.

There is, in my view, a theoretical reason for all this, which I will *briefly* mention. Firstly, while rightly emphasizing the importance of caste and gender, ideologues of the movement tend to conflate these non-class relations with class relations: oppressive caste and gender relations, and especially caste relations, are seen by them as necessarily indicative of some kind of feudalism. More importantly, they mistake feudal relations of exploitation for what are really capitalist relations at a low level of development of productive forces. This explains why the extent of feudal exploitation (as captured by their use of the concept of 'semi-feudalism') is overestimated, and why, therefore, politically, the movement is confined mainly to economically backward areas, ignoring vast swathes of the country reeling under capitalist, and especially neoliberal-capitalist, exploitation. They believe in a two-stage theory of revolution: a democratic revolution first, and a socialist revolution sometime in the future. Thus, effectively, the Naxalites now fight for a bourgeois society cleared of vestiges of feudalism. Many of them struggle for an authentic system of (liberal) democracy, one without autocratic and bureaucratic distortions, before any fight against capitalist relations as such can begin.[26] Their ideological-political focus on what they call feudalism will continue to keep millions of toiling people outside of their influence,[27] whose lives are adversely impacted by the bourgeoisie, including its so-called 'national' faction.[28] This will be the case *unless* the fight against localized feudal practices becomes a part of the fight against the capitalist system *as such*, whether the 'bearers' (Marx 1977, 92) of that system are 'national', monopoly, or imperialist capitalists. Indeed, their near-absence in, for example, Gujarat, which combines a vicious form of (politically supported) neoliberal capitalism with an equally virulent form of (politically supported) communalism, is a moot point to consider.

Secondly, there are the issues of caste and gender. The Naxalite movement has paid more attention to these issues than the traditional left. Yet, some critics say, patriarchal attitudes and practices persist within Naxal organizations (Mohanty 2006, 3164). Women are almost negligible in leadership positions. In terms of caste, the hard and dangerous work of handling guns is mainly done by dalits or people from the lower castes. Those who get killed belong mostly to these sections (Bhatia 2006, 3180). True, tribals, dalits, and other low-caste people comprise the bulk of their support base. But 'they are not [yet] adequately represented in the upper echelons of the party leadership' (Bhatia 2006, 3180). Culturally, while "song writing, tune setting and writing of poetry [generally] . . . centred around the SC (Scheduled Castes) and OBC (Other Backward Classes) *wadas* in the villages, . . . writing theory and speech making still remained an upper caste phenomenon" within the movement (Ilaiah 2004, 238).

Thirdly, the violence practiced by Maoist revolutionary squads, as a part of the Naxalite movement, must be seen as problematic on strategic and tactical grounds. Obtaining and keeping the right to vote is always a concession that has had to be struggled for by left-democratic forces. The ensuing liberal democratic process offers some limited possibilities for exposing the patently undemocratic practices of the Indian state, the ruling classes (domestic and foreign), and for educating the masses about the limits to what is possible within the system and about alternative anti-capitalist, anti-feudal programs. That the liberal democratic process provides some political space for pursuing people's causes is a factor yet to be fully recognized in the Naxalite political discourse (Mohanty 2006). It is not enough that Naxalite leaders and ideologues themselves know that the state (and the ruling classes) cannot meet the radical-democratic demands of the poor. To paraphrase Marx's *Thesis on Feuerbach* (Marx and Engels 1977, 13), whether the state and the ruling classes can meet the radical demands of the exploited classes cannot be (just) a '*scholastic* question'[29]; but, much rather, it must be resolved in practice (i.e., through their own struggles for their radical demands), and it is 'a *practical* question', therefore. And with Naxalite areas being among the poorest in the country, "there is no dearth of essential demands" to struggle for: there could be struggles for such things as publicly provided "schools, electricity, water and health centres" (Bhatia 2006, 3181), for a decent living wage and for the right to employment. The importance of the demands like these has increased under neoliberalism because of the state's and ruling classes' obsession with mindless economic growth, an obsession which has resulted in the sheer neglect of the living conditions of the poor. "However, these issues get eclipsed since most of the Naxalite groups do not wish to engage with the present government except as an enemy" (Bhatia 2006, 3181). This is because Naxalite leaders assume that their *theoretical* knowledge about the state (what it can and cannot do) is shared by the masses. This is a serious epistemological lapse. Democratic mass movements are necessary in struggling to get concessions from the state and the propertied classes.[30] They are also necessary for building solidarity and promoting class-consciousness among the exploited classes who must emerge as agents of their self-emancipation *in the process of* fighting for these concessions at multiple scales.

Indeed, "the success and popularity of the Naxalite movement itself owes more to the achievements of its open mass movements than to armed action" by secretly operating squads (Bhatia 2006, 3182). Sometimes secretive violent actions may have helped the mass movement. This happens when the party offers 'protection' to mass fronts (e.g., student or women organizations led by Naxalites) at open mass meetings: in many parts of the country, such as in Bihar, laborers did not even have the right to hold a meeting, as this outraged the landlords (Bhatia 2006, 3182). But such a relation between the party and mass movements is not without problems. For instance, if a mass organization is engaged in a struggle for ceiling surplus land, and if the party decides to 'annihilate' the landlord, the state is likely to target the members of the open front since they are the only visible actors. Thus, members of the mass front pay the price for actions taken by the underground party (Bhatia 2006). Further, where the Naxalite movement seeks to ensure justice by means of armed squads, this signifies that the beneficiaries of justice tend not to be involved in the process of obtaining justice.[31] The masses tend to think of the squads "as a substitute for their own struggle for justice" (Balagopal 2006, 3185). This can corrupt—some might say, has corrupted—the masses into receivers of justice rather than fighters for it in a process of *self-emancipation*. There was armed action in the early stages of the Naxalbari movement. But this was engaged in by peasants during direct action against landlords (e.g., occupying surplus land or destroying usury records). The use of secretive violent methods by squads is a different matter. It does make it difficult to launch non-electoral radical mass movements.

The Naxalites' armed action is being used by the state as a justification for killing Naxalite supporters who include the organic leaders of the exploited classes.[32] Continuous armed conflicts between state forces and Naxalites have also drastically reduced the space for other forms of struggle (non-violent struggles). In many areas, anyone who challenges the government about its inactions and who fights for legal rights (e.g., payment of minimum wages) runs the risk of being labeled a Naxalite. And, the 'Naxal label' means punishment.

The use of violence affects the political culture of the movement. First, the quality of the loyalty of the followers can be problematic. It becomes difficult to know whether the people are in it voluntarily or involuntarily (Bhatia 2006, 3181). Once one is labeled a Naxalite, it is difficult to return to normal life, relatively free from suspicion, fear, and death. So people depend on the party to help them, as they themselves are unable to deal with the police and the courts. Thus, many people may remain in the party because they need the party's protection (Bhatia 2006). Secondly, there is a culture of intolerance among the Naxalites toward those holding a different political view. This can be observed not only vis-à-vis political opponents from mainstream parties and parties of the parliamentary left, but also toward other Naxalite factions, which is often resolved through violent encounter. Further, many times, ordinary people are killed because they are seen as police informers. This has caused alienation of the Naxalites from a section of their own support-base, including the urban intelligentsia, and tribal and poor people (Sagar 2006, 3177).

6. CONCLUSION

The Naxalite movement originated because of a specific class structure. It has tried to change certain aspects of that structure, such as extra-economic aspects of class exploitation and unequal distribution of land. It is, therefore, arguably a radical social movement. I relate the emergence and continuation of this movement to twin developmental failures: failure of private sector development process and the failure of the post-colonial state, including in its neoliberal form, to bring benefits to vast sections of the (rural) population. I then briefly pose a much-neglected but potentially large question of the Naxalite movement itself as an alternative agent of development. So if the movement continues to exist, it is not just because of this twin failure but also because of the success of the Naxalites in providing some relief to the suffering masses. Having discussed this, I briefly point out major limitations of the movement itself. Acknowledging that it has a large following, I briefly make the argument that if more people and more areas are not under its influence, this is partly because of specific failures in the movement itself. One aspect of this is the failure to target the capitalist character of Indian society head on. This ideological-strategic deficiency is stark, especially under neoliberalism, which has become an important way in which imperialist institutions and companies attempt to entrench capitalist relations in new areas. The second aspect of the failure is tactical: a section of the movement exclusively focusing on armed struggle to bring about a change in the balance of power between landlords and masses. No one is saying class struggle is easy to mobilize and conduct. But it is difficult to reduce, conceptually and politically, *class* struggle to *military* struggle. There is no shortcut to revolutionary self-emancipation of the exploited.

In the process of making these arguments, I make two general points, critical of both the state and the Naxalites. One, the Naxalite movement is rooted in material conditions of deprivation, which are social-cultural and economic. Going beyond class reductionism, and the reductionism of identity politics, they have fruitfully combined class politics (albeit in a rather limited manner) as well as those of cultural oppression. Thus, the Naxalite movement shares important characteristics of what Veltmeyer (1997) calls "new peasant movements" in his research on peasants in Latin America (which, incidentally, also happens to have witnessed Maoist-inspired radical activity). Many people within the state agencies, and many middle-class people, do not consistently and fully understand Naxalites' pro-poor ideological significance. Partly influenced by a militaristic thinking, they homogenize the movement, ignoring that it is internally diverse in terms of its tactics, which change over time, from one area to another area, from one Naxalite group to another group. They associate the Naxalite movement exclusively with violence, and treat Naxalites merely/mainly as armed thugs, without any political and socio-economic program of development for the poor.[33]

Second, the material conditions of deprivation are produced dominantly by the specific ways in which capitalism works in the concrete conditions of India, which include social-economic remnants of feudalism, and formal democracy, within the system of global neoliberal capitalism. The Naxalites have thus not fully and consistently understood that the most important reason for rural distress, and indeed the distress of the majority of the country's population, is the *capitalist* character of the system, which is also mainly responsible for state's failure to mitigate some of the adverse effects of the system on the poor,[34] a fact increasingly clear under neoliberalism. Because of the Naxalites' inadequate understanding of the system's dynamics, their dominant focus has been mistakenly on the rural/agrarian issue (in backward regions) and on its so-called 'semi-feudal' shell.

NOTES

1. The underlying perspective prioritizes contradiction (Ollman 2003): between what happens and what can happen, between what the expectation/hope is (from state policies, for example) and what is actually delivered.
2. The epistemological importance of the Naxalite movement is that it raises extremely important theoretical questions. These include the theory of capitalism and feudalism (in less developed societies), (revolutionary) violence (in relation to class struggle/social movement), class (in relation to caste, gender and ethnicity), the state and democracy (in the post-colonial context), and development, and regionally uneven development. This chapter has, more or less, avoided a *theoretical* treatment of these questions. In my discussion of the movement in the chapter, I have generally restricted myself to the empirical level which is a part of my wider theoretical and empirical study of the movement in which some of these theoretical issues are addressed (e.g., capitalism, the state, and democracy in relation to Naxalism).
3. Thus, the Naxalite movement, which is a product of definite contradictions, represents a new contradiction: between what it can achieve and what it achieves.
4. This area is strategically important as it is not far off from Bangladesh, Nepal, and China.
5. CPI(M) has spread itself from the Telengana region of Andhra Pradesh to the tribal-dominated districts of adjoining Maharashtra, Chhatishgarh, Jharkhand, and Orissa.
6. Liberation has its bases primarily in Bihar and pockets of influence in Uttar Pradesh, West Bengal, Assam, Tamilnadu and Punjab, and Orissa.
7. Operated land is land owned plus land leased in minus land leased out.
8. The recent CPI(M)-led land struggle in Andhra Pradesh is an exception.
9. This conclusion is based on Prasad's study of Bihar villages, where Naxalites are active.
10. This is not to say that they have totally ignored the issue, however.

11. One of these, the Ranvir Sena (army), was formed in 1994 to answer the new assertiveness of the agricultural laborers with more effective repression, through the creation of a professional militia with better training, weaponry, and leadership. The Sena enjoys the protection of much of the political elite across party lines (Kumar 1999).
12. By March 2005, only 5.4 million acres were distributed in a country of 351 million acres of net sown area (GOI 2007, Tables 3.c and 3.3). Owners with more than 10 acres own 34.63% of the land and account for 12.78% of rural households including the landless (Bhalla 2007).
13. This statement from Bowles, interestingly, echoes Marx's (1976, 33) famous statement on relative poverty and relative wages in his *Wage-Labour and Capital*: "A house may be large or small; as long as the neighboring houses are likewise small, it satisfies all social requirements for a residence. But let there arise next to the little house a palace, and the little house shrinks into a hut . . . and the occupant of the relatively little house will always find himself more uncomfortable, more dissatisfied . . .". The process of capitalist development that the green revolution hastened created a condition in which millions of laborers and poor peasants became 'dissatisfied' in the Marx sense. This condition was a part of the overall climate that was behind the Naxalite movement. In fact, as discussed later, the fact that there has not been a stronger Naxalites-led mass movement in green revolution areas is ironic.
14. This also applies to the public distribution system or PDS which aimed at providing subsidized food to the poor.
15. Of course, policies such as this are expected to help the state to politically manage the adverse effects of neoliberalism on the poor who could pose a legitimacy threat to the system, a threat which is partly expressed, although not unambiguously, in the form of electoral reverses of parties in power. That NREGS did politically help the ruling Congress was clear in the recent election in which it was successful. Seen from a perspective that privileges contradiction, a pro-poor policy like NREGS has helped the Congress, the traditional party of big business, to return to power to implement *more* anti-poor neoliberal policies, which may, in turn, open up spaces for left struggles, including those by Naxalites (Das 2009).
16. The contradictory character is evident in a stark manner during the current crisis: economies dependent on external (e.g., imperialist) markets and having ignored domestic mass market (consumption needs of the vast majority) will be particularly vulnerable.
17. Shrinking income and consumption of the toiling classes is the characteristic aspect of neoliberalism *everywhere* (including in imperialist countries), not just in peripheral countries. There are two implications of this. Ideologically this means that capital has no real nationality (in many ways) (capitalists would not necessarily say, "We will be nice to Canadian or American people and nasty to Indian or Chinese people"). Politically, this means that there a potential basis for international solidarity of working class and peasants against capital, including its neoliberal *avatar*, everywhere and at all scales.
18. The fact that ruling class and the state use this phrase indicates that they admit that economic reforms are inhumane.
19. The daily net availability of foodgrains (food production plus import minus export) per person has gone down from 510 grammes in 1991–92 to 470 grammes in 1994–95 to 434 grammes in 2001–02 (Patnaik, 1999: Table 12; 2007: Table 4).
20. Patnaik (2007) provides statistical data on farmers' suicide in Andhra districts.

21. The percentage of the rural population that is officially poor is 27.09%; the urban figure is 23.62% (GOI 2005, Table 3.1). The rural infant mortality is 66 out of 1000, while the urban infant mortality is 38 out of 1000 in 2003 (GOI 2007, 19). The relative infant mortality gap between rural and urban areas—the ratio of the rural infant mortality rate to the urban infant mortality rate—has indeed increased between 1995 and 2003.
22. Andhra Pradesh is an exception. It is, geographically, the largest among all Naxal-affected states. It should be noted that poverty level is expected to be very high among the tribal population in Andhra districts where the Naxalite movement is strong.
23. Of course, there are numerous areas where the level of developmental distress is high (e.g., higher than the national average), and yet, there is no Naxal activity. Naxals have been active only in *some* of the distressed areas. The point is that where the level of distress is low, the Naxal-type movement is likely, showing that the Naxalite movement does not hang in the air: it is materially rooted. But objective conditions do not guarantee that a radical movement will occur, least of all, a given type of movement (e.g., Naxalism). There can be no one-to-one relation between development distress and a political activity, including Naxalism.
24. That the traditional Left has also played some role in slowing down neoliberalization (and in forcing the state to implement some pro-poor measures) is also un-deniable.
25. This refers to promises of development in government documents.
26. According to CPI(ML) Liberation, "Indian society is marked by four main contradictions—the contradiction between imperialism and Indian nation, that between feudalism and the broad masses of the people, between big capital and the Indian people, the working class in particular, and the contradiction among various sections of the ruling classes . . . [The] *principal* contradiction [is] between feudal remnants and the broad Indian masses, for the feudal remnants constitute the biggest stumbling block on the road to free and rapid development of productive forces in the country. *This determines the stage of our revolution—the stage of people's democratic revolution with agrarian revolution as its axis. [The]* primary aim of this democratic revolution will be to abolish all feudal remnants and the concomitant autocratic and bureaucratic distortions in the polity . . ." [http://cpiml.org/8th_ congress/partyprogramme.html; italics added (accessed on August 10, 2009)].

    The analysis of another major Naxalite stream—CPI(ML) New Democracy—is almost exactly the same. It quite clearly expresses its two-stage theory: "The Indian Revolution, taken as a whole, passes through *two distinct stages* of historical development, i.e. the people's democratic and the socialist revolution . . . How rapidly the socialist revolution will be completed will depend on the degree of our strength, the strength of the conscious and organized proletariat, the unity and organization of the Indian toilers under the hegemony of the proletariat and on the strength of the world socialist movement". And who will participate in the first stage of the revolution? "The people's democratic revolution under the leadership of the working class will establish a democratic dictatorship of the working class, the peasantry, the urban petty bourgeoisie and the *national bourgeoisie* under the leadership of the working majority of the Indian people". The new, people's democratic state will ensure the "*Protection of Industry and trade of national bourgeoisie*" [http://www.cpimlnd.org/party-documents, italics added (accessed August 10, 2009)].

27. These comprise the vast reserve army of laborers in rural areas (including those with small pieces of land) and in urban slums. This reserve army raises the level of exploitation of the currently employed through the mechanisms of low wages and overwork, despotically imposed by capital, and this reduces employment opportunities of those who are a part of the reserve army, as Marx argued in chapter 25 of *Capital* volume 1. What follows is that those who are employed *and* those who are not are both impacted by the capitalist system.
28. The 'national' faction will be a part of their people's democratic state.
29. Marxists have made the theoretical argument that the state will not cross some well-defined limits in terms of meeting the demands of exploited classes (Das 1996). Those who are not convinced by this *theoretical* answer may find the answer in and through practice (= struggle). It is interesting that feminists and anti-casteist thinkers and activists believe that the state is not as inflexible as Marxists think because it can meet a variety of *their* demands (see Gudavarthy 2005, 5417).
30. It is difficult to believe that sick, hungry, absolutely illiterate peasants can actively participate in an ideologically driven organized mass movement for self-emancipation.
31. This is not vastly dissimilar to the Left government giving some crumbs to the poor.
32. They are killed by landlord armies supported by mainstream political parties. They are also killed by the state's military forces or by state-sponsored civilian militias.
33. Of course, a segment of the movement is itself no less responsible for such a perception as it too seems to be eager to propagate armed struggle (Gupta 2006, 3172).
34. It is the capitalist system, characterized by increasing commodification and exploitation that creates such problems as landlessness, unemployment, poverty, and the like. And it is this system itself that puts severe limits on the state's financial ability to commit an adequate amount of resources in the form of anti-poverty policies to assist the poor.

REFERENCES

Balagopal, K. 2006. Chattisgarh: The physiognomy of violence. *Economic and Political Weekly* 41(21): 2183–2186.

Banerjee, S. 1984. *India's simmering revolution: The Naxalite uprising.* London: Zed.

———. 1996. Strategy and forms of political participation among left parties. In *Class formation and political transformation in post-colonial India*, edited by T. Sathyamurthy, 202–237. Delhi: Oxford University Press.

———. 2006. Beyond Naxalbari. *Economic and Political Weekly* 41(29): 3159–3163.

———. 2008. On the Naxalite movement: A report with a difference. *Economic and Political Weekly* 43(21): 10–12.

Bhalla, G. 2006. *Indian agriculture since Independence.* Delhi: National Book Trust.

Bhatia, B. 2006. On armed resistance. *Economic and Political Weekly* 41(29) 3179–3183.

Brass, P. 1994. *The politics of India since independence.* Cambridge: Cambridge University Press.

Brass, T. 2000. *Peasants, Populism and Postmodernism.* London: Frank Cass.

Chaudhuri, K. 2001. A Naxalite offensive in Orissa. *Frontline* 18:18. http://www.frontlineonnet.com/fl1818/fl181800.htm.

Cockburn, C. . ed. 1998. *The space between us: Negotiating gender and national identities in conflict*. London: Zed.

Cambridge, S. and J. Harriss, 2000. Reinventing India: Liberalisation, Hindu Nationalism and Popular democracy. Delhi: Oxford University Press.

Cox, K., and A. Mair 1991. From localised social structures to localities as agents. *Environment and Planning A* 23(2): 197–213.

Damas, M. 1991. *Approaching Naxalbari*. Calcutta: Radical Impression.

Das, R. 1996. State theories: A critical analysis. *Science and Society* 60(1): 27–57.

———. 1999. The spatiality of class and state power: The case of Indian land reforms. *Environment and Planning A* 31(12): 2103–2126.

———. 2000. The state-society relation: The case of an anti-poverty policy. *Environment and Planning C: Government and Policy* 18(6): 631–650.

———. 2002. The green revolution and poverty: A theoretical and empirical examination of the relation between technology and society. *Geoforum* 33(1): 55–72.

———. 2007. *Looking, but not seeing: State* and/as class in rural India. Special issue on Peasant, State and Class, *Journal of Peasant Studies* 34(3–4): 408–440.

———. 2009. What is the left to do in India? *Relay: A Socialist Project Review*, No. 26: 58–60.

Dhanagare, D. 1991. *Peasant movements in India*. Delhi: Oxford University Press.

Duyker, E. 1987. Tribal Guerillas: The Santhals of West Bengal and the Naxalite movement, Delhi; Oxford University Press.

Frankel, F. 1990. Caste, land and dominance in Bihar: breakdown of the Brahminical order. In *Dominance and state power,* vol. 1, edited by F. Frankel and M. Rao, 46–132. Delhi: Oxford University Press.

Giminez, M. 2005. Capitalism and the oppression of women: Marx revisited. *Science & Society* 69(1): 11–32.

GOI (Government of India). 2001. India: *Rural development statistics, 2000*. Hyderabad: National Institute of Rural Development.

———. 2005. *India: Rural Development Report*. Hyderabad: National Institute of Rural Development.

———. 2007. *India: Rural Development Report: 2006–2007*. Hyderabad: National Institute of Rural Development,.

Gudavarthy, A. 2005. Dalit and Naxalite movement in Andhra Pradesh. *Economic and Political Weekly* 40(51): 5410–5418.

Guha, R. 2007. Adivasis, Naxalites and democracy. *Economic and Political Weekly* 42(32): 3305–3312.

Gupta, T. 2006. Maoism in India. *Economic and Political Weekly* 41(29): 3172–3176.

Human Rights Watch. 1999. *Broken people: Caste violence against India's 'untouchables'*. New York: Human Rights Watch Organization.

Ilaiah, K. 2004. Caste, or class or caste-class: A study in Dalitbahujan consciousness and struggles in Andhra Pradesh in 1980s. In *Class, caste, and gender*, edited by M. Mohanty, 227–255. Delhi: Sage.

Jalal, A. 1995. *Democracy and authoritarianism in South Asia*. Cambridge: Cambridge University Press.

Khera, R. 2008. Empowerment guarantee act. *Economic and Political Weekly* 43(35): 8–10.

Kujur, R. 2006. Under development and Naxal movement. *Economic and Political Weekly* 41(7): 557–559.

Kumar, A. 1999. 'Massacres by landlord militia rock India's second most populous state', http://www.wsws.org/articles/1999/feb1999/ind2-f24.shtml

Liberation. 2003. Women agricultural labour struggles: Key issues. http://www.cpiml.org/liberation/year_2003/february. Accessed Dec. 20, 2007.

———. 2008. CAG audit interim report: NREGA being mocked in Spirit? http://www.cpiml.org/ liberation/year_2008/ February/ cag_nrega.html. Accessed Jan, 2008.

Louis, P. 2000. Shankarbigha revisited. *Economic and Political Weekly* 35(7): 507–509.

———. 2005. Jehanabad II: Viewing Bihar. *Economic and Political Weekly* 40(51): 5371–5372.

Marx, K. 1976. *Wage-labour and capital.* New York: International Publishers.

———. 1977. *Capital,* vol. 1. New York: Vintage.

Marx, K., and F. Engels 1977. *Selected works.* Moscow: Progress Publishers.

McDowell, L. 2008. Thinking through class and gender in the context of working class studies. *Antipode* 40(1): 20–24.

McIntyre, M. 2002. The co-production of race and class in Brazil and the United States. *Antipode* 34(2): 168–175.

Mehta, J. 2002. Give poverty a face, please. *Alternative Economic Survey: 2000–2001,* 29–34. Delhi: Rainbow Publishers.

Migdal, J. 1988. Strong Societies and Weak States: State Society Relations and State Capabilities in the Third World. Princeton: Princeton University Press.

Mohanty, M. 2006. Challenges of revolutionary violence. *Economic and Political Weekly* 41(29): 3163–3168.

Navlakha, G. 2006. Maoists in India. *Economic and Political Weekly* 41(22): 2186–2189.

Nathan, D. 1996. Agricultural labourer and the poor peasant in Bihar. In edited by T. Sathyamurthy, 151–178.

Ollman, B. 2003. *Dance of the dialectic.* Urbana: University of Illinois Press.

Omvedt, G. 1993. *Reinventing revolution.* London: Sharpe.

Patnaik, U. 1999. *The long transition.* Delhi: Tulika.

———. 2007. *The republic of hunger.* Gurgaon: Three Essays Collective.

Pushpendra. 2000. Liberalization and agrarian reforms: Some recent controversies. In *Land reforms in India,* vol. 5, edited by B. N. Sinha and Pushpendra, 45–63. New Delhi: Sage.

Rai, P. 2007. NREGA battling cancerous corruption. *India Together.* www.Indiatogether.org.

Ramakrishnan, V. 1999. A history of massacres. *Frontline* 16(5). http://www.thehindu.com/fline/fl1605/fl160500.htm.

Sagar. 2006. The spring and its thunder. *Economic and Political Weekly* 41(29): 3176–3178.

Samanta, A. 1984. *Left extremist movement in West Bengal.* Calcutta: Firma KLM Private Ltd.

Shah, G. 1991. Grass-roots mobilization in Indian politics. In *India's democracy,* edited by A. Kohli, 262–304. Hyderabad: Orient Longman.

Shiva, V. 1991. *The violence of the green revolution.* London: Zed.

Stiefel, M. and M. Wolfe 1994. *A voice for the excluded.* London: Zed.

Subramanian, S. 1998. Combating Naxalite violence. http://www.aapssindia.org/articles/art2/naxalite.html.

Tornquist, O. 1991. *What's wrong with Marxism: On peasants and workers in India and Indonesia.* Delhi: Manohar.

Veltmeyer, H. 1997. New social movements in Latin America. *Journal of Peasant Studies* 25(1): 139–169.

Wilson, K 1999. Patterns of accumulation and struggles of rural labour: Some aspects of agrarian change in Central Bihar. *Journal of Peasant Studies* 26(2–3): 316–354.

Contributors

Waquar Ahmed is a visiting assistant professor at the Department of Geography, Mount Holyoke College. He was the program coordinator of *Gene Campaign*, a non-governmental organization that works for the rights of farmers and indigenous peoples. His current research focuses on India's political economy, energy infrastructure and policy, foreign direct investments, and social movements.

Swapna Banerjee-Guha is a professor of Development Studies at the Tata Institute of Social Sciences, Mumbai, and an adjunct faculty in the Department of Economics at the University of Mumbai. She has a doctoral degree in Geography from Calcutta University. She conducted post-doctoral research as a Fulbright Fellow at the Johns Hopkins University in 1984. A visiting professor at the University of Vienna, visiting fellow at the Institute of Developing Economies, Japan, and visiting fellow at the Maison des Science de L' homme, Paris, she has traveled and lectured in several countries and supervised research students from various social science disciplines in India and abroad. A steering committee member of the International Critical Geography Group since its inception in 1997, Dr. Banerjee-Guha is a regular contributor to journals in India and abroad and has a number of books and more than 100 research articles to her credit. Her areas of interest are contemporary urban, social, and development issues at national and international levels.

Ipsita Chatterjee is an assistant professor at the Department of Geography and Environment, University of Texas at Austin. Chatterjee investigates contradictions of globalization in the context of capital-labor confrontation, state-market re-organization, and space-place re-ordering. She has published on issues relating to municipal neoliberalism and urban renewal, post-Fordist informalization, conflict and urban exclusion. She is currently working on class and class struggle beyond the factory.

Bharati Chaturvedi is the founder of Chintan Environmental Research and Action Group, a non-profit that addresses green justice and urban sustainability in India. She is a columnist for a leading Indian newspaper and writes for various other media, nationally and internationally. Bharti has masters degrees in history from Delhi University and international public policy from the School of Advanced International Studies, Johns Hopkins University. She is currently a Senior Fellow at the Synergos Institute, New York. She lives and works in Delhi.

Raju J. Das is an associate professor of geography at York University, Toronto, Canada. His research interests include political economy of development, globalization and rural labor, state theory, social movements, and social classes. He recently edited a special issue on peasant, state, and class for the *Journal of Peasant Studies*. His articles have been published in the *Transactions of the Institute of British Geographers*, *Political Geography*, and *Environment and Planning A*, among several others.

David Featherstone is a lecturer in human geography at the Department of Geographical and Earth Sciences, University of Glasgow. His book *Resistance, Space and Political Identities: the Making of Counter-Global Networks* was published by Wiley-Blackwell in 2008. His current research is focusing on the histories and geographies of solidarity and internationalism.

Vinay Gidwani is interested in capitalist transformations of agriculture and agroecologies and their inter-connections with cities through labor and capital flows. In attempting to understand various spatial resolutions of the 'agrarian question,' he foreground three areas of research: first, the cultural politics and geographies of work; second, the more-than-human constitution of social relations; and third, emergent terrains of injustice and struggle. He is presently working on urban and regional circuits of waste, and the labor processes that emerged around these, in the growth of metropolitan Delhi post 1930. Gidwani is the author, most recently, of *Capital, Interrupted: Agrarian Development and the Politics of Work in India* (Minnesota / Permanent Black, 2008).

Amitabh Kundu is professor of economics at the Jawaharlal Nehru University, New Delhi, India, where he has been is teaching for the past 30 years. He has been visiting professor/senior fellow at several universities in Europe and America and consultant to the World Bank, UNESCO (Division of Physical Heritage), the ILO and the Government of the Netherlands. His recent publications include *Urban Informal Sector* (ILO), *In the Name of Urban Poor* (Sage), *Inequality, Mobility and Urbanization: China and India* (ed. Manak) and *Poverty and Vulnerability in a Globalizing Metropolis: Ahmedabad* (ed. Manak).

Shipra Maitra has a doctoral degree from Jawaharlal Nehru University, New Delhi. Currently, she is the director of Amity College of Commerce & Finance, Amity University (Uttar Pradesh, India). She is also the visiting faculty in the School of Planning & Architecture (New Delhi). Her area of interest includes urban finance, municipal management, urban poverty, and land economics. She was associated with the University of Toronto as a Shastri-Canadian Fellow and the University of Amsterdam through the Exchange of Scholars' Programme. She has several national and international publications to her credit.

Rohit Negi teaches in the global studies program at the University of Illinois at Urbana Champaign. He has a PhD in geography from the Ohio State University. Negi's current research focuses on the political economy of contemporary resource extraction in sub-Saharan Africa. He has also published on the geoeconomics and geopolitics of the emerging Africa-Asia relationship.

Rupal Oza is the director of the women and gender studies program at Hunter College, CUNY. Her book, *The Making of Neoliberal India: Nationalism, Gender, and the Paradoxes of Globalization*, was published by Routledge, New York and from Women Unlimited, India. She has several articles in peer-reviewed journals. Her current project focuses on examining the link between special economic zones and the discourse of security in India.

Utsa Patnaik is Professor of Economics in the Centre for Economic Studies and Planning, Jawaharlal Nehru University and was one of the founder-members of the Centre at its inception in 1973. She has researched and written extensively on questions of transition of agrarian societies to industrialization both in a historical context and in contemporary times. Her publications include among other edited volumes: *Chains of Servitude—Bondage and Slavery in India* (1985, Orient Longman); *Agrarian Relations and Accumulation—the Mode of Production Debate* (1991, OUP); *The Agrarian Question in Marx and his Successors* (2007, Leftword Books) as well as a number of solely authored books: *Peasant Class Differentiation—A Study in Method* (1986 OUP), *The Long Transition—Essays on Political Economy* (1999, Tulika) and *The Republic of Hunger and Other Essays* (2008, Three Essays Collective). About 75 published papers include her critique of trade theory, of neo-liberal theory and policy and critique of poverty estimation methods.

Richard Peet is professor of geography at the Graduate School of Geography, Clark University, Worcester, Massachusetts. He is former editor of *Antipode: A Radical Journal of Geography*, former co-editor of *Economic Geography*, and present editor of the new journal *Human Geography.*

He has written some 100 journal articles, book chapters and other published pieces, and is the author of 15 books and monographs including *Modern Geographical Thought* (Blackwell, 1998), *Theories of Development* (Guilford, 2000 and 2008), *Unholy Trinity: The IMF, World Bank and WTO* (Zed, 2002) and *Geography of Power* (Zed, 2007).

Suman Sahai, who has had a distinguished scientific career in the field of genetics, was honored with the 2004 Borlaug Award for her outstanding contribution to agriculture and the environment. She has served as a faculty member at the Universities of Alberta and Chicago as also the University of Heidelberg. She returned to India and organized Gene Campaign, an organization dedicated to protecting farmers' rights and food and livelihood security. Suman Sahai chaired the Planning Commission Task Force on Agro Biodiversity and Genetically Engineered Organisms, for the Eleventh Plan. She has received several national awards and was appointed Knight of the Golden Ark (Netherlands) in 2001.

Index